Networks in the Knowledge Economy

Networks

in the Knowledge

Economy

Edited by

Rob Cross

Andrew Parker

Lisa Sasson

UNIVERSITY PRESS

2003

OXFORD
UNIVERSITY PRESS

Oxford   New York
Auckland   Bangkok   Buenos Aires   Cape Town   Chennai
Dar es Salaam   Delhi   Hong Kong   Istanbul   Karachi   Kolkata
Kuala Lumpur   Madrid   Melbourne   Mexico City   Mumbai   Nairobi
São Paulo   Shanghai   Taipei   Tokyo   Toronto

Copyright © 2003 by Oxford University Press, Inc.

Published by Oxford University Press, Inc.
198 Madison Avenue, New York, New York 10016

www.oup.com

Oxford is a registered trademark of Oxford University Press

Library of Congress Cataloging-in-Publication Data
Cross, Robert L., 1967–
Networks in the knowledge economy / edited by Rob Cross, Andrew Parker, Lisa Sasson.
    p. cm.
Includes bibliographical references and index.
ISBN 0-19-515950-0
1. Social networks. 2. Technology—Economic aspects. 3. Communication in learning and
scholarship. I. Parker, Andrew. II. Sasson, Lisa. III. Title.
HM741.C76 2003
302—dc21   2003045996

9 8 7 6 5 4 3 2 1

Printed in the United States of America
on acid-free paper

■ Acknowledgments

This work has been made possible by our affiliation with IBM's Institute for Knowledge-Based Organizations. This consortium provided us with invaluable opportunities to work with numerous leading organizations and learn specific ways that network analysis can be helpful to managers and practitioners. Further, the institute allowed us to develop a rich network with leading academics who have been studying networks from a scholarly perspective for decades. Though too numerous to list here, we are very grateful for the collaborations we have enjoyed with those enmeshed in both practice and scholarship.

Chapter 1
Burt, R. (1992). "The Social Structure of Competition." In *Structural Holes*. Cambridge, MA: Harvard University Press.

Chapter 2
Coleman, J. (1988). "Social Capital in the Creation of Human Capital." *American Journal of Sociology*, 94, pp. S95–S120.

Chapter 3
Krackhardt, D. (1992). "The Strength of Strong Ties: The Importance of *Philos* in Organizations." In N. Nohria & R. Eccles (Eds.), *Networks and Organizations: Structures, Form and Action*. Boston, MA: Harvard Business School Press, pp. 216–239.

Chapter 4
Granovetter, M. (1973). "The Strength of Weak Ties." *American Journal of Sociology*, 78, pp. 1360–1380.

Chapter 5
Rogers, E. (1995). "Diffusion Networks." In *Diffusion of Innovations* (4th ed.). New York: Free Press, pp. 281–334.

Chapter 6
Gladwell, M. (2000). "Designs for Working." *New Yorker*, pp. 60–70.

Chapter 7
Gladwell, M. (1999). "Six Degrees of Lois Weisberg." *New Yorker*, pp. 32–57.

Chapter 8
Cross, R., Parker, A., Prusak, L., & Borgatti, S. (2001). "Knowing What We Know: Supporting Knowledge Creation and Sharing in Social Networks." *Organizational Dynamics*, 30(2), pp. 100–120.

Chapter 9
Krackhardt, D., & Hanson, J. (1993, July–August). "Informal Networks: The Company behind the Chart." *Harvard Business Review*, 71(4), pp. 104–111.

Chapter 10
Cross, R., and L. Prusak (2002). "The People Who Make Organizations Go—or Stop." *Harvard Business Review*, 80(6), pp. 104–112.

Chapter 11
Cross, R., Borgatti, S., & Parker, A. (2002). "Making Invisible Work Visible: Using Social Network Analysis to Support Strategic Collaboration." *California Management Review*, 44(2), pp. 1–22.

Chapter 12
Brass, D. (1995). "A Social Network Perspective on Human Resources Management." In *Research in Personnel and Human Resources Management*, Vol. 13. Greenwich, CT: JAI Press, pp. 39–79.

Chapter 13
Krackhardt, D. (1994). "Constraints on the Interactive Organization as an Ideal Type." In C. Heckscher & A. Donnellon (Eds.), *The Post-Bureaucratic Organization: New Perspectives on Organizational Change*. Thousand Oaks, CA: Sage Publications, pp. 211–222.

◼ Contents

■ **Part III**

Managerial Implications of Social Networks in Organizations

■ Contributors

Stephen P. Borgatti is associate professor of organizational behavior at the Carroll School of Management, Boston College. He is the principal author of UCINET, the leading software package for social network analysis, and past president of the International Network for Social Network Analysis (INSNA), the professional association for social network researchers. Dr. Borgatti has published more than fifty journal articles in the area of social network theory and methodology.

Daniel J. Brass is J. Henning Hilliard Professor of Innovation Management at the University of Kentucky and is currently serving as associate editor of *Administrative Science Quarterly*. He received his Ph.D. in business administration from the University of Illinois-Urbana. He has published articles in such journals as *Administrative Science Quarterly, Academy of Management Journal, Academy of Management Review, Journal of Applied Psychology, Organization Science, Organizational Behavior and Human Decision Processes, Human Relations, Business Horizons, Organizational Behavior Teaching Review, Research in Personnel and Human Resources Management, Research in Politics and Society,* and *Research in Negotiation in Organizations*, as well as numerous book chapters. His research focuses on the antecedents and consequences of social networks in organizations.

Ronald Burt is a Hobart W. Williams Professor of Sociology and Strategy at the University of Chicago Graduate School of Business. His research activities include theory and research methodology, describing social structure of competitive advantage in careers, organizations, and markets. Dr. Burt received his Ph.D. in sociology from the University of Chicago.

James S. Coleman was a pioneer in mathematical sociology whose studies strongly influenced education policy in the United States. Coleman received his B.S. from Purdue University (1949) and his Ph.D. from Columbia University (1955), where he was a research associate in the

Bureau of Applied Social Research (1953–1955). While there, he was influenced by the style and ability of Paul Lazarsfeld to stimulate creative problem solving, an influence demonstrated in two major works: *Introduction to Mathematical Sociology* (1964) and *Mathematics of Collective Action* (1973). Coleman was a fellow at the Center for Advanced Study of Behavioral Science in Palo Alto, California (1955–1956), and then served as assistant professor of sociology at the University of Chicago (1956–1959). He was an associate and then a full professor in the department of social relations at Johns Hopkins University from 1959 to 1973 and then returned to Chicago as professor and senior study director at the National Opinion Research Center.

Rob Cross is an assistant professor of management in the McIntire School of Commerce. He also works as a research fellow with IBM's Institute for Knowledge Management where he directs the social network research program with a consortium of more than forty companies and government agencies. His research focuses on knowledge creation and sharing and specifically how relationships and informal networks in organizations can provide competitive advantage in knowledge-intensive work. He has consulted with such companies and organizations as Arthur Andersen, Aventis, Bank of Montreal, Bristol Myers, Capital One, Computer Sciences Corporation, Eli Lilly, IBM, Intel, IRS, McKinsey, Novartis, the National Security Agency, and others.

Malcolm Gladwell was born in England and grew up in Canada. He graduated with a degree in history from the University of Toronto in 1984. From 1987 to 1996, he was a reporter for the *Washington Post*, first as a science writer and then as New York City bureau chief. Since 1996, he has been a staff writer for the *New Yorker* magazine.

Mark S. Granovetter is a professor of sociology at Stanford University. He is working on a general treatment of economic sociology with the preliminary title "Society and Economy: The Social Construction of Economic Institutions." He is also working on a study on the origins and early development of the electricity industry in the United States.

Jeffrey R. Hanson is president of J. R. Hanson & Company, a management consulting firm in Bronxville, New York.

David Krackhardt is a professor of organizations at the Heinz School of Public Policy and Management and the Graduate School of Industrial Administration, Carnegie Mellon University. Prior appointments include faculty positions at Cornell's Graduate School of Management, the University of Chicago's Graduate School of Business, INSEAD (France), and Harvard Business School. His research focuses on how the theoretical insights and methodological innovations of network analysis can enhance our understanding of how organizations function.

Andrew Parker is a research consultant with the IBM Institute for Knowledge-Based Organizations (IKO) in Cambridge, Massachusetts. He is currently researching social capital within organizations. The project uses social network analysis—a set of tools for mapping important knowledge relationships between people and departments. Parker has worked with the IKO social network team to conduct network analysis in more than thirty different organizations. The research has covered top-level executive teams, functional departments, communities of practice, and recently merged companies. This research has helped these organizations develop insight into critical knowledge creation and sharing activities.

Laurence Prusak, a managing principal with IBM Global Services, is the founder and executive director of the Institute for Knowledge Management (IKM), a global consortium of member organizations engaged in advancing the practice of knowledge management through action research. Larry has extensive consulting experience, within the United States and internationally, in helping firms leverage and optimize their information and knowledge resources. He has also consulted with many U.S. and overseas government agencies and international organizations (NGOs).

Everett Rogers is a Regents' Professor in the Department of Communication and Journalism at the University of New Mexico. Professor Rogers is best known for his book, *Diffusion of Innovations*, published in its fourth edition in 1995. He is presently writing the fifth edition, which will focus on the diffusion of the Internet as an example of a critical innovation.

Lisa Sasson is a senior analyst at Aventis Pharmaceuticals in the Knowledge Management Department. She is currently focused on applying social network analysis methods within the context of alliance management and interorganizational collaboration. Prior to her work at Aventis, Sasson was an associate consultant at IBM's Institute for Knowledge Management, where she researched the role of knowledge management in strategic alliances, social network analysis, and management of expertise. She holds a graduate degree in international relations and an undergraduate degree in anthropology from Boston University.

Networks in the Knowledge Economy

Introduction

Rob Cross, Andrew Parker, and Lisa Sasson

Spend some time in most any organization today and you are sure to hear of the importance of networks, in one form or another, for getting work done. In this age of increasingly organic, flat, and flexible structures, many managers and scholars are using networks as a central organizing metaphor for twenty-first-century firms (e.g., Dimagio, 2001; Nohria & Ghoshal, 1997). In large part, this focus seems a product of two trends. First, over the past decade or so initiatives such as de-layering, TQM, reengineering, team-based structures, and outsourcing, to name a few, have been undertaken to promote organizational flexibility and efficiency (Hirschhorn & Gilmore, 1992; Hammer & Champy, 1993; Mohrman, Cohen, & Mohrman, 1995; Kerr & Ulrich, 1995). One outcome of these restructuring efforts is that information flow and work increasingly occur through informal networks of relationships rather than through channels tightly prescribed by formal reporting structures or detailed work processes.

Along with the drive to more organic structures in organizations we have also seen a rise in the prevalence and value of knowledge-intensive work (Quinn, 1992; Drucker, 1993). Early initiatives to support knowledge workers focused heavily on databases and organizational processes to ensure the capture and sharing of lessons and reusable work products (e.g., Stewart, 1997; O'Dell & Grayson, 1998; Ruggles, 1998; Davenport, Delong, & Beers, 1998). However, these investments rarely, if ever, had the intended impact on the effectiveness and efficiency of knowledge work. As a result, a "second wave" of knowledge-management advice is coming forth that pays a great deal more attention to knowledge embedded within employees and relationships in organizations (e.g., Brown & Duguid, 2000; Cross & Baird, 2000; Dixon, 2000; Von Krogh et al., 2000; Cohen & Prusak, 2001). Among other things, this work has illustrated the importance of trust and informal networks for knowledge creation and sharing within organizations.

We suggest that in today's de-layered, knowledge-intensive settings, most work of importance is heavily reliant on informal networks of employees within organizations. For example, networks sitting across core work processes, weaving together new product development initiatives or integrating strategic initiatives such as alliances or mergers can be critical to organizational effectiveness. They enable effective collaboration and integration of different expertise necessary for innovation. While such networks are generally not found on any formal organizational charts, they frequently can be sources of both strategic and operational success for an organization. However, outside of recent initiatives targeting communities of practice, there has been little focus on supporting work and effective collaboration within informal networks of employees (Wenger, 1998; Wenger & Snyder, 2000).

Social network analysis (SNA), a set of analytic tools that can be used to map networks of relationships, provides an important means of assessing and promoting collaboration in strategically important groups (see Scott, 2000, and Wasserman & Faust, 1994, for primers on the topic). Social network analysis allows one to conduct very powerful assessments of information sharing within a network with relatively little effort, thereby revealing both points where collaboration is effective and points where improvement is necessary. Unfortunately, many practitioners are unaware of the potential benefits that can be derived from systematically assessing important informal networks. Confined largely to academic pursuits, most writings on social network analysis are framed to advance science and are couched in a terminology that does not help managers understand ways to apply SNA to their own organizational concerns. This anthology was organized to provide readings on the application of social network analysis to managerial concerns. It is specifically concerned with networks *inside* of organizations, given the comparative lack of attention they have received in contrast to relationships between companies and advice on how to become a "networked organization." We will next briefly introduce social network analysis with a short case example. Following this we will frame the collection of readings organized by areas of importance to managers today.

■ Social Network Analysis

Social network analysis has roots in social science research that dates to the 1930s. The idea of drawing a picture of the connections among a specified group of people is often credited to Dr. J. L. Moreno (1934), an early social psychologist who envisioned mapping the entire population of New York City. Since that time, the field has grown significantly from a methodological standpoint with the advent of the personal computer and a global, multidisciplinary society of social network analysts called International Network of Social Network Analysts. Significant theoretical contributions have been made to the fields of sociology, social psychology, anthropology, epidemiology, and management studies, to name a few, by virtue of the application of social network techniques. In the field of management, interest has tended to focus heavily on issues of social capital (e.g., Burt, 2000; Leenders & Gabbay, 1999; Adler & Kwon, 2002); information flow in social networks (e.g., Allen, 1977; Monge & Contractor, 2000); and the informal structure of an organization (e.g., Krackhardt & Hanson, 1993; Nohria & Eccles, 1992; Lincoln, 1982). However, as social network analysis is often new to managers, we turn to an example of its use before framing this anthology.

Consider the information-sharing network of the top twenty executives in the exploration and production division of a large petroleum organization (this example is drawn from and discussed in more depth in Cross, Parker, Prusak, & Borgatti [2001]). In working with this group, we first obtained the formal organization chart, found in the top half of figure I.1, to see how the executives were hierarchically connected. We then asked each of the executives whom within the group they relied on for information to get their work done. From survey responses to this question we produced the social network diagram found in the bottom half of figure I.1. The connections between the people in the diagram indicate who obtains information from whom. As can quickly be seen, there is a significant difference between the formal and the informal organization. Although the organization chart provides clear information of who reports to whom, in this case it bears little resemblance to information flow and seemingly how work is getting done in this group.

Three points were particularly important in relation to information-sharing in this network. First, the SNA identified several midlevel managers who were important in terms of facilitating information flow. For example, it was a surprise to many executives in this group to find that Cole played such a central role with respect to overall information flow and as the only link between people within the production division and the rest of the network. It quickly became clear that if Cole left the group, the company would lose both his valuable knowledge and the relationships he had established that in many ways were holding the network together.

Second, the social network analysis helped to identify highly peripheral people. In particular, it became apparent that some of the senior people, for example, Jones, were too removed from day-to-day operations. It is often the case that when people move higher within an organization their work becomes more administrative, which makes them both less accessible and less knowledgeable about the day-to-day work of their subordinates. In this case, however, Jones had become difficult to access and his lack of responsiveness often slowed everyone down when important decisions needed to be made.

Finally, the SNA demonstrated the extent to which the production division (the subgroup on the top of the diagram) had become separated

Formal Organizational Structure of Exploration and Production Division

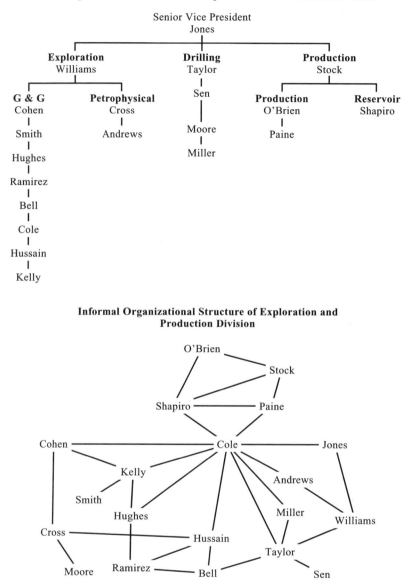

Figure I.1.
Formal versus informal structure in a petroleum organization. *Note*: Names have been disguised at the request of the company.

from the overall network. Part of the reason for this was that these people had recently been physically moved to a different floor in the building. They claimed that the physical separation had resulted in a loss of many of the serendipitous meetings between the production division and people in the other two divisions that occurred when they were co-located. As a result, the members of this network decided to introduce more structured means of coordinating their efforts to compensate for the loss of serendipitous communication.

■ Managerial Implications of Social Networks in Organizations

The above provides one example of how managers can use social network analysis in their organizations. In general, there are several managerial applications that seem to fall in one or more of three domains: (1) assessing individual and organizational social capital; (2) ensuring effective knowledge creation and sharing; and (3) analyzing the extent to which an organization's informal structure supports strategic objectives. We have framed this anthology to cover important readings in these areas and will touch briefly on the domains below.

Social Networks as Important Individual and Organizational Assets

Over the past decade there has been an increased interest in social capital, and specifically how relationships can confer important benefits to either individuals or organizations (see Burt, 2000; Adler & Kwon, 2002, and Leenders & Gabbay, 1999, for reviews). From this perspective, network analysis can be helpful for executives and managers in two unique ways. First, social network analysis provides a kind of X ray for assessing collaboration among employees or other units within an organization. By making often-invisible communication patterns visible, SNA helps inform interventions in which managers can engage to improve effectiveness of their groups.

Alternatively, when considered from the point of view of the individuals in the network, social network analysis can provide a great deal of insight into the health and effectiveness of one's personal network. Research shows that personal networks can be particularly important for finding a job (Granovetter, 1973), getting promoted (Burt, 1992), and obtaining information to do your work (Allen, 1977). Yet while almost everyone intuitively knows that their network is an important asset for them, it is very rare for executives to take time out to systematically assess this asset. Using social network analysis to understand hidden biases within one's network can be critical to executives in terms of decision-making, career advancement, and performance.

Social Network Implications for Knowledge Creation and Sharing

The flow of information and knowledge is the lifeblood of many organizations today. Social network analysis can be particularly effective for assessing and promoting collaboration in strategically important groups such as top leadership networks, strategic business units, new product development initiatives, communities of practice, joint ventures, and mergers. Despite the proliferation of various technologies and the explosion in accessible information, people learn how to do their work and acquire information much more prevalently through their networks than from information sources such as databases or files. Consider your own work. When was the last time that you started a project or solved a problem of significance without tapping others for information or advice? Or the last time you learned how to do something important in your work via a database?

Our research and that of others continues to show that people rely much more heavily on their networks than impersonal sources such as databases or file cabinets for information to do their work. One of the most consistent findings in the social science literature is that *whom* you know often has a great deal to do with *what* you come to know. Analytically, social network analysis can help identify points within a network that need to be addressed in order to improve information and knowledge flow. For example, important information brokers or boundary spanners that move information between different sections of an organization can be identified and leveraged in cost-effective ways to promote diffusion of ideas throughout a network. Alternatively, SNA can help identify heavily central people that might have become bottlenecks unnecessarily slowing the work of many others.

Managerial Implications of an Organization's Informal Structure

With flatter organizations very much in vogue, work is increasingly done in small groups that rely on their informal connections with the rest of the organization. It is important for managers to be able to assess and support informal networks within organizations to ensure alignment with corporate objectives. Unfortunately, critical informal networks often compete with and are fragmented by such aspects of organizations as formal structure, work processes, human resource practices, leadership style, and culture. This competition and fragmentation is particularly problematic in knowledge-intensive settings where management is counting on collaboration among employees with different expertise. Both practical experience and scholarly research indicate significant difficulty in getting people with different expertise, backgrounds, and problem-solving styles to effectively integrate their unique perspectives. Social network analysis provides a series of opportunities to ensure alignment of a given network with corporate objectives, in large part by making these patterns of interaction visible and thus actionable.

■ Conclusion

Put an organizational chart (the formal structure) in front of most any employee, from line-worker to executive, and they will tell you the boxes and lines do not reflect the way that work gets done in their organization. These people intuitively acknowledge the existence, importance, and power of the broad and diverse patterns of relationships that develop among a group of people over time. However, most organization members don't know how to effectively capture and analyze this informal structure in ways that can have a positive impact on organizational performance. Social network analysis gives us a unique way of looking at an individual's ties and the networks of relationships within an organization from a more concrete perspective. It makes the invisible web of relationships between people visible and thus helps managers make informed decisions for improving both their own and their group's performance.

■ References

Adler, P. S. & Kwon, S. (2000). "Social Capital: Prospects for a New Concept." *Academy of Management Review*, 27(1), pp. 17–40.

Allen, T. (1977). *Managing the Flow of Technology*. Cambridge, MA: MIT Press.

Brown, J. S., & Duguid, P. (2000). *The Social Life of Information*. Boston, MA: Harvard Business School Press.

Burt, R. (1992). *Structural Holes*. Cambridge, MA: Harvard University Press.

———. (2000). "The Network Structure of Social Capital." In R. Sutton and B. Staw (eds.), *Research in Organizational Behavior*. Greenwich, CT: JAI Press, pp. 325–433.

Cohen, D., & Prusak, L. (2001). *In Good Company: How Social Capital Makes Organizations Work*. Boston: Harvard Business School Press.

Cross, R., & Baird, L. (2000). "Technology Is Not Enough: Improving Performance by Building Organizational Memory." *Sloan Management Review*, 41(3), pp. 41–54.

Cross, R., Parker, A., Prusak, L., & Borgatti, S. (2001). "Knowing What We Know: Supporting Knowledge Creation and Sharing in Social Networks." *Organizational Dynamics*, 30(2), pp. 100–120.

Davenport, T., Delong, D., & Beers, M. (1998). "Successful Knowledge Management Projects." *Sloan Management Review*, Winter, pp. 43–57.

Dimagio, P. (2001). *The 21st Century Firm*. Princeton, NJ: Princeton University Press.

Dixon, N. (2000). *Common Knowledge: How Companies Thrive by Sharing What They Know*. Boston: Harvard Business School Press.

Drucker, P. (1993). *Post-Capitalist Society.* New York: Harper Collins.

Granovetter, M. (1973). "The Strength of Weak Ties." *American Journal of Sociology,* 78, pp. 1360–1380.

Hammer, M., & Champy, J. (1993). *Reengineering the Corporation: A Manifesto for Business Revolution.* New York: Harper Business.

Hirschhorn, L., & Gilmore, T. (1992). "The New Boundaries of the 'Boundaryless' Company." *Harvard Business Review,* May–June, pp. 104–115.

Kerr, S., and Ulrich, D. (1995). "Creating the Boundaryless Organization: The Radical Reconstruction of Organization Capabilities." *Planning Review,* 23(5), pp. 41–45.

Krackhardt, D., & Hanson, J. R. (1993). "Informal Networks: The Company behind the Chart." *Harvard Business Review,* 71, pp. 104–111.

Leenders, R., & Gabbay, S. (1999). *Corporate Social Capital and Liability.* Boston: Kluwar.

Lincoln, J. (1982). "Intra- (and Inter-) Organizational Networks." *Research in the Sociology of Organizations,* 1, pp. 1–38.

Mohrman, S., Cohen, S., & Mohrman, A. (1995). *Designing Team-Based Organizations: New Forms for Knowledge Work.* San Francisco, CA: Jossey-Bass.

Monge, P., & Contractor, N. (2000). "Emergence of Communication Networks." In F. Jablin & L. Putnam (eds.), *Handbook of Organizational Communication* (2nd ed.) Thousand Oaks, CA: Sage, pp. 440–502.

Moreno, J. L. (1934). *Who Shall Survive?* Washington, DC: Nervous and Mental Disease Publishing Company.

Nohria, N., & Eccles, R. (1992). *Networks and Organizations: Structure, Form, and Action.* Boston: Harvard Business School Press.

Nohria, N., & Ghoshal, S. (1997). *The Differentiated Network: Organizing Multi-National Corporations for Value Creation.* San Francisco, CA: Jossey-Bass.

O'Dell, C., & Grayson, C. J. (1998). *If Only We Knew What We Know.* New York: Free Press.

Quinn, J. (1992). *Intelligent Enterprises.* New York: Free Press.

Ruggles, R. (1998). "The State of the Notion: Knowledge Management in Practice." *California Management Review,* 40(3), pp. 80–89.

Scott, J. (2000). *Social Network Analysis* (2nd ed.). Thousand Oaks, CA: Sage.

Stewart, T. (1997). *Intellectual Capital: The New Wealth of Organizations.* New York: Doubleday.

Von Krogh, G., Ichijo, K., & Nonaka, I. (2000). *Enabling Knowledge Creation.* New York: Oxford University Press.

Wasserman, S., & Faust, K. (1994). *Social Network Analysis: Methods and Applications.* Cambridge: Cambridge University Press.

Wenger, E. (1998). *Communities of Practice.* Oxford: Oxford University Press.

Wenger, E., & Snyder, W. (2000). "Communities of Practice: The Organizational Frontier." *Harvard Business Review,* 137, pp. 139–145.

Part I

Social Networks as Important

Individual and Organizational Assets

1

The Social Structure of Competition

Ronald Burt

A player brings capital to the competitive arena and walks away with profit determined by the rate of return where the capital was invested. The market production equation predicts profit: invested capital, multiplied by the going rate of return, equals the profit to be expected from the investment. You invest a million dollars. The going rate of return is 10 percent. The profit is one hundred thousand dollars. Investments create an ability to produce a competitive product. For example, capital is invested to build and operate a factory. Rate of return is an opportunity to profit from the investment.

The rate of return is keyed to the social structure of the competitive arena and is the focus here. Each player has a network of contacts in the arena. Something about the structure of the player's network and the location of the player's contacts in the social structure of the arena provides a competitive advantage in getting higher rates of return on investment. This chapter is about that advantage. It is a description of the way in which social structure renders competition imperfect by creating entrepreneurial opportunities for certain players and not for others.[1]

Opportunity and Capital

A player brings at least three kinds of capital to the competitive arena. Other distinctions can be made, but three are sufficient here. First, the player has financial capital: cash in hand, reserves in the bank, investments coming due, lines of credit. Second, the player has human capital. Your natural qualities—charm, health, intelligence, and looks—combined with the skills you have acquired in formal education and job experience give you abilities to excel at certain tasks.

Third, the player has social capital: relationships with other players. You have friends, colleagues, and more general contacts through whom you receive opportunities to use your financial and human capital. I refer to opportunities in a broad sense, but I certainly mean to include the obvious examples of job promotions, participation in significant projects, influential access to important decisions, and so on. The social capital of people aggregates into the social capital of organizations. In a firm providing services—for example, advertising, brokerage, or consulting—there are people valued for their ability to deliver a quality product. Then there are "rainmakers," valued for their ability to deliver clients. Those who deliver the product do the work, and the rainmakers make it possible for all to profit from the work. The former represent the financial and human capital of the firm. The latter represent its social capital. More generally, property and human assets define the firm's production capabilities. Relations within and beyond the firm are social capital.

Distinguishing Social Capital

Financial and human capital are distinct in two ways from social capital. First, they are the property of individuals. They are owned in whole or in part by a single individual defined in law as capable of ownership, typically a person or corporation. Second, they concern the investment term in the market production equation. Whether held by a person or the fictive person of a firm, financial and human capital gets invested to create production capabilities. Investments in supplies, facilities, and people serve to build and operate a factory. Investments of money, time, and energy produce a skilled manager. Financial capital is needed for raw materials and production facilities. Human capital is needed to craft the raw materials into a competitive product.

Social capital is different on both counts. First, it is a thing owned jointly by the parties to a relationship. No one player has exclusive ownership rights to social capital. If you or your partner in a relationship withdraws, the connection, with whatever social capital it contained, dissolves. If a firm treats a cluster of customers poorly and they leave, the social capital represented by the firm-cluster relationship is lost. Second, social capital concerns rate of return in the market production equation. Through relations with colleagues, friends, and clients come the opportunities to transform financial and human capital into profit.

Social capital is the final arbiter of competitive success. The capital invested to bring your organization to the point of producing a superb product is as rewarding as the opportunities to sell the product at a profit. The investment to make you a skilled manager is as valuable as the opportunities—the leadership positions—you get to apply your managerial skills. The investment to make you a skilled scientist with state-of-the-art research facilities is as valuable as the opportunities—the projects—you get to apply those skills and facilities.

More accurately, social capital is as important as competition is imperfect and investment capital is abundant. Under perfect competition, social capital is a constant in the production equation. There is a single rate of return because capital moves freely from low-yield to high-yield investments until rates of return are homogeneous across alternative investments. When competition is imperfect, capital is less mobile and plays a more complex role in the production equation. There are financial, social, and legal impediments to moving cash between investments. There are impediments to reallocating human capital, both in terms of changing the people to whom you have a commitment and in terms of replacing them with new people. Rate of return depends on the relations in which capital is invested. Social capital is a critical variable. This is all the more true when financial and human capital are abundant—which in essence reduces the investment term in the production equation to an unproblematic constant.

These conditions are generic to the competitive arena, which makes social capital a factor as routinely critical as financial and human capital. Competition is never perfect. The rules of trade are ambiguous in the aggregate and everywhere negotiable in the particular. The allocation of opportunities is rarely made with respect to a single dimension of abilities needed for a task. Within an acceptable range of needed abilities, there are many people with financial and human capital comparable to your own. Whatever you bring to a production task, there are other people who could do the same job—perhaps not as well in every detail, but probably as well within the tolerances of the people for whom the job is done. Criteria other than financial and human capital are used to narrow the pool down to the individual who gets the opportunity. Those other criteria are social capital. New life is given to the proverb that says success is determined less by what you know than by whom you know. As a senior colleague once remarked (and Cole, 1992, chaps. 7–8, makes into an intriguing research program), "Publishing high-quality work is important for getting university resources, but friends are essential." Of those who are equally qualified, only a select few get the most rewarding opportunities. Of the products that are of comparably high quality, only some come to dominate their markets. The question is how.

Who and How

The competitive arena has a social structure: players trusting certain others, obligated to support certain others, dependent on exchange with certain others, and so on. Against this backdrop, each player has a network of contacts—everyone the player now knows, everyone the player has ever known, and all the people who know the player even though he or she doesn't know them. Something about the structure of the player's network and the location of the player's contacts in the social structure of the arena provides a competitive advantage in getting higher rates of return on investment.

Who

There are two routes into the social capital question. The first describes a network as your access to people with specific resources, which creates a correlation between theirs and yours. This idea has circulated as power, prestige, social resources, and more recently, social capital. Nan Lin and his colleagues provide an exemplar of this line of work, showing how the occupational prestige of a person's job is contingent on the occupational prestige of a personal contact leading to the job (Lin, 1982; Lin, Ensel, and Vaughn, 1981; Lin and Dumin, 1986). Related empirical results appear in Campbell, Marsden, and Hurlbert (1986), De Graaf and Flap (1988), Flap and De Graaf (1989), and Marsden and Hurlbert (1988). Coleman (1988) discusses the transmission of human capital across generations. Flap and Tazelaar (1989) provide a thorough review with special attention to social network analysis.

Empirical questions in this line of work concern the magnitude of association between contact resources and the actor's own resources, and variation in the association across kinds of relationships. Granovetter's (1973) weak tie metaphor, discussed in detail shortly, is often invoked to distinguish kinds of relationships.[2]

Network analysts will recognize this as an example of social contagion analysis. Network structure is not used to predict attitudes or behaviors directly. It is used to predict similarity between attitudes and behaviors (compare Barber, 1978, for a causal analysis). The research tradition is tied to the Columbia Sociology survey studies of social influence conducted during the 1940s and 1950s. In one of the first well-known studies, for example, Lazarsfeld, Berelson, and Gaudet (1944) show how a person's vote is associated with the party affiliations of friends. Persons claiming to have voted for the presidential candidate of a specific political party tend to have friends affiliated with that party. Social capital theory developed from this line of work describes the manner in which resources available to any one person in a population are contingent on the resources available to individuals socially proximate to the person.

Empirical evidence is readily available. People develop relations with people like themselves (for example, Fischer, 1982; Marsden, 1987; Burt, 1990). Wealthy people develop ties with other wealthy people. Educated people develop ties with one another. Young people develop ties with one another. There are reasons for this. Socially similar people, even in the pursuit of independent interests, spend time in the same places. Relationships emerge. Socially similar people have more shared interests. Relationships are maintained. Further, we are sufficiently egocentric to find people with similar tastes attractive. Whatever the etiology for strong relations between socially similar people, it is to be expected that the resources and opinions of any one individual will be correlated with the resources and opinions of his or her close contacts.

How

A second line of work describes social structure as capital in its own right. The first line describes the network as a conduit; the second line describes how networks are themselves a form of social capital. This line of work is less developed than the first. Indeed, it is little developed beyond intuitions in empirical research on social capital. Network range, indicated by size, is the primary measure. For example, Boxman, De Graaf, and Flap (1991) show that people with larger contact networks obtain higher-paying positions than people with small networks. A similar finding in social support research shows that persons with larger networks tend to live longer (Berkman and Syme, 1979).

Both lines of work are essential to a general definition of social capital. Social capital is at once the resources contacts hold and the structure of contacts in a network. The first term describes whom you reach. The second describes how you reach.

For two reasons, however, I ignore the question of who to concentrate on how. The first is generality. The question of who elicits a more idiographic class of answers. Predicting rate of return depends on knowing the resources of a player's contacts. There will be interesting empirical variation from one kind of activity to another, say, job searches versus mobilizing support for a charity, but the empirical generalization is obvious. Doing business with wealthy clients, however wealth is defined, has a higher margin than doing business with poor clients. I want to identify parameters of social capital that generalize beyond the specific individuals connected by a relationship.

The second reason is correlation. The two components in social capital should be so strongly correlated that I can reconstruct much of the phenomenon from whichever component more easily yields a general explanation. To the extent that people play an active role in shaping their relationships, then a player who knows how to structure a network to provide high opportunity knows whom to include in the network. Even if networks are passively inherited, the manner in which a player is connected within social structure says much about contact resources. I will show that players with well-structured networks obtain higher rates of return. Resources accumulate in their hands. People develop relations with people like themselves. Therefore, how a player is connected in social structure indicates the volume of resources held by the player and the volume to which the player is connected.[3]

The nub of the matter is to describe network benefits in the competitive arena in order to be able to describe how certain structures enhance those benefits. The benefits are of two kinds, information and control.

Opportunities spring up everywhere: new institutions and projects that need leadership, new funding initiatives looking for proposals, new jobs for which you know of a good candidate, valuable items entering the market for which you know interested buyers. The information benefits of a network define who knows about these opportunities, when they know, and who gets to participate in them. Players with a network optimally structured to provide these benefits enjoy higher rates of return to their investments because such players know about, and have a hand in, more rewarding opportunities.

Access, Timing, and Referrals

Information benefits occur in three forms: access, timing, and referrals. Access refers to receiving a valuable piece of information and knowing who can use it. Information does not spread evenly across the competitive arena. It isn't that players are secretive, although that too can be an issue. The issue is that players are unevenly connected with one another, are attentive to the information pertinent to themselves and their friends, and are all overwhelmed by the flow of information. There are limits to the volume of information you can use intelligently. You can keep up with only so many books, articles, memos, and news services. Given a limit to the volume of information that anyone can process, the network becomes an important screening device. It is an army of people processing information who can call your attention to key bits—keeping you up-to-date on developing opportunities, warning you of impending disasters. This second-hand information is often fuzzy or inaccurate, but it serves to signal something to be looked into more carefully.

Related to knowing about an opportunity is knowing whom to bring into it. Given a limit to the financing and skills that we possess individually, most complex projects will require coordination with other people as staff, colleagues, or clients. The manager asks, "Whom do I know with the skills to do a good job with that part of the project?" The capitalist asks, "Whom do I know who would be interested in acquiring this product or a piece of the project?" The department head asks, "Who are the key players needed to strengthen the department's position?" Add to each of these the more common question, "Whom do I know who is most likely to know the kind of person I need?"

Timing is a significant feature of the information received by the network. Beyond making sure that you are informed, personal contacts can make you one of the people who is informed early. It is one thing to find out that the stock market is crashing today. It is another to discover that the price of your stocks will plummet tomorrow. It is one thing to learn the names of the two people referred to the board for the new vice-presidency. It is another to discover that the job will be created and that your credentials could make you a serious candidate for the position. Personal contacts get significant information to you before the average person receives it. That early warning is an opportunity to act on the information yourself or to invest it back into the network by passing it on to a friend who could benefit from it.

These benefits involve information flowing from contacts. There are also benefits in the opposite flow. The network that filters information coming to you also directs, concentrates, and legitimates information about you going to others.

In part, this network does no more than alleviate a logistics problem. You can be in only a limited number of places within a limited amount of time. Personal contacts get your name mentioned at the right time in the right place so that opportunities are presented to you. Their referrals are a positive force for future opportunities. They are the motor expanding the third category of people in your network, the players you don't know who are aware of you. Consider the remark so often heard in recruitment deliberations: "I don't know her personally, but several people whose opinion I trust have spoken well of her."

Beyond logistics, there is the issue of legitimacy. Even if you know about an opportunity and can present a solid case for why you should get it, you are a suspect source of information. The same information has more legitimacy when it comes from someone inside the decision-making process who can speak to your virtues. Candidates offered the university positions with the greatest opportunity, for example, are people who have a strong personal advocate in the decision-making process, a person in touch with the candidate to ensure that both favorable information and responses to any negative information get distributed during the decision.

Benefit-Rich Networks

A player with a network rich in information benefits has contacts: (a) established in the places where useful bits of information are likely to air and (b) providing a reliable flow of information to and from those places.

Selecting Contacts
The second criterion is as ambiguous as it is critical. It is a matter of trust, of confidence in the information passed and the care with which contacts look out for your interests. Trust is critical precisely because competition is imperfect. The question is not whether to trust, but whom to trust. In a perfectly competitive arena, you can trust the system to provide a fair return on your investments. In the imperfectly competitive arena, you have only your personal contacts. The matter comes down to a question of interpersonal debt. If I do for her, will she for me? There is no general answer. The answer lies in the match between specific people. If a contact

feels that he is somehow better than you—a sexist male dealing with a woman, a racist white dealing with a black, an old-money matron dealing with an upwardly mobile ethnic—your investment in the relationship will be taken as proper obeisance to a superior. No debt is incurred. We use whatever cues can be found for a continuing evaluation of the trust in a relation, but we never know a debt is recognized until the trusted person helps us when we need it. With this kind of uncertainty, players are cautious about extending themselves for people whose reputation for honoring interpersonal debt is unknown. The more general point of trust as people meeting your expectations is illustrated in Barber's (1983) analysis of competence and duty as dimensions of trust relations in diverse institutions in American society.

Theory and research exist to identify trustworthy contacts. Strong relationships and mutual acquaintances tend to develop between people with similar social attributes such as education, income, occupation, and age (for example, Fischer, 1982; Burt, 1986, 1990; Marsden, 1987; and see note 4). Both factors are linked to trust. Trust is a component in the strong relationships, and mutual acquaintances are like an insurance policy through which interpersonal debt is enforced such that the other person can be deemed trustworthy (Nohria, 1991). Whether egocentrism, cues from presumed shared background and interests, or confidence in mutual acquaintances to enforce interpersonal debt, the operational guide to the formation of close, trusting relations seems to be that a person more like me is less likely to betray me. For the purposes here, I set the whole issue to one side as person-specific and presume that it is resolved by the able player.

Siting Contacts

That leaves the first criterion, establishing contacts where useful bits of information are likely to air. Everything else constant, a large, diverse network is the best guarantee of having a contact present where useful information is aired. This is not to say that benefits must increase linearly with size and diversity, a point to which I will return (figure 1.5), but only that, other things held constant, the information benefits of a large, diverse network are greater than the information benefits of a small, homogeneous network.

Size is the more familiar criterion. Bigger is better. Acting on this understanding, people can expand their networks by adding more and more contacts. They make more cold calls, affiliate with more clubs, attend more social functions. Numerous books and self-help groups can assist them in "networking" their way to success by putting them in contact with a large number of potentially useful, or helpful, or like-minded people. The process is illustrated by the networks in figure 1.1. The four-contact network at the left expands to sixteen contacts at the right. Rela-

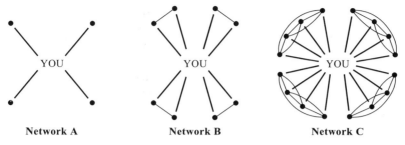

Network A   Network B   Network C

Figure 1.1.
Network expansion

tions are developed with a friend of each contact in network A, doubling the contacts to eight in network B. Snowballing through friends of friends, there are sixteen contacts in network C, and so on.

Size is a mixed blessing. More contacts can mean more exposure to valuable information, more likely early exposure, and more referrals. But increasing network size without considering diversity can cripple a network in significant ways. What matters is the number of nonredundant contacts. Contacts are redundant to the extent that they lead to the same people and so provide the same information benefits.

Consider two four-contact networks, one sparse, the other dense. There are no relations between the contacts in the sparse network, and strong relations between every contact in the dense network. Both networks cost whatever time and energy is required to maintain four relationships. The sparse network provides four nonredundant contacts, one for each relationship. No single one of the contacts gets the player to the same people reached by the other contacts. In the dense network, each relationship puts the player in contact with the same people reached through the other relationships. The dense network contains only one nonredundant contact. Any three are redundant with the fourth.

The sparse network provides more information benefits. It reaches information in four separate areas of social activity. The dense network is a virtually worthless monitoring device. Because the relations between people in that network are strong, each person knows what the other people know and all will discover the same opportunities at the same time.

The issue is opportunity costs. At minimum, the dense network is inefficient in the sense that it returns less diverse information for the same cost as that of the sparse network. A solution is to put more time and energy into adding nonredundant contacts to the dense network. But time and energy are limited, which means that inefficiency translates into opportunity costs. If I take four relationships as an illustrative limit on the number of strong relations that a player can maintain, the player in the dense network is cut off from three-fourths of the information provided by the sparse network.

■ Structural Holes

I use the term structural hole for the separation between nonredundant contacts. Nonredundant contacts are connected by a structural hole. A structural hole is a relationship of nonredundancy between two contacts. The hole is a buffer, like an insulator in an electric circuit. As a result of the hole between them, the two contacts provide network benefits that are in some degree additive rather than overlapping.

Empirical Indicators

Nonredundant contacts are disconnected in some way—either directly, in the sense that they have no direct contact with one another, or indirectly, in the sense that one has contacts that exclude the others. The respective empirical conditions that indicate a structural hole are cohesion and structural equivalence. Both conditions define holes by indicating where they are absent.

Under the cohesion criterion, two contacts are redundant to the extent that they are connected by a strong relationship. A strong relationship indicates the absence of a structural hole. Examples are father and son, brother and sister, husband and wife, close friends, people who have been partners for a long time, people who frequently get together for social occasions, and so on. You have easy access to both people if either is a contact. Redundancy by cohesion is illustrated at the top of figure 1.2. The three contacts are connected to one another and so provide the same network benefits. The presumption here—routine in network analysis since Festinger, Schachter, and Back's (1950) analysis of information flowing through personal relations and Homans's (1950) theory of social groups—is that the likelihood that information will move from one person to another is proportional to the strength of their relationship. Empirically, strength has two independent dimensions: frequent contact and emotional closeness (see Marsden and Hurlbert, 1988; Burt, 1990).

Structural equivalence is a useful second indicator for detecting structural holes. Two people are structurally equivalent to the extent that they have the same contacts. Regardless of the relation between structurally equivalent people, these people lead to the same sources of information and so are redundant. Cohesion concerns direct connection; structural equivalence concerns indirect connection by mutual contact. Redundancy by structural equivalence is illustrated at the bottom of figure 1.2. The three contacts have no direct ties with one another. They are nonredun-

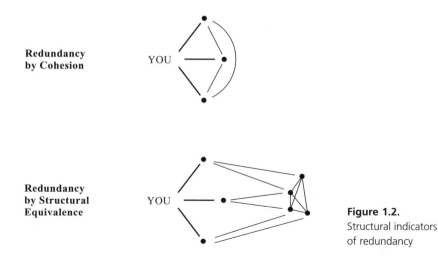

Redundancy by Cohesion

YOU

Redundancy by Structural Equivalence

YOU

Figure 1.2.
Structural indicators
of redundancy

dant by cohesion. But each leads you to the same cluster of more distant players. The information that comes to them, and the people to whom they send information, are redundant. Both networks in figure 1.2 provide one nonredundant contact at a cost of maintaining three.

The indicators are neither absolute nor independent. Relations deemed strong are only strong relative to others. They are our strongest relations. Structural equivalence rarely reaches the extreme of complete equivalence. People are more or less structurally equivalent. In addition, the criteria are correlated. People who spend a lot of time with the same other people often get to know one another. The mutual contacts responsible for structural equivalence set a stage for the direct connection of cohesion. The empirical conditions between two players will be a messy combination of cohesion and structural equivalence, present to varying degrees, at varying levels of correlation.

Cohesion is the more certain indicator. If two people are connected with the same people in a player's network (making them redundant by structural equivalence), they can still be connected with different people beyond the network (making them nonredundant). But if they meet frequently and feel close to one another, then they are likely to communicate and probably have contacts in common. More generally, and especially for fieldwork informed by attention to network benefits, the general guide is the definition of a structural hole. There is a structural hole between two people who provide nonredundant network benefits. If the cohesion and structural equivalence conditions are considered together, redundancy is most likely between structurally equivalent people connected by a strong relationship. Redundancy is unlikely, indicating a structural hole, between total strangers in distant groups. I will return to this issue again, to discuss the depth of a hole, after control benefits have been introduced.

The Efficient-Effective Network

Balancing network size and diversity is a question of optimizing structural holes. The number of structural holes can be expected to increase with network size, but the holes are the key to information benefits. The optimized network has two design principles.

Efficiency

The first design principle of an optimized network concerns efficiency: Maximize the number of nonredundant contacts in the network to maximize the yield in structural holes per contact. Given two networks of equal size, the one with more nonredundant contacts provides more benefits. There is little gain from a new contact redundant with existing contacts. Time and energy would be better spent cultivating new contacts to unreached people.[4] Maximizing the nonredundancy of contacts maximizes the structural holes obtained per contact.[5]

Efficiency is illustrated by the networks in figure 1.3. These reach the same people reached by the networks in figure 1.1, but in a different way. What expands in figure 1.1 is not the benefits but the cost of maintaining the network. Network A provides four nonredundant contacts. Network B provides the same number. The information benefits provided by the initial four contacts are redundant with benefits provided by their close friends. All that has changed is the doubled number of relationships maintained in the network. The situation deteriorates even further with the sixteen contacts in network C. There are still only four nonredundant contacts in the network, but their benefits are now obtained at a cost of maintaining sixteen relationships.

With a little network surgery, the sixteen contacts can be maintained at a fourth of the cost. As illustrated in figure 1.3, select one contact in each cluster to be a primary link to the cluster. Concentrate on maintaining the primary contact and allow direct relationships with others in the cluster to weaken into indirect relations through the primary contact. These players reached indirectly are secondary contacts. Among the redundant contacts in a cluster, the primary contact should be the one most easily maintained and most likely to honor an interpersonal debt to you in particular. The secondary contacts are less easily maintained or less likely to work for you (even if they might work well for someone else). The critical decision obviously lies in selecting the right person to be a primary contact. The importance of trust has already been discussed. With a trustworthy primary contact, there is little loss in information benefits from the cluster and a gain in the reduced effort needed to maintain the cluster in the network.

Repeating this operation for each cluster in the network recovers effort that would otherwise be spent maintaining redundant contacts. By reinvesting that saved time and effort in developing primary contacts to

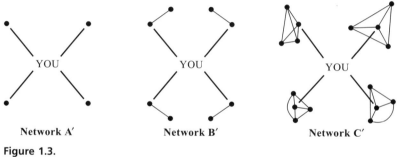

Figure 1.3.
Strategic network expansion

new clusters, the network expands to include an exponentially larger number of contacts while expanding contact diversity. The sixteen contacts in network C of figure 1.1, for example, are maintained at a cost of four primary contacts in network C′ of figure 1.3. Some portion of the time spent maintaining the redundant other twelve contacts can be reallocated to expanding the network to include new clusters.

Effectiveness

The second design principle of an optimized network requires a further shift in perspective: Distinguish primary from secondary contacts in order to focus resources on preserving the primary contacts. Here contacts are not people on the other end of your relations; they are ports of access to clusters of people beyond. Guided by the first principle, these ports should be nonredundant so as to reach separate, and therefore more diverse, social worlds of network benefits. Instead of maintaining relations with all contacts, the task of maintaining the total network is delegated to primary contacts. The player at the center of the network is then free to focus on properly supporting relations with primary contacts and expanding the network to include new clusters. The first principle concerns the average number of people reached with a primary contact; the second concerns the total number of people reached with all primary contacts. The first principle concerns the yield per primary contact. The second concerns the total yield of the network. More concretely, the first principle moves from the networks in figure 1.1 to the corresponding networks in figure 1.3. The second principle moves from left to right in figure 1.3. The target is network C′ in figure 1.3: a network of few primary contacts, each a port of access to a cluster of many secondary contacts.

Figure 1.4 illustrates some complexities in unpacking a network to maximize structural holes. The "before" network contains five primary contacts and reaches a total of fifteen people. However, there are only two clusters of nonredundant contacts in the network. Contacts 2 and 3 are

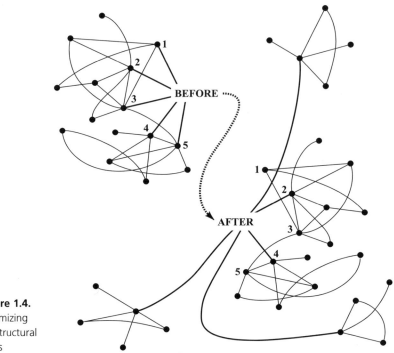

Figure 1.4.
Optimizing
for structural
holes

redundant in the sense of being connected with each other and reaching the same people (cohesion and structural equivalence criteria). The same is true of contacts 4 and 5. Contact 1 is not connected directly to contact 2, but he reaches the same secondary contacts; thus contacts 1 and 2 provide redundant network benefits (structural equivalence criterion). Illustrating the other extreme, contacts 3 and 5 are connected directly, but they are nonredundant because they reach separate clusters of secondary contacts (structural equivalence criterion). In the "after" network, contact 2 is used to reach the first cluster in the "before" network and contact 4 is used to reach the second cluster. The time and energy saved by withdrawing from relations with the other three primary contacts is reallocated to primary contacts in new clusters. The "before" and "after" networks are both maintained at a cost of five primary relationships, but the "after" network is dramatically richer in structural holes, and so network benefits.

Network benefits are enhanced in several ways. There is a higher volume of benefits, because more contacts are included in the network. Beyond volume, diversity enhances the quality of benefits. Nonredundant contacts ensure exposure to diverse sources of information. Each cluster of contacts is an independent source of information. One cluster, no matter how numerous its members, is only one source of information, because people connected to one another tend to know about the same things at about the same time. The information screen provided by multiple clusters of contacts is broader, providing better assurance that you, the player, will be informed of opportunities and impending disasters. Further, because nonredundant contacts are only linked through the central player, you are assured of being the first to see new opportunities created by needs in one group that could be served by skills in another group. You become the person who first brings people together, which gives you the opportunity to coordinate their activities. These benefits are compounded by the fact that having a network that yields such benefits makes you even more attractive as a network contact to other people, thus easing your task of expanding the network to best serve your interests.

Growth Patterns

A more general sense of efficiency and effectiveness is illustrated with network growth. In figure 1.5, the number of contacts in a player's network increases from left to right on the horizontal axis. The number who are nonredundant increases up the vertical axis. Observed network size increases on the horizontal, effective size up the vertical. Networks can be anywhere in the gray area. The maximum efficiency line describes networks in which each new contact is completely nonredundant with other contacts. Effective size equals actual size. Efficient-effective networks are in the upper right of the graph. The minimum efficiency line describes networks in which each new contact is completely redundant with other contacts; effective size equals one, regardless of multiple contacts in the network.

The two lines between the extremes illustrate more probable growth

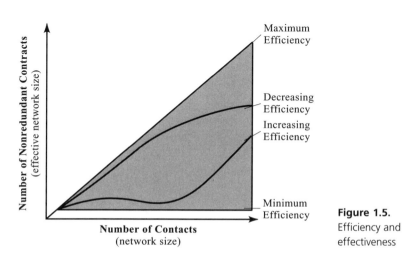

Figure 1.5.
Efficiency and effectiveness

patterns. The decreasing efficiency line shows players building good information benefits into their initial network, then relaxing to allow increasing redundancy as the network gets large. Friends of friends begin to be included. Comparisons across networks of different sizes suggest that this is the growth pattern among managers, though controls for time would be necessary to make the suggestion an inference.

The increasing efficiency line illustrates a different growth pattern. Initial contacts are redundant with one another. A foundation is established with multiple contacts in the same cluster. After the foundation is established, the player's network expands to include contacts in other clusters and effective size begins to increase. There are two kinds of clusters in which optimizing for saturation is wiser than optimizing for efficiency. The first is obvious. Leisure and domestic clusters are a congenial environment of low-maintenance, redundant contacts. Efficiency mixes poorly with friendship. Judging friends on the basis of efficiency is an interpersonal flatulence from which friends will flee. The second exception is a cluster of contacts where resources are dense. For the CEO, the board of directors is such a cluster. The university provost is similarly tied to the board of trustees. For the more typical manager, the immediate work group is such a cluster, especially with respect to funding authority within the group. These clusters are so important to the vitality of the rest of the network that it is worth treating each person in them as a primary contact, regardless of redundancy. Saturation minimizes the risk of losing effective contact with the cluster and minimizes the risk of missing an important opportunity anywhere in the cluster.

The more general point is that the probability of receiving network benefits from a cluster has two components, the probability that a contact will transmit information to you and the probability that it will be transmitted to the contact. I count on dense ties within a cluster to set the second probability to one. The probability of having a benefit transmitted to you therefore depends only on the strength of your relationship with a contact in the cluster. However, where the density of ties in an opportunity-rich cluster lowers the probability that your contact will know about an opportunity, there is value in increasing the number, and thus the redundancy, of contacts in the cluster so that total coverage of the cluster compensates for imperfect transmission within it.

Structural Holes and Weak Ties

Discontinuities in social structure have long been a subject of study in sociology. Fitting the structural hole argument into the history of sociological thought is not the task of this book, but one piece of contemporary history adds value to the argument here. Mark Granovetter's weak tie argument provides an illuminating aside on the information benefits of structural holes.

History

In the late 1960s and early 1970s at Harvard University, Harrison White, with a cluster of exceptional sociology graduate students, was engaged in studying the importance of the gaps, as opposed to the ties, in social structure. First came his celebrated work on chains of mobility (White, 1970), and later his work with colleagues, most notably Ronald Breiger and Scott Boorman, on concrete network models—blockmodels—of social structure (White, Boorman, and Breiger, 1976; see Burt, 1982:63–69, for review). The usual analysis of mobility describes patterns of mobility, or careers, created by people moving between positions in a social structure. White (1970) shifted perspective to focus on the hole, or opportunity, created when a person leaves a position. As people move up the hierarchy, they create opportunities for people below them. Chains of promotion move up a hierarchy. Chains of opportunity move down. Looking at social structure more generally, White, Boorman, and Breiger (1976, esp. pp. 732n, 737–740) stressed the structural hole metaphor as a substantive motivation for their network blockmodels. They focused on "zeroblocks" as an especially significant component in the relation pattern defining a position in social structure. It is clear from their analysis that they meant structural holes to be important for understanding network contingent action, as well as the task they addressed of clustering network elements into blocks (for example, see pp. 763ff., on the low rate of change in zero-blocks).

One of the students, Mark Granovetter, found a troubling result in his dissertation research. Hoping to link network structure to job searches, he interviewed men about how they found their current jobs and included sociometric items asking for the names of close contacts. The troubling result was that the men almost never found work through close contacts. When information on a job opportunity came through a personal contact, the contact was often distant, such as a high school acquaintance met by accident at a recent social event. He developed the point in a widely cited article, "The Strength of Weak Ties" (Granovetter, 1973), and in a book, *Getting a Job* (Granovetter, 1974).

Connecting the Two Arguments

The weak tie argument is elegantly simple. The stage is set with results familiar from the social psychology of Festinger and Homans circa 1950, discussed earlier with respect to cohesion indicators of structural holes. People live in a cluster of others with whom they have strong relations. Information circulates at a high velocity within these clusters. Each person tends to know what the other people know. The spread of information on new ideas and opportunities, therefore, must come through the weak ties that connect people in separate clusters. The weak ties so often ignored by social scientists are in fact a critical element of social structure. Hence the strength of weak ties. Weak ties are essential to the flow of information that integrates otherwise disconnected social clusters into a broader society.

The idea and its connection with structural holes is illustrated in figure 1.6. There are three clusters of players. Strong ties, indicated by solid lines, connect players within clusters. Dashed lines indicate two weak ties between players in separate clusters. One of the players, you, has a unique pattern of four ties: two strong ties within your cluster and a weak tie to a contact in each in the other clusters. There are three classes of structural holes in your network: (a) holes between the cluster around contact A and everyone in your own cluster (for example, the hole between contacts A and C); (b) holes between the cluster around contact B and everyone in your own cluster (for example, the hole between contacts B and C); and (c) the hole between contacts A and B.

Weak ties and structural holes seem to describe the same phenomenon. In figure 1.6, for example, they predict the same ranking of information benefits. You are best positioned for information benefits; contacts A and B are next, followed by everyone else. You have two weak ties, contacts A and B have one each, and everyone else has none. You have the largest volume of structural holes between your contacts; contacts A and B have fewer, and everyone else has few or none.

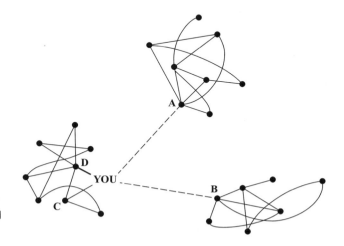

Figure 1.6.
Structural holes and
weak ties

The Strength of Structural Holes

The weak tie argument is simpler and already well known. Why complicate the situation with the structural hole argument? There are two reasons.

First, the causal agent in the phenomenon is not the weakness of a tie but the structural hole it spans. Tie weakness is a correlate, not a cause. The structural hole argument captures the causal agent directly and thus provides a stronger foundation for theory and a clearer guide for empirical research. Second, by shifting attention away from the structural hole responsible for information benefits to the strength of the tie providing them, the weak tie argument obscures the control benefits of structural holes. Control benefits augment and in some ways are more important than the information benefits of structural holes. Building both benefits into the argument speaks more clearly to the generality of the phenomenon under study. I will elaborate the first point, then move to the second in the next section.

The weak tie argument is about the strength of relationships at the same time that it is about their location. The two dashed lines in figure 1.6 are bridges. They are the only connection between two otherwise separate clusters of strongly interconnected players (compare Granovetter, 1973:1065, on weak ties as bridges). A bridge is at once two things. It is a chasm spanned and the span itself. By title and subsequent application, the weak tie argument is about the strength of relationships that span the chasm between two social clusters. The structural hole argument is about the chasm spanned. It is the latter that generates information benefits. Whether a relationship is strong or weak, it generates information benefits when it is a bridge over a structural hole.

Consider a cross-tabulation of ties by their strength and location. Your relationships can be sorted into two categories of strength. Strong ties are your most frequent and close contacts. Weak ties are your less frequent, less close contacts. Between these two categories, you have a few strong ties and many weak ties.

Now sort, by location, redundant ties within your social cluster versus nonredundant ties to people in other clusters. The nonredundant ties are your bridges to other clusters. From what we know about the natural etiology of relationships, bridges are less likely to develop than ties within clusters. The category of redundant ties includes your strong ties to close friends and colleagues, whom you see often, but it also includes their friends, and friends of friends, whom you meet only occasionally if at all. As you expand your inventory from your closest, most frequent contacts to your more distant ones, contacts tend to be people like yourself before you reach a sufficiently low level of relationship to include people from completely separate social worlds. This tendency varies from one person to the next, but it is in the aggregate the substance of the well-documented tendency already discussed for relations to develop between socially similar people. In figure 1.6, you are one of nine people in your social cluster. You have strong ties to two people. Through those two, you have weak ties to the other six people in the cluster. To keep the sociogram simple, I deleted the dashed lines for those ties and their equivalent inside the other clusters. The other six people in your cluster are friends of friends whom you know and sometimes meet but don't have the time or energy to include among your closest contacts. The cluster is clearly held together by strong ties. Everyone has two to five strong ties to others within the cluster. All nine people are likely to know about the same opportunities as expected in a cohesive cluster. Of the 36 possible connections among the nine people in the cluster, however, only 12 are solid line strong ties. The remaining two-thirds are weak ties between redundant friends of friends.

Now cross-tabulate the two classifications and take expected values. The result is given in table 1.1. Information benefits vary across the columns of the table and are higher through nonredundant ties. This is accurately represented in both the weak tie and the structural hole argument. But a quick reading of the weak tie argument, with its emphasis on the strength of a relationship, has led some to test the idea that information benefits covary inversely with the strength of ties. This is a correlation between the rows and columns of table 1.1, which is no correlation at all. In fact, the typical tie in table 1.1 is weak and provides redundant information. The correlation in a study population depends on the distribution of ties in the table, but there is no theoretical reason to expect a strong correlation between the strength of a relationship and the information benefits it provides.

The weak tie argument is about the two cells in the second column of the table. It predicts that nonredundant ties, the bridges that provide information benefits, are more likely weak than strong. In the second column of table 1.1, weak tie bridges are more likely than strong tie bridges. To simplify his argument, Granovetter makes this tendency absolute by ruling out strong tie bridges (the "rare" cell in table 1.1, the "forbidden triad" in Granovetter's argument, 1973: 1063). He (1973:1064) says, "A

Table 1.1
The Natural Distribution of Relationships

| Strength | Location in Social Structure | | Total |
	Redundant Tie within Cluster	Nonredundant Tie beyond Cluster	
Weak tie	many	some	more
Strong tie	some	rare	less
Total	more	less	

strong tie can be a bridge, therefore, only if neither party to it has any other strong ties, unlikely in a social network of any size (though possible in a small group). Weak ties suffer no such restriction, though they are certainly not automatically bridges. What is important, rather, is that all bridges are weak ties."

Bridge strength is an aside in the structural hole argument. Information benefits are expected to travel over all bridges, strong or weak. Benefits vary between redundant and nonredundant ties, the columns of table 1.1. Thus structural holes capture the condition directly responsible for the information benefits. The task for a strategic player building an efficient-effective network is to focus resources on the maintenance of bridge ties. Otherwise, and this is the correlative substance of the weak tie argument, bridges will fall into their natural state of being weak ties.

■ Control and the *Tertius Gaudens*

I have described how structural holes can determine who knows about opportunities, when they know, and who gets to participate in them. Players with a network optimized for structural holes, in addition to being exposed to more rewarding opportunities, are also more likely to secure favorable terms in the opportunities they choose to pursue. The structural holes that generate information benefits also generate control benefits, giving certain players an advantage in negotiating their relationships. To describe how this is so, I break the negotiation into structural, motivational, and outcome components (corresponding to the textbook distinction between market structure, market conduct, and market performance; for example, Caves, 1982). The social structure of the competitive arena defines opportunities; a player decides to pursue an opportunity and is sometimes successful. I will begin with the outcome.

Tertius Gaudens

Sometimes you will emerge successful from negotiation as the *tertius gaudens*. Taken from the work of Georg Simmel, the *tertius* role is useful here because it defines successful negotiation in terms of the social structure of the situation in which negotiation is successful. The role is the heart of Simmel's (1922) later analysis of the freedom an individual derives from conflicting group affiliations (see Coser, 1975, for elaboration).[6] The *tertius gaudens* is "the third who benefits" (Simmel, 1923: 154, 232).[7] The phrase survives in an Italian proverb, *Far i due litiganti, il terzo gode* (Between two fighters, the third benefits), and, in a more jovial Dutch wording, *de lachende derde* (the laughing third).[8] *Tertius, terzo,* or *derde,* the phrase describes an individual who profits from the disunion of others.

There are two *tertius* strategies: being the third between two or more players after the same relationship, and being the third between players in two or more relations with conflicting demands. The first, and simpler, strategy is the familiar one that occurs in economic bargaining between buyer and seller. When two or more players want to buy something, the seller can play their bids against one another to get a higher price. The strategy extends directly: a woman with multiple suitors or a professor with simultaneous offers of positions in rival institutions.

The control benefits of having a choice between players after the same relationship extends directly to choice between the simultaneous demands of players in separate relationships. The strategy can be seen between hierarchical statuses in the enterprising subordinate under the authority of two or more superiors: for example, the student who strikes her own balance between the simultaneous demands of imperious faculty advisers.[9] The bargaining is not limited to situations of explicit competition. In some situations, emerging as the *tertius* depends on creating competition. In proposing the concept of a role-set, for example, Merton (1957: 393–394) identifies this as a strategy to resolve conflicting role demands. Make simultaneous, contradictory demands explicit to the people posing them and ask them to resolve their—now explicit—conflict. Even where it doesn't exist, competition can be produced by defining issues such that contact demands become contradictory and must be resolved before you can meet their requests. Failure is possible. You might provide too little incentive for the contacts to resolve their differences. Contacts drawn from different social strata need not perceive one another's demands as carrying equal weight. Or you might provide too much incentive. Now aware of one another, the contacts could discover sufficient reason to cooperate in forcing you to meet their mutually agreed-upon demands (Simmel, 1902: 176, 180–181), calls attention to such failures). But if the strategy is successful, the pressure on you is alleviated and is replaced with an element of control over the negotiation. Merton (1957: 430) states the situation succinctly: the player at the center of the network, "originally at the focus of the conflict, virtually becomes a more or less influential bystander whose function it is to high-light the conflicting demands by members of his role-set and to make it a problem for them, rather than for him, to resolve *their* contradictory demands."

The strategy holds equally well with large groups. Under the rubric "divide and rule," Simmel (1902:185–186) describes institutional mechanisms through which the Incan and Venetian governments obtained advantage by creating conflict between subjects. The same point is illustrated more richly in Barkey's (1991) comparative description of state control in early seventeenth-century France and Turkey. After establishing the similar conditions in the two states at the time, Barkey asks why peasant-noble alliances developed in France against the central state while no analogous or substitutable alliances developed in Turkey. The two empires were comparable with respect to many factors that scholars have cited to

account for peasant revolt. They differed in one significant factor correlated with revolt—not in the structure of centralized state control but in
control strategy. In France, the king sent trusted representatives as agents
to collect taxes and to carry out military decisions in provincial populations. These outside agents, *intendants*, affected fundamental local decisions, and their intrusion was resented by the established local nobility.
Local nobility formed alliances with the peasantry against the central
state. In Turkey, the sultan capitalized on conflict among leaders in the
provinces. When a bandit became a serious threat to the recognized gov-
ernor, a deal was struck with the bandit to make him the legitimate gov-
ernor. Barkey (1991:710) writes: "At its extreme, the state could render a
dangerous rebel legitimate overnight by striking a bargain that ensured
new sources of revenue for the rebel and momentary relief from internal
warfare and, perhaps, an army or two for the state." The two empires
differed in their use of structural holes. The French king, assuming he had
absolute authority, ignored them. The Turkish sultan, promoting competition between alternative leaders, strategically exploited them. Conflict
within the Turkish empire remained in the province, rather than being
directed against the central state. As is characteristic of the control obtained via structural holes, the resulting Turkish control was more negotiated than was the absolute control exercised in France. It was also more
effective.

The Essential Tension

There is a presumption of tension here. Control emerges from the *tertius*
brokering tension between other players. No tension, no *tertius*.

It is easy to infer that the tension presumed is the tension between
combatants. There is certainly a *tertius*-rich tension between combatants.
Governors and bandits in the Turkish game played for life or death stakes.
A corporate executive listening to the control argument illustrates the
problem. Her colleagues, she explained, took pride in working together
in a spirit of partnership and goodwill. The *tertius* imagery rang true for
many firms she knew of, but not her own.

The reasoning is good. The conclusion is wrong. Promotions in the
firm are strongly correlated, and illuminatingly so for women, with the
structural holes in a manager's network.

The tension essential to the *tertius* is merely uncertainty. Separate the
uncertainty of control from its consequences. The consequences can be life
or death, in the extreme, or merely a question of embarrassment. Everyone knows you made an effort to get that job, but it went to someone
else. The *tertius* strategies can be applied to control with severe consequences or to control of little consequence. What is essential is that control
is uncertain, that no one can act as if he or she has absolute authority.
Where there is any uncertainty about whose preferences should dominate

a relationship, there is an opportunity for the *tertius* to broker the negotiation for control by playing demands against one another. There is no long-term contract that keeps a relationship strong, no legal binding that can secure the trust necessary to a productive relationship. Your network is a pulsing swirl of mixed, conflicting demands. Each contact wants your exclusive attention, your immediate response when a concern arises. All, to warrant their continued confidence in you, want to see you measure up to the values against which they judge themselves. Within this preference webwork, where no demands have absolute authority, the *tertius* negotiates for favorable terms.

The Connection with Information Benefits

Structural holes are the setting for *tertius* strategies. Information is the substance. Accurate, ambiguous, or distorted information is moved between contacts by the *tertius*. One bidder is informed of a competitive offer in the first *tertius* strategy. A player in one relationship is informed of demands from other relationships in the second *tertius* strategy.

The two kinds of benefits augment and depend on one another. Application of the *tertius* strategies elicits additional information from contacts interested in resolving the negotiation in favor of their own preferences. The information benefits of access, timing, and referrals enhance the application of strategy. Successful application of the *tertius* strategies involves bringing together players who are willing to negotiate, have sufficiently comparable resources to view one another's preferences as valid, but won't negotiate with one another directly to the exclusion of the *tertius*. Having access to information means being able to identify where there will be an advantage in bringing contacts together and is the key to understanding the resources and preferences being played against one another. Having that information early is the difference between being the one who brings together contacts versus being just another person who hears about the negotiation. Referrals further enhance strategy. It is one thing to distribute information between two contacts during negotiation. It is another thing to have people close to each contact endorsing the legitimacy of the information you distribute.

■ Entrepreneurs

I have described how the information and control benefits that are relevant to gaining an advantage in negotiating relationships are multiplicative. They augment and depend on one another and together emerge from the wellspring of structural holes in a network. But what prompts a player to pursue these benefits? Negotiation contains a motivational component.

The Issue of Motivation

Behavior of a specific kind converts opportunity into higher rates of return. The information benefits of structural holes might come to a passive player, but control benefits require an active hand in the distribution of information. Motivation is now an issue. Knowing about an opportunity and being in a position to develop it are distinct from doing something about it. The *tertius* plays conflicting demands and preferences against one another and builds value from their disunion. You enter the structural hole between two players to broker the relationship between them. Such behavior is not to everyone's taste. A player can respond in ways ranging from fully developing the opportunity to ignoring it. When you take the opportunity to be the *tertius*, you are an entrepreneur in the literal sense of the word—a person who generates profit from being between others. Both terms will be useful in these precise meanings; entrepreneur refers to a kind of behavior, the *tertius* is a successful entrepreneur.[10]

Both are distinct from behavior subsequent to emerging as the *tertius*. The *tertius* can choose to extract value from negotiated relations, or to add value, strengthening the relations for later profit. Some reinvestment is to be expected if the player's network is to remain intact. A nonprofit player, pursuing entrepreneurial opportunities just for the pleasure of being the one who brings others together to build value, could choose to reinvest it all. The issue at hand is not the uses to which profit is put. It is who chooses to have a hand in the distribution of profit.

Motivation can be traced to cultural images of good and evil. In *The Protestant Ethic and the Spirit of Capitalism*, Weber (1905, esp. pp. 166ff.) describes the seventeenth-century bourgeois Protestant as an individual seeking—in his religious duty, his Calvinist "calling"—the profit of sober, thrifty, diligent exploitation of opportunities for usury and trade. Kilby (1971) provides a review and criticism of research on culturally induced entrepreneurs.

Psychological need is another motive. McClelland (1961) describes the formation in childhood of a need to achieve as critical to later entrepreneurial behavior (a need that can also be cultivated later if desired [McClelland, 1975]). Without going into the etiology of motive, Schumpeter (1912:93) stresses nonutilitarian motives for entrepreneurship: "First of all, there is the dream and the will to found a private kingdom, usually, though not necessarily, also a dynasty. . . . Then there is the will to conquer: the impulse to fight, to prove oneself superior to others, to succeed for the sake, not of the fruits of success, but of the success itself. . . . Finally, there is the joy of creating, of getting things done, or simply of exercising one's energy and ingenuity."[11]

Opportunity and Motivation

These are powerful frameworks for understanding competition, but I don't wish to detour into the beliefs behind entrepreneurial behavior. I propose to leap over the motivation issue by taking the network as simultanously an indicator of entrepreneurial opportunity and of motivation. Psychological and cultural motives for entrepreneurial behavior have been conceptualized and studied without data on the social network surrounding the entrepreneur. Such data are the substance of the structural hole argument and, in three ways, carry their own answer to the question of motivation.

First, there is the clarity of an opportunity. The above are "push" explanations. Players are pushed by psychological need or cultural imperative to be entrepreneurs. There is also a "pull" explanation. Players can be pulled to entrepreneurial action by the promise of success. I do not mean that players are rational creatures expected to calculate accurately and act in their own interest. Nor do I mean to limit the scope of the argument to situations in which players act as if they are rational in that way. I mean simply that given two opportunities, any player is more likely to act on the one with the clearer path to success. The clarity of opportunity is its own motivation. As the number of entrepreneurial opportunities in a network increases, the odds of some being clearly defined by deep structural holes increases, and therefore the odds of entrepreneurial behavior increase. To be sure, a person whose abilities or values proscribe entrepreneurial behavior is unlikely to act, and someone inclined to entrepreneurial behavior is more likely to act or even to take the initiative to create opportunities.[12] Regardless of ability or values, however, within the broad range of acceptable behaviors, a person is unlikely to take entrepreneurial action if the probability of success is low. An observer might question the propriety of a scholar who negotiates with several universities offering a position, but the question is not an issue for the player with one offer.

There are also network analogues to the push explanations of motive. A person with a psychological need for entrepreneurial behavior is prone to building a network configured around such behavior. If I find a player with a network rich in the structural holes that make entrepreneurial behavior possible, I have a player willing and able to act entrepreneurially. But it is the rare person who is the sole author of a network. Networks are more often built in the course of doing something else. If your work, for example, involves meeting people from different walks of life, your network will end up composed of contacts who without you have no contact with one another. Even so, the network is its own explanation of motive. As the volume of structural holes in a player's network increases—regardless of the process that created them—the entrepreneurial behavior of making and negotiating relations between others becomes a way of life. This is a network analogue to the cultural explanation of motive. If all you know is entrepreneurial relationships, the motivation question is a nonissue. Being willing and able to act entrepreneurially is how you understand social life.

I will treat motivation and opportunity as one and the same. For reasons of a clear path to success, or the tastes of the player as the network's author, or the nature of the player's environment as author of the network, a network rich in entrepreneurial opportunity surrounds a player motivated to be entrepreneurial. At the other extreme, a player innocent of entrepreneurial motive lives in a network devoid of entrepreneurial opportunity.[13]

Measurement Implications

This detour into the issue of entrepreneurial motivation highlights a complexity that might otherwise obscure the association between structural holes and rates of return. Consider figure 1.7. Players are defined by their rate of return on investments (vertical axis) and the entrepreneurial opportunities of structural holes in their networks (horizontal axis).

The sloping line in the graph describes the hole effect of players rich in structural holes (horizontal axis) getting higher rates of return on investments (vertical axis). The increasingly positive slope of the line captures the increasing likelihood of *tertius* profit. A player invests in certain relationships. They need not all be high-yield relationships. The higher the proportion of relationships enhanced by structural holes, the more likely and able the entrepreneurial player, and so the more likely it is that the player's investments are in high-yield relationships. The result is a higher aggregate rate of return on investments.

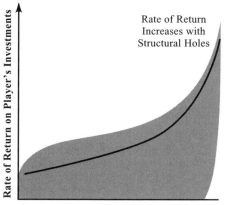

Rate of Return
Increases with
Structural Holes

Rate of Return on Player's Investments

Structural Holes in the Player's Network
few — entrepreneurial opportunities — many

Figure 1.7.
Rate of return and structural holes

I have shaded the area in the graph to indicate how I expect data to be distributed around the line of association. There is no imperative that says players have to take advantage of the benefits provided by structural holes. Players rich in entrepreneurial opportunity may choose to develop opportunities (and so appear in the upper right corner of the graph) or ignore them (and so appear in the lower right corner of the graph). Some players in figure 1.7 are above the line. Some are below. If players were perfectly rational, observations would be clustered around the line. Players would take advantage of any entrepreneurial opportunity presented to them. A control for differences in player motivation, such as a McClelland measure of need for achievement, would have the same effect. The point is not the degree of deviation from the line of association; it is the greater deviation below the line. Variable motivation creates deviations below the true hole effect on rate of return.

This emphasizes the relative importance for empirical research of deviations above and below the line of association. Observations in the lower right corner of the graph, players underutilizing their entrepreneurial opportunities, might be due to variation in motivation. Observations in the upper left corner are a severe test of the argument. Players who have opportunities can choose whether to develop them. Players without opportunities do not have that choice. Within the limits of measurement error, there should be no observations in the upper left corner of the graph.

■ Secondary Holes

This brings me to the third component in the negotiation: the social structural conditions that constitute entrepreneurial opportunity. I have linked opportunity to structural holes, but not with respect to the whole domain of relevant holes. Thus far, a network optimized for entrepreneurial opportunity has a vine-and-cluster structure. As illustrated in figures 1.3 and 1.4, a player has direct relations with primary contacts, each a port of access to a cluster of redundant secondary contacts. Structural holes between the primary contacts, or primary structural holes, provide information and control benefits. But the benefits they provide are affected by structural holes just beyond the border of the network. Structural holes among the secondary contacts within the cluster around each primary contact play a role in the *tertius* strategies. These are secondary structural holes.

Control Benefits and Secondary Structural Holes

The ultimate threat in negotiating a relationship is withdrawal: either severing your link to a former contact's cluster or transferring the primary relationship to a new person in the cluster. This threat depends on two

things. First, there must be alternatives, secondary contacts who are redundant with your primary contact and capable of replacing the primary
contact in your network. Examples include an alternative spouse in the
case of negotiating a conjugal relationship, an alternative job in the case
of negotiating with a truculent supervisor, or an alternative supplier in
the case of a firm renewing a contract with a past supplier. Second, there
must be structural holes among the secondary contacts. If there are no
contacts substitutable for your current primary contact, he or she is free
to impose demands—up to the limit of structural holes between primary
contacts. If your current primary contact is in collusion with whatever
substitutes exist, which eliminates structural holes you might exploit, he
or she is free to impose demands—again, up to the limit of structural
holes between primary contacts.

Consider figure 1.8. You are negotiating with a primary contact in a
cluster of redundant contacts indicated by dots enclosed by a circle. Situation A illustrates the familiar negotiation between buyer and seller. You
use the offer from one buyer to raise the other's offer.

Situation B illustrates the exact opposite condition. Here the redundant contacts are all connected by strong relations. This is the situation of
negotiating with a member of a social clique or cult. In the absence of
holes over which you can broker the connection between redundant contacts, your only recourse is to live with your contact's demands, dominate
the cluster, or cut the cluster from your network.

Network density is not the issue here. Situation C is a relatively low
density cluster (43 percent of the 28 relations within the cluster are marked

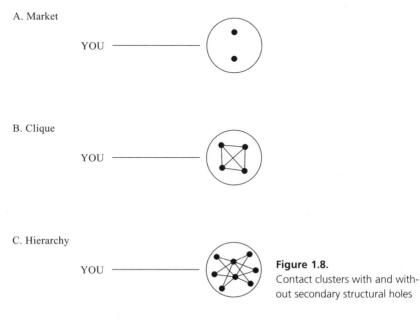

A. Market

YOU ——————

B. Clique

YOU ——————

C. Hierarchy

YOU ——————

Figure 1.8.
Contact clusters with and without secondary structural holes

with a line as strong), but contacts within the cluster are coordinated through their joint ties to two leaders in the center. It doesn't make sense to negotiate the price of a purchase in a department store by playing one sales clerk against another. They both answer to a higher authority. You have to make a purchase sufficiently large that it allows you to deal with someone higher in the organization. Then, as in situation C, you can develop the structural hole between the two leaders at the center of the circle and play one leader against the other.

Cluster Boundaries

Secondary contacts are a cluster of redundant players in the competitive arena beyond any one player's network. Players in the cluster are redundant by cohesion (strongly connected within the cluster) or by structural equivalence (connected with the same players beyond the cluster). Given redundancy within clusters, the more general statement is that players are redundant contacts in the same cluster to the extent that they are connected with the same clusters of redundant contacts.

The idea is illustrated in figure 1.9. Four identical networks are displayed at the top of the figure. Lines are relations, each circle indicates a cluster of redundant contacts, and the dark circle at the center is the player responsible for the network. Each network includes a primary contact in each of the six clusters.

The four central players are redundant. They are connected to the same clusters of redundant contacts and thus have the same information and control benefits. They might be connected to different people in each cluster, but their contacts are ports of access into the same six clusters. Rather than representing the four players with separate networks, it is more accurate to represent them as four redundant contacts within the dark circle in the network at the bottom of figure 1.9. Contacts are aggregated similarly within each of the clusters identified by letter.

The same comparison illustrates nonredundancy. Notice the two curved lines between the player and two clusters, B and E. Clusters B and E are rich in structural holes, so relations with any contact in them will be more easily negotiated than relations with the better-organized clusters, such as A, D, and F. Suppose that one of the central players decides to focus on these relations, leaving the other three to deal with clusters A, C, D, and E. The three are then no longer redundant with the first. The first is connected to clusters different from the ones in their networks.

This image of redundancy is analogous to the concept of substitutable producers in input-output economics. Two producers are substitutable in an economic network to the extent that they purchase similar volumes of the same kinds of supplies to make the commodity they sell. Suppliers are in turn substitutable to the extent that their product requires similar

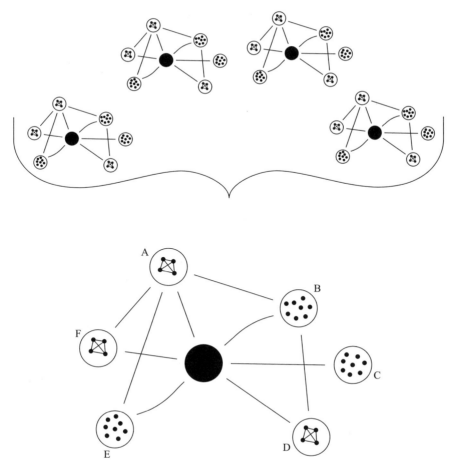

Figure 1.9.
Four redundant networks pooled as one network surrounding four substitutable players

volumes of the same kinds of supplies. Two bakers are substitutable to the extent that they use the same kinds of ingredients. They might purchase their flour and sugar from different vendors, but they are substitutable to the extent that they similarly purchase flour from one of the alternative flour vendors and sugar from one of the alternative sugar vendors. Two auto manufacturers are substitutable to the extent that they use the same proportions of metal, glass, rubber, and plastic to produce the cars they sell. Each manufacturer might purchase glass from a different vendor, but they similarly purchase glass from one or another of the available glass vendors to make their cars.

Redundancy as substitutability is analogous to the equivalence concept in network analysis but different from the often-used variations of structural and role equivalence. Structurally equivalent people have identical relations with the same people. This is too narrow a definition of redundancy. The dark circles in the four networks in figure 1.9 can have relations with completely different people within each cluster, which would make them redundant but not structurally equivalent. At the other extreme, role equivalent people have identically structured relations, regardless of the specific individuals with whom they have relations. This is too broad a definition of redundancy. For example, a person connected only to cluster A in figure 1.9 would be role equivalent to a person only connected to clusters D and F. They would be role equivalent in the sense of being outsiders connected to a clique; however, they are nonredundant because they are connected with different clusters of redundant contacts. Operationally, I am left with cluster boundaries defined a priori by some criterion.

The Depth of a Structural Hole

Secondary only refers to the remove of a hole from the central player. Primary holes are between a player's direct contacts, and secondary holes are between indirect contacts. Of the two kinds of holes, the latter are the more intense.

Let the depth of a structural hole be the ease with which it can be developed for control and information benefits. When the hole is deep between two individuals, it is easy to play them against one another with *tertius* strategies.

Depth is characterized in table 1.2 with combinations of the two indicators of holes: cohesion and equivalence. The columns contrast players who have no relationship with one another with players who meet frequently and feel emotionally close to one another (in other words, have a strong relationship). The rows contrast players in completely separate clusters with those who have equivalent ties to the same clusters (in other words, are close together in the same cluster).

Much of the table is clear from the cohesion and structural equivalence indicators for defining structural holes already discussed. There is a structural hole of some depth between the players in all conditions except the "no hole" cell. Redundancy is most likely between structurally equivalent people connected by a strong relationship. At the other extreme, there is a structural hole where both indicators show no connection: the "hole" cell in the upper left of table 1.2. Redundancy is unlikely between total strangers in distant clusters.

Cohesion is a good indicator. Where cohesion is low, there is a hole between the players. There is no hole where cohesion is high between players equivalently connected to the same clusters. There is also a hole between players in distant clusters connected by a strong relationship. The two players are ports into different clusters of information, but their strong tie means a strong flow of information between them. Playing them

Table 1.2
Depth of a Structural Hole between Players

Equivalent Ties to Clusters	Cohesion between Players	
	None	Strong
None	hole	shallow
Strong	deep	no hole

against one another turns on the extent to which their cluster interests override their commitment to each other.

Cohesion is an especially good indicator relative to equivalence. The first row of the table shows a hole between players in separate clusters. But the second row shows that the widest extremes of hole depth occur between players in the same cluster. The second row of the table is the usual axis of imperfect market competition. Players connected to the same clusters are redundant and so could replace one another in their respective networks. What I bring to your network, a contact connected to the same clusters that I reach could also bring to your network. I and the contact are substitutable producers; we are competitors in the same market. If I have strong relations with my colleagues, we collude to avoid people playing us against one another and you face a cluster like the one in figure 1.8B. If the relations are poor among my colleagues and myself, we are easy prey to being played against one another because we are so readily substitutable and you face a cluster like the one in figure 1.8A.

Equivalence is the frame and cohesion the indicator. Equivalent ties to the same clusters frame two players as competitors in the same market. Cohesion defines the depth of the hole between them. In terms of a regression model, the depth of the hole between two players increases with their equivalence, decreases with the strength of relation between them, and decreases sharply with the extent to which they are equivalent and strongly connected.

■ Structural Autonomy

The argument can now be summarized with a concept defining the extent to which a player's network is rich in structural holes, and thus rich in entrepreneurial opportunity, and thus rich in information and control benefits. The concept is structural autonomy. I will present the concept in a general way here.

The argument began with a generic production equation. Profit equals an investment multiplied by a rate of return. The benefits of a relationship can be expressed in an analogous form: time and energy invested to reach a contact multiplied by a rate of return. A player's entrepreneurial opportunities are enhanced by a relationship to the extent that (a) the player has invested substantial time and energy to secure a connection with the contact and (b) there are many structural holes around the contact ensuring a high rate of return on the investment. More specifically, rate of return concerns how and whom you reach with the relationship. Time and energy invested to reach a player with more resources generate more social capital. For the sake of argument, as explained in the discussion of social capital, I assume that a player with a network optimized for structural holes can identify suitably endowed contacts. My concern is the how of a relationship, defined by the structure of a network and its connection with the social structure of the competitive arena. Thus the rate of return keyed to structural holes is a product of the extent to which there are (a) many primary structural holes between the contact and others in the player's network and (b) many secondary structural holes between the contact and others outside the network who could replace the contact.

There is also the issue of structural holes around the player. As the holes around contacts provide information and control benefits to the player, holes around the player can be developed by contacts for their benefit. Consider your position as one of four disconnected players at the center of the network at the bottom of figure 1.9. Your contacts have the option of replacing you with one of your colleagues who provides the same network benefits that you do. To manage this uncertainty, you might develop relationships with your colleagues so that it would be difficult to play them off against you (an oligopoly strategy), or you might specialize in some way so that they no longer provide network benefits redundant with your own (a differentiation strategy). The point here is that your negotiating position is weaker than expected from the distribution of structural holes around contacts. Developing entrepreneurial opportunities depends on having numerous structural holes around your contacts and none attached to yourself.

These considerations come together in the concept of structural autonomy. Players with relationships free of structural holes at their own end and rich in structural holes at the other end are structurally autonomous. These are the players best positioned for the information and control benefits that a network can provide. These are the players to the far right of the graph in figure 1.7. Structural autonomy summarizes the action potential of the *tertius*'s network. The budget equation for optimizing structural autonomy has an upper limit set by the time and energy of the *tertius*, and a trade-off between the structural holes a new contact provides versus the time and energy required to maintain a productive relationship with the contact.[14]

■ Summary

This chapter's argument begins with the task of profit. Profit is generated by a production equation in which player investments are multiplied by the going rate of return. A million dollars invested at a 10 percent rate of return yields a hundred thousand dollar profit. Investments create an ability to produce a competitive product. Capital is invested, for example, to build and operate a factory. Rate of return is an opportunity to profit from the investment.

The rate of return is keyed to the social structure of the competitive arena. Each player has a network of contacts in the competitive arena. Certain players are connected to certain others, trusting of certain others, obligated to support certain others, dependent on exchange with certain others. Something about the structure of the player's network and the location of the player's contacts in the social structure of the arena defines the player's chances of getting higher rates of return on investment. The chances are enhanced by two kinds of network benefits, information and control, distinguished by the rows of the box in figure 1.10.

The substance of information benefits are access, timing, and referrals. The player's network provides access to information well beyond what the player could process alone. The network also provides that information early, which gives the player an advantage in acting on the information. These benefits concern information coming to the player from contacts. Referral benefits involve the opposite flow. The network that filters information coming to the player also directs, concentrates, and legitimates information received by others about the player. Referrals get the player's interests represented in a positive light, at the right time, in the right places.

Information benefits are maximized in a large, diverse network of trusted contacts. Trust is important with respect to the honoring of interpersonal debt by contacts but is an idiographic question answered by the social match between player and each contact individually. Network size and diversity under a presumption of trust are the general parameters to be optimized. The effective size of a network can be less than its observed size. Size is the number of primary contacts in a network; effective size is the number of nonredundant contacts. Two contacts are redundant to the extent that they provide the same information benefits to the player. Cohesion is an empirical indicator of redundancy. Contacts strongly connected to each other are likely to have similar information and so provide redundant benefit to the player. Structural equivalence is a second indicator. Contacts who, regardless of their relationships with one another, link the player to the same third parties have the same sources of information and so provide redundant benefit to the player. Structural holes are the gaps between nonredundant contacts. As a result of the hole between them, the two contacts provide network benefits that are in some

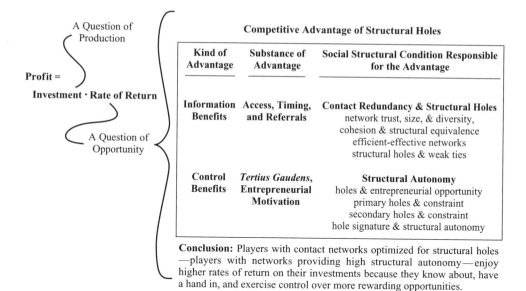

Figure 1.10.
Argument

degree additive rather than overlapping. A network optimized for information benefits can be described with respect to its contacts or its connections between contacts. A network rich in nonredundant contacts is rich in structural holes.

The structural holes that generate information benefits also generate control benefits, giving certain players an advantage in negotiating their relationships. Sociological theory offers a role describing people who derive control benefits from structural holes. It is the *tertius gaudens,* the third who benefits: a person who derives benefit from brokering relationships between other players. There are two *tertius* strategies. People can be played against one another when they compete for the same relationship: for example, two buyers after the same purchase. Second, people can be played against one another when they make conflicting demands on the same individual in separate relationships: a science professor's course demands, for example, being played by a student against the course demands of a humanities professor. There is a presumption of tension here, but the essential tension is not the hostility of combatants; it is merely uncertainty. Separating the uncertainty of control from its consequences, *tertius* strategies apply similarly to negotiating control that has severe consequences or to negotiating control that is of little consequence. What is essential is that the control is uncertain, that no one can act as if he or she has absolute authority in the relationship under negotiation. In the swirling mix of preferences characteristic to social networks, where no demands have absolute authority, the *tertius* negotiates for favorable terms.

The information and control benefits are multiplicative, augmenting and dependent on one another, together emerging from the wellspring of structural holes in a network. Structural holes are the setting for *tertius* strategies. Information is the substance. Accurate, ambiguous, or distorted information is moved between contacts by the *tertius*. One bidder is informed of a competitive offer in the first strategy. A player in one relationship is informed of demands from other relationships in the second strategy.

The final task of this chapter is to bring the argument together in a definition, relevant to empirical research, of the extent to which a player's network is rich in structural holes, and thus in entrepreneurial opportunity, and thus in information and control benefits. Each of a player's relationships is treated as an investment on which structural holes determine the rate of return. A player's entrepreneurial opportunities are enhanced by a relationship to the extent that (a) the player has invested substantial time and energy to secure a connection with the contact and (b) there are many structural holes around the contact ensuring a high rate of return on the investment. The rate of return keyed to structural holes is a product of the extent to which there are (a) many primary structural holes between the contact and others in the player's network and (b) many secondary structural holes between the contact and others outside the network who could replace the contact. There are also the structural holes around the player. As the holes around contacts provide information and control benefits to the player, holes around the player can be developed by contacts for their benefit.

These considerations come together in the concept of structural autonomy. Players with relationships free of structural holes at their own end and rich in structural holes at the other end are structurally autonomous. These are the players best positioned for the information and control benefits that a network can provide. Structural autonomy summarizes the action potential of the *tertius*'s network. The budget equation for optimizing structural autonomy has an upper limit set by the *tertius*'s time and energy, and a trade-off between the structural holes a new contact provides versus the time and energy required to maintain a productive relationship with the contact. The summary conclusion is that players with networks optimized for structural holes—players with networks providing high structural autonomy—enjoy higher rates of return on their investments because they know about, have a hand in, and exercise control over more rewarding opportunities.

The reasoning isn't new. The argument draws on social psychological studies of negotiation, economic studies of imperfect competition, and, most especially, sociological studies of roles and statuses in social structure.

What is new is the expression of competitive advantage—in economic, political, or social arenas—in terms of structural holes as an elemental unit clearly defined in theory and readily operationalized for empirical research.

■ Notes

1. I refer to people and organizations in the competitive arena as "players." Richard Swedberg has commented that I use the term to denote a very active actor, seeking out contacts and opportunities. He gently suggested that the term had a touch of frivolity that I might do well to eliminate with a more neutral term such as "actor." I have used the more neutral term in more general discussion (Burt, 1982), but for the topic of competition, I prefer the term "player." It better fits my felt-reality of the phenomenon. More than implying activity, it is a term of peer recognition: "Yes, he's a player." He's a presence in the game. If you have the motivation, resources, and skills to compete, you're a player; otherwise, you're scenery. Everyone is a player in some arenas, scenery in most. This chapter is about the social structural conditions that give certain players a competitive advantage.

2. Coleman's (1988:S105–S108, S109–S116) argument for the importance of network closure in the transmission of human capital between generations is an illustrative alternative to Granovetter's weak tie metaphor. The weak tie metaphor is that weaker ties are most important to transmission. The work spawned by Lazarsfeld focuses on strong ties. Coleman emphasizes the importance of strong ties reinforced by other ties. Although the argument is not grounded in network models of Simmel's conflicting group-affiliation metaphor, the resemblance is obvious. For example, parents are presumed to prefer that their children obtain at least the minimal education required to graduate from high school. Relying on attribute data, Coleman (1988:S114–S115) shows that children in Catholic high schools—where parents are presumed to be closely connected with one another and other parents, and so constrain the choices of their children—have lower drop-out rates than do children in public high schools. Network analysis improves the power of such arguments, by providing: (a) concrete measures of the extent to which parents (versus others, such as peers) are structurally positioned to constrain the choices of specific children, and (b) formal theory creating more precise, testable understandings of how constraint operates. These points are both illustrated in the forthcoming argument.

3. Network contagion measures of social capital will always be a valuable addition to the application of the general definition to the situation of a specific individual. For example, a person with a poorly structured network that includes just one well-placed contact can do well through that contact's sponsorship regardless of how well the person's network as a whole is structured. We will also see the downside. Being known as someone's minion, dependent on their sponsorship, limits the minion's attractiveness as a social capital addition in other networks. Relations require an investment of time and trust that in this case depend entirely on the sponsor's support. The minion isn't a serious player

independently shaping the course of events in the arena. This makes the minion role adhesive. It holds the player with dependence on the sponsor's support. It cauterizes the development of relations with other players through which the dependence could be made more negotiable.

4. This point is significant because it contradicts the natural growth of contact networks. Left to the normal course of events, a network will accumulate redundant contacts. Friends introduce you to their friends and expect you to like them. Business contacts introduce you to their colleagues. You will like the people you meet in this way. The factors that make your friends attractive make their friends attractive because like seeks out like. Your network grows to include more and more people. These relations come easily, they are comfortable, and they are easy to maintain. But these easily accumulated contacts do not expand the network so much as they fatten it, weakening its efficiency and effectiveness by increasing contact redundancy and tying up time. The process is amplified by spending time in a single place: in your family, or neighborhood, or in the office. The more time you spend with any specific primary contact, the more likely you will be introduced to their friends. Evidence of these processes can be found in studies of balance and transitivity in social relations (see Burt, 1982:55–60, for review) and in studies of the tendency for redundant relations to develop among physically proximate people (for example, the suggestively detailed work of Festinger, Schachter, and Back, 1950; or the work with more definitive data by Fischer, 1982, on social contexts, and Feld, 1981, 1982, on social foci). Here I ignore the many day-to-day tactical issues critical to maintaining a network.

5. The number of structural holes is not increased directly, but is likely to increase. The presumption through all this is that the time and energy to maintain relationships is limited and that the constant pressure to include new contacts will use all the time and energy available (as in the preceding note). Although structural holes are not increased directly by maximizing nonredundant contacts, they can be expected to increase indirectly through the reallocation of time and energy from maintaining redundant contacts to acquiring new nonredundant contacts (as illustrated in figure 1.4).

6. This theme is often grouped with Durkheim's (1893) argument for the liberating effect of a division of labor, but it is useful here to distinguish the two arguments. Simmel focuses on the liberating quality of competition between multiple affiliations, which is our concern. Durkheim focuses on the liberating quality of interdependent affiliations. Integration, rather than competition, is Durkheim's theme. That theme continues in Blau's (1977) analysis of crosscutting social circles, in which he argues that conflict between strata becomes increasingly difficult as affiliations provide people with alternative stratification hierarchies. Flap (1988) provides a network-oriented review of such work, building from anthropology and political science, to study the "crisscross" effect inhibiting violence.

7. Georg Simmel introduced this phrase in papers on the importance of group size, translated and published by Albion Small in the *American Journal of Sociology* (Simmel, 1896:393–394, 1902:174–189). A later version was translated by Wolff (Simmel, 1923:154–169, 232–234).

8. I am grateful to Anna Di Lellio for calling my attention to the Italian proverb and Hein Schreuder for calling my attention to the Dutch expression.

The idea of exploiting a structural hole is viscerally familiar to all audiences, but interestingly varied across cultures in phrasing the profit obtained (an interesting site for a Zelizer, 1989, kind of analysis).

9. This point is nicely exemplified in Simmel's (1896:394) discussion of subordination comparing the freedom of two medieval subordinate positions, the bondsman ("unfree") and the vassal: "An essential difference between the medieval 'unfree' men and the vassals consisted in the fact that the former had and could have only one master, while the latter could accept land from different lords and could take the oath of fealty to each. By reason of the possibility of placing themselves in the feudal relation to several persons the vassals won strong security and independence against the individual lords. The inferiority of the position of vassalage was thereby to a considerable degree equalized."

10. The literal meaning of entrepreneur as broker continues today, but only as one of many narrow meanings in the term's more general, ambiguous meaning of anyone who sets out to accomplish or undertake a task. Before it was watered down, the term enjoyed a long history in its literal meaning as a reference to individuals who obtained their profit by coordinating the activities of others. The term comes from the French verb *entreprendre*, meaning literally "to take, grasp, or snatch" (*prendre*) from "between" (*entre*). In the mid-1500s, entrepreneurs were the men who organized and led military expeditions. Similar to the English privateer, the French entrepreneur was a private agent commissioned to coordinate the recruitment, arming, and transportation of men for a military junket with some promise of profitable booty. The reference to military projects expanded by the 1700s to refer to general contractors for large government projects. Entrepreneurs were the men who organized labor and materials for civil and military projects such as harbors, fortifications, bridges, roads, and buildings. Today's ambiguous meaning of entrepreneur as anyone who undertakes a task comes from the works of French political economists in the middle of the eighteenth century (Belidor, Cantillon, Quesnay, Baudeau, Turgot) describing individuals who undertook projects at risk of being unprofitable because of buying and selling at uncertain prices. Hoselitz (1951) provides a fascinating social etymology of the term (also Redlich, 1949, both of which appeared in the regrettably discontinued journal *Explorations in Entrepreneurial History*, produced until the late 1960s through Harvard's Research Center in Entrepreneurial History). The term's use in economics and business seems little more precise than its use in the general population (for example, see Cochran, 1968, for a quick sketch; Peterson, 1981, for a detailed review), but the literal meaning is sometimes visible. For example, see Peterson's (1981:66ff.) Schumpeterian review of entrepreneurial action as a process of bringing together in a novel way previously separate factors of production or see Kirzner's (1973, esp. pp. 75–87, 126–131, 205–211; and 1979, esp. chap. 3) comparison of his concept of entrepreneur with that of others in economic theory. There is a distinct quality of the *tertius* in Kirzner's successful entrepreneur, for example (1973:48). "Pure entrepreneurial profit is the difference between the two sets of prices. It is not yielded by exchanging something the entrepreneur values less for something he values more highly. It comes from discovering sellers and buyers of something for which the latter will pay more than the former demand."

11. I am grateful to Richard Swedberg for giving me the benefit of his care-

ful study of Schumpeter in calling my attention to these passages. Their broader scope and context are engagingly laid out in his biography of Schumpeter (Swedberg, 1991). The passages can also be found in the Schumpeter selection included in Parsons et al.'s (1961:513) *Theories of Society*.

12. I am reminded of a colleague who found none of the three local banks willing to finance a mortgage on the house he wished to buy. Eventually the mortgage was financed jointly by the three banks, a mortgage my colleague obtained by going to the loan officer in each bank and indicating that each other loan officer was willing to sign off on the loan if he would. With sufficient entrepreneurial motivation, opportunities to emerge as the *tertius* can be created where they don't already exist.

13. I am begging the question of how opportunity and motivation are connected. I emphasize the causal priority of opportunity. The opposite emphasis is traditional in sociology. In his foreword to the English version of Weber's (1905: 8) analysis, R. H. Tawney put the matter succinctly: "Why insist that causation can work in only one direction? Is it not a little artificial to suggest that capitalist enterprise had to wait, as Weber appears to imply, till religious changes had produced a capitalist spirit? Would it not be equally plausible, and equally one-sided, to argue that the religious changes were themselves merely the result of economic movements?" I see no asymmetric resolution to this problem; entrepreneurial opportunity and motivation are reciprocally causal items. Kilby's (1971) edited volume and Wilken's (1979) historical comparative analysis are useful references for detailed discussion of the problem. Here I emphasize opportunity because I can analyze it in a rigorous way with network concepts and describe a great variety of empirical events. Given a rigorous concept of entrepreneurial opportunity, the next analytical step is to study motivational differences between individuals who take advantage of their opportunities and individuals who do not.

14. This sentence is the starting point for an optimization model in which the benefits of a contact are weighed against the cost of maintaining a relation with the contact, subject to a time and energy budget constraint on the aggregate of contacts in a network. The work is beyond the scope of this discussion, but I want to remove an ostensible barrier to such work and in the process highlight a scope limitation to my argument. Marks (1977) provides a cogent argument against the energy scarcity metaphor so often used to justify discussions of role negotiations. Instead of viewing roles as energy debilitating, Marks argues for an "expansion" view in which energy is created by performing roles (compare Sieber, 1974). Marks and Sieber discuss the advantages of performing multiple roles. Both are responding to the energy scarcity arguments used to motivate discussions of mechanisms by which people manage role strain (most notably, Merton, 1957; Goode, 1960). To quote Goode (1960:485), a person "cannot meet all these demands to the satisfaction of all the persons who are part of his total role network. Role strain—difficulty in meeting given role demands—is therefore normal. In general, the person's total role obligations are overdemanding." I have borrowed the theme of overdemanding role obligations. The *tertius* budget constraint concerns both the time and energy cost of maintaining existing relations and the opportunity costs of contacts lost because of redundancy. However, my argument only concerns negotiations within a single role. The mechanisms

used to manage role strain, such as segregating role relations in time and space, could also be used by the *tertius* to manage conflict to his or her own advantage, but I am ignoring that possibility, and so limiting the scope of my argument, to focus on the situation in which *tertius* negotiates conflicting demands that have to be met simultaneously.

■ References

Barber, Bernard. 1978. Inequality and occupational prestige: Theory, research, and social policy. *Sociological Inquiry* 48:75–88.

Barber, Bernard. 1983. *The Logic and Limits of Trust*. New Brunswick, N.J.: Rutgers University Press.

Barkey, Karen. 1991. Rebellious alliances: the state and peasant unrest in early seventeenth century France and the Ottoman empire. *American Sociological Review* 56:699–715.

Berkman, Lisa F., and S. Leonard Syme. 1979. Social networks, host resistance, and mortality: A nine-year follow-up study of Alameda County residents. *American Journal of Epidemiology* 109:186–204.

Blau, Peter M. 1977. *Heterogeneity and Inequality*. New York: Free Press.

Boxman, Ed A. W., Paul M. De Graaf, and Hendrik D. Flap. 1991. The impact of social and human capital on the income attainment of Dutch managers. *Social Networks* 13:51–73.

Burt, Ronald S. 1982. *Toward a Structural Theory of Action*. New York: Academic Press.

Burt, Ronald S. 1986. A note on sociometric order in the General Social Survey network data. *Social Networks* 8:149–174.

Burt, Ronald S. 1990. Kinds of relations in American discussion networks. Pp. 411–451 in *Structures of Power and Constraint*, ed. C. Calhoun, M. W. Meyer, and W. R. Scott. New York: Cambridge University Press.

Campbell, Karen E., Peter V. Marsden, and Jeanne S. Hurlbert. 1986. Social resources and socioeconomic status. *Social Networks* 8:97–117.

Caves, Richard E. 1982. *American Industry: Structure, Conduct, Performance*. Englewood Cliffs, N.J.: Prentice Hall.

Cochran, Thomas C. 1968. Entrepreneurship. Pp. 87–90 in *International Encyclopedia of the Social Sciences*, vol. 5. New York: Macmillan.

Cole, Stephen. 1992. *Making Science*. Cambridge, Mass.: Harvard University Press.

Coleman, James S. 1988. Social capital in the creation of human capital. *American Journal of Sociology* 94:S95–S120.

Coser, Rose Laub. 1975. The complexity of roles as a seedbed of individual autonomy. Pp. 237–263 in *The Idea of Social Structure*, ed. L. A. Coser. New York: Harcourt, Brace, Jovanovich.

De Graaf, Nan D., and Hendrik D. Flap. 1988. With a little help from my friends. *Social Forces* 67:453–472.

Durkheim, Emile. (1893) 1933. *The Division of Labor in Society*. Translated by G. Simpson. New York: Free Press.

Feld, Scott L. 1981. The focused organization of social ties. *American Journal of Sociology* 86:1015–1035.

Feld, Scott L. 1982. Social structural determinants of similarity. *American Sociological Review* 47:797–801.

Festinger, Leon, Stanley Schachter, and Kurt W. Back. 1950. *Social Pressures in Informal Groups*. Stanford: Stanford University Press.

Fischer, Claude S. 1982. *To Dwell among Friends*. Chicago: University of Chicago Press.

Flap, Hendrik D., and Nan D. De Graaf. 1989. Social capital and attained occupational status. *Netherlands Journal of Sociology* 22:145–161.

Flap, Hendrik D., and F. Tazelaar. 1989. The role of informal social networks on the labor market: flexibilization and closure. Pp. 99–118 in *Flexibilization of the Labor Market*, ed. H. Flap. Utrecht: ISOR, University of Utrecht.

Goode, William J. 1960. A theory of role strain. *American Sociological Review* 25: 483–496.

Granovetter, Mark S. 1973. The strength of weak ties. *American Journal of Sociology* 78:1360–1380.

Granovetter, Mark S. 1974. *Getting a Job*. Cambridge, Mass.: Harvard University Press.

Homans, George C. 1950. *The Human Group*. New York: Harcourt, Brace and World.

Hoselitz, Bert F. 1951. The early history of entrepreneurial history. *Explorations in Entrepreneurial History* 3:193–220.

Kilby, Peter, ed. 1971. *Entrepreneurship and Economic Development*. New York: Free Press.

Kirzner, Israel M. 1973. *Competition and Entrepreneurship*. Chicago: University of Chicago Press.

Lazarsfeld, Paul F., Bernard Berelson, and Hazel Gaudet. 1944. *The People's Choice*. New York: Columbia University Press.

Lin, Nan, 1982. Social resources and instrumental action. Pp. 131–145 in *Social Structure and Network Analysis*, ed. P. V. Marsden and Nan Lin. Beverly Hills, Calif.: Sage.

Lin, Nan, and Mary Dumin. 1986. Access to occupations through social ties. *Social Networks* 8:365–385.

Lin, Nan, Walter M. Ensel, and John C. Vaughn. 1981. Social resources and strength of ties. *American Sociological Review* 46:393–405.

Marks, Stephen R. 1977. Multiple roles and role strain: some notes on human energy, time, and commitment. *American Sociological Review* 42:921–936.

Marsden, Peter V. 1987. Core discussion networks of Americans. *American Sociological Review* 52:122–131.

Marsden, Peter V., and Jeanne S. Hurlbert. 1988. Social resources and mobility outcomes: A replication and extension. *Social Forces* 67:1038–1059.

McClelland, David C. 1961. *The Achieving Society*. Princeton: Van Nostrand.

McClelland, David C. 1975. *Power*. New York: Irvington.

Merton, Robert K. (1957) 1968. Continuities in the theory of reference group behavior. Pp. 335–440 in *Social Theory and Social Structure*. New York: Free Press.

Nohria, Nitin. 1991. Structural equivalence as an occasion for the production of trust. Paper presented at the Euro-American conference "Boundaries and Units."

Parsons, Talcott, Edward Shils, Kaspar D. Naegele, and Jesse R. Pitts. 1961. *Theories of Society*. New York: Free Press.

Peterson, Richard A. 1981. Entrepreneurship and organization. Pp. 65–83 in *Handbook of Organizational Design*, vol. 1, ed. P. C. Nystrom and W. H. Starbuck. New York: Oxford University Press.

Redlich, Fritz. 1949. The origins of the concepts of "entrepreneur" and "creative entrepreneur." *Explorations in Entrepreneurial History* 1:1–7.

Schumpeter, Joseph A. (1912) 1961. *The Theory of Economic Development*. Trans. R. Opie. Cambridge, Mass.: Harvard University Press.

Sieber, Sam D. 1974. Toward a theory of role accumulation. *American Sociological Review* 39:567–578.

Simmel, Georg. 1896. Superiority and subordination as subject-matter of sociology, II. Trans. A. Small. *American Journal of Sociology* 2:392–415.

Simmel, Georg. 1902. The number of members as determining the sociological form of the group, II. Trans. A. Small. *American Journal of Sociology* 8:158–96.

Simmel, Georg. (1922) 1955. *Conflict and Web of Group Affiliations*. Trans. K. H. Wolff and R. Bendix. New York: Free Press.

Simmel, Georg. (1923) 1950. *The Sociology of Georg Simmel*. Trans. K. H. Wolff. New York: Free Press.

Swedberg, Richard. 1991. *Schumpeter—A Biography*. Princeton: Princeton University Press.

Weber, Max. (1904–1905) 1930. *The Protestant Ethic and the Spirit of Capitalism*. Trans. T. Parsons. New York: Charles Scribner's Sons.

White, Harrison C. 1970. *Chains of Opportunity*. Cambridge, Mass.: Harvard University Press.

White, Harrison C., Scott Boorman, and Ronald L. Breiger. 1976. Social structure from multiple networks, I, Blockmodels of roles and positions. *American Journal of Sociology* 81:730–780.

Wilken, Paul H. 1979. *Entrepreneurship*. Norwood, N.J.: Ablex.

Zelizer, Viviana A. 1989. The social meaning of money: "Special monies." *American Journal of Sociology* 95:342–377.

2

Social Capital in the Creation of Human Capital

James S. Coleman

There are two broad intellectual streams in the description and explanation of social action. One, characteristic of the work of most sociologists, sees the actor as socialized and action as governed by social norms, rules, and obligations. The principal virtues of this intellectual stream lie in its ability to describe action in social context and to explain the way action is shaped, constrained, and redirected by the social context.

The other intellectual stream, characteristic of the work of most economists, sees the actor as having goals independently arrived at, as acting independently, and as wholly self-interested. Its principal virtue lies in having a principle of action, that of maximizing utility. This principle of action, together with a single empirical generalization (declining marginal utility), has generated the extensive growth of neoclassical economic theory, as well as the growth of political philosophy of several varieties: utilitarianism, contractarianism, and natural rights.[1]

In earlier works (Coleman 1986a, 1986b), I have argued for and engaged in the development of a theoretical orientation in sociology that includes components from both these intellectual streams. It accepts the principle of rational or purposive action and attempts to show how that principle, in conjunction with particular social contexts, can account not only for the actions of individuals in particular contexts but also for the development of social organization. In the present paper, I introduce a conceptual tool for use in this theoretical enterprise: social capital. As background for introducing this concept, it is useful to see some of the criticisms of and attempts to modify the two intellectual streams.

Criticisms and Revisions

Both these intellectual streams have serious defects. The sociological stream has what may be a fatal flaw as a theoretical enterprise: the actor has no "engine of action." The actor is shaped by the environment, but there are no internal springs of action that give the actor a purpose or direction. The very conception of action as wholly a product of the environment has led sociologists themselves to criticize this intellectual stream, as in Dennis Wrong's (1961) "Oversocialized Conception of Man in Modern Sociology."

The economic stream, on the other hand, flies in the face of empirical reality: persons' actions are shaped, redirected, constrained by the social context; norms, interpersonal trust, social networks, and social organization are important in the functioning not only of the society but also of the economy.

A number of authors from both traditions have recognized these difficulties and have attempted to impart some of the insights and orientations of the one intellectual stream to the other. In economics, Yoram Ben-Porath (1980) has developed ideas concerning the functioning of what he calls the "F-connection" in exchange systems. The F-connection is families, friends, and firms, and Ben-Porath, drawing on literature in anthropology and sociology, as well as economics, shows the way these forms of social organization affect economic exchange. Oliver Williamson has, in a number of publications (e.g., 1975, 1981), examined the conditions under which economic activity is organized in different institutional forms, that is, within firms or in markets. There is a whole body of work in economics, the "new institutional economics," that attempts to show, within neoclassical economic theory, both the conditions under which particular economic institutions arise and the effects of these institutions (i.e., of social organization) on the functioning of the system.

There have been recent attempts by sociologists to examine the way social organization affects the functioning of economic activity. Baker (1983) has shown how, even in the highly rationalized market of the Chicago Options Exchange, relations among floor traders develop, are maintained, and affect their trades. More generally, Granovetter (1985) has engaged in a broad attack on the "undersocialized concept of man" that characterizes economists' analysis of economic activity. Granovetter first criticizes much of the new institutional economics as crudely functionalist because the existence of an economic institution is often explained merely by the functions it performs for the economic system. He argues that, even in the new institutional economics, there is a failure to recognize the importance of concrete personal relations and networks of relations—what he calls "embeddedness"—in generating trust, in establishing expectations, and in creating and enforcing norms.

Granovetter's idea of embeddedness may be seen as an attempt to introduce into the analysis of economic systems social organization and social relations not merely as a structure that springs into place to fulfill an economic function, but as a structure with history and continuity that give it an independent effect on the functioning of economic systems.

All this work, both by economists and by sociologists, has constituted a revisionist analysis of the functioning of economic systems. Broadly, it can be said to maintain the conception of rational action but to superimpose on it social and institutional organization—either endogenously generated, as in the functionalist explanations of some of the new institutional economists, or as exogenous factors, as in the more proximate causally oriented work of some sociologists.

My aim is somewhat different. It is to import the economists' principle of rational action for use in the analysis of social systems proper, including but not limited to economic systems, and to do so without discarding social organization in the process. The concept of social capital is a tool to aid in this. In this paper, I introduce the concept in some generality and then examine its usefulness in a particular context, that of education.

■ Social Capital

Elements from these two intellectual traditions cannot be brought together in a pastiche. It is necessary to begin with a conceptually coherent framework from one and introduce elements from the other without destroying that coherence.

I see two major deficiencies in earlier work that introduced "exchange theory" into sociology, despite the pathbreaking character of this work. One was the limitation to microsocial relations, which abandons the principal virtue of economic theory, its ability to make the micro-macro transition from pair relations to system. This was evident both in Homans's (1961) work and in Blau's (1964) work. The other was the attempt to introduce principles in an ad hoc fashion, such as "distributive justice" (Homans 1964, p. 241) or the "norm of reciprocity" (Gouldner 1960). The former deficiency limits the theory's usefulness, and the latter creates a pastiche.

If we begin with a theory of rational action, in which each actor has control over certain resources and interests in certain resources and events, then social capital constitutes a particular kind of resource available to an actor.

Social capital is defined by its function. It is not a single entity but a variety of different entities, with two elements in common: they all consist of some aspect of social structures, and they facilitate certain actions of actors—whether persons or corporate actors—within the structure. Like other forms of capital, social capital is productive, making possible the achievement of certain ends that in its absence would not be possible. Like physical capital and human capital, social capital is not completely fungible but may be specific to certain activities. A given form of social capital that is valuable in facilitating certain actions may be useless or even harmful for others.

Unlike other forms of capital, social capital inheres in the structure of relations between actors and among actors. It is not lodged either in the actors themselves or in physical implements of production. Because purposive organizations can be actors ("corporate actors") just as persons can, relations among corporate actors can constitute social capital for them as well (with perhaps the best-known example being the sharing of information that allows price-fixing in an industry). However, in the present paper, the examples and area of application to which I will direct attention concern social capital as a resource for persons.

Before I state more precisely what social capital consists of, it is useful to give several examples that illustrate some of its different forms.

1. Wholesale diamond markets exhibit a property that to an outsider is remarkable. In the process of negotiating a sale, a merchant will hand over to another merchant a bag of stones for the latter to examine in private at his leisure, with no formal insurance that the latter will not substitute one or more inferior stones or a paste replica. The merchandise may be worth thousands, or hundreds of thousands, of dollars. Such free exchange of stones for inspection is important to the functioning of this market. In its absence, the market would operate in a much more cumbersome, much less efficient fashion.

Inspection shows certain attributes of the social structure. A given merchant community is ordinarily very close, both in the frequency of interaction and in ethnic and family ties. The wholesale diamond market in New York City, for example, is Jewish, with a high degree of intermarriage. Participants in the business live in the same community in Brooklyn and go to the same synagogues. It is essentially a closed community.

Observation of the wholesale diamond market indicates that these close ties, through family, community, and religious affiliation, provide the insurance that is necessary to facilitate the transactions in the market. If any member of this community defected through substituting other stones or through stealing stones in his temporary possession, he would lose family, religious, and community ties. The strength of these ties makes possible transactions in which trustworthiness is taken for granted and trade can occur with ease. In the absence of these ties, elaborate and expensive bonding and insurance devices would be necessary—or else the transactions could not take place.

2. The *International Herald Tribune* of June 21–22, 1986, contained an article on page 1 about South Korean student radical activism. It describes the development of such activism: "Radical thought is passed on in clandestine 'study circles,' groups of students who may come from the same high school or hometown or church. These study circles . . . serve as the basic organizational unit for demonstrations and other protests. To avoid detection, members of different groups never meet, but communicate through an appointed representative."

This description of the basis of organization of this activism illustrates social capital of two kinds. The "same high school or hometown or church" provides social relations on which the "study circles" are later built. The study circles themselves constitute a form of social capital—a cellular form of organization that appears especially valuable for facilitating opposition in any political system intolerant of dissent. Even where political dissent is tolerated, certain activities are not, whether the activities are politically motivated terrorism or simple crime. The organization that makes possible these activities is an especially potent form of social capital.

3. A mother of six children who recently moved with husband and children from suburban Detroit to Jerusalem described as one reason for doing so the greater freedom her young children had in Jerusalem. She felt safe in letting her eight-year-old take the six-year-old across town to school on the city bus and felt her children to be safe in playing without supervision in a city park, neither of which she felt able to do where she lived before.

The reason for this difference can be described as a difference in social capital available in Jerusalem and suburban Detroit. In Jerusalem, the normative structure ensures that unattended children will be "looked after" by adults in the vicinity, while no such normative structure exists in most metropolitan areas of the United States. One can say that families have available to them in Jerusalem social capital that does not exist in metropolitan areas of the United States.

4. In the Kahn El Khalili market of Cairo, the boundaries between merchants are difficult for an outsider to discover. The owner of a shop that specializes in leather will, when queried about where one can find a certain kind of jewelry, turn out to sell that as well—or, what appears to be nearly the same thing, to have a close associate who sells it, to whom he will immediately take the customer. Or he will instantly become a money changer, although he is not a money changer, merely by turning to his colleague a few shops down. For some activities, such as bringing a customer to a friend's store, there are commissions; for others, such as money changing, there is merely the creation of obligations. Family relations are important in the market, as is the stability of proprietorship. The whole market is so infused with relations of the sort I have described that it can be seen as an organization, no less so than a department store. Alternatively, one can see the market as consisting of a set of individual merchants, each having an extensive body of social capital on which to draw, through the relationships of the market.

The examples above have shown the value of social capital for a number of outcomes, both economic and noneconomic. There are, however, certain properties of social capital that are important for understanding how it comes into being and how it is employed in the creation of human capital. First, a comparison with human capital, and then an examination of different forms of social capital, will be helpful for seeing these properties.

■ Human Capital and Social Capital

Probably the most important and most original development in the economics of education in the past 30 years has been the idea that the concept of physical capital as embodied in tools, machines, and other productive equipment can be extended to include human capital as well (see Schultz 1961; Becker 1964). Just as physical capital is created by changes in materials to form tools that facilitate production, human capital is created by changes in persons that bring about skills and capabilities that make them able to act in new ways.

Social capital, however, comes about through changes in the relations among persons that facilitate action. If physical capital is wholly tangible, being embodied in observable material form, and human capital is less tangible, being embodied in the skills and knowledge acquired by an individual, social capital is less tangible yet, for it exists in the *relations* among persons. Just as physical capital and human capital facilitate productive activity, social capital does as well. For example, a group within which there is extensive trustworthiness and extensive trust is able to accomplish much more than a comparable group without that trustworthiness and trust.

■ Forms of Social Capital

The value of the concept of social capital lies first in the fact that it identifies certain aspects of social structure by their functions, just as the concept "chair" identifies certain physical objects by their function, despite differences in form, appearance, and construction. The function identified by the concept of social capital is the value of these aspects of social structure to actors as resources that they can use to achieve their interests.

By identifying this function of certain aspects of social structure, the concept of social capital constitutes both an aid in accounting for different outcomes at the level of individual actors and an aid toward making the micro-to-macro transitions without elaborating the social structural details through which this occurs. For example, in characterizing the clandestine study circles of South Korean radical students as constituting social capital that these students can use in their revolutionary activities, we assert that the groups constitute a resource that aids in moving from individual protest to organized revolt. If, in a theory of revolt, a resource that accomplishes this task is held to be necessary, then these study circles are grouped together with those organizational structures, having very different origins, that have fulfilled the same function for individuals with revolutionary goals in other contexts, such as the *Comités d'action lycéen* of the French student revolt of 1968 or the workers' cells in tsarist Russia described and advocated by Lenin ([1902] 1973).

It is true, of course, that for other purposes one wants to investigate the details of such organizational resources, to understand the elements that are critical to their usefulness as resources for such a purpose, and to examine how they came into being in a particular case. But the concept of social capital allows taking such resources and showing the way they can be combined with other resources to produce different system-level behavior or, in other cases, different outcomes for individuals. Although, for these purposes, social capital constitutes an unanalyzed concept, it signals to the analyst and to the reader that something of value has been produced for those actors who have this resource available and that the value depends on social organization. It then becomes a second stage in the analysis to unpack the concept, to discover what components of social organization contribute to the value produced.

In previous work, Lin (1988) and De Graaf and Flap (1988), from a perspective of methodological individualism similar to that used in this paper, have shown how informal social resources are used instrumentally in achieving occupational mobility in the United States and, to a lesser extent, in West Germany and the Netherlands. Lin focused on social ties, especially "weak" ties, in this role. Here, I want to examine a variety of resources, all of which constitute social capital for actors.

Before examining empirically the value of social capital in the creation of human capital, I will go more deeply into an examination of just what it is about social relations that can constitute useful capital resources for individuals.

Obligations, Expectations, and Trustworthiness of Structures

If A does something for B and trusts B to reciprocate in the future, this establishes an expectation in A and an obligation on the part of B. This obligation can be conceived as a credit slip held by A for performance by B. If A holds a large number of these credit slips, for a number of persons with whom A has relations, then the analogy to financial capital is direct. These credit slips constitute a large body of credit that A can call in if necessary—unless, of course, the placement of trust has been unwise and these are bad debts that will not be repaid.

In some social structures, it is said that "people are always doing things for each other." There are a large number of these credit slips outstanding, often on both sides of a relation (for these credit slips appear often not to be completely fungible across areas of activity, so that credit slips of B held by A and those of A held by B are not fully used to cancel each other out). The El Khalili market in Cairo, described earlier, constitutes an extreme case of such a social structure. In other social structures where individuals are more self-sufficient and depend on each other less, there are fewer of these credit slips outstanding at any time.

This form of social capital depends on two elements: trustworthiness of the social environment, which means that obligations will be repaid, and the actual extent of obligations held. Social structures differ in both these dimensions, and actors within the same structure differ in the second. A case that illustrates the value of the trustworthiness of the environment is that of the rotating-credit associations of Southeast Asia and elsewhere. These associations are groups of friends and neighbors who typically meet monthly, each person contributing to a central fund that is then given to one of the members (through bidding or by lot), until, after a number of months, each of the n persons has made n contributions and received one payout. As Geertz (1962) points out, these associations serve as efficient institutions for amassing savings for small capital expenditures, an important aid to economic development.

But without a high degree of trustworthiness among the members of the group, the institution could not exist—for a person who receives a payout early in the sequence of meetings could abscond and leave the others with a loss. For example, one could not imagine a rotating-credit association operating successfully in urban areas marked by a high degree of social disorganization—or, in other words, by a lack of social capital.

Differences in social structures in both dimensions may arise for a variety of reasons. There are differences in the actual needs that persons have for help, in the existence of other sources of aid (such as government welfare services), in the degree of affluence (which reduces aid needed from others), in cultural tendencies to lend aid and ask for aid (see Banfield 1967), in the closure of social networks, in the logistics of social contacts (see Festinger, Schachter, and Back 1963), and in other factors. Whatever the source, however, individuals in social structures with high levels of obligations outstanding at any time have more social capital on which they can draw. The density of outstanding obligations means, in effect, that the overall usefulness of the tangible resources of that social structure is amplified by their availability to others when needed.

Individual actors in a social system also differ in the number of credit slips outstanding on which they can draw at any time. The most extreme examples are in hierarchically structured extended family settings, in which a patriarch (or "godfather") holds an extraordinarily large set of obligations that he can call in at any time to get what he wants done. Near this extreme are villages in traditional settings that are highly stratified, with certain wealthy families who, because of their wealth, have built up extensive credits that they can call in at any time.

Similarly, in political settings such as a legislature, a legislator in a position with extra resources (such as the Speaker of the House of Representatives or the majority leader of the Senate in the U.S. Congress) can, by effective use of resources, build up a set of obligations from other legislators that makes it possible to get legislation passed that would otherwise be stymied. This concentration of obligations constitutes social capital that is useful not only for this powerful legislator but also in getting an increased level of action on the part of a legislature. Thus, those members of legislatures among whom such credits are extensive should be more powerful than those without extensive credits and debits because they can use the credits to produce bloc voting on many issues. It is well recognized, for example, that in the U.S. Senate, some senators are members of what is called "the Senate Club," while others are not. This in effect means that some senators are embedded in the system of credits and debits, while others, outside the club, are not. It is also well recognized that those in the club are more powerful than those outside it.

Information Channels

An important form of social capital is the potential for information that inheres in social relations. Information is important in providing a basis for action. But acquisition of information is costly. At a minimum, it requires attention, which is always in scarce supply. One means by which information can be acquired is by use of social relations that are maintained for other purposes. Katz and Lazarsfeld (1955) showed how this operated for women in several areas of life in a midwestern city around 1950. They showed that a woman with an interest in being in fashion but no interest in being on the leading edge of fashion used friends who she knew kept up with fashion as sources of information. Similarly, a person who is not greatly interested in current events but who is interested in being informed about important developments can save the time of reading a newspaper by depending on a spouse or friends who pay attention to such matters. A social scientist who is interested in being up-to-date on research in related fields can make use of everyday interactions with colleagues to do so, but only in a university in which most colleagues keep up-to-date.

All these are examples of social relations that constitute a form of social capital that provides information that facilitates action. The relations in this case are not valuable for the "credit slips" they provide in the form of obligations that one holds for others' performances or for the trustworthiness of the other party but merely for the information they provide.

Norms and Effective Sanctions

When a norm exists and is effective, it constitutes a powerful, though sometimes fragile, form of social capital. Effective norms that inhibit crime make it possible to walk freely outside at night in a city and enable old persons to leave their houses without fear for their safety. Norms in a community that support and provide effective rewards for high achievement in school greatly facilitate the school's task.

A prescriptive norm within a collectivity that constitutes an especially important form of social capital is the norm that one should forgo self-interest and act in the interests of the collectivity. A norm of this sort, reinforced by social support, status, honor, and other rewards, is the social capital that builds young nations (and then dissipates as they grow older), strengthens families by leading family members to act selflessly in "the family's" interest, facilitates the development of nascent social movements through a small group of dedicated, inward-looking, and mutually rewarding members, and in general leads persons to work for the public good. In some of these cases, the norms are internalized; in others, they are largely supported through external rewards for selfless actions and disapproval for selfish actions. But, whether supported by internal or external sanctions, norms of this sort are important in overcoming the public good problem that exists in collectivities.

As all these examples suggest, effective norms can constitute a powerful form of social capital. This social capital, however, like the forms described earlier, not only facilitates certain actions; it constrains others. A community with strong and effective norms about young persons' behavior can keep them from "having a good time." Norms that make it possible to walk alone at night also constrain the activities of criminals (and in some cases of noncriminals as well). Even prescriptive norms that reward certain actions, like the norm in a community that says that a boy who is a good athlete should go out for football, are in effect directing energy away from other activities. Effective norms in an area can reduce innovativeness in an area, not only deviant actions that harm others but also deviant actions that can benefit everyone. (See Merton [1968, pp. 195–203] for a discussion of how this can come about.)

■ Social Structure That Facilitates Social Capital

All social relations and social structures facilitate some forms of social capital; actors establish relations purposefully and continue them when they continue to provide benefits. Certain kinds of social structure, however, are especially important in facilitating some forms of social capital.

Closure of Social Networks

One property of social relations on which effective norms depend is what I will call closure. In general, one can say that a necessary but not sufficient condition for the emergence of effective norms is action that imposes external effects on others (see Ullmann-Margalit 1977; Coleman 1987).

Norms arise as attempts to limit negative external effects or to encourage positive ones. But, in many social structures where these conditions exist, norms do not come into existence. The reason is what can be described as lack of closure of the social structure. Figure 2.1 illustrates why. In an open structure like that of figure 2.1a, actor A, having relations with actors B and C, can carry out actions that impose negative externalities on B or C or both. Since they have no relations with one another but with others instead (D and E), they cannot combine forces to sanction A in order to constrain the actions. Unless either B or C is sufficiently harmed and sufficiently powerful vis-à-vis A to sanction alone, A's actions can continue unabated. In a structure with closure, like that of figure 2.1b, B and C can combine to provide a collective sanction or either can reward the other for sanctioning A. (See Merry [1984] for examples of the way gossip, which depends on closure of the social structure, is used as a collective sanction.)

In the case of norms imposed by parents on children, closure of the structure requires a slightly more complex structure, which I will call intergenerational closure. Intergenerational closure may be described by a simple diagram that represents relations between parent and child and relations outside the family. Consider the structure of two communities, represented by figure 2.2. The vertical lines represent relations across generations, between parent and child, while the horizontal lines represent relations within a generation. The point labeled A in both figure 2.2a and figure 2.2b represents the parent of child B, and the point labeled D represents the parent of child C. The lines between B and C represent the relations among children that exist within any school. Although the other relations among children within the school are not shown here, there exists a high degree of closure among peers, who see each other daily, have expectations toward each other, and develop norms about each other's behavior.

The two communities differ, however, in the presence or absence of links among the parents of children in the school. For the school represented by figure 2.2b, there is intergenerational closure; for that represented by figure 2.2a, there is not. To put it colloquially, in the lower

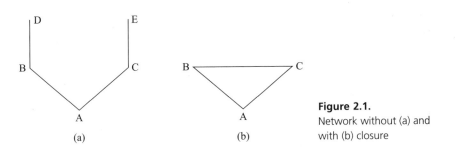

Figure 2.1.
Network without (a) and with (b) closure

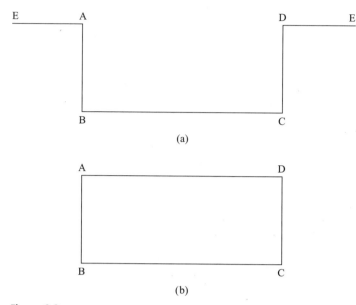

Figure 2.2.
Network involving parents (A, D) and children (B, C) without (a) and with (b) intergenerational closure

community represented by 2.2b, the parents' friends are the parents of their children's friends. In the other, they are not.

The consequence of this closure is, as in the case of the wholesale diamond market or in other similar communities, a set of effective sanctions that can monitor and guide behavior. In the community in figure 2.2b parents *A* and *D* can discuss their children's activities and come to some consensus about standards and about sanctions. Parent *A* is reinforced by parent *D* in sanctioning his child's actions; beyond that, parent *D* constitutes a monitor not only for his own child, *C*, but also for the other child, *B*. Thus, the existence of intergenerational closure provides a quantity of social capital available to each parent in raising his children— not only in matters related to school but in other matters as well.

Closure of the social structure is important not only for the existence of effective norms but also for another form of social capital: the trustworthiness of social structures that allows the proliferation of obligations and expectations. Defection from an obligation is a form of imposing a negative externality or another. Yet, in a structure without closure, it can be effectively sanctioned, if at all, only by the person to whom the obligation is owed. Reputation cannot arise in an open structure, and collective sanctions that would ensure trustworthiness cannot be applied. Thus, we may say that closure creates trustworthiness in a social structure.

Appropriable Social Organization

Voluntary organizations are brought into being to aid some purpose of those who initiate them. In a housing project built during World War II in an eastern city of the United States, there were many physical problems caused by poor construction: faulty plumbing, crumbling sidewalks, and other defects (Merton, n.d.). Residents organized to confront the builders and to address these problems in other ways. Later, when the problems were solved, the organization remained as available social capital that improved the quality of life for residents. Residents had resources available that they had seen as unavailable where they had lived before. (For example, despite the fact that the number of teenagers in the community was smaller, residents were *more* likely to express satisfaction with the availability of teenage babysitters.)

Printers in the New York Typographical Union who were monotype operators formed a Monotype Club as a social club (Lipset, Trow, and Coleman 1956). Later, as employers looked for monotype operators and as monotype operators looked for jobs, both found this organization an effective employment referral service and appropriated the organization for this purpose. Still later, when the Progressive Party came into power in the New York Union, the Monotype Club served as an organizational resource for the Independent Party as it left office. The Monotype Club subsequently served as an important source of social capital for the Independents to sustain the party as an organized opposition while it was out of office.

In the example of South Korean student radicals used earlier, the study circles were described as consisting of groups of students from the same high school or hometown or church. Here, as in the earlier examples, an organization that was initiated for one purpose is available for appropriation for other purposes, constituting important social capital for the individual members, who have available to them the organizational resources necessary for effective opposition. These examples illustrate the general point that an organization, once brought into existence for one set of purposes, can also aid others, thus constituting social capital available for use.

It is possible to gain insight into some of the ways in which closure and appropriable social organization provide social capital by use of a distinction made by Max Gluckman (1967) between simplex and multiplex relations.[2] In the latter, persons are linked in more than one context (neighbor, fellow worker, fellow parent, coreligionist, etc.), while in the former, persons are linked through only one of these relations. The central property of a multiplex relation is that it allows the resources of one relationship to be appropriated for use in others. Sometimes the resource is merely information, as when two parents who see each other as neighbors exchange information about their teenagers' activities; sometimes it is the obligations that one person owes a second in relationship X, which the second person can use to constrain the actions of the first in relationship Y. Often it is resources in the form of other persons who have obligations in one context that can be called on to aid when one has problems in another context.

Social Capital in the Creation of Human Capital

The preceding pages have been directed toward defining and illustrating social capital in general. But there is one effect of social capital that is especially important: its effect on the creation of human capital in the next generation. Both social capital in the family and social capital in the community play roles in the creation of human capital in the rising generation. I will examine each of these in turn.

Social Capital in the Family

Ordinarily, in the examination of the effects of various factors on achievement in school, "family background" is considered a single entity, distinguished from schooling in its effects. But there is not merely a single "family background"; family background is analytically separable into at least three different components: financial capital, human capital, and social capital. Financial capital is approximately measured by the family's wealth or income. It provides the physical resources that can aid achievement: a fixed place in the home for studying, materials to aid learning, the financial resources that smooth family problems. Human capital is approximately measured by parents' education and provides the potential for a cognitive environment for the child that aids learning. Social capital within the family is different from either of these. Two examples will give a sense of what it is and how it operates.

John Stuart Mill, at an age before most children attend school, was taught Latin and Greek by his father, James Mill, and later in childhood would discuss critically with his father and with Jeremy Bentham drafts of his father's manuscripts. John Stuart Mill probably had no extraordinary genetic endowments, and his father's learning was no more extensive than that of some other men of the time. The central difference was the time and effort spent by the father with the child on intellectual matters.

In one public school district in the United States where texts for school use were purchased by children's families, school authorities were puzzled to discover that a number of Asian immigrant families purchased *two* copies of each textbook needed by the child. Investigation revealed that the family purchased the second copy for the mother to study in order to help her child do well in school. Here is a case in which the human capital of the parents, at least as measured traditionally by years of schooling, is low, but the social capital in the family available for the child's education is extremely high.

These examples illustrate the importance of social capital within the family for a child's intellectual development. It is of course true that children are strongly affected by the human capital possessed by their parents. But this human capital may be irrelevant to outcomes for children if parents are not an important part of their children's lives, if their human capital is employed exclusively at work or elsewhere outside the home. The social capital of the family is the relations between children and parents (and, when families include other members, relationships with them as well). That is, if the human capital possessed by parents is not complemented by social capital embodied in family relations, it is irrelevant to the child's educational growth that the parent has a great deal, or a small amount, of human capital.[3]

I will not differentiate here among the forms of social capital discussed earlier but will attempt merely to measure the strength of the relations between parents and child as a measure of the social capital available to the child from the parent. Nor will I use the concept in the context of the paradigm of rational action, as, for example, is often done in use of the concept of human capital to examine the investments in education that a rational person would make. A portion of the reason for this lies in a property of much social capital not shown by most forms of capital (to which I will turn in a later section): its public goods character, which leads to underinvestment.

Social capital within the family that gives the child access to the adult's human capital depends both on the physical presence of adults in the family and on the attention given by the adults to the child. The physical absence of adults may be described as a structural deficiency in family social capital. The most prominent element of structural deficiency in modern families is the single-parent family. However, the nuclear family itself, in which one or both parents work outside the home, can be seen as structurally deficient, lacking the social capital that comes with the presence of parents during the day, or with grandparents or aunts and uncles in or near the household.

Even if adults are physically present, there is a lack of social capital in the family if there are not strong relations between children and parents. The lack of strong relations can result from the child's embeddedness in a youth community, from the parents' embeddedness in relationships with other adults that do not cross generations, or from other sources. Whatever the source, it means that whatever *human* capital exists in the parents, the child does not profit from it because the *social* capital is missing.

The effects of a lack of social capital within the family differ for different educational outcomes. One for which it appears to be especially important is dropping out of school. With the *High School and Beyond* sample of students in high schools, table 2.1 shows the expected dropout rates for students in different types of families when various measures of social and human capital in the family and a measure of social capital in the community are controlled statistically.[4] An explanation is necessary for the use of number of siblings as a measure of lack of social capital. The number of siblings represents, in this interpretation, a dilution of adult attention to the child. This is consistent with research results for measures of achievement and IQ, which show that test scores decline with sib position, even when total family size is controlled, and that scores decline with number of children in the family. Both results are consistent with the view that younger sibs and children in large families have less adult attention, which produces weaker educational outcomes.

Item 1 of table 2.1 shows that when other family resources are controlled, the percentage of students who drop out between spring of the sophomore year and spring of the senior year is 6 percentage points higher for children from single-parent families. Item 2 of table 2.1 shows that the rate is 6.4 percentage points higher for sophomores with four

Table 2.1
Dropout Rates between Spring, Grade 10, and Spring, Grade 12, for Students Whose Families Differ in Social Capital, Controlling for Human Capital and Financial Capital in the Family

	Percentage dropping out	Difference in percentage points
1. Parents' presence		
Two parents	13.1	6.0
Single parent	19.1	
2. Additional children		
One sibling	10.8	6.4
Four siblings	17.2	
3. Parents and children		
Two parents, one sibling	10.1	12.5
One parent, four siblings	22.6	
4. Mother's expectation for child's education		
Expectation of college	11.6	8.6
No expectation of college	20.2	
5. Three factors together		
Two parents, one sibling, mother expects college	8.1	22.5
One parent, four siblings, no college expectation	30.6	

Estimates taken from logistic regression reported more fully in table 2.2.

siblings than for those with otherwise equivalent family resources but only one sibling. Or, taking these two figures together, we can think of the ratio of adults to children as a measure of the social capital in the family available for the education of any one of them. Item 3 of table 2.1 shows that for a sophomore with four siblings and one parent, and an otherwise average background, the rate is 22.6%; with one sibling and two parents, the rate is 10.1%—a difference of 12.5 percentage points.

Another indicator of adult attention in the family, although not a pure measure of social capital, is the mother's expectation of the child's going to college. Item 4 of the table shows that for sophomores without this parental expectation, the rate is 8.6 percentage points higher than for those with it. With the three sources of family social capital taken together, item 5 of the table shows that sophomores with one sibling, two parents, and a mother's expectation for college (still controlling on other resources of family) have an 8.1% dropout rate; with four siblings, one parent, and no expectation of the mother for college, the rate is 30.6%.

These results provide a less satisfactory test than if the research had been explicitly designed to examine effects of social capital within the family. In addition, table A1 in the Appendix shows that another variable that should measure social capital in the family, the frequency of talking with parents about personal experiences, shows essentially no relation to dropping out. Nevertheless, taken all together, the data do indicate that social capital in the family is a resource for education of the family's children, just as is financial and human capital.

Social Capital outside the Family

The social capital that has value for a young person's development does not reside solely within the family. It can be found outside as well, in the community consisting of the social relationships that exist among parents, in the closure exhibited by this structure of relations, and in the parents' relations with the institutions of the community.

The effect of this social capital outside the family on educational outcomes can be seen by examining outcomes for children whose parents differ in the particular source of social capital discussed earlier, intergenerational closure. There is not a direct measure of intergenerational closure in the data, but there is a proximate indicator. This is the number of times the child has changed schools because the family moved. For families that have moved often, the social relations that constitute social capital are broken at each move. Whatever the degree of intergenerational closure available to others in the community, it is not available to parents in mobile families.

The logistic regression carried out earlier and reported in table A1 shows that the coefficient for number of moves since grade 5 is 10 times its standard error, the variable with the strongest overall effect of any variable in the equation, including the measures of human and financial capital in the family (socioeconomic status) and the crude measures of family social capital introduced in the earlier analysis. Translating this into an effect on dropping out gives 11.8% as the dropout rate if the family has not moved, 16.7% if it has moved once, and 23.1% if it has moved twice.

In the *High School and Beyond* data set, another variation among the schools constitutes a useful indicator of social capital. This is the distinctions among public high schools, religiously based private high schools, and nonreligiously based private high schools. It is the religiously based high schools that are surrounded by a community based on the religious organization. These families have intergenerational closure that is based on a multiplex relation: whatever other relations they have, the adults are members of the same religious body and parents of children in the same school. In contrast, it is the independent private schools that are typically least surrounded by a community, for their student bodies are collections of students, most of whose families have no contact.[5] The choice of private school for most of these parents is an individualistic one, and, although they back their children with extensive human capital, they send their children to these schools denuded of social capital.

In the *High School and Beyond* data set, there are 893 public schools, 84 Catholic schools, and 27 other private schools. Most of the other private schools are independent schools, though a minority have religious foundations. In this analysis, I will at the outset regard the other private schools as independent private schools to examine the effects of social capital outside the family.

The results of these comparisons are shown in table 2.2. Item 1 of the table shows that the dropout rates between sophomore and senior years are 14.4% in public schools, 3.4% in Catholic schools, and 11.9% in other private schools. What is most striking is the low dropout rate in Catholic schools. The rate is a fourth of that in the public schools and a third of that in the other private schools.

Adjusting the dropout rates for differences in student-body financial, human, and social capital among the three sets of schools by standardizing the population of the Catholic schools and other private schools to the student-body backgrounds of the public schools shows that the differences are affected only slightly. Furthermore, the differences are not due to the religion of the students or to the degree of religious observance. Catholic students in public school are only slightly less likely to drop out than non-Catholics. Frequency of attendance at religious services, which is itself a measure of social capital through intergenerational closure, is strongly related to dropout rate, with 19.5% of public school students who rarely or never attend dropping out compared with 9.1% of those who attend often. But this effect exists apart from, and in addition to, the effect of the school's religious affiliation. Comparable figures for Catholic school

Table 2.2
Dropout Rates between Spring, Grade 10, and Spring, Grade 12,
for Students from Schools with Differing Amounts of Social Capital
in the Surrounding Community

	Public	Catholic	Other private schools
1. Raw dropout rates	14.4	3.4	11.9
2. Dropout rates standardized to average public school sophomore[a]	14.4	5.2	11.6
	Non-Catholic religious		**Independent**
3. Raw dropout rates for students[b] from independent and non-Catholic religious private schools	3.7		10.0

[a]The standardization is based on separate logistic regressions for these two sets of schools, using the same variables listed in n. 4. Coefficients and means for the standardization are in Hoffer (1986, tables 5 and 24).

[b]This tabulation is based on unweighted data, which is responsible for the fact that both rates are lower than the rate for other private schools in item 1 of the table, which is based on weighted data.

students are 5.9% and 2.6%, respectively (Coleman and Hoffer 1987, p. 138).

The low dropout rates of the Catholic schools, the absence of low dropout rates in the other private schools, and the independent effect of frequency of religious attendance all provide evidence of the importance of social capital outside the school, in the adult community surrounding it, for this outcome of education.

A further test is possible, for there were eight schools in the sample of non-Catholic private schools ("other private" in the analysis above) that have religious foundations and over 50% of the student body of that religion. Three were Baptist schools, two were Jewish, and three were from three other denominations. If the inference is correct about the religious community's providing intergenerational closure and thus social capital and about the importance of social capital in depressing the chance of dropping out of high school, these schools also should show a lower dropout rate than the independent private schools. Item 3 of table 2.2 shows that their dropout rate is lower, 3.7%, essentially the same as that of the Catholic schools.[6]

The data presented above indicate the importance of social capital for the education of youth, or, as it might be put, the importance of social capital in the creation of human capital. Yet there is a fundamental difference between social capital and most other forms of capital that has strong implications for the development of youth. It is this difference to which I will turn in the next section.

Physical capital is ordinarily a private good, and property rights make it possible for the person who invests in physical capital to capture the benefits it produces. Thus, the incentive to invest in physical capital is not depressed; there is not a suboptimal investment in physical capital because those who invest in it are able to capture the benefits of their investments. For human capital also—at least human capital of the sort that is produced in schools—the person who invests the time and resources in building up this capital reaps its benefits in the form of a higher paying job, more satisfying or higher status work, or even the pleasure of greater understanding of the surrounding world—in short, all the benefits that schooling brings to a person.

But most forms of social capital are not like this. For example, the kinds of social structures that make possible social norms and the sanctions that enforce them do not benefit primarily the person or persons whose efforts would be necessary to bring them about but benefit all those who are part of such a structure. For example, in some schools where there exists a dense set of associations among some parents, these are the result of a small number of persons, ordinarily mothers who do not hold full-time jobs outside the home. Yet these mothers themselves experience only a subset of the benefits of this social capital surrounding the school. If one of them decides to abandon these activities—for example, to take a full-time job—this may be an entirely reasonable action from a personal point of view and even from the point of view of that household with its children. The benefits of the new activity may far outweigh the losses that arise from the decline in associations with other parents whose children are in the school. But the withdrawal of these activities constitutes a loss to all those other parents whose associations and contacts were dependent on them.

Similarly, the decision to move from a community so that the father, for example, can take a better job may be entirely correct from the point of view of that family. But, because social capital consists of relations among persons, other persons may experience extensive losses by the severance of those relations, a severance over which they had no control. A part of those losses is the weakening of norms and sanctions that aid the school in its task. For each family, the total cost it experiences as a consequence of the decisions it and other families make may outweigh the benefits of those few decisions it has control over. Yet the beneficial consequences to the family of those decisions made by the family may far outweigh the minor losses it experiences from them alone.

It is not merely voluntary associations, such as a PTA, in which underinvestment of this sort occurs. When an individual asks a favor from another, thus incurring an obligation, he does so because it brings him a needed benefit; he does not consider that it does the other a benefit as well by adding to a drawing fund of social capital available in a time of need. If the first individual can satisfy his need through self-sufficiency, or through aid from some official source without incurring an obligation, he will do so—and thus fail to add to the social capital outstanding in the community.

Similar statements can be made with respect to trustworthiness as social capital. An actor choosing to keep trust or not (or choosing whether to devote resources to an attempt to keep trust) is doing so on the basis of costs and benefits he himself will experience. That his trustworthiness will facilitate others' actions or that his lack of trustworthiness will inhibit others' actions does not enter into his decision. A similar but more qualified statement can be made for information as a form of social capital. An individual who serves as a source of information for another because he is well informed ordinarily acquires that information for his own benefit, not for the others who make use of him. (This is not always true. As Katz and Lazarsfeld [1955] show, "opinion leaders" in an area acquire information in part to maintain their positions as opinion leaders.)

For norms also, the statement must be qualified. Norms are intentionally established, indeed as means of reducing externalities, and their benefits are ordinarily captured by those who are responsible for establishing them. But the capability of establishing and maintaining effective norms depends on properties of the social structure (such as closure) over which one actor does not have control yet are affected by one actor's action. These are properties that affect the structure's capacity to sustain effective norms yet ordinarily do not enter into an individual's decision that affects them.

Some forms of social capital have the property that their benefits can be captured by those who invest in them; consequently, rational actors will not underinvest in this type of social capital. Organizations that produce a private good constitute the outstanding example. The result is that there will be in society an imbalance in the relative investment in organizations that produce private goods for a market and those associations and relationships in which the benefits are not captured—an imbalance in the sense that if the positive externalities created by the latter form of social capital could be internalized, it would come to exist in greater quantity.

The public goods quality of most social capital means that it is in a fundamentally different position with respect to purposive action than are most other forms of capital. It is an important resource for individuals and may affect greatly their ability to act and their perceived quality of life. They have the capability of bringing it into being. Yet, because the benefits of actions that bring social capital into being are largely experienced by persons other than the actor, it is often not in his interest to bring it into being. The result is that most forms of social capital are created or destroyed as by-products of other activities. This social capital arises or disappears without anyone's willing it into or out of being and is thus even less recognized and taken account of in social action than its already intangible character would warrant.

There are important implications of this public goods aspect of social capital that play a part in the development of children and youth. Because the social structural conditions that overcome the problems of supplying these public goods—that is, strong families and strong communities—are much less often present now than in the past, and promise to be even less present in the future, we can expect that, ceteris paribus, we confront a declining quantity of human capital embodied in each successive generation. The obvious solution appears to be to attempt to find ways of overcoming the problem of supply of these public goods, that is, social capital employed for the benefit of children and youth. This very likely means the substitution of some kind of formal organization for the voluntary and spontaneous social organization that has in the past been the major source of social capital available to the young.

Conclusion

In this paper, I have attempted to introduce into social theory the concept of social capital, paralleling the concepts of financial capital, physical capital, and human capital—but embodied in relations among persons. This is part of a theoretical strategy that involves use of the paradigm of rational action but without the assumption of atomistic elements stripped of social relationships. I have shown the use of this concept through demonstrating the effect of social capital in the family and in the community in aiding the formation of human capital. The single measure of human capital formation used for this was one that appears especially responsive to the supply of social capital, remaining in high school until graduation versus dropping out. Both social capital in the family and social capital outside it, in the adult community surrounding the school, showed evidence of considerable value in reducing the probability of dropping out of high school.

In explicating the concept of social capital, three forms were identified: obligations and expectations, which depend on trustworthiness of the social environment, information-flow capability of the social structure, and norms accompanied by sanctions. A property shared by most forms of social capital that differentiates it from other forms of capital is its public good aspect: the actor or actors who generate social capital ordinarily capture only a small part of its benefits, a fact that leads to underinvestment in social capital.

Table A1
Logistic Regression Coefficients and Asymptotic Standard Errors for Effects of Student Background Characteristics on Dropping out of High School between Sophomore and Senior Years, 1980–82, Public School Sample

	b	SE
Intercept	−2.305	.169
Socioeconomic status	−.460	.077
Black	−.161	.162
Hispanic	.104	.138
Number of siblings	.180	.028
Mother worked while child was young	−.012	.103
Both parents in household	−.415	.112
Mother's expectation for college	−.685	.103
Talk with parents	.031	.044
Number of moves since grade 5	.407	.040

Source: Taken from Hoffer (1986).

■ **Notes**

I thank Mark Granovetter, Susan Shapiro, and Christopher Winship for criticisms of an earlier draft, which aided greatly in revision.

1. For a discussion of the importance of the empirical generalization to economics, see Black, Coats, and Goodwin (1973).

2. I am especially grateful to Susan Shapiro for reminding me of Gluckman's distinction and pointing out the relevance of it to my analysis.

3. The complementarity of human capital and social capital in the family for a child's development suggests that the statistical analysis that examines the effects of these quantities should take a particular form. There should be an interaction term between human capital (parents' education) and social capital (some combination of measures such as two parents in the home, number of siblings, and parents' expectations for child's education). In the analysis reported, here, however, a simple additive model without interaction was used.

4. The analysis is carried out by use of a weighted logistic model with a random sample of 4,000 students from the public schools in the sample. The variables included in the model as measures of the family's financial, human, and social capital were socioeconomic status (a single variable constructed of parents' education, parents' income, father's occupational status, and household possessions), race, Hispanic ethnicity, number of siblings, number of changes in school due to family residential moves since fifth grade, whether mother worked before the child was in school, mother's expectation of child's educational attainment,

frequency of discussions with parents about personal matters, and presence of both parents in the household. The regression coefficients and asymptotic standard errors are given in the App. table A1. An analysis with more extensive statistical controls, including such things as grades in school, homework, and number of absences, is reported in Hoffer (1986, table 25), but the effects reported in table 2.1 and subsequent text are essentially unchanged except for a reduced effect of mother's expectations. The results reported here and subsequently are taken from Hoffer (1986) and from Coleman and Hoffer (1987).

5. Data from this study have no direct measures of the degree of intergenerational closure among the parents of the school to support this statement. However, the one measure of intergenerational closure that does exist in the data, the number of residential moves requiring school change since grade 5, is consistent with the statement. The average number of moves for public school students is .57; for Catholic school students, .35; and for students in other private schools, .88.

6. It is also true, though not presented here, that the lack of social capital in the family makes little difference in dropout rates in Catholic schools—or, in the terms I have used, social capital in the community compensates in part for its absence in the family. See Coleman and Hoffer (1987, chap. 5).

■ References

Baker, Wayne. 1983. "Floor Trading and Crowd Dynamics." Pp. 107–28 in *Social Dynamics of Financial Markets*, edited by Patricia Adler and Peter Adler. Greenwich, Conn.: JAI.

Banfield, Edward. 1967. *The Moral Basis of a Backward Society*. New York: Free Press.

Becker, Gary. 1964. *Human Capital*. New York: National Bureau of Economic Research.

Ben-Porath, Yoram. 1980. "The F-Connection: Families, Friends, and Firms and the Organization of Exchange." *Population and Development Review* 6:1–30.

Black, R. D. C., A. W. Coats, and C. D. W. Goodwin, eds. 1973. *The Marginal Revolution in Economics*. Durham, N.C.: Duke University Press.

Blau, Peter. 1964. *Exchange and Power in Social Life*. New York: Wiley.

Coleman, James S. 1986a. "Social Theory, Social Research, and a Theory of Action." *American Journal of Sociology* 91:1309–35.

———. 1986b. *Individual Interests and Collective Action*. Cambridge: Cambridge University Press.

———. 1987. "Norms as Social Capital." Pp. 133–55 in *Economic Imperialism*, edited by Gerard Radnitzky and Peter Bernholz. New York: Paragon.

Coleman, J. S., and T. B. Hoffer. 1987. *Public and Private Schools: The Impact of Communities*. New York: Basic.

De Graaf, Nan Dirk, and Hendrik Derk Flap. 1988. "With a Little Help from My Friends." *Social Forces* 67 (in press).

Festinger, Leon, Stanley Schachter, and Kurt Back. 1963. *Social Pressures in Informal Groups*. Stanford, Calif.: Stanford University Press.

Geertz, Clifford. 1962. "The Rotating Credit Association: A 'Middle Rung' in Development." *Economic Development and Cultural Change* 10:240–63.

Gluckman, Max. 1967. *The Judicial Process among the Barotse of Northern Rhodesia*, 2d ed. Manchester: Manchester University Press.

Gouldner, Alvin. 1960. "The Norm of Reciprocity: A Preliminary Statement." *American Sociological Review* 25:161–78.

Granovetter, Mark. 1985. "Economic Action, Social Structure, and Embeddedness." *American Journal of Sociology* 91:481–510.

Hoffer, T. B. 1986. *Educational Outcomes in Public and Private High Schools*. Ph.D. dissertation. University of Chicago, Department of Sociology.

Homans, George. 1974. *Social Behavior: Its Elementary Forms*, rev. ed. New York: Harcourt, Brace & World.

Katz, E., and P. Lazarsfeld. 1955. *Personal Influence*. New York: Free Press.

Lenin, V. I. (1902) 1973. *What Is to Be Done*. Peking: Foreign Language Press.

Lin, Nan. 1988. "Social Resources and Social Mobility: A Structural Theory of Status Attainment." In *Social Mobility and Social Structure*, edited by Ronald Breiger. Cambridge: Cambridge University Press.

Lipset, Seymour, M. Trow, and J. Coleman. 1956. *Union Democracy*. New York: Free Press.

Merry, Sally, E. 1984. "Rethinking Gossip and Scandal." Pp. 271–302 in *Toward a General Theory of Social Control*. Vol. 1, *Fundamentals*, edited by Donald Black. New York: Academic.

Merton, Robert K. 1968. *Social Theory and Social Structure*, 2d ed. New York: Free Press.

———. n.d. "Study of World War II Housing Projects." Unpublished manuscript. Columbia University, Department of Sociology.

Schultz, Theodore. 1961. "Investment in Human Capital." *American Economic Review* 51 (March): 1–17.

Ullmann-Margalit, Edna. 1977. *The Emergence of Norms*. Oxford: Clarendon.

Williamson, Oliver. 1975. *Markets and Hierarchies*. New York: Free Press.

———. 1981. "The Economics of Organization: The Transaction Cost Approach." *American Journal of Sociology* 87:548–77.

Wrong, Dennis. 1961. "The Oversocialized Conception of Man in Modern Sociology." *American Sociological Review* 26:183–93.

3

The Strength of Strong Ties

The Importance of *Philos* in Organizations

David Krackhardt

Theory

In 1973, Mark Granovetter proposed that weak ties are often more important than strong ties in understanding certain network-based phenomena. His argument rests on the assumption that strong ties tend to bond similar people to each other and these similar people tend to cluster together such that they are all mutually connected. The information obtained through such a network tie is more likely to be redundant, and the network is therefore not a channel for innovation. By contrast, a weak tie more often constitutes a "local bridge" to parts of the social system that are otherwise disconnected, and therefore a weak tie is likely to provide new information from disparate parts of the system. Thus, this theory argues, tie strength is curvilinear with a host of dependent variables: no tie (or an extremely weak tie) is of little consequence; a weak tie provides maximum impact, and a strong tie provides diminished impact.

Subsequent research has generally supported Granovetter's theory (Granovetter 1982), but two issues have been neglected in the research stream. First, there is considerable ambiguity as to what constitutes a strong tie and what constitutes a weak tie. Granovetter laid out four identifying properties of a strong tie: "The strength of a tie is a (probably linear) combination of the amount of time, the emotional intensity, the intimacy (mutual confiding), and the reciprocal services which characterize the tie" (1973:1361). This makes tie strength a linear function of four quasi-independent indicators. At what point is a tie to be considered weak? This is not simply a question for the methodologically curious. It is an important part of the theory itself, since the theory makes a curvilinear prediction. If we happen to be on the very left side of the continuum of tie strength, then increasing the strength of the tie (going from no tie to weak tie) will increase the relevant information access. On the other hand, at some point making the ties stronger will theoretically decrease their impact. How do we know where we are on this theoretical curve? Do all four indicators count equally toward tie strength?

In practice, tie strength has been measured many different ways. Some scholars have measured strong ties as reciprocated nominations, weak ties as unreciprocated nominations, and no ties as no nominations (Friedkin 1980). Other measures have included recency of contact (Lin, Dayton, and Greenwald 1978). Sometimes labels such as "friend," "relative," or "neighbor" are used to identify strong ties (Erickson and Yancey 1980; Lin, Ensel, and Vaughn 1981). Others (Granovetter 1973:1371) have simply used frequency of interaction as a surrogate for tie strength. One may intuitively agree that these strong ties are clearly *stronger* than the set of weak ties as measured. But it is clear that all of these measures capture the essence of what Granovetter meant when he spoke of the category "strong ties."

The Psychology of Strong Ties

The second issue that has been all but ignored since Granovetter's seminal article is the affective character of strong ties. Of the four characteristics of strong ties, two of these—emotional intensity and intimacy—are inherently subjective and interpretive. A third, "reciprocal services," is perhaps behavioral, but one could argue that the equitable exchange implied by this term is also a subjective criterion. Only the first criterion, time spent in the relationship, is clearly objective.

Again, this is not simply a measurement issue. Granovetter's theory draws on the psychological theory of balance (Heider 1958; Newcomb 1961). From this theory, Granovetter notes that given a triad of actors, *A*, *B*, and *C*, if *A* is strongly tied to *B* and to *C*, then it is likely that the triad will be balanced: that is, *B* and *C* will be strongly tied to each other also. There is certainly evidence of this effect (see, for example, Davis 1979). But what has been forgotten in this research effort is that the underlying rationale for balance is psychological.[1] Heider uses words like "stress," "tension," and "disharmony" to describe what happens to a person who faces an unbalanced situation. These disquieting affective states presumably motivate the individual to resolve the imbalance. Moreover, the tendency to resolve an unbalanced triad is strongest when the strength of affective attachment is strong. Once triads are balanced, no local bridge can exist. In other words, Granovetter's claim that strong ties do not constitute local bridges is dependent on balance, which in turn is influenced by the affective component of those ties. Yet we seldom see affective dimensions captured in the operationalizations of strong ties.

The Strength of Strong Ties

In his review of a decade of research on the strength-of-weak-ties hypothesis, Granovetter (1982) rightly pointed out that strong ties can play an important role, and that role should not be ignored. In fact, he noted:

"Weak ties provide people with access to information and resources beyond those available in their own social circles; but strong ties have *greater motivation* to be of assistance and are typically more easily available" (113; emphasis mine). Citing Pool (1980), he further asserted that strong ties are more likely to be useful to the individual when that individual is in an insecure position. Granovetter concluded from his review of the research (1982:113–117) that people in insecure positions are more likely to resort to the development of strong ties for protection and uncertainty reduction. In a parallel argument, Krackhardt and Stern (1988) posited that the pattern of friendship ties within an organization will be critical to an organizations ability to deal with crises. Through a set of organizational simulations, they demonstrated that an organization characterized by friendship ties that cut across departmental boundaries is better suited to adapting to environmental changes and uncertainty.

This chapter will build on that theme: the strength of strong ties in cases of severe change and uncertainty. People resist change and are uncomfortable with uncertainty. Strong ties constitute a base of trust that can reduce resistance and provide comfort in the face of uncertainty. Thus it will be argued that change is not facilitated by weak ties but rather by a particular type of strong tie. To develop this theme, I will draw from Granovetter's original idea of what constitutes a strong tie and his later ideas about how strong ties are useful. First, I will replace the definition of tie strength as a continuous variable with a set of conditions for a particular type of tie, a tie I will call *philos*, the Greek word for friend. (I will reserve the word "friend" for other uses, to be explained shortly.)

A *Philos* Relationship

Since the concept of strong ties has been clouded with ambiguity and inconsistency, I will use the Greek word *philos* to designate a particular type of tie that, because of its special character, has implications that make it different from other types of ties. Grammatically, I will use *philos* as a noun, and rules governing its use will be similar to that of the word "friend." That is, one may say "*A* is a *philos* to *B*" or, in the symmetrical case, "*A* and *B* are *philos*." I will define a *philos* relationship as one that meets the following three necessary and sufficient conditions:

1. *Interaction*. For *A* and *B* to be *philos*, *A* and *B* must interact with each other. The implication of this component is that there will be a high probability that each will have access to information that the other has, since such frequent interactions will provide opportunities to exchange such information.
2. *Affection*. For *A* to be a *philos* of *B*, *A* must like *B*, *A* must feel affection for *B*. This evaluative component allows much of the important

balance predictions of Heider and transitive closure predictions of Granovetter to hold. Heider (1958:202) also made predictions about the symmetry of the "liking" relationship, and one may assume that in most cases such relationships are symmetrical. However, one can imagine occasions when affection is not reciprocated, resulting in an asymmetric relationship.

3. *Time*. A and B, to be *philos*, must have a history of interactions that have lasted over an extended period of time. That is, there is no such thing as instant *philos*. One implication here is that *philos* relationships cannot be studied in laboratory experiments. While one can induce short-term affective states and study "liking" (e.g., Byrne 1971), the study of *philos* is relegated to the field, where relationships have sufficient time to develop.

Note that I have not eliminated the psychological, affective quality of the relationship in defining *philos*. In fact, it is explicitly there, and to remove it destroys the predictions I would like to make from the relationship. While the definition of *philos* is not precisely the same as Granovetter's definition of strong ties, one may safely infer that *philos* relations constitute strong ties as Granovetter saw them.

The combination of these qualities are defined to be *philos*. But they also actively combine to make a theoretical prediction, one of *trust*. Interaction creates *opportunity* for the exchange of information, some of which may be confidential. Affection creates *motivation* to treat the other in positive ways, or at least not to do something that would hurt the person (because to do otherwise would create imbalance and consequent feelings of stress, disharmony, tension). And time creates the *experience* necessary to allow each person to predict how the other will use any shared information. These are the ingredients of trust. Granovetter has argued that the structure of embedded relationships in a social system is a necessary part of sociological inquiry to systematic change: "The embeddedness argument stresses instead the role of concrete personal relations and structures (or 'networks') or such relations in generating trust and discouraging malfeasance" (1985:490). With this article, Granovetter has switched emphasis from the strength of weak ties to the strength of strong *philos* ties. I predict that the *philos* relations will be the critical ones in generating trust and discouraging malfeasance.

The three components are necessary for *philos* because without any one of them the basis for trust falls apart. Without current interaction, there is little opportunity to share critical or confidential information. Without the history, there is no experience to know how the other will use the confidential information or who he or she will share it with. Without the positive affect, there is less motivation to maintain Heiderian balance, to share confidential information or to refrain from malfeasance.

Etic *Philos* versus Emic Friends

The underlying construct here is the well-defined *philos*. The concept most closely associated with this idea in the English language is that of friend. Unfortunately, as Fischer (1982) has pointed out, the term "friend" is not well defined. In particular, he noted that the term means different things to different people. Based on a set of questionnaire responses about people's acquaintances, Fischer suggested that people use the label "friend" to denote a relationship devoid of any other formal designation (like "father"). However, within the set of coworkers, he found that friends were those with whom one had "sociable interaction" and with whom one would "discuss personal matters," ideas at least consistent with my notion of *philos*.

The correspondence between *philos* and friend can be best related to the anthropological dichotomy between etic and emic definitions. *Philos* is a theoretical construct, an etic concept with precise if abstract meaning. "Friend" is an emic construct, a word whose true meaning is embedded in the minds of those people in our society who use it frequently. As Fischer notes, we cannot abandon the term "friend" in the pursuit of science simply because the term has an imprecise definition: "It is too important a 'folk concept,' an idea that people use to order their worlds. And, it is too much a part of our own intellectual apparatus" (1982:288).

I will not try to define the folk meaning of friend. Instead, I will assume that the emic word "friend" is an estimate of the etic concept *philos*, just as a sample statistic is an estimate of a population parameter. The extent to which these two constructs match is a question worth exploring. As with all estimates, there will be error; I cannot even assure the reader that the estimate is unbiased. But the face validity of the idea that friends are people who like each other, have known each other for a reasonable time, and frequently interact with each other is at least minimally defensible. I will insist on differentiating between friend and *philos* because it is important to keep the distinction between the etic concept and the emic estimator of that concept.

What follows is a case study of a firm that underwent a union certification campaign. Just prior to this campaign, network data were collected in this firm (see Krackhardt 1990 for a description of the network study). Following the campaign, interviews were conducted with six key informants who provided information about the events that led to the initiation of the union attempt and to the eventual failure of the campaign itself. I will provide an account of the critical events that occurred and relate these events to two kinds of strong (at least frequent) ties, the friendship and advice networks. These events underscore the importance that *philos* relationships (as measured by friendships) play over and above strong but affectless working relationships, such as the advice relationship, in the course of organizational change.

A small entrepreneurial firm, called here Silicon Systems, is located on the West Coast of the United States in an area known for its many small, start-up firms as well as some more established ones. Silicon Systems' business involved the sales, installation, and maintenance of state-of-the-art information systems in client organizations. Its clients ranged from local banks to schools to medium-sized manufacturing firms to research and development (R&D) labs. Until recently, its largest competitors, firms such as IBM and AT&T, focused their marketing efforts on the neighboring metropolitan areas. But recently the growth potential of Silicon Systems' market had attracted the attention of these competitors. According to Silicon Systems' top managers, the small firm's competitive edge rested in its ability to respond more efficiently to idiosyncratic customer demands.

Silicon Systems was wholly owned in equal shares by the three top managers. All employees worked in the single-story building owned by the company. They saw one another regularly, although installers worked many days at client sites rather than in the office. Thus Silicon Systems employees were familiar with one another to varying degrees, and each employee had an opinion about every other employee, with the occasional exception of new hires.

The firm had grown from three people to thirty-six in fifteen years. Much of this growth occurred in the five years preceding the study. Most of these years had been profitable, and the owners anticipated no downward trend in their business.

The Networks of Strong Ties

With the exception of a few employees who had just joined the firm, all of the 36 employees knew one another to some degree and conversed occasionally. Granovetter (1973:1371) defined weak ties as those who interact more than once per year and less than twice per week. He operationalized strong ties as those who interacted at least twice per week. By his criteria, all the employees in Silicon Systems would be considered at least weakly tied to one another.

The presence or absence of weak ties, therefore, is not a viable question in this context. Instead, the focus in this case will be on the presence or absence of various types of strong ties. And, in particular, I claim that the affective component of the strong tie is important in understanding the dynamics surrounding crises or changes in organizations. To demonstrate this, I will distinguish between two types of strong (that is, frequent) ties: a network of advice interactions stemming from routine work problems and a network of *philos* relationships in the firm.

Consistent with my cognitive theme, the network information obtained in this case study was based on the actors' own perceptions about who was related to whom in the firm. Each person provided his or her own estimate of the entire structure (Krackhardt 1987) of both a *philos* and an advice network. These maps are represented as "cognitive cubes," or more formally, $R_{i,j,k}$, where i is the sender of the relation, j is the receiver of the relation, and k is the perceiver of the relation. The directions for the "advice" section of the questionnaire were as follows:

> In this section, you will find a set of similar questions with a list of people after each question. The question is: "Who would this person go to for help or advice at work?" That is, if this person had a question or ran into a problem at work, who would they likely go to, to ask for advice or help? Please answer the question by placing a check next to the names of all the people the person is likely to go to. . . . Some people may go to several people for help or advice. Some may go only to one person. Some may not go to anyone, in which case do not check anyone's name under that question.

These directions were followed by 36 questions (e.g., "Who would Cindy Stalwart go to for help or advice at work?"), each asking the same question about a different employee. Each of these 36 questions was followed by a list of 35 names, any number of which the respondent could check off in response to the question.

Similarly, another section of the questionnaire asked about friendships. The directions for this section paralleled those in the previous section: ". . . This time the question is: "Who would this person consider to be a personal friend?" Please place a check next to all the names of those people who that person would consider to be a friend of theirs."

Again, the question was repeated 36 times, once for each employee's name (e.g., "Who would Abe consider to be a personal friend?"), and each question was followed by a list of 35 names from which the respondent could check any number.

The three-dimensional data from these questionnaires allow two different types of aggregations to be formed, each represented in a twodimensional matrix. The first aggregation creates what will be referred to as the "actual network." The second aggregation is a simple slice of the cognitive cube and will be referred to as the "perceived network." Specific definitions follow.

Actual Network

The actual network for both the friendship and advice relations will be identified by an asterisk: $R^*_{i,j}$ (see Krackhardt 1990 for more details). This network is defined as follows:

$$R^*_{i,j} = 1 \text{ if } R_{i,j,i} = 1 \text{ and } R_{i,j,j} = 1;$$
$$0 \text{ otherwise.}$$

That is, both i and j must agree that i goes to j for help and advice before the relation $i \rightarrow j$ in actual advice network is recognized. Similarly, both i and j must agree that i considers j a friend before the $i \rightarrow j$ link is recorded as existing in the actual friendship network.

Perceived Network and Cognitive Accuracy

In the network study prior to the union certification campaign, I found that the individual's ability to accurately reconstruct the advice network predicted that person's reputational power in the organization (Krack-hardt 1990). I argue that having accurate knowledge of the informal organization gave the employee a competitive edge in any political endeavor. In the current case study, I will refer to the accuracy scores of individuals who were critical players in the pre-union activities and in the union drive itself because these scores shed light on the political perspicacity of key employees.

The degree to which a respondent was accurate in his or her perceptions of the networks was simply defined as the correlation between the individual's perceived network and the actual network, as defined earlier. The individual k's perceived network is denoted $R_{ki,j}$, and the correlation with $R^*_{i,j}$ from here on will be referred to as person k's accuracy score.[2]

Centrality

The three most common measures of centrality—degree, closeness, and betweenness—are compared and reviewed by Freeman (1979). I will restrict my discussion to degree and betweenness centrality. Degree centrality is the simplest form of centrality and comes in two forms: indegree and outdegree. The indegree of an actor in the network is the number of other people who choose that actor in the particular relationship. For example, Steve, the president, had an indegree of 19 in the actual advice relationship (see table 3.1). This meant that 19 employees went to Steve for help and advice at work. Outdegree is the number of people chosen by the actor. For example, Steve had an outdegree of 7 on the actual advice relationship, meaning that he went to seven others for help and advice. The indegree and outdegree of an actor are often good indicators of the informal status that the individual has in the organization. For example, people with high indegrees in the advice relationship are those with experience and know-how to give advice. Those with high outdegrees tend to reach out to others.

Betweenness is somewhat more complicated in its definition. Using Freeman's (1979) notation, betweenness centrality is defined as follows:[3]

$$C_B(k) = \frac{2\Sigma_i^n \ \Sigma_j^n \left(\dfrac{g_{ij}(k)}{g_{ij}} \right)}{n^2 - 3n + 2}$$

for all unordered triples i, j, k, where $i < j$, n is the number of nodes in the network, $g_{ij}(k)$ is the number of geodesics (shortest paths) between nodes i and j in the network, and $g_{ij}(k)$ is the number of geodesics from i to j that include k. To the extent that k lies on the shortest paths between each pair (i, j), then k would be said to have high betweenness centrality. Thus a person with high betweenness is in a position to act as gatekeeper for information that flows through the network. Moreover, betweenness is an indication of the nonredundancy of the source of information. To the extent that a person is connected to otherwise disconnected parts of the network, and therefore has access to different, nonredundant sources of information, that person will have a higher betweenness score.

The difference between degree and betweenness is illustrated in figures and 3.1a and 3.1b. Each figure describes a set of relationships (indicated with lines) among a set of people (indicated with capital letters). In figure 3.1a, persons C, D, G, and H have the highest degree centrality, with 4 indegrees and outdegrees each (the choices are assumed to be symmetric in this hypothetical example, so that indegrees and outdegrees are equal). Each of the remaining people has degree centrality of 3. In contrast to these degree measures, betweenness indicators suggest that a different set of people occupy prominent positions in figure 3.1a. Persons E and F are between 4/9 of other pairs of people, for a betweenness score of .444. Persons C, D, G, and H are between less than 20% of the pairs of people, for a betweenness score of .185. The remaining people have 0 betweenness. It is E and F's position with their access to *separate* groups that gives them such high betweenness scores.

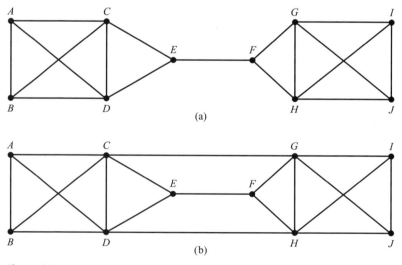

(a)

(b)

Figure 3.1.
Two sociograms illustrating differences in centrality

But if we add merely two lines to figure 3.1a to connect C with G and D with H (see figure 3.1b), we destroy this advantage that E and F shared. E and F's betweenness drops from .444 to .056; C, D, G, and H's betweenness barely changes from .185 to .190 (the remaining points are still 0). By adding these lines, the groups on each side are no longer dependent on the E-F bridge. In fact, the entire structure is more wedded together so that no point enjoys the particularly central position that E and F did in figure 3.1a.

It is worth noting the parallel between the betweenness measure of centrality and Granovetter's concept of a local bridge. A local bridge is a property of a tie; the numerical value of a local bridge (referred to as its *degree*) is equal to the shortest alternative path between the two points connected by the bridge (say, A and B) if that bridge were to be removed. The more that the others around A and B are tied together by direct or relatively short alternative paths, the lower the value or degree of the local bridge between A and B. Betweenness is an attribute of a node in the graph; local bridge degree is an attribute of a tie. But both measure the degree to which the actors reach disparate and unconnected parts of the social system. The higher the degree of the local bridges a person is connected to, the higher that person's betweenness score will be. Thus I refer to the betweenness of actors in these networks in my discussion of the union certification campaign at Silicon Systems, keeping in mind this relationship to Granovetter's idea of the importance of such bridges.

■ The Unionization Attempt: A Case Study

Four months after the network data were fed back to the firm, Silicon Systems was confronted with an unexpected dilemma. The National Labor Relations Board (NLRB) called the president of the firm (Steve) to inform him that the NLRB was granting a petition by a national union to hold a certification election at Silicon Systems. This news came as a total surprise to top management. They felt nervous about the outcome and extremely sensitive about what this meant about the future of the firm. Further, they asked me to refrain from talking to anyone at the firm about the union or the union drive.

After the union drive was completed, I approached the top management of the firm for permission to interview some key people about what had happened. At that time, I talked to three people who were involved in the process on the condition that no one's identity be divulged. Subsequently, top management gave me permission to interview three more employees to verify the information obtained in the first set of interviews. The six informants were interviewed at length about their view of the union and the events surrounding the certification drive. The interviews were primarily unstructured, but specific questions were always included:

"What were the key events in the certification campaign?" "Who were the main players (both for and against the union)?" "Why do you think the union failed to gain certification?" The six people represented a spectrum of employees in terms of their own support for the union and in terms of their longevity with the firm (one person had been there for over 15 years, one had been there for less than a year). Because of the sensitivity of this issue, none of the information below is attributed to any individual in the firm. All accounts reported here represent a consensus of the informants.

By the time top management found out about the employees' union interests, enough employees had signed union authorization cards that the NLRB granted the union's request to have a certification election in two months' time. The three owners were highly concerned, since they believed that they would lose a distinct advantage they had over their larger competitors if the firm became unionized. They consulted labor lawyers to find out what options they had. Their lawyers informed them that there were legal constraints on what they could do to actively discourage certification without risking an unfair-labor-practices judgment. They decided that they would work within these constraints to provide what information they could to support management's position. However, the fate of the certification campaign depended largely on the dynamic forces between the union officials and the nonmanagement employees, especially those in the bargaining unit itself.

Representatives of neither the union nor the NLRB were willing to divulge what percentage of the bargaining unit had signed authorization cards. But an official of the union did confirm that, as a matter of policy, they do not request an election unless they have at least 55% of the bargaining unit signed up. Moreover, according to this official, the union prided itself on not losing certification elections. The union does not ask the NLRB to conduct an election unless it feels certain it will win. Election campaigns are costly, and the union does not like to lose face.

During the two-month campaign period, the national union held several organizing meetings. Gripes were aired about the firm. As is typical in such cases, debates ensued around the pros and cons of unionization. Feelings strengthened as the vote grew closer.

To understand the dynamics involved, it will be useful to refer to individual employees in the context of their positions in both the formal organization and the informal networks. The pseudonyms for these employees and their respective formal positions in the organizational chart are given in figure 3.2. The advice network and friendship network are displayed in figures 3.3, and 3.4, respectively. In the advice network (figure 3.3), arrows indicate the direction of the advice relationship. For example, the arrow from Bob to Chris (near the top of the figure) indicates that Bob goes to Chris for help and advice. A double-headed arrow, such as the one found between Vic and Rick, indicates that each actor goes to

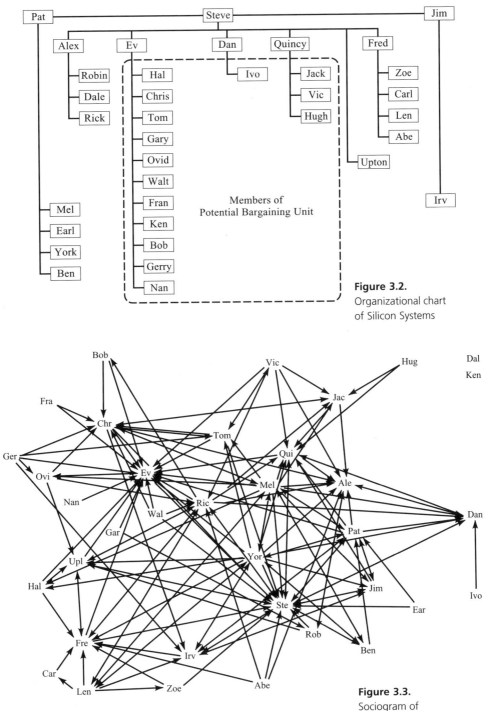

Figure 3.2.
Organizational chart of Silicon Systems

Figure 3.3.
Sociogram of advice network

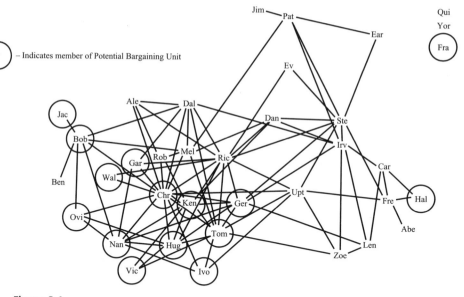

Figure 3.4.
Sociogram of friendship network

the other for help and advice. The friendship network does not display arrows, because the majority of friendship relations are symmetrical. With the exception of isolates, the placement of the actors in these figures is determined by a multidimensional scaling (MDS) of the graph-theoretic path distances between actors in the network.[4] The MDS solution tends to put the central actors in the middle of the figure and the more peripheral actors scattered around the sides.

In addition to these pictoral representations, degree and betweenness centrality scores and accuracy scores are provided in tables 3.1 and 3.2. Employees names are arranged in the tables in descending order of betweenness centrality. Three employees chose not to fill out the questionnaire, and consequently no accuracy score could be calculated for them. These missing accuracy scores are indicated by an "M" in tables 3.1 and 3.2. I was able to calculate centralities for those employees even though they did not fill out the questionnaire because I had estimates of their relations based on other employees' perceptions.

The Key Players in Management: Steve and Ev

Steve was the founder and president of this company. He knew all of its operations. As noted earlier, in the advice network his indegree was 19 and outdegree was 7 (see figure 3.3 and table 3.1). It is no surprise that he was the recipient of so many requests for help and advice. The fact

Table 3.1
Centralities and Accuracy on the Advice Network

		Centralities			Accuracy (rank)	
ID	Name	Indegree	Outdegree	Betweenness		
5	Ev	19.	1	0.20130	0.485	(3)
19	Steve	19.	7.	0.16405	0.411	(20)
24	Rick	6.	11.	0.08208	M	(M)
13	Mel	5.	15.	0.06711	M	(M)
6	Fred	9.	3.	0.06249	0.459	(7)
17	Quincy	10.	3.	0.05753	0.514	(1)
25	York	5.	15.	0.05551	0.391	(22)
30	Dan	7.	3.	0.05488	0.430	(10)
29	Chris	7.	6.	0.05263	0.384	(23)
16	Pat	7.	9.	0.03259	0.420	(16)
27	Alex	11.	2.	0.03217	0.397	(21)
12	Len	3.	7.	0.02444	0.212	(33)
35	Irv	6.	5.	0.01912	M	(M)
10	Jack	5.	2.	0.01593	0.332	(30)
21	Upton	7.	3.	0.01373	0.413	(19)
20	Tom	4.	3.	0.00834	0.378	(24)
18	Robin	2.	3.	0.00799	0.436	(9)
15	Ovid	2.	4.	0.00469	0.429	(12)
22	Vic	1.	6.	0.00375	0.352	(28)
33	Gerry	0.	5.	0.00274	0.302	(32)
7	Gary	0.	2.	0.00195	0.423	(14)
1	Abe	0.	4.	0.00139	0.482	(4)
36	Jim	5.	4.	0.00111	0.417	(17)
26	Zoe	1.	2.	0.00073	0.475	(5)
8	Hal	2.	3.	0.00067	0.371	(27)
2	Bob	1.	2.	0.00024	0.333	(29)
23	Walt	0.	4.	0.00024	0.417	(18)
28	Ben	2.	4.	0.00000	0.499	(2)
3	Carl	1.	1.	0.00000	0.374	(26)
32	Fran	0.	2.	0.00000	0.378	(25)
31	Earl	0.	2.	0.00000	0.423	(15)
34	Hugh	0.	2.	0.00000	0.470	(6)
9	Ivo	0.	1.	0.00000	0.442	(8)
14	Nan	0.	1.	0.00000	0.314	(31)
11	Ken	0.	0.	0.00000	0.429	(11)
4	Dale	0.	0.	0.00000	0.426	(13)

Table 3.2
Centralities and Accuracy on the Friendship Network

ID	Name	Centralities			Accuracy (rank)	
		Indegree	Outdegree	Betweenness		
29	Chris	12.	16.	0.16202	0.362	(11)
2	Bob	6.	4.	0.10899	0.344	(15)
24	Rick	11.	9.	0.10573	M	(M)
19	Steve	8.	6.	0.10472	0.349	(14)
21	Upton	5.	4.	0.09101	0.356	(12)
6	Fred	4.	2.	0.08981	0.334	(18)
35	Irv	8.	7.	0.07368	M	(M)
16	Pat	5.	4.	0.07013	0.323	(23)
13	Mel	6.	7.	0.06695	M	(M)
20	Tom	10.	10.	0.06651	0.363	(10)
33	Gerry	8.	7.	0.06615	0.381	(8)
4	Dale	8.	7.	0.05218	0.331	(20)
11	Ken	9.	7.	0.02812	0.384	(7)
14	Nan	5.	7.	0.02504	0.188	(31)
34	Hugh	6.	7.	0.01955	0.407	(3)
3	Carl	2.	4.	0.01792	0.391	(5)
30	Dan	5.	5.	0.01377	0.442	(1)
12	Len	2.	4.	0.00944	0.329	(21)
26	Zoe	3.	2.	0.00695	0.414	(2)
18	Robin	4.	4.	0.00280	0.333	(19)
9	Ivo	3.	2.	0.00268	0.398	(4)
15	Ovid	4.	3.	0.00240	0.302	(25)
27	Alex	3.	3.	0.00230	0.336	(17)
7	Gary	3.	2.	0.00118	0.311	(24)
5	Ev	2.	1.	0.00000	0.292	(26)
22	Vic	1.	3.	0.00000	0.275	(28)
8	Hal	1.	2.	0.00000	0.155	(33)
23	Walt	1.	2.	0.00000	0.352	(13)
36	Jim	1.	1.	0.00000	0.221	(29)
10	Jack	1.	1.	0.00000	0.200	(30)
31	Earl	0.	2.	0.00000	0.380	(9)
28	Ben	0.	1.	0.00000	0.292	(27)
1	Abe	0.	1.	0.00000	0.387	(6)
32	Fran	0.	0.	0.00000	0.325	(22)
17	Quincy	0.	0.	0.00000	0.341	(16)

that Steve reached out to seven employees on a regular basis for help and advice underscored his management style: he liked to stay in touch with what was going on in the firm, especially among his management team members, to whom most of his outdegree ties are pointed. He also enjoyed the second highest betweenness score, indicating that his ties were spread out among various groups within the firm. As indicated by his accuracy score, Steve's knowledge of the advice network was somewhat below the median in the firm. His lack of a better understanding of many of the informal advice ties can be attributed to his lack of attention to the rank and file of the firm.

An interesting contrast to Steve's managerial style was provided by Ev, the technical expert in the firm. Ev supervised the installation of much of the most sophisticated equipment in the field. His critical role in the organization was underscored by the fact that he had the highest betweenness score in the advice network—even higher than that of Steve. Ev's ability to solve problems in the field made him indispensable to a wide variety of people within the firm. His outdegree score, however, was 1 (Steve). His approach was more that of the engineer—the problem solver—than that of the manager. People came to him with problems, and he solved them or told others how to solve them. Ev did not see as part of his job that he had to seek out others' opinions, advice, or help. But by being so close to where the action was, he was in a good position to observe the informal advice network. His accuracy score reflected this good position: he had the third-highest accuracy in the advice network at Silicon Systems.

While no one questioned Ev's technical skills, some of the installers who worked for Ev indicated discontent with his managerial style. In fact, unbeknownst to top management at the time, dissatisfaction with Ev had spawned union interest on the part of several of the installers. As a result, contact was made secretly with a national union to organize the firm.

The installers' feelings toward Ev are illustrated in his position in the friendship network (figure 3.4). Ev had only 2 indegrees (two people considered him a personal friend), neither of whom were people who worked with him in the field. His betweenness in the friendship 0. Moreover, Ev's accuracy score for the friendship network was the eighth-lowest in the firm. Not only was friendship something he failed to engage in at work; he also paid little attention to it among others who worked for him or around him.

In contrast, Steve had 8 indegrees in the friendship network (eight people considered him a personal friend), and those who chose him were reasonably spread out, as he had the fourth-highest betweenness score. Despite his central position, however, his accuracy score was only slightly above the median for the firm, again because he tended to pay more attention to the top of the organization than to the rank and file. His lack of familiarity with the bottom of the organization led to his overwhelming sense of surprise and betrayal when he was informed by the NLRB that a union drive was under way.

Key Members of the Potential Bargaining Unit: Chris, Hal, Ovid, and Jack

The most central person in the friendship network was Chris, with 12 indegrees, 16 outdegrees, and a betweenness score of .162, substantially higher than the next-closest score. He had a more accurate assessment of the friendship network than anyone in management except Dan. Chris had been with the firm for a number of years, and his experience as a veteran installer was appreciated. But because his technical skills were not as strong as Ev's, Chris did not enjoy as central a position in the advice network as Ev did. In the field, however, Chris was often informally put in charge of a group of people to install some computer equipment, and his coworkers preferred working with him to working with Ev.

Before the union was contacted, Chris was very supportive of the union's goals. He was concerned about issues of pay and job security for himself and his fellow installers. While he was not the one who contacted the union, he had discussed with his colleagues the possibility of joining a union.

After the union was contacted, Chris took a back seat to others who were organizing on behalf of the union. He did not lead the organizing meetings, and he said very little publicly. Several fellow employees turned to him for guidance on this issue, but he resisted taking a leadership role. His reticence stemmed from two sources. First, the union made little effort to get him involved. While the union officials spent time with employees at the local bars and other locations, they never approached Chris with plans about his own role in the process. Second, Chris had strong feelings of ambivalence about the union. As noted earlier, he felt positive toward the union issues of pay and fair treatment by supervisors, but he also felt loyalty to the firm itself. He had been with the firm for a number of years, and he had grown to like his job and his coworkers. He did not want to be part of something that he thought might potentially damage the firm. Rather than attempt to lead his colleagues in any particular direction, he chose to remain in the background and did not actively involve himself in the debates at the meetings. As the vote approached, he felt more and more torn. Less than three weeks before the certification vote, he resigned from the firm rather than face the pressures of publicly committing on the union issue. He rejoined the company two days after the certification vote was taken.

Strong prounion positions were held by three key members of the potential bargaining unit: Ovid, Jack, and Hal. All three men had less betweenness centrality than the two antiunion employees, Mel and Robin. All three had a poorer cognitive picture of the friendship network than

Robin (Mel did not fill out the questionnaire, so his cognitive accuracy score was not available). Jack and Hal had minimal friendship ties to others in the potential bargaining unit. While Ovid strongly favored the union, he was very quiet about it, to the point that only a few people knew where he actually stood on the issue. It also was known that he was to leave shortly after the vote, so his influence was diminished. Jack was vocal about his dissatisfaction with how the company treated him. But his position on the periphery of the friendship network (see figure 3.4, on the extreme left) aptly describes his lack of informal influence with most of his colleagues. He was considered someone who had a grudge and who was motivated by his own personal agenda to be pro-union.

The most central actor in the union's attempt at organizing everyone was Hal. He was the union's original contact with the firm, and he was the instigator for the drive. He was the union's key spokesman at the organizing meetings, many of which he ran personally. He told the union representatives that he could get enough of his coworkers to vote for the union to assure a victory for the union. For the union's part, it obviously and publicly chose Hal to lead the employees in the organization attempt.

As one can see in figure 3.4 (on the right-hand side), Hal was not a central actor in the friendship network. It was true that Hal was the most enthusiastic supporter of the union, which is largely why the union officials selected him. However, he was not the person who wielded the most informal influence among his colleagues. In fact, he was seen by several members of the potential bargaining unit as a "loose cannon" and not "one of the guys."

Other Key Players: Robin and Mel

There was considerable antiunion feeling in the company, but none of it was located in the bargaining unit being organized. The key nonmanagement company supporters included Robin and Mel. Both were considered "one of the guys" and would often go drinking at local bars with people from the bargaining unit. They were vehemently opposed to the union and told people so. As can be seen in figure 3.4, Robin and Mel were friends with each other, as well as with several of the members of the bargaining unit, including Chris. In fact, their friendship with Chris contributed to Chris's ambivalence toward the union. Thus while they were not formally part of the bargaining unit, they wielded considerable informal influence within that group.

At the start of the two-month campaign, the union had the interest and lukewarm support of a majority of the people in the bargaining unit. In the opinion of several people who were interviewed for this study, the company would have lost the election had it been held on the first day of the campaign. While it is not known exactly how many people were prounion at the start, according to a union spokesperson interviewed, at least eight of the fifteen members of the potential bargaining unit had signed authorization cards.

Over the two months, the incessant pushing on the part of Hal (and to some extent Jack), instead of rallying support, served only to alienate several coworkers. This, combined with the antiunion position of Mel and Robin, led to a gradual deterioration of support for the union over the campaign period. In the end, the union was defeated in the certification election by a vote of twelve to three.

■ Discussion

What this study shows is that the key players in the advice network were not the key actors in the friendship network. Most striking is Ev's relative status in the friendship network. He was connected to the president (Steve) and another, peripheral employee. None of the employees who worked with him in the field was connected to him in the friendship network. By contrast, Chris was the most central actor in the friendship network. Chris was an installer with friendships that cut across functional and hierarchical boundaries. But his position in the advice network was relatively minor.

Chris's ambivalence stemmed from his feelings about the union in conjunction with his feelings about his friends, Mel and Robin. That is, he felt strongly that the union provided important protection for him and his fellow workers. He had been a voice in favor of contacting a union before the certification campaign began. But as his friend started to argue intensively against the union, he experienced the stress and tension that Heider predicted in such an imbalanced situation. Chris and Mel had a strong mutual "advice" tie also (that is, Chris would go to Mel for advice and vice versa). But, according to his closest associates, this work-based tie was not what contributed to Chris's discomfort in this situation. The informants I talked with would always refer to Chris's friends as influential on his behavior in this case. The only work-based relationship they discussed as influential in Chris's behavior was his relationship with Ev (his supervisor). If anything, this relationship with Ev, who was strongly opposed to the union, prompted Chris to be more inclined to support the union. Again, this is consistent with Heider's prediction: Since Chris's evaluation of Ev was negative and Ev's evaluation of the union was negative, Heider would predict that Chris would be positively disposed toward the union.

Davis (1963) noted that Heider's balance theory could be used to derive predictions about "cross-pressure" responses (Berelson, Lazarsfeld, and McPhee 1954). Cross-pressure situations arise when people are linked to groups that differ in their evaluations in important ways. Chris was in a prototypical cross-pressure situation. Davis quoted Berelson et al. (284): "An individual who is characterized by any type of cross-pressure is likely to change his mind in the course of the campaign, to make up his mind late, and occasionally, to leave the field and not to vote at all."

Putting this in balance-theory language, Davis himself wrote: "To the extent that *Person* has a positive bond to *Other*$_1$ and also to *Other*$_2$ . . . , it becomes increasingly difficult for him to adopt a stable attitude toward *X*" (1963:205). He further noted that the stronger the bond between *Person* and *Others*, the more difficult it is to resolve his attitude toward *X*. *Philos* bonds are particularly strong, since they involve strong affect and also have been invested in for some time. In Chris's case, it was because of the *history and affection* for his colleagues, some of whom (like Ovid) were strongly in favor of the union and others of whom (like Rob and Mel) were strongly opposed to the union, that Chris felt those cross-pressures and finally decided to withdraw from the decision.

It is impossible to know all the reasons for the union's failure to organize Silicon Systems. But according to the informants, a significant part of the failure was due to the fact that the union selected ineffective, non-powerful people to represent it in the process. While Hal and Jack were enthusiastic and articulate supporters of the union and its cause, they were not considered influential among their peers. Note that they were connected to their peers through the advice network: Hal to five people and Jack to six (see figure 3.3). But they were marginal players in the friendship network: Hal had two connections (neither of them to other members of the potential bargaining unit), and Jack had only one (see figure 3.4). As with Chris, when people spoke of Jack and Hal's roles in the process, they referred to affective qualities of friendship—or lack of it—in discussing how little influence each had in swaying the opinions of his coworkers.

Moreover, the union failed to recognize and address the influence that Robin and Mel had over members of the bargaining unit. In contrast to Hal and Jack, Rob and Mel had several friendship connections to members of the potential bargaining unit, most notably Chris. It is clear from figure 3.4 that Chris could have played an influential role in the process, if he had chosen to do so. His sympathies were with the union, but his alliances were torn. The union officials chose to ignore Chris. Had they co-opted and convinced him to take an active prounion role, others in the unit might have followed suit and voted for certification.

The Power of an Outsider

Thus we note that some people *behaved* in ways that indicated support for the union; others behaved in ways that indicated support for the management position. But the fact that the individuals *behaved* in particular ways is not enough. They had to be influential, also, for this behavior to be leveraged into actual support. This influence, this leverage, comes from the actors' positions in the *philos* network vis-à-vis others who were to have the final vote on this issue.

An outsider, such as the union in this instance, does not have either a formal or an informal position of influence from which to change people's thinking. But an outsider can acquire knowledge of such positions that others hold. For an outsider, the friendship network (figure 3.4) provides a map of potential influence. Knowledge of this map provides the outsider with an increased power base with which to accomplish his or her goals.

These conclusions stem largely from references to the friendship network, not the advice network, for two reasons. First, those people interviewed often referred to friendships in talking about who was influential in the campaign. Second, there are theoretical justifications for expecting friendships to be key in the certification drive. Krackhardt and Stern (1988) suggested that friendship links embody trust and that trust leads to cooperation under times of crises or radical change and uncertainty. When radical change requires trust to implement, affect can play an important role in determining where the power lies. In relatively tranquil times, however, work gets done in an organization by well-practiced and routine procedures. When exceptions to the routine are common, the process by which these exceptions are handled becomes part of the routine. In such times the patterns of daily or weekly interactions over work flow problems become the building blocks of power in the organization. Those who know how to handle the routine exceptions are the ones who know how to get things done and will assume powerful roles (Crozier 1964).

Second, it was clear that affective evaluations and resulting trust dominated the process because the union drive amounted to a major change for the organization—an organizational crisis, from management's point of view. The advice network reflected technical expertise and routine work-flow knowledge. The proposed change was nonroutine; advice on this critical issue was sought from those one trusted (as friends), not from technical experts.

I would speculate that had union officials had access to the information in figure 3.4, they might have revised their strategy in their attempt to organize Silicon Systems. While they did not have access to structural power, they could have developed a more accurate assessment of power by asking the same friendship questions used in this research. Their lack of awareness of the *philos* network, in other words, represented a lost opportunity for gaining power as an outsider.

My earlier study results show that accuracy in assessing the *advice* network, not the friendship network, was significantly related to reputational power of the members of the firm (Krackhardt 1990). In this study, however, I argue that power is enhanced through an understanding of the *philos* network. This seeming contradiction makes sense in light of the theoretical arguments just made. At the time that the network and power data were being collected, the firm had not experienced any tumultuous events or environmental jolts. In answering questions about influence and power, employees were responding according to their experiences in their day-to-day lives in the organization. As in the case of Ev, those people central to the advice network, the experts, are likely to derive power from such routine situations. On the other hand, the certification move was an attempt to introduce a significant change in the organization (from both management's and workers' perspectives). Dealing with this change did not require routine information. It required trust, which is better represented in a *philos* network than in an affectively neutral advice network.

Conclusion

We opened this chapter by noting that Granovetter's strength-of-weak ties hypothesis had found support in the literature but that the support had left some issues unaddressed. Our study did not set out to test or expand the weak-ties hypothesis but attempted to refocus on the importance of strong ties within an organization. In particular, using Granovetter's own logic, we can see how strong ties may become important in organizations when they are spread out among the players.

But a critical part of networks rests in a forgotten aspect of the strong-ties argument: The affect level of these ties cannot be ignored. Frequent interactions that are not part of the *philos* relations are not going to have the same effect as those that are. Someone, even an outsider, who understands the structure of *philos* ties within an organization will be much more able to anticipate political resistance and facilitate change.

Just as I opened by referring to Mark Granovetter, it is fitting that I close with a reference to his current work. In his keynote speech at the 1990 INSNA conference, Granovetter admitted that he tried to escape the label of a social networker and move on to "more substantive interests in stratification, economic sociology and sociological theory" (Granovetter 1990). But, he went on, no matter which substantive avenue he traveled, a review of the literature in that area led him to rediscover the importance of networks in understanding the social phenomena under scrutiny. Granovetter's current thinking differs especially with that of economists who seek to explain forces toward equilibria: "This means talking seriously about how changes occur. And what happens in such a dynamic account is that you have to look at how people make use of their location in social networks to mobilize resources in order to achieve their economic goals."

If change were simply dependent on new information, then weak ties would be preeminent. But when it comes to major change, change that may threaten the status quo in terms of power and the standard routines of how decisions are made, then resistance to that change must be addressed before predictions can be made about the success of that change effort. A major resource that is required to bring about such change is trust in the propagators of that change. Change is the product of strong, affective, and time-honored relationships. Change is the product of *philos*.

■ Notes

1. An alternative to the psychological explanation has been offered by Davis (1968:548). He suggests that groups cluster on attributes having less to do with sentiment and more to do with the social categories they belong to or to the fact that organizations are naturally divided into subgroups that facilitate balanced clusters of interaction. This is an interesting conjecture, one that deserves more systematic study. Nonetheless, there is some evidence suggesting that Heider's explanation is at least part of the picture. Krackhardt and Kilduff (1990) explored the friendship patterns within a small firm. The patterns of friendship did not clump into easily identifiable groups, as Davis would have predicted. But, consistent with balance theory, when an individual disagreed with his or her friends about their evaluations of others in the workplace, there was a strong tendency for that person to be relatively disaffected with his or her experience at the organization.

2. Since person k has some input into the definition of $R^*_{i,j}$, that is, when $i = k$ or when $j = k$, these "local ties" were excluded from person k's accuracy score. For a more thorough discussion, see Krackhardt 1990:350.

3. Betweenness is calculated from the underlying graph of the asymmetric relation R*. That is, the asymmetric relation is made symmetrical first before the betweenness score is computed. See Krackhardt 1990:351 for more details.

4. The program used here was an adaptation of Lingoes and Roskam's (1973) MINISSA package. See Kruskal and Wish's (1978) discussion of MDS and the various packages available.

■ References

Berelson, B. R., Paul F. Lazarsfeld, and W. N. McPhee. 1954. *Voting: A Study of Opinion Formation in a Presidential Campaign*. Chicago: University of Chicago Press.

Byrne, D. 1971. *The Attraction Paradigm*. New York: Academic Press.

Crozier, M. 1964. *The Bureaucratic Phenomenon*. Chicago: University of Chicago Press.

Davis, James A. 1963. "Structural Balance, Mechanical Solidarity and Interpersonal Relations." *American Journal of Sociology* 68:444–463.

———. 1968. "Social Structures and Cognitive Structures." In R. P. Abelson, E. Anderson, N. J. McGuire, T. M. Newcomb, M. J. Rosenberg, and P. H. Tannenbaum, eds. *Theories of Cognitive Consistency: A Source Book*. Chicago: Rand McNally.

———. 1979. "The Davis/Holland/Lernhardt Studies: An Overview." In Paul W.

Holland and Samuel Lernhardt, eds. *Perspectives on Social Network Research.* New York: Academic Press.

Erickson, E., and W. Yancey. 1980. "Class, Sector and Income Determination." Unpublished paper, Department of Sociology, Temple University.

Fischer, Claude S. 1982. "What Do We Mean by 'Friend'? An Inductive Study." *Social Networks* 3:287–306.

Freeman, Linton C. 1979. "Centrality in Social Networks: Conceptional Clarification." *Social Networks* 1:215–239.

Friedkin, N. E. 1980. "A Test of Structural Features of Granovetter's Strength of Weak Ties Theory." *Social Networks* 2:22–41.

Granovetter, M. S. 1973. "The Strength of Weak Ties." *American Journal of Sociology* 78:1360–1380.

———. 1982. "The Strength of Weak Ties: A Network Theory Revisited." In P. V. Marsden and Nan Lin, eds. *Social Structure and Network Analysis.* Beverly Hills: Sage.

———. 1985. "Economic Action and Social Structure: The Problem of Embededness." *American Journal of Sociology* 91(3):481–510.

———. 1990. "The Myth of Social Network Analysis as a Special in the Social Sciences." INSNA Conference, San Diego.

Heider, Fritz. 1958. *The Psychology of Interpersonal Relations.* New York: Wiley.

Krackhardt, David. 1987. "Cognitive Social Structures." *Social Networks* 9:109–134.

———. 1990. "Assessing the Political Landscape: Structure, Cognition, and Power in Organizations." *Administrative Science Quarterly* 35:342–369.

Krackhardt, David, and Martin Kilduff. 1990. "Friendship Patterns and Culture: The Control of Organizational Diversity." *American Anthropologist* 92(1):142–154.

Krackhardt, David, and Robert Stern. 1988. "Informal Networks and Organizational Crisis: An Experimental Simulation." *Social Psychology Quarterly* 51: 123–140.

Kruskal, Joseph B., and Myron Wish. 1978. *Multidimensional Scaling.* Beverly Hills: Sage.

Lin, N., P. W. Dayton, and P. Greenwald. 1978. "Analyzing the Instrumental Use of Relations in the Context of Social Structure." *Sociological Methods and Research* 7:149–166.

Lin, N., W. M. Ensel, and J. C. Vaughn. 1981. "Social Resources and Strength of Ties: Structural Factors in Occupational Status Attainment." *American Sociological Review* 46:393–405.

Lingoes, J. C., and Edward E. Roskam. 1973. "A Mathematical and Empirical Analysis of Two Multidimensional Scaling Algorithms." *Psychometrika* 38:93.

Newcomb, J. M. 1961. *The Aquaintance Process.* New York: Holt, Reinhart and Winston.

Pool, I. 1980. "Comment on Mark Granovetter's 'The Strength of Weak Ties': A Network Revisited." Presented at the Annual Meetings of the International Communications Association, Acapulco, May.

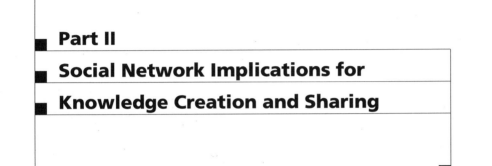

Part II

Social Network Implications for

Knowledge Creation and Sharing

4

The Strength of Weak Ties

Mark S. Granovetter

A fundamental weakness of current sociological theory is that it does not relate micro level interactions to macro level patterns in any convincing way. Large-scale statistical, as well as qualitative, studies offer a good deal of insight into such macro phenomena as social mobility, community organization, and political structure. At the micro level, a large and increasing body of data and theory offers useful and illuminating ideas about what transpires within the confines of the small group. But how interaction in small groups aggregates to form large-scale patterns eludes us in most cases.

I will argue in this paper that the analysis of processes in interpersonal networks provides the most fruitful micro-macro bridge. In one way or another, it is through these networks that small-scale interaction becomes translated into large-scale patterns and that these, in turn, feed back into small groups.

Sociometry, the precursor of network analysis, has always been curiously peripheral—invisible, really—in sociological theory. This is partly because it has usually been studied and applied only as a branch of social psychology; it is also because of the inherent complexities of precise network analysis. We have had neither the theory nor the measurement and sampling techniques to move sociometry from the usual small-group level to that of larger structures. While a number of stimulating and suggestive studies have recently moved in this direction (Bott 1957; Mayer 1961; Milgram 1967; Boissevain 1968; Mitchell 1969), they do not treat structural issues in much theoretical detail. Studies which do so usually involve a level of technical complexity appropriate to such forbidding sources as the *Bulletin of Mathematical Biophysics*, where the original motivation for the study of networks was that of developing a theory of neural, rather than social, interaction (see the useful review of this literature by Coleman 1960; also Rapoport 1963).

The strategy of the present paper is to choose a rather limited aspect of small-scale interaction—the strength of interpersonal ties—and to show, in some detail, how the use of network analysis can relate this aspect to

such varied macro phenomena as diffusion, social mobility, political organization, and social cohesion in general. While the analysis is essentially
qualitative, a mathematically inclined reader will recognize the potential
for models; mathematical arguments, leads, and references are suggested
mostly in footnotes.

■ The Strength of Ties

Most intuitive notions of the "strength" of an interpersonal tie should be
satisfied by the following definition: the strength of a tie is a (probably
linear) combination of the amount of time, the emotional intensity, the
intimacy (mutual confiding), and the reciprocal services which characterize the tie.[1] Each of these is somewhat independent of the other, though
the set is obviously highly intracorrelated. Discussion of operational measures of and weights attaching to each of the four elements is postponed
to future empirical studies.[2] It is sufficient for the present purpose if most
of us can agree, on a rough intuitive basis, whether a given tie is strong,
weak, or absent.[3]

Consider, now, any two arbitrarily selected individuals—call them A
and B—and the set, $S = C, D, E, \ldots$, of all persons with ties to either *or*
both of them.[4] The hypothesis which enables us to relate dyadic ties to
larger structures is the stronger the tie between A and B, the larger the
proportion of individuals in S to whom they will *both* be tied, that is,
connected by a weak or strong tie. This overlap in their friendship circles
is predicted to be least when their tie is absent, most when it is strong,
and intermediate when it is weak.

The proposed relationship results, first, from the tendency (by definition) of stronger ties to involve larger time commitments. If A-B and
A-C ties exist, then the amount of time C spends with B depends (in part)
on the amount A spends with B and C, respectively. (If the events "A is
with B" and "A is with C" were independent, then the event "C is with
A and B" would have probability equal to the product of their probabilities. For example, if A and B are together 60% of the time, and A and C
40%, then C, A, and B would be together 24% of the time. Such independence would be less likely after than before B and C became acquainted.)
If C and B have no relationship, common strong ties to A will probably
bring them into interaction and generate one. Implicit here is Homans's
idea that "the more frequently persons interact with one another, the
stronger their sentiments of friendship for one another are apt to be"
(1950, p. 133).

The hypothesis is made plausible also by empirical evidence that the
stronger the tie connecting two individuals, the more similar they are, in
various ways (Berscheid and Walster 1969, pp. 69–91; Bramel 1969, pp. 9–
16; Brown 1965, pp. 71–90; Laumann 1968; Newcomb 1961, chap. 5;

Precker 1952). Thus, if strong ties connect A to B and A to C, both C and B, being similar to A, are probably similar to one another, increasing the likelihood of a friendship once they have met. Applied in reverse, these two factors—time and similarity—indicate why weaker A-B and A-C ties make a C-B tie less likely than strong ones: C and B are less likely to interact and less likely to be compatible if they do.

The theory of cognitive balance, as formulated by Heider (1958) and especially by Newcomb (1961, pp. 4–23), also predicts this result. If strong ties A-B and A-C exist, and if B and C are aware of one another, anything short of a positive tie would introduce a "psychological strain" into the situation since C will want his own feelings to be congruent with those of his good friend, A, and similarly, for B and *his* friend, A. Where the ties are weak, however, such consistency is psychologically less crucial. (On this point see also Homans [1950, p. 255] and Davis [1963, p. 448].)

Some direct evidence for the basic hypothesis exists (Kapferer 1969, p. 229 n.; Laumann and Schuman 1967; Rapoport and Horvath 1961; Rapoport 1963).[5] This evidence is less comprehensive than one might hope. In addition, however, certain inferences from the hypothesis have received empirical support. Description of these inferences will suggest some of the substantive implications of the above argument.

Weak Ties in Diffusion Processes

To derive implications for large networks of relations, it is necessary to frame the basic hypothesis more precisely. This can be done by investigating the possible triads consisting of strong, weak, or absent ties among A, B, and any arbitrarily chosen friend of either or both (i.e., some member of the set S, described earlier). A thorough mathematical model would do this in some detail, suggesting probabilities for various types. This analysis becomes rather involved, however, and it is sufficient for my purpose in this paper to say that the triad which is most *unlikely* to occur, under the hypothesis stated above, is that in which A and B are strongly linked, A has a strong tie to some friend C, but the tie between C and B is absent. This triad is shown in figure 4.1. To see the consequences of this assertion, I will exaggerate it in what follows by supposing that the triad shown *never* occurs—that is, that the B-C tie is always present (whether weak or

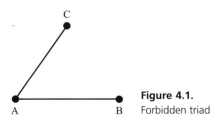

Figure 4.1.
Forbidden triad

strong), given the other two strong ties. Whatever results are inferred from this supposition should tend to occur in the degree that the triad in question tends to be absent.

Some evidence exists for this absence. Analyzing 651 sociograms, Davis (1970, p. 845) found that in 90% of them, triads consisting of two mutual choices and one nonchoice occurred less than the expected random number of times. If we assume that mutual choice indicates a strong tie, this is strong evidence in the direction of my argument.[6] Newcomb (1961, pp. 160–65) reports that in triads consisting of dyads expressing mutual "high attraction," the configuration of three strong ties became increasingly frequent as people knew one another longer and better; the frequency of the triad pictured in figure 4.1 is not analyzed, but it is implied that processes of cognitive balance tended to eliminate it.

The significance of this triad's absence can be shown by using the concept of a "bridge"; this is a line in a network which provides the *only* path between two points (Harary, Norman, and Cartwright 1965, p. 198). Since, in general, each person has a great many contacts, a bridge between *A* and *B* provides the only route along which information or influence can flow from any contact of *A* to any contact of *B,* and, consequently, from anyone connected *indirectly* to *A* to anyone connected indirectly to *B.* Thus, in the study of diffusion, we can expect bridges to assume an important role.

Now, if the stipulated triad is absent, it follows that, except under unlikely conditions, *no strong tie is a bridge.* Consider the strong tie *A-B*: if *A* has another strong tie to *C*, then forbidding the triad of figure 4.1 implies that a tie exists between *C* and *B*, so that the path *A-C-B* exists between *A* and *B*; hence, *A-B* is not a bridge. A strong tie can be a bridge, therefore, *only if* neither party to it has any *other* strong ties, unlikely in a social network of any size (though possible in a small group). Weak ties suffer no such restriction, though they are certainly not automatically bridges. What is important, rather, is that all bridges are weak ties.

In large networks it probably happens only rarely, in practice, that a specific tie provides the *only* path between two points. The bridging function may nevertheless be served *locally.* In figure 4.2*a*, for example, the tie *A-B* is not strictly a bridge, since one can construct the path *A-E-I-B* (and others). Yet *A-B* is the shortest route to *B* for *F, D,* and *C.* This function is clearer in figure 4.2*b*. Here, *A-B* is, for *C, D,* and others, not only a local bridge to *B* but, in most real instances of diffusion, a much more likely and efficient path. Harary et al. point out that "there may be a distance [length of path] beyond which it is not feasible for *u* to communicate with *v* because of costs or distortions entailed in each act of transmission. If *v* does not lie within this critical distance, then he will not receive messages originating with *u*" (1965, p. 159). I will refer to a tie as a "local bridge of degree *n*" if *n* represents the shortest path between its two points (other than itself) and *n* > 2. In figure 4.2*a*, *A-B* is a local bridge of degree 3, in 4.2*b*, of degree 13.

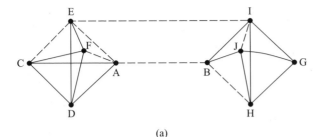

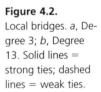

(a)

(b)

Figure 4.2.
Local bridges. *a*, Degree 3; *b*, Degree 13. Solid lines = strong ties; dashed lines = weak ties.

As with bridges in a highway system, a local bridge in a social network will be more significant as a connection between two sectors to the extent that it is the only alternative for many people—that is, as its degree increases. A bridge in the absolute sense is a local one of infinite degree. By the same logic used above, only weak ties may be local bridges.

Suppose, now, that we adopt Davis's suggestion that "in interpersonal flows of most any sort the probability that 'whatever it is' will flow from person *i* to person *j* is (*a*) directly proportional to the number of all-positive (friendship) paths connecting *i* and *j*; and (*b*) inversely proportional to the length of such paths" (1969, p. 549).[7] The significance of weak ties, then, would be that those which are local bridges create more, and shorter, paths. Any given tie may, hypothetically, be removed from a network; the number of paths broken and the changes in average path length resulting between arbitrary pairs of points (with some limitation on length of path considered) can then be computed. The contention here is that removal of the average weak tie would do more "damage" to transmission probabilities than would that of the average strong one.[8]

Intuitively speaking, this means that whatever is to be diffused can reach a larger number of people, and traverse greater social distance (i.e., path length),[9] when passed through weak ties rather than strong. If one tells a rumor to all his close friends, and they do likewise, many will hear the rumor a second and third time, since those linked by strong ties tend to share friends. If the motivation to spread the rumor is dampened a bit on each wave of retelling, then the rumor moving through strong ties is much more likely to be limited to a few cliques than that going via weak ones; bridges will not be crossed.[10]

Since sociologists and anthropologists have carried out many hundreds of diffusion studies—Rogers's 1962 review dealt with 506—one might suppose that the above claims could easily be put to test. But this is not so, for several reasons. To begin with, though most diffusion studies find that personal contacts are crucial, many undertake no sociometric investigation. (Rogers discusses this point.) When sociometric techniques *are* used, they tend to discourage the naming of those weakly tied to the respondent by sharply limiting the numbers of choices allowed. Hence, the proposed importance of weak ties in diffusion is not measured. Even when more sociometric information is collected, there is almost never an attempt to directly retrace the exact interpersonal paths traversed by an (idea, rumor, or) innovation. More commonly, the time when each individual adopted the innovation is recorded, as is the number of sociometric choices he received from others in the study. Those receiving many choices are characterized as "central," those with few as "marginal"; this variable is then correlated with time of adoption and inferences made about what paths were probably followed by the innovation.

One point of controversy in diffusion studies can be related to my argument. Some scholars have indicated that early innovators are marginal, that they "underconform to norms to such a degree that they are perceived as highly deviant" (Rogers 1962, p. 197). Others (e.g., Coleman, Katz, and Menzel [1966] on the adoption of a new drug by doctors) find that those named more frequently adopt an innovation substantially earlier. Becker (1970) tries to resolve the question of whether early innovators are "central" or "marginal" by referring to the "perceived risks of adoption of a given innovation." His study of public health innovations shows that when a new program is thought relatively safe and uncontroversial (as with the drug of Coleman et al.), central figures lead in its adoption; otherwise, marginal ones do (p. 273). He explains the difference in terms of a greater desire of "central" figures to protect their professional reputations.

Kerckhoff, Back, and Miller (1965) reach a similar conclusion in a different type of study. A Southern textile plant had been swept by "hysterical contagion": a few, then more and more workers, claiming bites from a mysterious "insect," became nauseous, numb, and weak, leading to a plant shutdown. When the affected workers were asked to name their three best friends, many named one another, but the very *earliest* to be stricken were social isolates, receiving almost no choices. An explanation, compatible with Becker's, is offered: since the symptoms might be thought odd, early "adopters" were likely to be found among the marginal, those less subject to social pressures. Later, "it is increasingly likely that some persons who are socially integrated will be affected. . . . The contagion enters social networks and is disseminated with increasing rapidity" (p. 13). This is consistent with Rogers's comment that while the *first* adopters of innovations are marginal, the next group, "early adopters," "are a more integrated part of the local social system than the innovators" (1962, p. 183).

"Central" and "marginal" individuals may well be motivated as claimed; but if the marginal are genuinely so, it is difficult to see how they can ever spread innovations successfully. We may surmise that since the resistance to a risky or deviant activity is greater than to a safe or normal one, a larger number of people will have to be exposed to it and adopt it, in the early stages, before it will spread in a chain reaction. Individuals with many weak ties are, by my arguments, best placed to diffuse such a difficult innovation, since some of those ties will be local bridges.[11] An initially unpopular innovation spread by those with *few* weak ties is more likely to be confined to a few cliques, thus being stillborn and never finding its way into a diffusion study.

That the "marginal" innovators of diffusion studies might actually be rich in *weak* ties is possible, given the usual sociometric technique, but in most cases this is purely speculative. Kerckhoff and Back, however, in a later more detailed analysis of the hysteria incident, indicate that besides asking about one's "three best friends," they also asked with whom workers ate, worked, shared car pools, etc. They report that five of the six workers earliest affected "are social isolates when friendship choices are used as the basis of analysis. Only 1 of the 6 is mentioned as a friend by *anyone* in our sample. This is made even more striking when we note that these 6 women are mentioned with considerable frequency when other bases for choice are used. In fact, they are chosen more frequently on a 'non-friendship' basis than are the women in any of the other categories" (1968, p. 112).

This finding lends credence to the weak-tie argument but is inconclusive. A somewhat different kind of diffusion study offers more direct support: the "small-world" investigations of Milgram and his associates. The name of these studies stems from the typical comment of newly introduced individuals who discover some common acquaintance; this situation is generalized in an attempt to measure, for arbitrarily chosen pairs of individuals in the United States, how long a path of personal contacts would be needed to connect them. A booklet is given to randomly designated senders who are asked to forward it toward some named target person, via someone the sender knows personally who would be more likely than himself to know the target. The new recipient then advances the booklet similarly; eventually it reaches the target or someone fails to send it on. The proportion of such chains completed has ranged from 12% to 33% in different studies, and the number of links in completed chains has ranged from two to ten, averaging between five and eight (Milgram 1967; Travers and Milgram 1969; Korte and Milgram 1970).

Each time someone forwards a booklet he also sends a postcard to the researchers, indicating, among other things, the relationship between himself and the next receiver. Two of the categories which can be chosen are "friend" and "acquaintance." I will assume that this corresponds to "strong" and "weak" ties. In one of the studies, white senders were asked to forward the booklet to a target who was Negro. In such chains, a crucial point was the *first* sending of the booklet from a white to a Negro. In 50% of the instances where the white described this Negro as an "acquaintance," the chain was ultimately completed; completion rate fell to 26%, however, when the white sent the booklet to a Negro "friend." (My computation is based on unpublished data kindly supplied by Charles Korte. See Korte [1967] and Korte and Milgram [1970].) Thus, weaker interracial ties can be seen to be more effective in bridging social distance.

Another relevant study, by Rapoport and Horvath (1961), is not exactly one of diffusion but is closely related in that it traces out paths along which diffusion *could* take place. They asked each individual in a Michigan junior high school ($N = 851$) to list his eight best friends in order of preference. Then, taking a number of random samples from the group (sample size, an arbitrary number, was nine), they traced out, for each sample, and averaged over all the samples, the total number of people reached by following along the network of first and second choices. That is, the first and second choices of each sample member were tabulated, then the first and second choices of *these* people were added in, etc., counting, at each remove, *only* names not previously chosen, and continuing until no new people were reached. The same procedure was followed using second and third choices, third and fourth, etc., up to seventh and eighth. (The theoretical connection of this tracing procedure to diffusion is discussed by Rapoport [1953*a*, 1953*b*, and especially 1954].)

The smallest total number of people were reached through the networks generated by first and second choices—presumably the strongest ties—and the largest number through seventh and eighth choices. These findings correspond to my assertion that more people can be reached through weak ties. A parameter in their mathematical model of the sociogram, designed to measure, approximately, the overlap of acquaintance circles, declined monotonically with increasing rank order of friends.[12]

■ Weak Ties in Egocentric Networks

In this section and the next, I want to discuss the general significance of the above findings and arguments at two levels: first that of individuals, then that of communities. These discussions make no pretense of being comprehensive; they are meant only to illustrate possible applications.

In recent years, a great deal of literature has appeared analyzing the impact on the behavior of individuals of the social networks in which they are embedded. Some of the studies have emphasized the ways in which behavior is shaped and constrained by one's network (Bott 1957; Mayer 1961; Frankenberg 1965), others the ways in which individuals can manipulate these networks to achieve specific goals (Mayer 1966; Boissevain 1968; Kapferer 1969). Both facets are generally supposed to be affected by the structure of one's network. Bott argued that the crucial variable is that of whether one's friends tend to know one another ("closeknit" network) or not ("loose-knit" network). Barnes makes this dichotomy into a continuous variable by counting the number of ties observed in the network formed by ego and his friends and dividing it by the ratio of possible ones; this figure then corresponds to what is often called network "density" (Barnes 1969; Tilly 1969).[13]

Epstein (1969) points out, however, that different *parts* of ego's network may have different density. He calls those with whom one "interacts most intensely and most regularly, and who are therefore also likely to come to know one another," the "effective network"; the "remainder constitute the *extended* network" (pp. 110–11). This is close to saying, in my terms, that one's strong ties form a dense network, one's weak ties a less dense one. I would add that one's weak ties which are not local bridges might as well be counted with the strong ties, to maximize separation of the dense from the less dense network sectors.

One point on which there is no general agreement is whether ego's network should be treated as composed only of those to whom he is tied directly or should include the contacts of his contacts and/or others. Analyses stressing encapsulation of an individual by his network tend to take the former position, those stressing manipulation of networks, the latter, since information or favors available through direct contacts may depend on who *their* contacts are. I would argue that by dividing ego's network into that part made up of strong and nonbridging weak ties on the one hand and that of bridging weak ties on the other, both orientations can be dealt with. Ties in the former part should tend to be to people who not only know one another but also have few contacts not tied to ego as well. In the "weak" sector, however, not only will ego's contacts not be tied to one another, they *will* be tied to individuals not tied to ego. Indirect contacts are thus typically reached through ties in this sector; such ties are then of importance not only in ego's manipulation of networks but also in that they are the channels through which ideas, influences, or information socially distant from ego may reach him. The fewer indirect contacts one has the more encapsulated he will be in terms of knowledge of the world beyond his own friendship circle; thus, bridging weak ties (and the consequent indirect contacts) are important in both ways.

I will develop this point empirically by citing some results from a labor-market study I have recently completed. Labor economists have long been aware that American blue-collar workers find out about new jobs more through personal contacts than by any other method. (Many studies are reviewed by Parnes [1954, chap. 5].) Recent studies suggest that this is also true for those in professional, technical, and managerial positions (Shapero, Howell, and Tombaugh 1965; Brown 1967; Granovetter 1970). My study of this question laid special emphasis on the nature of the *tie* between the job changer and the contact person who provided the necessary information.

In a random sample of recent professional, technical, and managerial job changers living in a Boston suburb, I asked those who found a new job through contacts how often they *saw* the contact around the time that he passed on job information to them. I will use this as a measure of tie strength.[14] A natural a priori idea is that those with whom one has strong ties are more motivated to help with job information. Opposed to this greater motivation are the structural arguments I have been making: those to whom we are weakly tied are more likely to move in circles different from our own and will thus have access to information different from that which we receive.

I have used the following categories for frequency of contact: often = at least twice a week; occasionally = more than once a year but less than twice a week; rarely = once a year or less. Of those finding a job through contacts, 16.7% reported that they saw their contact often at the time, 55.6% said occasionally, and 27.8% rarely ($N = 54$).[15] The skew is clearly to the weak end of the continuum, suggesting the primacy of structure over motivation.

In many cases, the contact was someone only marginally included in the current network of contacts, such as an old college friend or a former workmate or employer, with whom sporadic contact had been maintained (Granovetter 1970, pp. 76–80). Usually such ties had not even been very strong when first forged. For work-related ties, respondents almost invariably said that they never saw the person in a nonwork context.[16] Chance meetings or mutual friends operated to reactivate such ties. It is remarkable that people receive crucial information from individuals whose very existence they have forgotten.[17]

I also asked respondents where their contacts *got* the information they transmitted. In most cases, I traced the information to its initial source. I had expected that, as in the diffusion of rumors or diseases, long paths would be involved. But in 39.1% of the cases, information came directly from the prospective employer, whom the respondent already knew; 45.3% said that there was one intermediary between himself and the employer; 12.5% reported two; and 3.1% more than two ($N = 64$). This suggests that for some important purposes it may be sufficient to discuss, as I have, the egocentric network made up of ego, his contacts, and *their* contacts. Had long information paths been involved, large numbers might have found out about any given job, and no particular tie would have been crucial. Such a model of job-information flow actually does correspond to the economists' model of a "perfect" labor market. But those few who did acquire information through paths with more than one intermediary tended to be young and under the threat of unemployment; influence was much less likely to have been exerted by their contact on their behalf. These respondents were, in fact, more similar to those using *formal* intermediaries (agencies, advertisements) than to those hearing through short paths: both of the former are badly placed and dissatisfied in the labor market, and both receive information without influence. Just as reading about a job in the newspaper affords one no recommendation in applying for it, neither does it to have heard about it fifth hand.

The usual dichotomy between "formal" or mass procedures and diffusion through personal contacts may thus be invalid in some cases where, instead, the former may be seen as a limiting case of long diffusion chains. This is especially likely where information of instrumental significance is involved. Such information is most valuable when earmarked for one person.

From the individual's point of view, then, weak ties are an important resource in making possible mobility opportunity. Seen from a more macroscopic vantage, weak ties play a role in effecting social cohesion. When a man changes jobs, he is not only moving from one network of ties to another but also establishing a link between these. Such a link is often of the same kind which facilitated his own movement. Especially within professional and technical specialties which are well defined and limited in size, this mobility sets up elaborate structures of bridging weak ties between the more coherent clusters that constitute operative networks in particular locations. Information and ideas thus flow more easily through the specialty, giving it some "sense of community," activated at meetings and conventions. Maintenance of weak ties may well be the most important consequence of such meetings.

Weak Ties and Community Organization

These comments about sense of community may remind us that in many cases it is desirable to deal with a unit of analysis larger than a single individual. I would like to develop my argument further by analyzing, in this section, why some communities organize for common goals easily and effectively whereas others seem unable to mobilize resources, even against dire threats. The Italian community of Boston's West End, for example, was unable to even *form* an organization to fight against the "urban renewal" which ultimately destroyed it. This seems especially anomalous in view of Gans's description of West End social structure as cohesive (1962).

Variations in culture and personality are often cited to explain such anomalies. Gans contrasts "lower"-, "working"-, and "middle"-class sub-cultures, concluding that only the last provides sufficient trust in leaders and practice in working toward common goals to enable formation of an effective organization. Thus, the working-class West End could not resist urban renewal (1962, pp. 229–304). Yet, numerous well-documented cases show that *some* working-class communities have mobilized quite success-fully against comparable or lesser threats (Dahl 1961, pp. 192–99; Keyes 1969; Davies 1966, chap. 4).[18] I would suggest, as a sharper analytical tool, examination of the network of ties comprising a community to see whether aspects of its structure might facilitate or block organization.

Imagine, to begin with, a community completely partitioned into cliques, such that each person is tied to every other in his clique and to none outside. Community organization would be severely inhibited. Leaf-letting, radio announcements, or other methods could insure that every-one was *aware* of some nascent organization; but studies of diffusion and mass communication have shown that people rarely *act* on mass-media information unless it is also transmitted through personal ties (Katz and Lazarsfeld 1955; Rogers 1962); otherwise one has no particular reason to think that an advertised product or an organization should be taken se-riously. Enthusiasm for an organization in one clique, then, would not spread to others but would have to develop independently in *each one* to insure success.

The problem of trust is closely related. I would propose that whether a person trusts a given leader depends heavily on whether there exist intermediary personal contacts who can, from their own knowledge, as-sure him that the leader is trustworthy, and who can, if necessary, inter-cede with the leader or his lieutenants on his behalf. Trust in leaders is integrally related to the *capacity to predict and affect their behavior*. Leaders, for their part, have little motivation to be responsive or even trustworthy toward those to whom they have no direct or indirect connection. Thus, network fragmentation, by reducing drastically the number of paths from any leader to his potential followers, would inhibit trust in such leaders. This inhibition, furthermore, would not be entirely irrational.

Could the West End's social structure really have been of this kind? Note first that while the structure hypothesized is, by definition, extremely fragmented, this is evident only at a macroscopic level—from an "aerial view" of the network. The local phenomenon is cohesion. (Davis [1967] also noted this paradox in a related context.) An analyst studying such a group by participant observation might never see the extent of fragmen-tation, especially if the cliques were not earmarked by ethnic, cultural, or other visible differences. In the nature of participant observation, one is likely to get caught up in a fairly restricted circle; a few useful contacts are acquired and relied on for introduction to others. The "problem of entry into West End society was particularly vexing," Gans writes. But eventually, he and his wife "were welcomed by one of our neighbors and became friends with them. As a result they invited us to many of their evening gatherings and introduced us to other neighbors, relatives and friends. . . . As time went on . . . other West Enders . . . introduced me to relatives and friends, although *most* of the social gatherings at which I participated were those of our *first* contact and their circle" (1962, pp. 340–41; emphasis supplied). Thus, his account of cohesive groups is not *inconsistent* with overall fragmentation.

Now, suppose that all ties in the West End were either strong or absent and that the triad of figure 4.1 did not occur. Then, for any ego, all his friends were friends of one another and all their friends were ego's friends as well. Unless each person was strongly tied to *all* others in the community, network structure did indeed break down into the isolated cliques posited above. (In terms of Davis's mathematical treatment, the overall network was "clusterable," with unique clusters [1967, p. 186].) Since it is unlikely that anyone could sustain more than a few dozen strong ties, this would, in fact, have been the result.

Did strong ties take up enough of the West Enders' social time to make this analysis even approximately applicable? Gans reported that "sociability is a routinized gathering of a relatively unchanging peer group of family members and friends that takes place several times a week." Some "participate in informal cliques and in clubs made up of unrelated people. . . . In number, and in the amount of time devoted to them, however, these groups are much less important than the family circle" (1962, pp. 74, 80). Moreover, two common sources of weak ties, formal organizations and work settings, did not provide them for the West End; organization membership was almost nil (pp. 104–7), and few worked within the area itself, so that ties formed at work were not relevant to the community (p. 122).

Nevertheless, in a community marked by geographic immobility and lifelong friendships (Gans 1962, p. 19), it strains credulity to suppose that each person would not have known a great many others, so that there would have been *some* weak ties. The question is whether such ties were bridges.[19] If *none* were, then the community would be fragmented in exactly the same way as described above, except that the cliques would then contain weak as well as strong ties. (Again, this follows from Davis's analysis of "clusterability," with strong and weak ties called "positive" and absent ones "negative" [1967].) Such a pattern is made plausible by the lack of ways in the West End to *develop* weak ties other than by meeting friends of friends (where "friend" includes relatives)—in which case the new tie is automatically not a bridge. It is suggested, then, that for a community to have many weak ties which bridge, there must be several distinct ways or contexts in which people may form them. The case of Charlestown, a working-class community which successfully organized against the urban renewal plan of the same city (Boston) against which the West End was powerless, is instructive in this respect: unlike the West

End, it had a rich organizational life and most male residents worked within the area (Keyes 1969, chap. 4).

In the absence of actual network data, all this is speculation. The hard information needed to show either that the West End was fragmented or that communities which organized successfully were not, and that both patterns were due to the strategic role of weak ties, is not at hand and would not have been simple to collect. Nor has comparable information been collected in *any* context. But a theoretical framework has, at least, been suggested, with which one could not only carry out analyses post hoc but also *predict* differential capacity of communities to act toward common goals. A rough principle with which to begin such an investigation might be: the more local bridges (per person?) in a community and the greater their degree, the more cohesive the community and the more capable of acting in concert. Study of the origins and nature (strength and content, for example) of such bridging ties would then offer unusual insight into the social dynamics of the community.

■ Micro and Macro Network Models

Unlike most models of interpersonal networks, the one presented here is not meant primarily for application to small, face-to-face groups or to groups in confined institutional or organizational settings. Rather, it is meant for linkage of such small-scale levels with one another and with larger, more amorphous ones. This is why emphasis here has been placed more on weak ties than on strong. Weak ties are more likely to link members of *different* small groups than are strong ones, which tend to be concentrated within particular groups.

For this reason, my discussion does not lend itself to elucidation of the internal structure of small groups. This point can be made more clearly by contrasting the model of this paper to one with which it shares many similarities, that of James Davis, Paul Holland, and Samuel Leinhardt (hereafter, the DHL model) (Davis 1970; Davis and Leinhardt 1971; Holland and Leinhardt 1970, 1971a, 1971b; Davis, Holland, and Leinhardt 1971; Leinhardt 1972). The authors, inspired by certain propositions in George Homans's *Human Group* (1950), argue that "the central proposition in structural sociometry is this: *Interpersonal choices tend to be transitive—if P chooses O and O chooses X, then P is likely to choose X*" (Davis et al. 1971, p. 309). When this is true without exception, a sociogram can be divided into cliques in which every individual chooses every other; any asymmetric choices or nonchoices are *between* such cliques, and asymmetry, if present, runs only in one direction. A partial ordering of cliques may thus be inferred. If mutual choice implies equal, and asymmetric choice unequal, status, then this ordering reflects the stratification structure of the group (Holland and Leinhardt 1971a, pp. 107–14).

One immediate difference between this model and mine is that it is cast in terms of "choices" rather than ties. Most sociometric tests ask people whom they *like* best or would *prefer* to do something with, rather than with whom they actually spend time. If transitivity is built more into our cognitive than our social structure, this method might overstate its prevalence. But since the DHL model could recast in terms of ties, this is not a conclusive difference.

More significant is the difference in the application of my argument to transitivity. Let P choose O and O choose X (or equivalently, let X choose O and O choose P): then I assert that transitivity—P choosing X (or X, P)—is most likely when both ties—P-O and O-X are strong, least likely when both are weak, and of intermediate probability if one is strong and one weak. Transitivity, then, is claimed to be a function of the strength of ties rather than a general feature of social structure.

The justification of this assertion is, in part, identical with that offered earlier for the triad designated A-B-C. In addition, it is important to point out here that the DHL model was designed for small groups, and with increasing size of the group considered, the rationale for transitivity weakens. If P chooses O and O chooses X, P should choose X out of consistency; but if P does not *know* or barely knows X, nonchoice implies no inconsistency. For the logic of transitivity to apply, a group must be small enough so that any person knows enough about every other person to be able to decide whether to "choose" him, and encounters him often enough that he feels the need for such a decision. Including weak ties in my model, then, lessens the expectation of transitivity and permits analysis of intergroup relationships and also of amorphous chunks of social structure which an analyst may ferret out as being of interest but which are not easily defined in terms of face-to-face groups. Anthropologists have recently referred to such chunks as "quasi-groups" (Mayer 1966; Boissevain 1968).

Since, as I have argued above, weak ties are poorly represented in sociograms, there is little in the DHL empirical studies—which apply statistical tests to sociometric data—to confirm or disconfirm my argument on transitivity. One finding does lend itself to speculation, however. Leinhardt (1972) shows that the sociograms of schoolchildren conform more and more closely to the transitive model as they become older, sixth graders being the oldest tested. He interprets this as reflecting cognitive development—increasing capacity to make use of transitive logic. If my assertion is correct, an alternative possibility would be that children develop stronger ties with increasing age. This is consistent with some theories of child development (see especially Sullivan 1953, chap. 16) and would imply, on my argument, greater transitivity of structure. Some support for this explanation comes from Leinhardt's finding that proportion of choices which were mutual was positively correlated with both grade level and degree of transitivity. In these sociograms, with an average of only about four choices per child, it seems likely that most mutual choices reflected strong ties (see n. 6, above).

Conclusion

The major implication intended by this paper is that the personal experience of individuals is closely bound up with larger-scale aspects of social structure, well beyond the purview or control of particular individuals. Linkage of micro- and macrolevels is thus no luxury but of central importance to the development of sociological theory. Such linkage generates paradoxes: weak ties, often denounced as generative of alienation (Wirth 1938), are here seen as indispensable to individuals' opportunities and to their integration into communities; strong ties, breeding local cohesion, lead to overall fragmentation. Paradoxes are a welcome antidote to theories which explain everything all too neatly.

The model offered here is a very limited step in the linking of levels; it is a fragment of a theory. Treating only the *strength* of ties ignores, for instance, all the important issues involving their content. What is the relation between strength and degree of specialization of ties, or between strength and hierarchical structure? How can "negative" ties be handled? Should tie strength be developed as a continuous variable? What is the developmental sequence of network structure over time?

As such questions are resolved, others will arise. Demography, coalition structure, and mobility are just a few of the variables which would be of special importance in developing micro-macro linkage with the help of network analysis; how these are related to the present discussion needs specification. My contribution here is mainly, then, exploratory and programmatic, its primary purpose being to generate interest in the proposed program of theory and research.

Notes

This paper originated in discussions with Harrison White, to whom I am indebted for many suggestions and ideas. Earlier drafts were read by Ivan Chase, James Davis, William Michelson, Nancy Lee, Peter Rossi, Charles Tilly, and an anonymous referee; their criticisms resulted in significant improvements.

1. Ties discussed in this paper are assumed to be positive and symmetric; a comprehensive theory might require discussion of negative and/or asymmetric ties, but this would add unnecessary complexity to the present, exploratory comments.

2. Some anthropologists suggest "multiplexity," that is, multiple contents in a relationship, as indicating a strong tie (Kapferer 1969, p. 213). While this

may be accurate in some circumstances, ties with only one content or with diffuse content may be strong as well (Simmel 1950, pp. 317–29). The present definition would show most multiplex ties to be strong but also allow for other possibilities.

3. Included in "absent" are both the lack of any relationship and ties without substantial significance, such as a "nodding" relationship between people living on the same street, or the "tie" to the vendor from whom one customarily buys a morning newspaper. That two people "know" each other by name need not move their relation out of this category if their interaction is negligible. In some contexts, however (disasters, for example), such "negligible" ties might usefully be distinguished from the absence of one. This is an ambiguity caused by substitution, for convenience of exposition, of discrete values for an underlying continuous variable.

4. In Barnes's terminology, the union of their respective primary stars (1969, p. 58).

5. The models and experiments of Rapoport and his associates have been a major stimulus to this paper. In 1954 he commented on the "well-known fact that the likely contacts of two individuals who are closely acquainted tend to be more overlapping than those of two arbitrarily selected individuals" (p. 75). His and Horvath's 1961 hypothesis is even closer to mine: "One would expect the friendship relations, and therefore the overlap bias of the acquaintance circles, to become less tight with increasing numerical rank-order" (p. 290), i.e., best friend, second-best friend, thirdbest, etc. Their development of this hypothesis, however, is quite different, substantively and mathematically, from mine (Rapoport 1953a, 1953b, 1954, 1963; Rapoport and Horvath 1961).

6. This assumption is suggested by one of Davis's models (1970, p. 846) and made explicitly by Mazur (1971). It is not obvious, however. In a free-choice sociometric test or a fixed-choice one with a large number of choices, most strong ties would probably result in mutual choice, but some weak ones might, as well. With a small, fixed number of choices, most mutual choices should be strong ties, but some strong ties might show up as asymmetric. For a general discussion of the biases introduced by sociometric procedures, see Holland and Leinhardt (1971b).

7. Though this assumption seems plausible, it is by no means self-evident. Surprisingly little empirical evidence exists to support or refute it.

8. In a more comprehensive treatment it would be useful to consider to what extent a *set* of weak ties may be considered to have bridging functions. This generalization requires a long, complex discussion and is not attempted here (see Harary et al. 1965, pp. 211–16).

9. We may define the "social distance" between two individuals in a network as the number of lines in the shortest path from one to another. This is the definition of "distance" between points in graph theory (Harary et al. 1965, pp. 32–33, 138–41). The exact role of this quantity in diffusion and epidemic theory is discussed by Solomonoff and Rapoport (1951).

10. If a damping effect is not specified, the whole population would hear the rumor after a sufficiently large number of retellings, since few real networks include totally self-contained cliques. The effective difference between using weak and strong ties, then, is one of people reached per unit of (ordinal) time.

This could be called "velocity" of transmission. I am indebted to Scott Feld for this point.

11. These individuals are what are often called, in organizational analysis, "liaison persons," though their role here is different from the one usually discussed. (Compare the concept in graph theory of a "cut point"—one which, if removed from a graph, disconnects one part from another [Harary 1965].) In general, a bridge has one liaison person on each side, but the existence of a liaison person does not imply that of a bridge. For local bridges, the concept of local liaisons could be developed. In a more microscopically oriented discussion I would devote more time to the liaison role. For now, I only point out that, under the present assumptions, a person can be a liaison between two network sectors *only* if all his ties into one or both are weak.

12. This parameter, θ, measures such overlap in the following sense: it is zero in a random net—one in which individuals choose others at random—and is one in a net made up entirely of cliques disconnected each from every other. Intermediate values of θ, however, do not have a good intuitive interpretation in terms of individuals, but only with reference to the particular mathematical model defining the parameter; thus it does not correspond precisely to my arguments about friendship overlap.

13. But if the crucial question is really whether ego's *friends* know each other, this measure should probably be computed after ego and his ties have been subtracted from the network; distortions caused by failure to do so will be especially great in small networks. It is important to note, also, that in *non*egocentric networks, there is no simple correspondence between density and any "average" measure of the extent to which the various egos have friends who know one another. "Density," as used here, should not be confused with the "ax-one density" of Rapoport's models—the number of choices issuing from each node of a network.

14. Although this measure corresponds only to the first of the four dimensions in my definition, supplementary anecdotal evidence from interviews makes it likely that, in this case, the entire definition is satisfied by this measure. At the time of research, it had not occurred to me that tie strength would be a useful variable.

15. The numbers reported are small because they represent a random subsample of 100, who were interviewed personally, of the total sample of 282. The personal interview allowed more detailed questioning. Comparisons between the mail sample and the interview sample on the large number of items which were put to both show almost no significant differences; this suggests that results observed in the smaller sample on those items put to it alone would not be much different in the mail sample.

16. Often when I asked respondents whether a friend had told them about their current job, they said, "Not a friend, an acquaintance." It was the frequency of this comment which suggested this section of the paper to me.

17. Donald Light has suggested to me an alternative reason to expect predominance of weak ties in transfer of job information. He reasons that most of any given person's ties are weak, so that we should expect, on a "random" model, that most ties through which job information flows should be weak. Since baseline data on acquaintance networks are lacking, this objection remains inconclusive. Even if the premise were correct, however, one might still expect

that greater motivation of close friends would overcome their being outnumbered. Different assumptions yield different "random" models; it is not clear which one should be accepted as a starting point. One plausible such model would expect information to flow through ties in proportion to the time expended in interaction; this model would predict much more information via strong ties than one which merely counted all ties equally.

18. This point was brought to my attention by Richard Wolfe.

19. See Jane Jacobs's excellent, intuitive discussion of bridging ties ("hop-skip links") in community organization (1961, chap. 6.)

■ References

Barnes, J. A. 1969. "Networks and Political Process." In *Social Networks in Urban Situations*, edited by J. C. Mitchell. Manchester: Manchester University Press.

Becker, Marshall. 1970. "Sociometric Location and Innovativeness." *American Sociological Review* 35 (April): 267–82.

Berscheid, E., and E. Walster. 1969. *Interpersonal Attraction*. Reading, Mass.: Addison-Wesley.

Boissevain, J. 1968. "The Place of Non-Groups in the Social Sciences." *Man 3* (December): 542–56.

Bott, Elizabeth. 1957. *Family and Social Network*. London: Tavistock.

Bramel, D. 1969. "Interpersonal Attraction, Hostility and Perception." In *Experimental Social Psychology*, edited by Judson Mills. New York: Macmillan.

Brown, David. 1967. *The Mobile Professors*. Washington, D.C.: American Council on Education.

Brown, Roger. 1965. *Social Psychology*. New York: Free Press.

Coleman, J. S. 1960. "The Mathematical Study of Small Groups." In *Mathematical Thinking in the Measurement of Behavior*, edited by H. Solomon. Glencoe: Free Press.

Coleman, J. S., E. Katz, and H. Menzel. 1966. *Medical Innovation: A Diffusion Study*. Indianapolis: Bobbs-Merrill.

Dahl, Robert. 1961. *Who Governs?* New Haven, Conn.: Yale University Press.

Davies, J. C. 1966. *Neighborhood Groups and Urban Renewal*. New York: Columbia University Press.

Davis, James A. 1963. "Structural Balance, Mechanical Solidarity and Interpersonal Relations." *American Journal of Sociology* 68 (January): 444–62.

———. 1967. "Clustering and Structural Balance in Graphs." *Human Relations* 20 (May): 181–87.

———. 1969. "Social Structures and Cognitive Structures." In R. P. Abelson et al., *Theories of Cognitive Consistency*. Chicago: Rand McNally.

———. 1970. "Clustering and Hierarchy in Interpersonal Relations." *American Sociological Review* 35 (October): 843–52.

Davis, James A., P. Holland, and S. Leinhardt. 1971. "Comment." *American Sociological Review* 36 (April): 309–11.

Davis, James A., and S. Leinhardt. 1971. "The Structure of Positive Interpersonal Relations in Small Groups." In *Sociological Theories in Progress*. Vol. 2, edited by J. Berger, M. Zelditch, and B. Anderson. Boston: Houghton Mifflin.

Epstein, A. 1969. "The Network and Urban Social Organization." In *Social Networks in Urban Situations*, edited by J. C. Mitchell. Manchester: Manchester University Press.

Frankenberg, R. 1965. *Communities in Britain*. Baltimore: Penguin.

Gans, Herbert. 1962. *The Urban Villagers*. New York: Free Press.

Granovetter, M. S. 1970. "Changing Jobs: Channels of Mobility Information in a Suburban Community." Doctoral dissertation, Harvard University.

Harary, F. 1965. "Graph Theory and Group Structure." In *Readings in Mathematical Psychology*. Vol. 2, edited by R. Luce, R. Bush, and E. Galanter. New York: Wiley.

Harary, F., R. Norman, and D. Cartwright. 1965. *Structural Models*. New York: Wiley.

Heider, F. 1958. *The Psychology of Interpersonal Relations*. New York: Wiley.

Holland, Paul, and S. Leinhardt. 1970. "Detecting Structure in Sociometric Data." *American Journal of Sociology* 76 (November): 492–513.

———. 1971*a*. "Transitivity in Structural Models of Small Groups." *Comparative Group Studies* 2:107–24.

———. 1971*b*. "Masking: The Structural Implications of Measurement Error in Sociometry." Mimeographed. Pittsburgh: Carnegie-Mellon University.

Homans, George. 1950. *The Human Group*. New York: Harcourt, Brace & World.

Jacobs, Jane. 1961. *The Death and Life of Great American Cities*. New York: Random House.

Kapferer, B. 1969. "Norms and the Manipulation of Relationships in a Work Context." In *Social Networks in Urban Situations*, edited by J. C. Mitchell. Manchester: Manchester University Press.

Katz, E., and P. Lazarsfeld. 1955. *Personal Influence*. New York: Free Press.

Kerckhoff, A., and K. Back. 1968. *The June Bug: A Study of Hysterical Contagion*. New York: Appleton-Century-Crofts.

Kerckhoff, A., K. Back, and N. Miller. 1965. "Sociometric Patterns in Hysterical Contagion." *Sociometry* 28 (March): 2–15.

Keyes, L. C. 1969. *The Rehabilitation Planning Game*. Cambridge, Mass.: M.I.T. Press.

Korte, Charles. 1967. "Small-World Study (Los Angeles): Data Analysis." Mimeographed. Poughkeepsie, N.Y.: Vassar College.

Korte, Charles, and Stanley Milgram. 1970. "Acquaintance Networks between Racial Groups." *Journal of Personality and Social Psychology* 15 (June): 101–8.

Laumann, Edward. 1968. "Interlocking and Radial Friendship Networks: A Cross-sectional Analysis." Mimeographed. Ann Arbor: University of Michigan.

Laumann, Edward, and H. Schuman. 1967. "Open and Closed Structures." Paper prepared for the 1967 ASA meeting. Mimeographed.

Leinhardt, Samuel. 1972. "Developmental Change in the Sentiment Structure of Childrens' Groups." *American Sociological Review* 37 (April): 202–12.

Mayer, Adrian. 1966. "The Significance of Quasi-Groups in the Study of Complex Societies." In *The Social Anthropology of Complex Societies*, edited by M. Banton. New York: Praeger.

Mayer, Phillip. 1961. *Townsmen or Tribesmen?* Capetown: Oxford.

Mazur, B. 1971. "Comment." *American Sociological Review* 36 (April): 308–9.

Milgram, Stanley. 1967. "The Small-World Problem." *Psychology Today* 1 (May): 62–67.

Mitchell, J. Clyde. 1969. *Social Networks in Urban Situations*. Manchester: Manchester University Press.

Newcomb, T. M. 1961. *The Acquaintance Process*. New York: Holt, Rinehart & Winston.

Parnes, Herbert. 1954. *Research on Labor Mobility*. New York: Social Science Research Council.

Precker, Joseph. 1952. "Similarity of Valuings as a Factor in Selection of Peers and Near-Authority Figures." *Journal of Abnormal and Social Psychology* 47, suppl. (April): 406–14.

Rapoport, Anatol. 1953*a*. "Spread of Information through a Population with Socio-Structural Bias. I. Assumption of Transitivity." *Bulletin of Mathematical Biophysics* 15 (December): 523–33.

———. 1953*b*. "Spread of Information through a Population with Socio-Structural Bias. II. Various Models with Partial Transitivity." *Bulletin of Mathematical Biophysics* 15 (December): 535–46.

———. 1954. "Spread of Information through a Population with Socio-Structural Bias. III. Suggested Experimental Procedures." *Bulletin of Mathematical Biophysics* 16 (March): 75–81.

———. 1963. "Mathematical Models of Social Interaction." In *Handbook of Mathematical Psychology*. Vol. 2, edited by R. Luce, R. Bush, and E. Galanter. New York: Wiley.

Rapoport, A., and W. Horvath. 1961. "A Study of a Large Sociogram." *Behavioral Science* 6:279–91.

Rogers, Everett. 1962. *Diffusion of Innovations*. New York: Free Press.

Shapero, Albert, Richard Howell, and James Tombaugh. 1965. *The Structure and Dynamics of the Defense R & D Industry*. Menlo Park, Calif.: Stanford Research Institute.

Simmel, Georg. 1950. *The Sociology of Georg Simmel*. New York: Free Press.

Solomonoff, Ray, and A. Rapoport. 1951. "Connectivity of Random Nets." *Bulletin of Mathematical Biophysics* 13 (June): 107–17.

Sullivan, Harry Stack. 1953. *The Interpersonal Theory of Psychiatry*. New York: Norton.

Tilly, Charles. 1969. "Community:City:Urbanization." Mimeographed. Ann Arbor: University of Michigan.

Travers, Jeffrey, and S. Milgram. 1969. "An Experimental Study of the 'Small-World' Problem." *Sociometry* 32 (December): 425–43.

Wirth, Louis. 1938. "Urbanism as a Way of Life." *American Journal of Sociology* 44 (July): 1–24.

5

Diffusion Networks

Everett Rogers

Every herd of wild cattle has its leaders, its influential heads.
—*Gabriel Tarde*, The Laws of Imitation

Here we explore what is known about diffusion networks and how they function to convey innovation-evaluation information to decrease uncertainty about a new idea. We begin with a discussion of *opinion leadership*, the degree to which an individual is able informally to influence other individuals' attitudes or overt behavior in a desired way with relative frequency. Opinion leaders are individuals who lead in influencing others' opinions about innovations. The behavior of opinion leaders is important in determining the rate of adoption of an innovation in a system. In fact, the S-shape of the diffusion curve occurs because once opinion leaders adopt and tell others about the innovation, the number of adopters per unit of time takes off. We explore in this chapter the role of social modeling in diffusion networks, and how interpersonal communication drives the diffusion process through creating a "critical mass" of adopters.

Opinion Leadership in the Diffusion of Modern Math

Insight into the nature of opinion leadership is provided by a study of the spread of an important educational innovation, modern math, among the thirty-eight school superintendents in Allegheny County, Pennsylvania, which is essentially the city of Pittsburgh.

The innovation of modern math began in the early 1950s when top mathematicians in the United States completely overhauled the nature of mathematics training being offered in public schools. Out of their efforts came modern math, a radically new approach to mathematics packaged to include textbooks, audiovisual aides designed for teaching the new concepts, and summer institutes to retrain school teachers in the new subject matter. The innovation spread relatively quickly because of powerful federal sponsorship by the National Science Foundation and the U.S. Department of Education. Modern math was widely hailed by educators as a major improvement. It was quite different from the "old" math in that it used set theory, Venn diagrams, and an emphasis upon probability. Math teachers had to learn an entirely new approach to their subject.

Modern math entered the schools of Allegheny County through one school superintendent, shown in figure 5.1 as "I," who adopted it in 1958. This innovator was a sociometric isolate in that he had no interpersonal network links with any of the other school superintendents in the Pittsburgh area. Innovators like "I" are frequently disdained by their fellow members in a local system. They interact primarily with cosmopolite friends who are outside of the local system.

Figure 5.1 is a sociogram, a communication map tracing the network links in the diffusion of an innovation. The arrows show the patterns of friendship among the superintendents. The shaded area encircles six friends who constitute a clique or informal friendship group. The superintendents in this clique interact more with each other than they do with outsiders.

This clique played a central role in the diffusion of modern math in Pittsburgh's schools. Once the clique members (especially the three main opinion leaders who decided to use the innovation in 1959 and 1960) adopted, the rate of adoption of modern math began to climb rapidly in the system. Figure 5.1 shows there was only one adopter in 1958 (the innovator), five by the end of 1959, fifteen by 1960, twenty-seven by 1961, thirty-five by 1962, and thirty-eight by the end of 1963. The rapid spurt in 1959, 1960, and 1961 appeared to occur as a direct result of the opinion leaders' behavior.

Later in the this chapter we show that opinion leaders are highly conforming to the norms of their system. We see support for this generalization in the present case. The cosmopolite innovator was *too* innovative to serve as an appropriate role model for the other thirty-seven superintendents; they waited to adopt until the three opinion leaders in the six-member clique favored the innovation. A change agent responsible for diffusing another innovation in Allegheny County should concentrate promotional efforts on these opinion leaders.

Further, figure 5.1 shows a rather high degree of homophily in the time of adoption of modern math by the superintendents. Many of the friendship arrows are between superintendents who adopted in the same year or within one year of each other. When two superintendents in a dyadic relationship adopted in different years, the difference is slight, suggesting that in this case the source is different enough from the receiver to be perceived as competent but not so much different as to be an inappropriate role model.

This case illustration is based on Richard O. Carlson (1965).

◼ Models of Mass Communication Flows

In order to understand better the nature of opinion leadership and diffusion networks, we now examine several models of mass communication flows, roughly in the temporal sequence of their entrance on the stage of communication study.

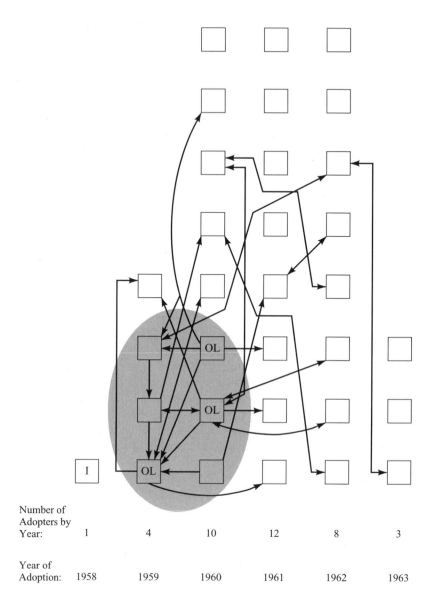

Number of
Adopters by
Year: 1   4   10   12   8   3

Year of
Adoption: 1958   1959   1960   1961   1962   1963

Figure 5.1.
Opinion leadership patterns in the diffusion of modern math among school superintendents in Allegheny County, Pennsylvania. *Note*: For the sake of simplicity, only thirty-
two of the thirty-eight superintendents who adopted modern math are shown. Two
adopters in 1960 and four adopters in 1961 are not shown here. The three opinion
leaders are identified as "OL," and the innovator is labeled "I." *Source*: Constructed
from data provided by Carlson (1965).

Hypodermic Needle Model

The *hypodermic needle model* postulated that the mass media had direct, immediate, and powerful effects on a mass audience. The mass media in the 1940s and 1950s were perceived as a powerful influence on behavior change. The omnipotent media were pictured as conveying messages to atomized masses of individuals (Katz and Lazarsfeld, 1955). Evidence of the power of the mass media was drawn from such historical events as (1) the role of the Hearst newspapers in arousing public support for the Spanish-American War, (2) the power of Nazi leader Joseph Goebbels's propaganda apparatus during World War II in Europe, and (3) the influence of Madison Avenue advertising on consumer and voting behavior in the United States.

Eventually, when more sophisticated methods were used in communication research, considerable doubt was cast on the hypodermic needle model. This survey research was directed by Paul F. Lazarsfeld of Columbia University, a pioneering mass communication scholar (Rogers, 1994). The hypodermic needle model was based primarily on intuitive theorizing from unique historical events and was too simple, too mechanistic, and too gross to give an accurate account of mass media effects.

Two-Step Flow Model

The decisive end of the hypodermic needle model resulted serendipitously from a classic study of the 1940 presidential election in Erie County, Ohio (Lazarsfeld, Berelson, and Gaudet, 1944). This inquiry was designed with the hypodermic needle model in mind and was aimed at analyzing the role of the mass media in changing political decisions. A panel study conducted with a sample of 600 voters over the six months prior to the November election found, to the researchers' surprise, that very few voting choices were directly influenced by the mass media. "This study went to great lengths to determine how the mass media brought about such changes. To our surprise we found the effect to be rather small. . . . People appeared to be much more influenced in their political decisions by face-to-face contact with other people . . . than by the mass media directly" (Lazarsfeld and Menzel, 1963). Instead the data suggested "that ideas often *flow* from radio and print *to* opinion leaders and *from* these to the less active sections of the population" (Lazarsfeld, Berelson, and Gaudet, 1944). The first step, from media sources to opinion leaders, is mainly a transfer of *information*, whereas the second step, from opinion leaders to their followers, also involves the spread of interpersonal *influence*. This *two-step flow hypothesis* suggested that communication messages flow from a source, via mass media channels, to opinion leaders, who in turn pass them on to followers. This model has since been tested for a variety of communication behaviors, including the diffusion of innovations, and found generally to provide some useful understandings of the flow of mass communication.

The two-step flow model helped focus attention upon the interface between mass media channels and interpersonal communication channels. The model implied that the mass media were not so powerful nor so direct as was previously thought. Of course an individual can be exposed to a new idea through either mass media or interpersonal channels, and then engage in communication exchanges about the innovation with peers. The mass communication process does not necessarily consist of just two steps. In some instances there may be only one step, as when the mass media have a direct impact on an individual. In other instances a multistage communication process may occur.

Different communication sources/channels function at different stages in an individual's innovation-decision process. The original two-step flow model did not recognize the role of different communication sources/channels at various stages in the innovation-decision process. We know that individuals pass from (1) *knowledge* of an innovation, to (2) *persuasion*, to (3) a *decision* to adopt or reject, to (4) *implementation*, and then to (5) *confirmation* of this decision. Mass media channels are primarily knowledge-creators, whereas interpersonal networks are more important in persuading individuals to adopt or reject. This notion was masked in the original statement of the two-step model because the time sequence involved in an individual's decision-making process was ignored. Such source/channel differences between the knowledge and persuasion stages usually exist for *both* opinion leaders and followers. Thus, the opinion leaders are not the only individuals to use mass media channels, as the original statement of the two-step flow model suggested.

The two-step flow model as it was originally postulated did not tell us enough. The flow of communication in a mass audience is far more complicated than just two steps. What is known about the mass communication process is too detailed to be expressed in one sentence or in two steps. Nevertheless, one important intellectual benefit from the two-step flow hypothesis occurred in communication study: a focus upon opinion leadership.

■ Homophily-Heterophily in Communication Networks

Understanding of the nature of communication flows through interpersonal networks is enhanced by the concepts of homophily and heterophily. The structure of *who* relays messages to *whom* is brought out in such network analysis.

Homophily and Heterophily

A fundamental principle of human communication is that the exchange of ideas occurs most frequently between individuals who are alike, or homophilous. *Homophily* is the degree to which a pair of individuals who communicate are similar. The similarity may be in certain attributes, such as beliefs, education, social status, and the like. The conceptual label of homophily was given to this phenomenon several decades ago by Paul F. Lazarsfeld and Robert K. Merton (1964), but the general idea of homophilous behavior was noted almost a century ago by Gabriel Tarde (1903): "Social relations . . . are much closer between individuals who resemble each other in occupation and education." *Heterophily* is the degree to which pairs of individuals who interact are different in certain attributes. Heterophily is the opposite of homophily.

Homophily occurs frequently because communication is more effective when source and receiver are homophilous. When two individuals share common meanings, beliefs, and mutual understandings, communication between them is more likely to be effective. Individuals enjoy the comfort of interacting with others who are similar. Talking with those who are markedly different from ourselves requires more effort to make communication effective. Heterophilous communication between dissimilar individuals may cause cognitive dissonance because an individual is exposed to messages that are inconsistent with existing beliefs, an uncomfortable psychological state. Homophily and effective communication breed each other. The more communication there is between members of a dyad, the more likely they are to become homophilous;[1] the more homophilous two individuals are, the more likely that their communication will be effective. Individuals who depart from the homophily principle and attempt to communicate with others who are different from themselves often face the frustration of ineffective communication. Differences in technical competence, social status, beliefs, and language lead to mistaken meanings, thereby causing messages to be distorted or to go unheeded.

A study of the diffusion of computers among the top administrators in 127 Pittsburgh suburban communities found that these innovations mainly spread by means of interpersonal networks. The networks mainly connected city officials whose municipalities were neighboring and who were most similar in formal education and length of governmental experience (Kearns, 1992). Again, we see that most diffusion networks are homophilous.

But heterophilous communication has a special informational potential, even though it may occur only rarely. Heterophilous network links often connect two cliques, thus spanning two sets of socially dissimilar individuals in a system. These heterophilous interpersonal links are especially important in carrying information about innovations, as is implied in Granovetter's (1973) theory of the strength of weak ties. So, homophilous communication may be frequent and easy but may not be so crucial as the less frequent heterophilous communication in diffusing innovations. Homophily accelerates the diffusion process but limits the spread of an innovation to individuals connected in the same network.

Homophily as a Barrier to Diffusion

Homophily can act as an invisible barrier to the flow of innovations within a system. New ideas usually enter a system through higher-status and more innovative members. A high degree of homophily means that these elite individuals interact mainly with each other, and thus the innovation does not "trickle down" to non-elites. Homophilous diffusion patterns cause new ideas to spread horizontally, rather than vertically, within a system. Homophily therefore can act to slow down the rate of diffusion in a system. If homophily is a barrier to diffusion, change agents should work with different sets of opinion leaders in a system. If the interpersonal networks in a system were characterized by a high degree of heterophily, a change agent could concentrate attention on only a few opinion leaders near the top in social status and innovativeness. This is seldom the case.

Available evidence suggests Generalization 1: *Interpersonal diffusion networks are mostly homophilous.* For instance, individuals of highest status in a system seldom interact directly with those of lowest status. Likewise, innovators seldom converse with laggards. Although this homophily pattern in interpersonal networks acts to slow the diffusion of innovations within a system, it also has benefits. For example, a high-status opinion leader might be an inappropriate role model for someone of lower status, so interaction between them might not be beneficial to the latter. An illustration of this point comes from an investigation by Van den Ban (1963) in a Netherlands agricultural community. He found that only 3 percent of the opinion leaders had farms smaller than fifty acres in size, but 38 percent of all farms in the community were smaller than fifty acres. The wisest farm management decision for the large farmers was to purchase mechanized farm equipment, such as tractors and milking machines, as a substitute for hired labor, which was expensive. The best economic choice for the smaller farmers, however, was to ignore the expensive equipment and concentrate on intensive horticultural farming that required a great deal of labor per acre. As might be expected, however, the small farmers were following the example of the opinion leaders with large farms, even though the example was inappropriate for their situation. In this case a greater degree of homophily, so that small farmers would interact mainly with opinion leaders who were themselves small farmers, would have been beneficial.

An illustration of homophilous and heterophilous diffusion networks is provided by Rao, Rogers, and Singh (1980), who studied two Indian villages. One village was very innovative, while the other village had more traditional norms. Diffusion networks for a new rice variety were more homophilous in the traditional village. The opinion leaders here were elderly and had little formal education. In comparison, the opinion leaders in the innovative village were younger, highly educated, and of a high social caste. In the more traditional village, diffusion network links were highly homophilous; Brahmins talked to Brahmins, Harijans talked to Harijans, and so forth. But in the progressive village, the new rice variety started at the top of the social structure and then spread rapidly downward across the caste lines through heterophilous network links. So the heterophilous network links aided rapid diffusion.

Following are generalizations about characteristics of opinion leaders and followers under various degrees of heterophily in a system:

Generalization 2: *When interpersonal diffusion networks are heterophilous, followers seek opinion leaders of higher socioeconomic status.*

Generalization 3: *When interpersonal diffusion networks are heterophilous, followers seek opinion leaders with more formal education.*

Generalization 4: *When interpersonal diffusion networks are heterophilous, followers seek opinion leaders with a greater degree of mass media exposure.*

Generalization 5: *When interpersonal diffusion networks are heterophilous, followers seek opinion leaders who are more cosmopolite.*

Generalization 6: *When interpersonal diffusion networks are heterophilous, followers seek opinion leaders with greater change agent contact.*

Generalization 7: *When interpersonal diffusion networks are heterophilous, followers seek opinion leaders who are more innovative.*

These six generalizations indicate a general tendency for followers to seek information and advice from opinion leaders who are perceived as more technically competent than themselves. When heterophily occurs, it is usually in the direction of a greater degree of competency, but not *too* much greater. We should not forget that the general pattern of interpersonal networks is one of homophily in diffusion networks. This homophily means that the dyadic followers of opinion leaders usually learn appropriate lessons about an innovation through their ties with their near-peer opinion leaders. But these homophilous diffusion networks also slow the percolation of an innovation through the structure of a social system.

■ **Measuring Opinion Leadership and Network Links**

Four main methods of measuring opinion leadership and diffusion network links have been used in the past: (1) sociometric, (2) informants' ratings, (3) self-designating techniques, and (4) observation (table 5.1).

The *sociometric* method consists of asking respondents whom they

Table 5.1
**Advantages and Limitations of Four Methods of Measuring Opinion
Leadership in Diffusion Networks**

Measurement method	Description	Questions asked	Advantages	Limitations
1. Sociometric method	Ask system members to whom they go for advice and information about an idea.	Who is your leader?	Sociometric questions are easy to administer and are adaptable to different types of settings and issues. Highest validity	Analysis of sociometric data can be complex. Requires a large number of respondents to locate a small number of opinion leaders. Not applicable to sample designs where only a portion of the social system is interviewed.
2. Informants' ratings	Subjectively selected key informants in a system are asked to designate opinion leaders.	Who are leaders in this system?	A cost-saving and time-saving method as compared to sociometric method	Each informant must be thoroughly familiar with the system.
3. Self-designating method	Ask each respondent a series of questions to determine the degree to which he/she perceives himself/herself to be an opinion leader.	Are you a leader in this system?	Measures the individual's perceptions of her/his opinion leadership, which influence her/his behavior	Dependent upon the accuracy with which respondents can identify and report their self-images.
4. Observation	Identify and record communication network links as they occur.	None	High validity	Obtrusive, works best in a very small system and may require much patience by the observer.

sought (or hypothetically might seek) for information or advice about a given topic, such as a particular innovation. Opinion leaders are those members of a system who receive the greatest number of sociometric choices (and thus who are involved in the largest number of network links). Undoubtedly, the sociometric technique is a highly valid measure of opinion leadership, as it is measured through the perceptions of followers. It necessitates, however, interrogating a large number of respondents to locate a small number of opinion leaders. And the sociometric method is most applicable when all members of a social system provide network data, rather than when a small sample within the total population is contacted.[2]

It is common to specify the number of sociometric network partners who can be named by a respondent; for example, "Who are the *three* (or four, or five) other women in this village with whom you have discussed family planning methods?" Such limited-choice questioning leads a respondent to name only the strongest network partners. It is possible that others with whom a respondent converses less often may exchange information with the respondent that is most crucial in the diffusion process. Perhaps sociometric questions should allow an unlimited number of choices, letting the respondent name any number of network partners with whom a topic is discussed. Another approach is to conduct a roster study, in which each respondent is presented with a list of all the other members of the system and asked whether he or she talks with each of them, and how often. The roster technique has the advantage of measuring weak as well as strong links.

An alternative to using sociometry to identify opinion leaders is to ask key *informants* who are especially knowledgeable about the networks in a system. Often a handful of informants can identify the opinion leaders in a system, with a precision that is almost as accurate as sociometric techniques, particularly when the system is small and the informants are well-informed.

The *self-designating* technique asks respondents to indicate the tendency for others to regard them as influential. A typical self-designating question is: "Do you think people come to you for information or advice more often than to others?" The self-designating method depends upon the accuracy with which respondents can identify and report their self-images. This measure of opinion leadership is especially appropriate when interrogating a random sample of respondents in a system, a sampling design that often precludes effective use of sociometric methods.

A fourth means of measuring opinion leadership is *observation*, in which an investigator identifies and records the communication behavior in a system. One advantage of observation is that the data usually have a high degree of validity. If network links are appropriately observed, there is no doubt about whether they occur or not. Observation works best in a very small system, where the observer can actually see and record interpersonal interactions as they occur. Unfortunately, in such small systems observation may be a very obtrusive data-gathering technique. Because the members of a system know they are being observed, they may act differently.[3] Further, an observer may need to be very patient if the diffusion network behavior that he or she wants to observe occurs only rarely.

In practice, observation is seldom used to measure diffusion networks and opinion leadership. By far the most popular means of measurement is survey sociometry.

When two or three types of opinion leadership measurement have been utilized with the same respondents, positive correlations among the measures have been obtained, although these relationships are far from perfect. This finding suggests that the choice of any one of the four methods can be based on convenience, as all four are about equally valid.

In a typical distribution of opinion leadership in a social system, a few individuals receive a great deal of opinion leadership, while most individuals have none or very little. The most influential opinion leaders are key targets for the efforts of change agents.

■ Monomorphic and Polymorphic Opinion Leadership

Is there one set of all-purpose opinion leaders in a system, or are there different opinion leaders for different issues? *Polymorphism* is the degree to which an individual acts as an opinion leader for a variety of topics. Its opposite, *monomorphism*, is the degree to which an individual acts as an opinion leader for only a single topic. The degree of polymorphic opinion leadership in a given social system seems to vary with such factors as the diversity of the topics on which opinion leadership is measured, whether system norms are innovative or not, and so on. An analysis of opinion leadership among housewives in Decatur, Illinois, for four different topics (fashions, movies, public affairs, and consumer products) by Katz and Lazarsfeld (1955) found that one-third of the opinion leaders exerted their influence in more than one of the four areas. Other studies report more, or less, polymorphism. For instance, village leaders in Third World countries are frequently opinion leaders for health, agricultural, and educational ideas, as well as political and moral issues in the community.

■ Characteristics of Opinion Leaders

How do opinion leaders differ from their followers? The following seven generalizations summarize a considerable volume of empirical studies designed to answer this question. In each we refer to "opinion leaders" and "followers" as if opinion leadership were a dichotomy and as if all non-leaders were followers. These oversimplifications are necessary for the sake of clarity.

External Communication

Generalization 8: *Opinion leaders have greater exposure to mass media than their followers*. The original conception of the two-step flow hypothesis stated that opinion leaders attend more to mass media channels (Lazarsfeld, Berelson, and Gaudet, 1944). Opinion leaders gain their perceived competency by serving as an avenue for the entrance of new ideas into their system. The external linkage may be provided via mass media channels, by the leader's cosmopoliteness, or by the leader's greater change agent contact.

Generalization 9: *Opinion leaders are more cosmopolite than their followers.*

Generalization 10: *Opinion leaders have greater change agent contact than their followers.*

Accessibility

For opinion leaders to spread messages about an innovation, they must have extensive interpersonal network links with their followers. Opinion leaders must be socially accessible. One indicator of such accessibility is social participation; face-to-face communication about new ideas occurs at meetings of formal organizations and through informal discussions.

Generalization 11: *Opinion leaders have greater social participation than their followers.*

Socioeconomic Status

We expect that a follower typically seeks an opinion leader of somewhat higher status, as suggested in Generalization. So opinion leaders, on the average, should be of higher status than their followers. This point was stated by Gabriel Tarde (1903): "Invention can start from the lowest ranks of the people, but its extension depends upon the existence of some lofty social elevation."

Generalization 12: *Opinion leaders have higher socioeconomic status than their followers.*

Innovativeness

If opinion leaders are to be recognized by their peers as competent and trustworthy experts about innovations, the opinion leaders should adopt new ideas before their followers. There is strong empirical support for Generalization 13: *Opinion leaders are more innovative than their followers.* But opinion leaders are not necessarily innovators. Sometimes they are, but often they are not. At first glance, there appears to be contradictory evidence as to whether or not opinion leaders are innovators. What explains this apparent paradox? We must consider the effect of system norms on the innovativeness of opinion leaders, because the degree to which opinion leaders are innovative depends in large part on their followers.

Innovativeness, Opinion Leadership, and System Norms

How can opinion leaders be most conforming to system norms and at the same time lead in the adoption of new ideas? The answer is expressed as Generalization 14: *When a social system's norms favor change, opinion leaders are more innovative, but when the norms do not favor change, opinion leaders are not especially innovative.* In systems with more traditional norms, the opinion leaders are usually a separate set of individuals from the innovators. The innovators are perceived with suspicion and often with disrespect by the members of such systems, who do not trust their sense of judgment about innovations. For instance, in a study of Colombian farmers in traditional villages, Rogers with Svenning (1969) found that opinion leaders were only slightly more innovative than their followers and were older and less cosmopolite. But in progressive villages, opinion leaders were young and innovative. So the system's norms determine whether or not opinion leaders are innovators.

Data from inquirie in various nations support the notion of opinion leaders as highly conforming to system norms. For instance, Herzog, Stanfield, Whiting, and Svenning (1968) concluded from their study of Brazilian villages that "[i]n the most traditional communities, neither the leaders nor their followers are innovative, and as a result, the community remains traditional. In the most modern communities, community norms favor innovativeness and both the leaders and followers are innovative. In the middle range communities, where modernization is just getting underway, divisions occur and the community opinion leaders lead the way toward modernization, by trying new ideas before the other farmers in the community."

A common error made by change agents is that they select opinion leaders who are too innovative. Change agents work through opinion leaders in order to close the heterophily gap with their clients. But if opinion leaders are too much more innovative than the average client, the heterophily that formerly existed between the change agent and his or her clients now exists between the opinion leaders and their followers. Innovators are poor opinion leaders in systems with traditional norms: They are too elite and too change-oriented. The innovator serves as an unrealistic model for the average client, and he or she knows this. The norms of the system determine which adopter category the opinion leaders in a system belong to.

A parallel case to that among farmer opinion leaders is found in the case of the former "laboratory schools" in the United States. These schools were usually affiliated with a college of education, located on a university campus, and served to introduce new teaching methods. The first lab school was founded by John Dewey at the University of Chicago around 1900 and served as the site for implementing his radical ideas in elementary education, such as "learning by doing" and "teach the whole child"

(Rogers, 1994). Like the Dewey School, the typical lab school was wealthy, and its student body was composed of bright faculty children. Supposedly, the lab school was an attempt to demonstrate educational innovations that would then spread to other schools. But the lab schools, with their enriched environments and talented students, were perceived as too different by the average school. Teachers and administrators would visit the lab schools, impelled by curiosity, but went away unconvinced of the innovations they had observed. As a result, laboratory schools throughout the United States have fallen into disrepute as a means of educational diffusion. Almost all of them have been terminated. They were failures in demonstrating the usefulness of educational innovations.

Sometimes change agents identify potentially effective opinion leaders among their clients, but they concentrate their contacts too much on these leaders, who become innovators and lose their former followers. The relationship of respect between opinion leaders and their followers is a delicate balance. If an opinion leader becomes too innovative, or adopts a new idea too quickly, followers may begin to doubt the opinion leader's judgment. One role of the opinion leader in a social system is to help reduce the uncertainty about an innovation for his or her followers. To fulfill this role, the opinion leader should demonstrate prudent judgment in decisions about adopting new ideas. So the opinion leader must continually look over his or her shoulder and consider where the rest of the system is at regarding new ideas.

The opinion leader's influence in a social system may vary not only on the basis of his or her innovativeness relative to the norms of the system but also on the basis of the nature of the innovation that is diffusing. An interesting illustration of the role of opinion leaders in the diffusion of a high-uncertainty innovation and a low-uncertainty innovation is provided by Marshall Becker's (1970) survey of ninety-five directors of local health departments.[4] The low-uncertainty innovation was a measles immunization program, a new idea that fit easily with the purpose of health departments and that was compatible with the professional norms of the directors of the health departments (who were medical doctors). The measles immunization program spread quickly among the health departments of study. The innovators in adopting this new program were the opinion leaders among the ninety-five health department directors. The adoption behavior of the opinion leaders served to speed up the diffusion process.

The high-uncertainty innovation was diabetes screening, a program that was a radical departure from the usual activities of public health departments. This innovation was socially risky because it infringed upon an activity usually performed by medical doctors in private practice (screening for chronic diseases). So this innovation did not fit with the norms of the public health system. The innovators in adopting this innovation were not opinion leaders; instead they were the directors of health departments whom their peers rated as socially marginal. The opinion leaders knew about this innovation, but they waited to adopt. Once the innovators had implemented the innovation of diabetes screening and found that its social risks were not excessive, the opinion leaders adopted. The innovation of diabetes screening then diffused rapidly, but only after a slow start.

Becker (1970) interpreted these findings to mean that the time at which an individual adopted an innovation depended on whether or not the individual was an opinion leader, and whether the innovation was considered highly risky or not. Typically, innovative individuals hold back in adopting a high-uncertainty innovation to maintain their opinion leadership.

Becker's (1970) investigation of health department directors is distinctive in that the respondents were heads of organizations. Can organizations have opinion leadership, as individuals do? A study by Jack Walker (1966) suggested that innovations can diffuse from organization to organization through interorganizational networks in a parallel process to that among individuals in a social system.[5] The organizations studied by Professor Walker were the fifty state governments in America. Each state was scored as to its innovativeness in adopting (such as by enacting a new state law) each of eighty-eight new state programs in welfare, health, education, conservation, highways, civil rights, police, and the like. Each adoption by a state amounted to offering a new service, establishing a new regulation, or creating a new state agency. Examples are having a gasoline tax, enacting a civil rights bill, providing for slaughterhouse inspection, and having a state health board. The five most innovative states, Walker (1971) found, were New York, Massachusetts, California, New Jersey, and Michigan. The pioneering states, which Professor Walker called the national league, have large populations and are urbanized and industrialized. Perhaps they face social problems some years before the more rural and smaller states and therefore enact new types of laws to cope with these problems. They are also richer states, so they have the resources to adopt innovations.

In each region of the United States, certain states emerged as opinion leaders; once they adopted a new program, other states in their region followed their lead. If an innovation was first adopted by a state other than one of these leader states, it then spread to the other states slowly or not at all. Thus, a network communication structure existed for innovation diffusion among the American states.

In a further analysis, Walker (1971) gathered sociometric data from personal interviews with state officials in ten of the states in order to determine the diffusion networks linking the American states. State officials looked to their immediate neighbors when searching for information about innovations: "State administrators communicate most readily with their counterparts in states that they believe have similar resources, social problems, and administrative styles" (Walker, 1971). For instance, Iowa officials followed Michigan's and California's lead in certain innovations, although they were much more influenced by Wisconsin, a bordering state to Iowa that was considered a more appropriate model. Walker (1971) found that the follower states in his study often copied the exact wording of a law previously adopted by an opinion leader state, including, in several cases, a typographical error! Wisconsin ranked tenth on Walker's index of innovativeness; Iowa ranked twenty-ninth among the fifty states.

In summary, one can think of the diffusion process among the fifty American states as beginning with a new law that is adopted by one or more of the five "national league" states. After a few years, the new law may be adopted by one of the regional opinion leader states. Then the innovative law spreads rapidly among the surrounding states in that region. Note that the opinion leader states generally mediated between the five innovators and the other forty-five states. They provided connectedness to the nationwide diffusion network. Here we are beginning to look at more than just the characteristics of individual opinion leaders versus followers. We have taken a step toward gaining an improved understanding of diffusion networks by looking at the network structure of the system.

■ Networks in the Diffusion of a Medical Drug

Early diffusion scholars simply counted the number of network links reported for each individual in a system, in order to measure the degree of opinion leadership, and then determined the characteristics of opinion leaders and followers. In this type of investigation individuals were the units of analysis, even though the variable of opinion leadership was measured for individuals as the number of interpersonal choices they received. They next began using diffusion network *links* as units of analysis. This intellectual shift was a profound change in the nature of diffusion research. Such network analysis allowed deeper understanding of the previously hidden interpersonal mechanisms of the diffusion process.

The first diffusion investigation to explore the nature of diffusion networks was the classic study by James S. Coleman, Katz, and Menzel (1966) of a new drug's spread among medical doctors. This splendid investigation is distinctive in the insightful way in which Coleman and his colleagues investigated the interpersonal networks that impel the diffusion process. Like previous diffusion scholars, Coleman and others first studied various independent variables related to individual innovativeness (the month of adoption of the new drug tetracycline—code-named Gammanym—by medical doctors). Unlike most previous scholars, however, Coleman and his coresearchers included various indicators of network communication behavior among their independent variables of study; they found these network variables to be the most important predictors of innovativeness (more important than such individual characteristics as age, cosmopoliteness, and socioeconomic status).

But Coleman, Katz, and Menzel (1996) did not stop there, as previous diffusion researchers had done. Instead, they studied the way in which interpersonal networks explained the nature of the diffusion process. In this way, they departed from the previous reliance of diffusion scholars on the individual as the unit of analysis; they pioneered in using diffusion network links as their units of data analysis. This methodological advance provided important understandings of the interpersonal mechanisms creating the S-shaped diffusion curve.

Tetracycline was a powerful antibiotic drug, widely used in the treatment of acute conditions. The innovation had a potential for almost daily use by a physician in general practice. Tetracycline's efficacy in any particular case could be quickly and easily determined. The new drug seemed to be the approximate equivalent for doctors of what hybrid corn meant to Iowa farmers: A major change in previous behavior, whose results (in terms of relative advantage) were strikingly evident. Unlike the Iowa farmers, who adopted hybrid corn for themselves, the medical doctors were making adoption decisions for their patients. So the doctors may have faced less risk in adopting tetracycline; they could hardly have lost their medical practice because of the new drug. But the farmers had to pay for the hybrid corn they planted and faced the prospect of crop failure.

Only two months after the new drug became available, 15 percent of the doctors tried it, and four months later this figure reached 50 percent (Coleman, Katz, and Menzel, 1966). Undoubtedly, the perceived attributes of tetracycline affected its rapid rate of adoption (it reached almost complete adoption by the doctors in the Illinois cities of study in only seventeen months) and emphasized the importance of peer networks in its diffusion. Although there was the usual uncertainty in a doctor's first use of the new drug, its results were strikingly positive and almost all of the interpersonal network messages about the innovation encouraged other doctors to adopt. Practically no discontinuance of tetracycline occurred during the seventeen-month period of its diffusion. Tetracycline was an ideal innovation to trace as it spread through diffusion networks in the four medical communities of study.

Coleman, Katz, and Menzel (1966) found that innovativeness in adopting the new drug was associated with several measures of network *interconnectedness* (defined as the degree to which the units in a social system are linked by interpersonal networks) for their sample of medical doctors:

1. Affiliation with a hospital as a regular staff member.
2. More frequent attendance at hospital staff meetings.
3. Sharing an office with one or more other doctors.
4. Being named sociometrically as a source of information and advice by other doctors.
5. Being named sociometrically by other doctors as someone with whom they discussed their patients' cases.

6. Being named sociometrically as a best friend by other doctors.
7. Reciprocating the sociometric network links reported by other doctors who chose a respondent as a discussion partner.

For each of these seven network variables, doctors with more network links were the most innovative in adopting tetracycline, while doctors who were isolates (that is, who received no sociometric choices from their peers) were latest in adopting the new drug (figure 5.2). In fact, the degree of network interconnectedness of a physician was a better predictor of innovativeness than any of the other independent variables investigated by Coleman, Katz, and Menzel (1966), such as a doctor's personal characteristics, exposure to communication channels, patients' average incomes, and the like. "Between-people" variables were more important than the "within-people" variables. Among the various network connectedness measures, the best predictor of innovativeness was the friendship variable (the sixth variable in the list above); in fact, more than half of the forty-six isolate doctors (who received only one or no friendship sociometric

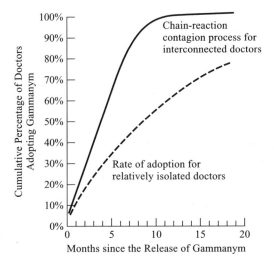

Figure 5.2.
The rate of adoption for interconnected doctors "took-off" in a snowballing contagion process, while the rate of adoption for relatively isolated doctors approached a straight line. *Note*: The rates of adoption above are a generalized and somewhat stylized version of the actual rates of adoption of tetracycline reported by Coleman, Katz, and Menzel (1966, p. 89) for interconnected versus isolated doctors, for each of the seven network measures. The chain-reaction contagion process occurs for interconnected doctors because they are closely linked by interpersonal networks.
Source: Based on Coleman, Katz, and Menzel (1966).

choices and who practiced medicine alone rather than in an office partnership) had still not adopted the new drug ten months after it began to diffuse in the medical community (Coleman, Katz, and Menzel 1966). In comparison, at this same ten-month point, almost all of the interconnected doctors (who received two or more network choices) had adopted tetracycline.

Coleman, Katz, and Menzel (1966) explained the greater innovativeness of the interconnected doctors on the basis of a chain-reaction kind of contagion process that seemed to take place during the early months of the diffusion process for tetracycline. Figure 5.2 shows that the S-curve for the interconnected doctors takes off rapidly in a kind of snowballing process: An early adopter conveys his or her personal experience with the innovation to two or more of his or her peers, who each may then adopt, and, in the next time period, interpersonally convey their subjective experience with the new idea to two or more other doctors, and so on. Within several months, almost all of the interconnected doctors have adopted, and their rate of adoption then necessarily begins to level off. This contagion process occurred because of the interpersonal networks that linked the medical doctors, thus providing communication avenues for the exchange of subjective evaluations of the innovation.

The chain-reaction snowballing of adoption did not happen, however, for the relatively isolated individuals, who lacked peer-network contacts from which to learn about others' subjective evaluations of the innovation. So the isolated individuals' rate of adoption is almost a straight line, curving slightly because the number of new adopters in each period remains a constant percentage of those who have not already adopted the innovation (see figure 5.2). There is no sudden take-off in the rate of adoption for the isolated individuals. But eventually most or all of these isolated individuals adopted. Interconnected doctors were more innovative in adopting the new drug because of their interpersonal networks: "The impact [of networks] upon the integrated doctors was quick and strong; the impact upon isolated doctors was slower and weaker, but not absent" (Coleman, Katz, and Menzel, 1966).

When the doctors were confronted with making a decision about the new drug in an ambiguous situation that did not speak for itself, they turned to each other for information that would help them make sense out of the new idea. Thus, the meaning of the new drug was socially constructed. Doctors closely linked in networks tended to interpret the innovation similarly. In the case of tetracycline, the medical community studied by Coleman, Katz, and Menzel (1966) gradually arrived at a positive perception of the innovation. This shared opinion led the interconnected doctors to adopt the new drug more rapidly, but eventually the medical community's favorable view of the innovation trickled out to the relatively isolated doctors on the social margins of the network. We see that diffusion is a very social process.

We conclude this discussion with Generalization 15, which states *The network interconnectedness of an individual in a social system is positively related to the individual innovativeness.* If individuals are convinced to adopt new ideas by the experience of near-peers with an innovation, then the more interpersonal communication an individual has with such near-peers, the more innovative the individual will be in adopting the new idea.

In recent years, several scholars reanalyzed the Coleman and others' drug diffusion data in order to question and extend several of the original conclusions about the role of social networks in the diffusion process. Ronald S. Burt (1980 and 1987) concluded that the similarity in the time of adoption of tetracycline by two doctors was not due mainly to a network link but rather to "structural equivalence" (which occurs when two individuals occupy the same social space in the structure of a network). Peter V. Marsden and Joel Podolny (1990) also reanalyzed the data using the technique of event history analysis. They concluded that network variables had little influence on doctors' innovativeness in adopting tetracycline. Finally, Thomas W. Valente (1991, 1993, and 1994) reanalyzed the data using a threshold model, in which each doctor has an individual threshold of resistance to the medical innovation which has to be overcome by network influences about the innovation from near-peers. Valente (1993) found that a combination of external influence from cosmopolite sources (particularly medical journals) plus the network interconnectedness of doctors best explained their innovativeness in adopting tetracycline. These recent reanalyses of the drug diffusion data illustrate how several scholars, each with a unique theoretical model and with distinctive methodological tools, come to different conclusions about the way in which network influences explain the adoption of an innovation.

This case illustration is based upon Coleman, Katz, and Menzel (1966).

Diffusion Networks

As we have just shown, the heart of the diffusion process is the modeling and imitation by potential adopters of their near peers' experiences who have previously adopted a new idea. In deciding whether or not to adopt an innovation, individuals depend mainly on the communicated experience of others much like themselves who have already adopted. These subjective evaluations of an innovation mainly flow through interpersonal networks. We must understand the nature of networks if we are to understand fully the diffusion of innovations.

Evidence for the importance of network influences on individuals in the diffusion of innovations comes from investigations in Third World villages. For example, Rogers and Kincaid (1981) studied the diffusion of several different family planning innovations in twenty-five Korean villages. They found that certain of these villages were "pill villages," others were "IUD villages," and one of the villages was a "vasectomy village." In a "pill village" all of the adopters of family planning methods were using oral contraceptive pills, and, similarly in the other villages of study, all contraceptive adopters were using the same family planning method.

Certainly such amazing homogeneity in choice of contraceptive innovation could not have occurred by chance. Each of the Korean villages had been the target of the same national family planning program, in which a standard cafeteria of contraceptive methods were promoted throughout the country.

Closer study by Rogers and Kincaid (1981) disclosed that in an "IUD village," for example, certain opinion leaders had first adopted a particular family planning innovation, the IUD, and their experiences were then shared with fellow villagers via interpersonal networks. The result, after several years of diffusion, was the tendency for every adopter in that village to be using the same method of family planning. These findings suggest that in Korea, the diffusion of family planning mainly occurs within villages, even though the government program was aimed at the national population.

Further evidence of this point came from the wide range in the percent of married, fertile-aged couples adopting family planning (Rogers and Kincaid, 1981). In some villages, more than 50 percent of the target audience had adopted. In other villages, the rate of adoption was only 10 or 15 percent. Such differences trace to the nature of intravillage communication networks. So an individual's network links are one important predictor of the individual's adoption of an innovation.

Similar clustering of adopters of an innovation has been observed in other settings. For example, William H. Whyte (1954) noted that window air conditioners were adopted by clusters of neighboring houses in a Philadelphia suburb. In the mid-1950s, the diffusion of air conditioners was well under way in America. Adoption of this relatively expensive item of household equipment was easily identifiable in the aerial photographs that Whyte took, as the air conditioners protruded out the windows of the Philadelphia row houses in the suburb that he studied. When Whyte followed up with personal interviews with the adopters of window air conditioners, he found that neighboring adopters seldom had purchased an identical brand of the cooling equipment. Satisfied adopters told their network partners about the pleasures of air conditioning, but they did not push the particular brand of equipment that they had adopted. Instead, they said that all brands of air conditioners were pretty much alike.

■ Patient Zero and Sexual Networks in the Early Spread of AIDS

The first Americans with AIDS were diagnosed by medical doctors in New York, San Francisco, and Los Angeles and reported to the Centers for Disease Control and Prevention (CDC) in May 1981. All of the patients were gay young men, otherwise in a state of good health. Many had a rare kind of skin cancer, Karposi's Sarcoma, previously only found in old men of Mediterranean descent.

Others died of an unusual form of pneumonia. The new epidemic baffled the CDC investigators. When they interviewed the first forty patients to be diagnosed with AIDS symptoms, they found that nineteen of these men who lived in Los Angeles were linked by sexual contact with the twenty-one other patients who resided in San Francisco, New York, and elsewhere in the United States. Clearly, something was being transmitted from man to man through sexual contact. What could it be? The CDC investigators checked out various lubricants used in gay sex. They also looked into poppers and other types of drugs.

The forty patients with the mystery disease had one quality in common. They said they had sexual contacts with an average of 227 different individuals per year, with one patient reporting 1,560 sexual contacts. The CDC researchers identified one of the forty AIDS patients, whom they called "Patient Zero," as playing a particularly key role in the diffusion network. He named seventy-two different male partners during 1979 to 1981. Eight were among the other thirty-nine AIDS patients. Further, Patient Zero connected the Los Angeles cluster with the New York cluster of AIDS patients.

Patient Zero was named Gaetan Dugas. He was a flight attendant for Air Canada and traveled widely. He was strikingly handsome and had a hyperactive sexual drive. These special characteristics represented a lethal factor in the sexual network for early AIDS transmission. Similarly in England, two of the first British patients with AIDS were homosexual airline stewards. And in India and East Africa, truck drivers and commercial sex workers at truck stops played a major role in spreading AIDS during the first phase of its diffusion.

The CDC investigators invited Professor Alden S. Klovdahl, a noted network scholar at Australian National University, to analyze the data on the network links among the 40 men with AIDS. Klovdahl used a special computer program, ORTEP, similar to that used by chemists to visualize molecular structures. On one of the three dimensions of the network of the 40 men, Klovdahl plotted the date at which each individual reported the onset of AIDS symptoms (figure 5.3). Now the crucial role of Patient Zero was even more apparent. While he was not the first individual with AIDS (he was the sixth), once Patient Zero got AIDS, many others soon followed. His eight direct sexual contacts in turn linked him to eight other men with AIDS, who in turn linked him to ten more of the men. So in three steps, Patient Zero infected twenty-six (63 percent) of the thirty-nine other individuals with AIDS. Figure 5.3 indicates that some individuals seem to have infected others who reported AIDS symptoms earlier than their infectors. This is possible because of the different lengths of individuals' infection periods (the time from being infected with the virus until the individual has AIDS symptoms).

The computer graphics of Klovdahl's computer program allowed the CDC researchers to better understand the nature of the AIDS network among the forty men. The CDC assumed that a virus was being transmitted through sexual contact and that it caused an immune deficiency in the human body which allowed various infections to run unchecked. Later, this explanation was sup-

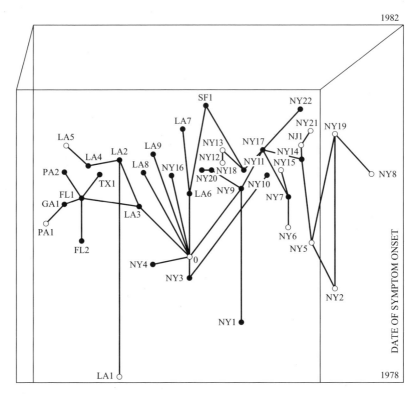

Figure 5.3.
A three-dimensional sociogram of the sexual links among the first forty gay men with AIDS, showing the key role of Patient Zero (near the center of the network). *Note:* The vertical axis represents the date at which AIDS symptoms were first diagnosed for each respondent. A designation of "LA1" indicates the respondent was the first individual in Los Angeles to experience the onset of AIDS symptoms. *Source:* Klovdahl (1985).

ported by other evidence, and AIDS was given its name, Acquired Immune Deficiency Syndrome.

Based on Klovdahl (1985) and on personal discussions with Alden S. Klovdahl.

Communication Network Analysis

A *communication network* consists of interconnected individuals who are linked by patterned flows of information. Networks have a certain degree of structure, of stability. This patterned aspect of networks provides predictability to human behavior. The study of networks helps illuminate *communication structure*, the differentiated elements that can be recognized in the patterned communication flows in a system. This communication structure is so complex that in any but a very small system even the members of the system do not understand the communication structure of which they are part. There are so many possible network links in a system that a problem of information overload is caused for the individual who tries to detect the communication structure. For instance, in a social system with 100 members, 4,950 network links are possible (computed by the formula $(\frac{N[N-1]}{2})$ where N is the number of individuals in the system). In a system of 200 members, 19,900 network links are possible; with 1,000 members, almost a half-million links are possible. A computer is necessary to analyze the patterns among these myriad of network links. *Communication network analysis* is a method of research that identifies the communication structure in a system by using interpersonal communication relationships as the units of analysis in analyzing network data about communication flows.

Methods of network analysis identify individuals in cliques on the basis of their communication proximity in network links, so that individuals who are closer are assigned to the same clique. *Communication proximity* is the degree to which two linked individuals in a network have personal communication networks that overlap. A *personal communication network* consists of those interconnected individuals who are linked by patterned communication flows to a given individual. One can think of each individual possessing such a personal network, consisting of the set of other individuals to whom the focal individual is linked in network relationships. The focal individual's behavior is determined, in part, by information and influence that is communicated through the individual's personal network.

Some personal networks consist of a set of individuals, all of whom interact with each other; these are *interlocking personal networks*. In contrast, *radial personal networks* consist of a set of individuals linked to a focal individual but not interacting with each other. Such radial personal networks are less dense and more open,[6] and thus allow the focal individual to exchange information with a wider environment. Obviously, such radial networks are particularly important in the diffusion of innovations because the links reach out into the entire system, while an interlocking network is more ingrown in nature.

The Strength of Weak Ties Theory

The general notion of classifying network links on the basis of the degree to which they convey information began with Mark S. Granovetter's (1973) theory of "the strength of weak ties." This network scholar sought to determine how people living in the Boston suburb of Newton got jobs. Granovetter gathered data from a sample of 282 respondents who had taken new jobs within the past year. To his surprise, most of these individuals said that they heard about their positions from heterophilous individuals who were not very close friends. These "weak ties" occurred with individuals "only marginally included in the current network of contacts, such as an old college friend or a former workmate or employer, with whom sporadic contact had been maintained" (Granovetter, 1973). Chance meetings with such acquaintances sometimes reactivated these weak ties, leading to the exchange of job information with the individual. Sometimes the lead to a new job came from a complete stranger.

An example of successful job searching through weak network links was an accountant who flew to Boston to attend a convention. The accountant shared a taxi at Logan Airport with a Bostonian businessman. They began a conversation, and the businessman disclosed that his company was seeking to hire an accountant. You can imagine what happened next. The accountant, who later resided in Newton, was one of Granovetter's respondents.

Only 17 percent of Granovetter's Newton respondents said they found their new jobs through close friends or relatives.[7] Why were weak ties so much more important than strong network links? Because an individual's close friends seldom know much that the individual does not also know. One's intimate friends are usually friends of each other's, forming a close-knit clique (an interlocking personal network). Such an ingrown system is an extremely poor net in which to catch new information from one's environment. Much more useful as a channel for gaining such information are an individual's more distant (weaker) acquaintances; they are more likely to possess information that the individual does not already possess, such as about a new job or about an innovation. Weak ties connect an individual's small clique of intimate friends with another, distant clique; as such, weak ties are often bridging links,[8] connecting two or more cliques. If these weak ties were somehow removed from a system, the result would be an unconnected set of separate cliques. So even though weak ties are not frequent paths for the flow of communication messages, the information flowing through them plays a crucial role for individuals and for the system. This great importance of weak ties in conveying new information is why Granovetter (1973) called his theory "the [informational] strength of weak [network] ties."

This weak-versus-strong-ties dimension is more precisely defined as *communication proximity*, the degree to which two individuals in a network have overlapping personal communication networks. Weak ties are low in communication proximity because they connect two individuals who do not share network links with a common set of other individuals. At least some degree of heterophily must be present in network links for the diffusion of innovations to occur. Low-proximity weak ties are often heterophilous, and this is the reason for their central importance in the diffusion process. For example, Liu and Duff (1972) and Duff and Liu (1975) found that a family planning innovation spread rather quickly among the members of small cliques of Filipino housewives. But this new idea did not diffuse throughout the total community until information about the contraceptive was conveyed by weak ties from one tight-knit clique to another. The weak ties were usually heterophilous on socioeconomic status, thus linking, for example, a higher-status clique with a lower-status clique.

We summarize this discussion with Generalization 16: *The information-exchange potential of communication network links is negatively related to their degree of (1) communication proximity and (2) homophily*. Heterophilous links of low proximity (Granovetter's weak ties), while rare, play a crucial role in the flow of *information* about an innovation. This information may also be *influential* if it consists of a personal evaluation of an innovation by an individual who has already adopted it. Perhaps there is a strength-of-weak-ties component in networks that convey information about an innovation and a "strength of *strong* ties" in networks that convey interpersonal influence. Certainly the influence potential of network ties with an individual's intimate friends is stronger than the opportunity for influence from an individual's weak ties with seldom-contacted acquaintances. Closely linked peers in an interlocking network seldom exert their potential influence because this type of homophilous, high-proximity personal network is seldom activated by information about an innovation. An individual's intimates rarely possess much information that the individual does not already know. Information must flow into such an interlocking network to provide energy for further information exchange.

Who Is Linked to Whom in Networks?

Generalization 17 states: *Individuals tend to be linked to others who are close to them in physical distance and who are relatively homophilous in social characteristics*. Individuals form network links that require the least effort and that are most rewarding. Both spatial and social proximity can be indicators of least effort. Communication network links with neighboring and homophilous partners are relatively easy and require little effort. But we have just shown that such low-effort network links are usually of limited value for obtaining information about innovations. In contrast, heterophilous links with socially and spatially distant others are usually stronger in carrying information about new ideas to an individual. Easy network links are thus of less informational value.

The implication for individuals in managing their personal networks, if they wish to improve their reception of information, is to break out of the comfort of close links and to form more heterophilous and spatially distant network links.

Joining a protest, demonstration, social movement, or some other form of activism amounts to adopting an innovation, although in this case the new idea is an ideology rather than a hardware technology. An illustration of this point is provided by Doug McAdam's (1986) study of university students who joined the 1964 Mississippi Freedom Summer project. Hundreds of young people volunteered to travel to Mississippi to register black voters and to dramatize their denial of civil rights. They gave up their opportunity for summer jobs to support themselves while in the South. They lived with black families, enduring their poverty and fear. Three of the Freedom Summer activists were killed by segregationists that included Mississippi law enforcement officers. The volunteers endured arrests, beatings, and bombings. Certainly the adoption of volunteering for the 1964 Freedom Summer was a major decision. Recruitment of the volunteers typically resulted from a speech by a civil rights activist at a meeting on a university campus; then the recruit filled out a five-page application form and was personally interviewed by a recruiter for Freedom Summer.

Twenty years later, Professor Doug McAdam, a sociologist at the University of Arizona, obtained access to the applications of 720 volunteers and 239 other students who were selected but who then withdrew prior to departing for Mississippi in 1964. McAdam also conducted in-depth personal interviews with eighty of the participants and withdrawals from the Freedom Summer project. The application form asked each student to list the names of ten people that they wished to be kept informed of their summer activities. These data allowed McAdam to measure each student's network links (1) with others who went on the Mississippi Freedom Summer and (2) with students who withdrew. Further, indirect network links could be measured, such as with a student who was not named directly but who was named by someone else that a respondent named. These indirect network ties were weak ties (Granovetter, 1973).

Weak ties did not have much impact in explaining whether a student volunteer went to Mississippi or withdrew. Neither did such other variables as prior activism, race, distance from Mississippi, college major, or other personal characteristics. Being male, of older age, and active in campus organizations were somewhat related to participation in Freedom Summer versus withdrawal. But by far the best predictor of going to Mississippi was having strong network relationships with other participants or to a Freedom Summer activist. Having a close friend who withdrew from the project influenced a respondent to also withdraw. Some of the withdrawals resulted from the opposition of parents or other adults. One example is a freshman woman who said: "I heard an SNCC [Student Nonviolent Coordinating Committee] person speak . . . at [the university] and was absolutely mesmerized. It was like I now had a mission in life. I remember filling out the application and racing back to my dorm to call my parents, thinking, of course, that they would be as thrilled with my 'mission' as I was." But the student's mother started crying, and her father threatened to stop paying for tuition. Faced with these negative influences, the student withdrew from Freedom Summer.

As in the adoption of technological innovations, the diffusion of an ideological innovation is a social process. Interpersonal network links, more than any other single factor, explain whether or not university students risked their lives by participating in the 1964 Mississippi Freedom Summer. Perhaps because an ideological innovation does not have a material referent (that is, hardware) to the extent that a technological innovation does, its social construction through interpersonal communication with others is especially important.

A crucial concept in understanding the social nature of the diffusion process is the *critical mass*, a point in the process when diffusion becomes self-sustaining. The notion of the critical mass comes from scholars of social movements, and in recent years the concept has become useful in studies of the diffusion of interactive innovations.

This case illustration is based upon McAdam (1986) and McAdam and Paulson (1993).

■ The Critical Mass in the Adoption of Interactive Innovations

The rate of adoption of interactive media such as electronic messaging systems, fax, and teleconferencing often displays a certain distinctive quality called the critical mass. The *critical mass* occurs at the point at which enough individuals have adopted an innovation so that the innovation's further rate of adoption becomes self-sustaining. The interactive quality of the new media creates a certain degree of interdependence among the adoption decisions of the members of a system. An interactive innovation is of little use to an adopting individual unless other individuals with whom the adopter wishes to communicate also adopt. Thus, a critical mass of individuals must adopt an interactive communication technology before it has utility for the average individual in the system. With each additional adopter, the utility of an interactive communication technology increases for all adopters. An illustration is provided by the very first individual to adopt a telephone in the 1870s. This interactive technology had no utility until a second individual also adopted. Until a critical mass occurs at a relatively early stage in the diffusion process, the rate of adoption is slow. After a critical mass is achieved, the rate of adoption accelerates (figure 5.4).

Interactivity is the degree to which participants in a communication process can exchange roles in, and have control over, their mutual discourse (Williams, Rice, and Rogers, 1988). *Mutual discourse* is the degree to which a given communication act is based on a prior series of communication acts. Thus, each message in a sequence of exchanges affects the next message in a kind of cumulative process. *Exchange of roles* means

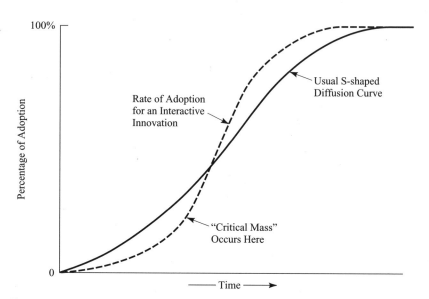

Figure 5.4.
The rate of adoption (1) for a usual innovation and (2) for an interactive innovation, showing the critical mass. *Note*: The *critical mass* occurs at the point at which enough individuals have adopted an innovation so that the innovation's further rate of adoption becomes self-sustaining.

the empathic ability of individual A to take the position of individual B (and thus to perform B's communication acts), and vice versa. Having *control* means the extent to which an individual can choose the timing, content and sequence of a communication act, search out alternative choices, enter the content into storage for other users, and perhaps create new communication capabilities (Williams, Rice, and Rogers, 1988). Such control of the communication process is broadly shared in the case of interactive communication.

Interactive communication technologies facilitate multidirectional information exchanges. In the case of noninteractive innovations, the earlier adopters have a *sequential* interdependence effect on later adopters. As more and more individuals in a system adopt, the noninteractive innovation is perceived as increasingly beneficial to future adopters. But in the case of interactive innovations, not only do earlier adopters influence later adopters, but later adopters also influence earlier adopters, in a process of *reciprocal* interdependence (Markus, 1990). The benefits from each additional adoption of an interactive innovation increase not only for all future adopters but also for each previous adopter. The distinctive aspect of interactive communication technologies, in a diffusion sense, is "reciprocal interdependence, in which later adopters influence earlier adopters as well as the other way around" (Markus, 1990). So the benefits of an interactive innovation flow backward in time to previous adopters, as well as forward in time to future adopters.

Diffusion of an Interactive Innovation: BITNET and INTERNET

BITNET and INTERNET are typical of new communication technologies that are interactive in nature; a kind of interpersonal communication occurs via an electronic communication channel rather than face-to-face. Examples of interactive communication technologies are e-mail (like BITNET and INTERNET), telephones, and, to a certain extent, fax.

BITNET stands for "Because It's Time NETwork." This interconnection of university computers was begun in 1981 by Ira Fuchs, the vice chancellor for university systems at CUNY (the City University of New York), and Greydon Freemen, director of the computer center at Yale University. Both university campuses had made considerable use of local computer networking on their own campuses, which seemed to fit with the collaborative nature of much academic work. BITNET began when the two university computer centers were connected via a leased telephone line, thus allowing anyone at either of the two university local networks to exchange messages that were typed into a computer. By the end of the first year, 1981, four additional universities joined BITNET. Each subscribing university joined by leasing a telephone line to the nearest university that already belonged to BITNET. Here we see an illustration of sequential interdependence; each additional adopting university increased the benefits of BITNET for every institution that was a potential adopter through a decreased initial cost of adoption. The first adopters of BITNET were elite East Coast institutions, who were highly competitive in applying for government and foundation research grants. They had the usual characteristics of innovators.

Then, in 1982, the University of California at Berkeley leased a long, expensive telephone line to join BITNET. This adoption was key to opening up BITNET to other West Coast universities, and a number joined shortly, each paying a part of the transcontinental phone line. This is an illustration of reciprocal interdependence, in which each additional adopter increases the utility of the innovation for both future adopters and previous adopters. Suddenly, the rate of adoption of BITNET took off; by 1983, nineteen universities joined. Then, between 1984 and 1985, BITNET doubled in size every six months. Telephone-leased lines to Canadian, European, and Japanese universities were established. Federal R&D laboratories also joined BITNET, and connections to ARPANET (a prior electronic network of defense-related R&D organizations) were established. Eventually, in the early 1990s, BITNET joined with numerous other networks to form INTERNET, an electronic network of networks. At this point, an academic person at a U.S. research university could safely assume that any other such individual with whom they wished to communicate could be reached via BITNET.

The growth of computer networks has increased at an exponential rate in recent years. The main impetus for this expansion was the formation of INTER-

NET, a network linking over 20,000 existing computer networks, including BIT-NET. The origins of INTERNET go back to ARPANET, which was created in 1969 to allow U.S. Department of Defense contractors to share computer services. E-mail was added as an afterthought but soon came to be the dominant function for the network's users. ARPANET was designed in the Cold War era to survive a nuclear attack, so there was no single control point. When INTERNET was formed out of ARPANET in 1983, it continued this many-to-many, decentralized network structure. Thousands and thousands of computers are linked by telephone lines through thousands and thousands of different network paths. A particular message courses its way toward its intended destination, passed along from computer to computer. So nobody really runs INTERNET. Such is the true nature of a network.

By mid-1993, INTERNET connected 15,000,000 computers, a number that was doubling annually. These INTERNET users included people in 200 nations, and 800 million messages were transmitted during 1994. What do people use INTERNET for? Authors collaborate in writing books on INTERNET. Some users fall in love and plan their weddings on the network. Other individuals utilize the humor bulletin boards, some of which feature soft porn. Many users seek, and exchange, information about a particular topic. A computer company offers free use of its new computer to those who wish to try it out with their own software programs, linked to the new computer via INTERNET. Many INTERNET users are university professors and R&D workers who exchange technical information with other members of their invisible college.

What if someone "misbehaves" on INTERNET? They quickly receive negative feedback until they change their behavior. For instance, one company sent copies of its catalog of products to a large number of INTERNET users. This inappropriate act led to an immediate and critical response from thousands of network participants. The catalog company evidently had not realized that a network is a two-way street. Such "mailbox bombing" occurs when individuals send thousands of messages to someone's e-mail account in order to overload it, as punishment for misconduct on INTERNET. So the decentralized network has a self-policing function. Even though no single authority is in charge of INTERNET, social norms are upheld.

Gurbaxani (1990) fit various curves to the data on rate of adoption for BIT-NET and concluded that the distribution closely approximated an S-shaped curve. The critical mass occurred just after 1982, when UC Berkeley joined BIT-NET. "Once the critical mass was reached, however, the growth rate increased dramatically to where the number of nodes doubled every six months" (Gurbaxani, 1990). A crucial strategy for managers of an interactive innovation is to identify those units in a system whose adoption will most rapidly influence potential users to subscribe: In the present case, UC Berkeley, a highly respected California university, triggered the critical mass with its adoption of BITNET. Once it adopted, many other universities followed. With each additional adopter, the innovation of BITNET became more valuable to each future adopter, and to every previous adopter. Then, when BITNET joined with other computer networks in INTERNET, the total number of users skyrocketed because of reciprocal interdependence.

This case illustration is based on Gurbaxani (1990) and on various other sources.

Background of the Concept of the Critical Mass

The notion of the critical mass originated in physics, where it was defined as the amount of radioactive material necessary to produce a nuclear reaction.[9] "An atomic pile 'goes critical' when a chain reaction of nuclear fission becomes self-sustaining" (Schelling, 1978). Various illustrations of critical mass situations, in which a process becomes self-sustaining after some threshold point has been reached, abound in everyday life. A single log in a fireplace will not continue to burn by itself; a second log must be present so that each log reflects its heat onto the other. When the ignition point is reached, the fire takes off, and the two logs will burn to ashes.

The critical mass bears on the relationship between the behavior of individuals and the larger system of which they are part. It thus centers on a crucial cross-level analysis that is "characteristic of a large part of the social sciences, especially the more theoretical part" (Schelling, 1978). "The principle of 'critical mass' is so simple that it is no wonder that it shows up in epidemiology, fashion, survival and extinction of species, language systems, racial integration, jaywalking, panic behavior, and political movements" (Schelling, 1978).

The concept of the critical mass is so fundamental to an understanding of such a wide range of human behavior because individuals' actions often depend on how many other individuals around them are behaving in a particular way (Schelling, 1978). Much of the theory and research concerning the critical mass in recent decades was inspired by Mancur Olson's (1965) *Logic of Collective Action*: "Even if all the individuals in a large group are rational and self-interested, and would gain if, as a group, they acted to achieve their common interest or objective, they would still not voluntarily act to achieve that common or group interest." This seeming irrationality has attracted a great deal of attention to the study of collective action by communication scholars, sociologists, social psychologists, economists, and scholars of public opinion. Why is individual behavior in a system so seemingly illogical? The basic reason is that each individual acts in ways that are rational in pursuing *individual* goals without fully considering that he or she might be disadvantaging the system at the *collective* level.

Olson's (1965) "logic of collective action" is similar to Garrett Hardin's (1968) "tragedy of the commons," in which each individual pursues a rational course of behavior that ironically drives the system (that is, the "commons") to disaster. Hardin's concept derives its name from the commons pasture in Medieval European villages, which was filled to its grazing capacity. Each herdsman calculated that the addition of one more animal would not exceed the capacity of the commons. But each of several hundred herdsmen calculated similarly, with a result of excessive grazing, erosion, and destruction of the commons pasture. A contemporary analogue occurs in the use of air conditioners by urban dwellers during a heat wave. "Each individual is most comfortable using his/her air conditioner at full power; yet if everyone does so, the result is a power overload that leaves everyone with no cooling at all" (Brewer, 1985).

Watching While Being Watched

Now consider a new electronic messaging system being introduced in an organization. This electronic messaging system has greater and greater utility for all users as additional individuals adopt. If the first adopters were to think only of their own *immediate* benefits, rather than about how they might *eventually* benefit, or how their organization might benefit, no one would adopt and the S-shaped diffusion process for the innovation would never begin. Until there is a critical mass of adopters, an interactive innovation has little advantage (and considerable disadvantage) for individual adopters. So we see another illustration of individual/system relationships, as in the previously discussed case of the logic of collective action and the tragedy of the commons. When a critical number of individuals have adopted an interactive innovation, a further rate of diffusion becomes self-sustaining. The critical mass is thus a kind of tipping point or social threshold in the diffusion process. After the critical mass is reached, the social system encourages further adoption by individual members of the system.

The notion that individuals adopt an innovation in part on the basis of their expectations regarding others' future adoption is suggested by Allen (1983): "It seems likely that individuals base their choice on what they expect the others to decide. Thus, the individual's effort to decide hinges upon 'watching the group'—the other members in the community of actual/potential subscribers—to discern what the group choice may be. . . . The outcome for the group then turns literally upon everybody watching while being watched."

The critical mass can also affect *discontinuance* of an interactive innovation, as well as adoption. As noted previously, diffusion theory allows for a certain degree of one-directional interdependence in individuals' decisions to adopt: Later adopters are influenced by earlier adopters (but not vice versa). For noninteractive innovations, this one-way influence relationship is called sequential interdependence. The notion of a critical mass implies that reciprocal interdependence also occurs, in which early adopters are influenced by later adopters (and discontinuers and rejecters), as well as vice versa. "As users defect, the benefits to the remaining users will decrease and the costs increase, thus stimulating further defection" (Markus, 1987). Thus, just as the critical mass affects the rate of adoption of an interactive innovation, it may also affect the rate of discontinuance by speeding up this process.

For example, consider an individual in an organization who stops responding to e-mail messages. This discontinuance of the e-mail system soon becomes evident to other individuals who are sending electronic messages to the discontinuer. They conclude that e-mail is no longer an effective way to reach the discontinuer. Thus everyone else becomes slightly more likely to discontinue using e-mail. So discontinuance of the interactive innovation by one individual may lead eventually to a critical mass of discontinuers, and then to complete rejection of e-mail by the entire organization.

Until this point in our discussion of the critical mass, we have treated all adopters as equivalent in their influence potential. Obviously they are not. A small number of highly influential individuals who adopt a new idea may represent a stronger critical mass than a very large number of individual adopters who have little influence. The critical mass typically includes the opinion leaders in a system, which implies that the communication network structure of the system is vitally involved in contributing to the power of the critical mass in the diffusion process of interactive innovations.

Individual Thresholds for Adoption

A *threshold* is the number of other individuals who must be engaged in an activity before a given individual will join that activity (Granovetter, 1978; Markus, 1987). In the case of the diffusion of an innovation, a threshold is reached when an individual is convinced to adopt as the result of knowing that some minimum number of other individuals in the system (or, more likely, in the individual's personal communication network) have adopted, and are satisfied with their use of the innovation. Notice that a threshold is at the *individual* level of analysis, whereas the critical mass operates at the *system* level. Individuals have adoption thresholds; systems such as communities and organizations have a critical mass. Individual thresholds explain the microlevel process through which aggregated individual decisions make up the critical mass in a system.

Granovetter (1978) provided an illustration of how the two-level phenomenon of individual thresholds and system-level critical mass are interrelated:

Imagine 100 people milling around in a square—a potential riot situation 1. Suppose their riot thresholds are distributed as follows:

There is one individual with threshold 0, one with threshold 1, one with threshold 2, and so on up to the last individual with threshold 99. This is a distribution of thresholds. The outcome is clear and could be described as a "bandwagon" or "domino" effect: The person with threshold 0, the "instigator," engages in riot behavior—breaks a window, say. This activates the person with threshold 1. The activity of these two people then activates the person with threshold 2, and so on, until all 100 people have joined.

If we removed the individual with threshold 1 and replaced the individual by someone with threshold 2, the riot would end with just one rioter. No critical mass would be reached.

Threshold models assume that an individual decision to adopt an innovation depends on the number of other individuals in the system who have already made the behavior change (Krassa, 1988). Although the conceptual notion of a distribution of individual thresholds facilitates our understanding of the diffusion process (especially for an interactive innovation), few empirical studies of this topic have been conducted. Thomas W. Valente (1991, 1993, and 1994) has pioneered in advancing our understanding of thresholds (and critical mass) in the diffusion of innovations.

Why Do Individuals Adopt Prior to the Critical Mass?

A key question in understanding the role of the critical mass in the diffusion process is why an individual adopts an interactive technology before the point at which a critical mass is reached. At any earlier point, the perceived cost of adopting the innovation outweighs its perceived benefits. An early adopting individual may decide to adopt in anticipation that the innovation's rate of adoption will take off in the near future when others adopt, although past diffusion research suggests that most individuals do not adopt an innovation until after learning of their peers' successful experiences (Rogers, 1986).

Typical adoption behavior is illustrated by a Korean woman, a respondent in a diffusion survey conducted by Rogers and Kincaid (1981) in 1973 who adopted a family planning innovation (figure 5.5). As an increasing percentage of her personal network (the dozen other women in her village with whom she talked most often about family planning) adopted family planning methods, she gradually was influenced to adopt. The percentage of network partners who had adopted rose from 33 percent in 1969 to 50 percent in 1970 and 1971 and to 62 percent in 1972, when a "tipping point" (the respondent's individual threshold) was reached. Then the respondent adopted. The Korean villages in the study were systems in which, in Allen's (1983) words, everybody was watching while being watched in the process of family planning diffusion.

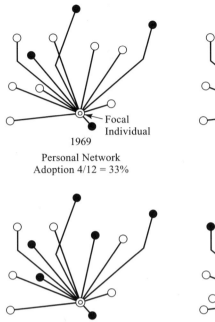
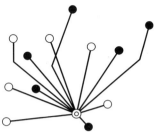
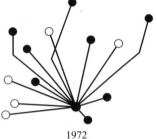

1969
Personal Network
Adoption 4/12 = 33%

1970
Personal Network
Adoption 6/12 = 50%

1971
Personal Network
Adoption 6/12 = 50%

1972
Personal Network
Adoption 8/13 = 62%

Figure 5.5.
Illustration of an individual's threshold for adoption (indexed as the percentage of adopters in the individual's personal communication network) of family planning innovations for a woman in a Korean village. *Note*: The Korean woman who is the focal individual in this personal communication network of a dozen village women adopted a family planning innovation only after half of her network partners adopted, in 1972. Thus this individual had a relatively high threshold of resistance to family planning methods, resistance that had to be overcome by extensive network influence from near-peers who had adopted previously. *Source*: Rogers and Kincaid (1981).

The threshold for adoption varies for different individuals in a system, which explains the S-shaped diffusion curve. The innovators who adopt an innovation first have a very low threshold for adoption, attributable to their venturesomeness. Later adopters have higher thresholds (that is, stronger resistance to the innovation) that are reached only when many other individuals in their personal network have adopted. Whereas later adopters are much more heavily socialized into the local system, innovators, due to their cosmopolite orientation, are almost social isolates in the system. Individual thresholds for adoption are normally distributed, thus creating the S-curve of diffusion.

Valente (1994) showed that network thresholds can be used to classify individuals according to (1) their innovativeness with respect to their system and (2) their innovativeness with respect to their personal network partners. This type of analysis locates individuals who have adopted early in the diffusion process but late relative to their personal network partners. Similarly, Valente's analysis showed that some individuals were late adopters who were exposed to the innovation through their network partners but who still did not adopt. Other individuals were late adopters because of a lack of network exposure to the innovation. Here we see the analytical advantages of exploring the individual's innovativeness as a function of his/her network partners' innovativeness in adopting an innovation.

The general point here is expressed in Generalization 18: *An individual is more likely to adopt an innovation if more of the other individuals in his or her personal network have adopted previously* (Rogers and Kincaid, 1981). Diffusion is highly social in nature: An individual's threshold for adoption is reached when a certain number of the individual's peers have adopted. Innovators, having a very low threshold, adopt an innovation relatively early and thus launch the diffusion process for an innovation in a system. By adopting early, the innovators help other, later-adopting individuals to reach their adoption thresholds. When the critical mass in the rate of adoption of an interactive innovation is reached, the percentage of all individuals' network partners takes a sudden jump, triggering a much more rapid rate of adoption thereafter.

To explain the effect of the critical mass on the adoption behavior of a system's members, we utilized thinking about microlevel personal communication networks. Many key questions about the critical mass can only be answered by investigating the networks through which the critical mass occurs and by which it exerts its effects. For example, in our discussion of the Korean woman's adoption of family planning (see figure 5.5), we measured her adoption threshold as the percentage of her personal communication network partners who adopted prior to her. We did not measure her adoption threshold as the percentage of all of the other thirty-eight women in her *village*, as she did not communicate about family planning with two-thirds of these fellow villagers. Measures of individuals' adoption thresholds are more precise when measured at the personal network level than at the level of the entire system.

The notion of a critical mass calls for important modifications of diffusion theory in the particular case of interactive innovations. The critical mass may also occur for noninteractive innovations. For example, a new article of clothing becomes fashionable when a critical mass of social elites begins wearing it. The fashionable dressers are watching while being watched. Other individuals then rapidly adopt the new fashion, which will eventually be supplanted by a yet newer clothing fashion. Yesterday's fashions are sold in second hand stores and at garage sales.

A good deal of interdependence occurs among the adopters of any innovation in the sense that adopters influence their peers to adopt by providing them with a positive (or negative) evaluation of the innovation. Such peer influence usually makes the diffusion curve take off somewhere between the 5 percent and 20 percent level of adoption. Once this take-off is achieved, little additional promotion of the innovation is needed, as further diffusion is self-generated by the innovation's own social momentum. This explanation for the S-shaped curve of adoption for a noninteractive innovation sounds much like the critical mass. What is different in the special case of interactive innovations is that there is a built-in "forcing quality" in the adopter-to-decider relationship, which stems from the reciprocal interdependence of interactive innovations. "It takes two to tango," as Katz (1962) pointed out. At least two.

The Critical Mass in the Diffusion of Fax

Since 1983, when the diffusion of facsimile ("fax") machines began, the rate of adoption has been more rapid than that for personal computers or VCRs, and it rivals that of cellular telephones in the United States. This rapid diffusion of fax occurred, however, after a wait of 150 years while the technology was shaped into its present form, the appropriate telephone infrastructure to support fax was put in place, and a critical mass of users slowly accumulated.

Fax was invented in 1843 by Alexander Bain, a Scottish clockmaker who called it a recording telegraph because the message was transmitted over telegraph lines. There were no adopters. A century later, in 1948, RCA announced a fax machine that transmitted messages via radio waves; it was called ultra-fax. During the 1960s, Xerox manufactured a fax machine called a "telecopier" that was sold to the Associated Press, UPI, and Reuters news agencies to send photographs and documents over telephone lines to mass media newsrooms. But at this point, accessing phone lines still required operator assistance, telecopiers were slow (it took eight minutes to transmit a single page), and the machines emitted an unpleasant smell.

Next, automatic telephone dialing and direct connection of a fax machine to regular phone lines was allowed. Faster transmission was demanded by users. A fax machine scans a page and converts the material on it into electric signals, which are sent over phone lines. The time required for telephone transmission limited the speed of sending a fax. A universal standard was adopted by the manufacturers of fax machines in 1965. But the equipment was still relatively expensive, about $8,000. The price began to fall and transmission speed increased when Japanese companies entered the market around 1980. Sharp introduced the first low-priced machine ($2,000) in 1984, and large companies in the United States began to buy fax machines. About 80,000 machines were sold that year. The price of a fax machine began to drop further in ensuing years, to $500 in 1980, and to $250 in 1993. It was estimated that a single page could be faxed from Los Angeles to Washington, D.C., for as little as a dime, compared to a first-class stamp of 29 cents. The main advantage of sending a fax is speed; so it mainly competes with overnight mail, which is much more expensive, depends on a third party for delivery, and does not provide a written confirmation that the message has been received, as does fax. A fax message conveys a sense of urgency to the individual receiving it, that the message must be important.

Although the fax boom began in the United States around 1983, the rate of adoption remained quite slow until 1987, the year in which a critical mass of users occurred. About one million machines were sold in 1987, and in 1989, two million fax units were adopted. Starting in 1987, Americans began to assume that "everybody else" had a fax machine (Holmlöv and Warneryd, 1990). "What is your fax number?" became a common query among American businesspeople. Fax numbers began to appear on individuals' business cards. Dating services used fax messages, and many takeout restaurants, such as pizza shops, began to encourage customers to fax in their orders. One U.S. company markets special fax stationery via ads transmitted by fax and promises a Sony Walkman to anyone who supplies the company with 100 fax numbers. Fax advertising makes up about 1 percent of all fax transactions. In recent years, some states passed legislation banning all junk mail by fax.

So it took 150 years for fax to become an overnight success!

This case illustration is based upon Holmlöv and Warneryd (1990) and various other sources.

Strategies for Getting to Critical Mass

What are some possible strategies that may be used to reach critical mass for an innovation in a system?

1. Target top officials in an organization's hierarchy for initial adoption of the interactive innovation. For example, when the president of an organization champions an interactive technology and is the first to adopt and utilize the new medium to send messages to other individuals in the organization, an obvious meta-communication message is implied: Other individuals should adopt the new technology to respond to the president's electronic messages. In 1982, a photograph of Stanford University president Donald Kennedy using a new electronic mail system appeared in the university's faculty newsletter. It was a clear signal that professors should adopt the e-mail system.

   Clearly, the organizational context for the critical mass can be important in providing organizational pressures to adopt an interactive innovation. An organization's hierarchy, reward system, and regulations can encourage, or discourage, the adoption of a new idea. The organization can provide resources for the adoption of an interactive technology and thus lower individuals' perceived cost of adopting.

2. Shape individuals' perceptions of the innovation; for example, by implying that adoption of the innovation is inevitable, that the innovation is very desirable, or that the critical mass has already occurred or will occur soon.

3. Introduce the innovation to intact groups in the system whose members are likely to adopt at once. The city of Santa Monica, California, an upper-middle-class community adjoining Los Angeles, launched Public Electronic Network (PEN) in 1989. It was one of the first municipal electronic communication systems in the United States that was free to citizens. The PEN project provided computer bulletin boards to individuals, including the members of a neighborhood watch group, a PTA, and a church group. Many members of these intact groups adopted at the same time, thus helping achieve a critical mass.

4. Provide incentives for early adoption of the interactive innovation, at least until the critical mass is reached.

"The most direct approach [to reaching critical mass] is to give the service free to a selected group of people for a limited time" (Rohlfs, 1974). An illustration of this strategy is provided by the French government, which in the 1980s gave free Minitel units to hundreds of thousands of heavy telephone users. Although very expensive, this strategy for achieving critical mass was successful. Within a dozen years, more than 6 million French households (about 25 percent of all telephone subscribers) had adopted the Minitel videotext system. Videotext is a system of delivering colored frames of information to a home or office television or computer screen by means of a cable or telephone line. The Minitel experience is all the more noteworthy because other attempts to introduce videotext services, in the United States and elsewhere, have been unsuccessful. Despite very heavy initial investments, these efforts failed to achieve a critical mass of users.

■ Minitel in France: Getting to Critical Mass

The French Minitel system consists of a microcomputer function, a small screen, and a connection to a home or office telephone in order to provide electronic telephone directory services. In addition to linking a telephone subscriber to France's 35 million phone numbers, Minitel provides weather, home banking, ticket reservation, teleshopping, games, and other information services. But the function that helped most in getting Minitel to critical mass was completely unplanned by the French engineers who designed the system: Conversational chatting on the *messagerie* bulletin boards. Minitel was designed as a kind of newspaper, but it functions most importantly as a kind of interactive telephonic service.

By 1993, 6 million French telephone subscribers had adopted Minitel, about 25 percent of the total, and the number of Minitel users was continuing to increase at 24 percent per year. More than a billion connections were made by Minitel users each year. The amazing success of Minitel is all the more impressive in comparison to other videotext systems in the world, none of which have been adopted by even 10 percent as many users. Minitel's success was achieved in the first three or four years of its diffusion, by the mid-1980s, when it reached a critical mass of users. How did Minitel get to critical mass?

The story begins with a vision of France as an information society and as a major world producer of computer-related technology. This vision statement was expressed by Simon Nora and Alain Mine in their 1978 report, *The Computerization of Society*, which became a best-selling book in France. The French felt threatened by the British Prestel system, which the French feared would become the world standard for videotext. The French telephone system at this time was simply awful and was very underused. The French telecommunications agency launched a trial of a new videotext system in Vélizy, a Paris suburb, in 1981. At this point, the system was called Antiope, a name that caused public confusion with the animal by a similar name. French newspapers felt that Antiope was unfair government competition in delivering the news, and threatened legal action against the government telecommunications agency.

The new videotext system was renamed "Minitel," and the pilot project at Vélizy was expanded to several other relatively wealthy areas in France. Soon Minitel service was available in an entire province. Then the Minitel project was expanded to another province, and within five years, Minitel was available nationwide. French Telécom provided an annual subsidy of $800 million to launch Minitel, hoping that this huge investment would be returned once a critical mass of adopters was achieved. By 1990, Minitel broke even and since then has earned a return on investment of 8 to 12 percent per year.

The monthly charges for using Minitel were not separated from regular telephone usage on subscribers' bills, so most individuals did not actually know how much they were paying for Minitel. Actually, the monthly bills of Minitel subscribers are about 150 percent those of non-Minitel phone subscribers, so there is a considerable extra cost.

French Telécom also provided incentives to various companies that used Minitel to connect with their customers. An example of such kiosk services is a newsstand from which a Minitel subscriber can order *Le Monde* or some other newspaper delivered to his or her home address. Business use of Minitel is considerable; 95 percent of French companies with more than 500 employees have adopted Minitel.

Despite these incentives, the rate of adoption for Minitel during the early 1980s was discouragingly slow for French Telécom, who wanted to achieve a high level of use and thus regain its huge investment of about $1.8 billion as quickly as possible. In October 1981, a key event of a completely unplanned nature occurred. Some computer hackers in the city of Strasbourg began to exchange chatty messages via Minitel. These live conversations took place via a *messagerie* service that the computer pirates called Gretel, identified by a logo of a heart with fluttering eyelashes. Participants in this electronic mail system were anonymous (even the monthly billing from French Telécom does not indicate which services were used), and much of the message content was sex related. The Telécom design engineers were scandalized and threatened to close Gretel down. But Minitel Rosé ("Pink Minitel") rapidly became too popular to kill. Within a year, chatting bulletin boards on Minitel were receiving 1,200 calls per day, with an average length of one hour per call, at a cost of $12 (U.S.) per hour. Pink Minitel was addictive; one French woman ran up a monthly bill of $14,000. Soon the sex-related messaging services on Minitel represented 8 percent of all calls, 19 percent of the time spent using Minitel, 22 percent of total sales, and half of Minitel's profits. Minitel was now well on its way to reaching critical mass. French people use the *messageries* as the electronic equivalent of singles bars. In a nation known for its love of talk and its talk of love, perhaps Pink Minitel should not have come as a surprise to the engineers who designed the Minitel system. The names of the Minitel Rosé messaging services imply their soft pornographic content: Sextel, Désiropolis, Aphrodite, Aíme-Moi. Minitel subscribers must pay for such titillation: French Telécom imposed a special extra tax of 33 percent on users of Minitel Rosé.

French Telécom made Minitel so easy to adopt that discontinuance was also very easy. About 20 percent of the 6 million adopters of this videotext system do not use it at all, and another 30 percent of adopters use it very little. Some 20 percent of subscribers only use Minitel for telephone directory services. Heaviest users are white-collar employees. Minitel has only negligible use in rural areas of France. Public Minitel terminals are available in post offices throughout France to provide electronic directory services.

The key to the success of Minitel was in getting to a critical mass of users rapidly, and the unplanned role of Minitel Rosé drove this early rate of adoption.

This case illustration draws on Kramer (1993) and numerous other published accounts of the diffusion of Minitel.

Social Learning Theory

A social psychological theory with direct applicability to diffusion networks is social learning theory. Most psychological approaches to human learning look within the individual to understand how learning occurs.

But the social learning approach looks outside of the individual at a specific type of information exchanges with others to explain how behavior changes. The intellectual leader of social learning theory is Professor Albert Bandura (1977) of Stanford University.

The central ideal of social learning theory is that an individual learns from another by means of observational modeling; that is, one observes another person's behavior and then does something similar. The observer's behavior is not exactly the same as the model's, which would be simple imitation or blind mimicry. Rather, in social modeling the observer extracts the essential elements from an observed behavior pattern in order to perform a similar behavior. Modeling allows the learner to adapt the observed behavior (much like the reinvention of an innovation).

The basic perspective of social learning theory is that the individual can learn from observation of other people's activities, so the individual does not necessarily have to experience a verbal exchange of information for the individual's behavior to be influenced by the model. Thus, nonverbal communication is important in behavior change (as well as verbal communication). Because social learning theory recognizes external factors to the individual as important in behavior change, it is essentially social, by viewing communication as a cause of behavior change. The individual can learn a new behavior by observing another individual in person or via the mass media (especially visual media like television or film). Social modeling often occurs through interpersonal networks, but it can also occur through a public display by someone with whom one is unacquainted. Ideally, an individual learns more from a social model if the model is positively rewarded for the behavior that is displayed rather than punished.

Social learning and diffusion have much in common: Both theories seek to explain how individuals change their overt behavior as a result of communication with other individuals. Both theories stress information exchange as essential to behavior change and view network links as the main explanation of how individuals alter their behavior.

Sociologists at the University of Arizona (Hamblin, Jacobson, and Miller, 1973; Hamblin and others, 1979; Pitcher, Hamblin, and Miller, 1978; Kunkel, 1977) have applied social learning theory to the diffusion of innovations, such as the rate of airplane hijackings. Their viewpoint is that "[d]iffusion models portray society as a huge learning system where individuals are continually behaving and making decisions through time but not independently of one another. . . . Everyone makes his own decisions, not just on the basis of his own individual experiences, but to a large extent on the basis of the observed or talked about experiences of others" (Hamblin and others, 1979).

While there is a basic similarity between social learning theory and the diffusion of innovations, there are also important differences.

1. In comparison to social learning research, diffusion research has been more aggregate in the way that the effects of modeling are measured (as either adoption or rejection of an innovation). Social learning perspectives would encourage diffusion researchers to measure more exactly *what* the individual learns through a network link with an adopter of an innovation. This detailed learning might include what resources of time, money, effort, skills, and mastery of technical jargon are necessary for the individual to adopt an innovation. Will the innovation solve the focal individual's perceived problem/need? What is the innovation's relative advantage over previous practice? How satisfied is the adopter-peer with the innovation? Such issues as these would focus diffusion research on the informational content that is exchanged in diffusion networks.
2. A diffusion perspective, if more fully brought into social learning research, might provide greater attention to time as a variable in behavior change, thus helping social learning focus more centrally on behavior change as a *process*.
3. Both social learning and recent diffusion research recognize that the individual does not always exactly mimic the model (as is implied by reinvention). Instead, the individual learner-adopter usually abstracts or generalizes the information learned from the model.
4. Both social learning and diffusion researchers have recently emphasized the exchange/convergence aspects of behavior change, emphasizing interpersonal information exchange as the basis for behavior change.

■ Summary

Opinion leadership is the degree to which an individual is able to influence informally other individuals' attitudes or overt behavior in a desired way with relative frequency. Opinion leaders play an important role in diffusion networks. The concept of opinion leadership originated as part of the *two-step flow model*, which hypothesized that communication messages flow from a source, via mass media channels, to opinion leaders, who in turn pass them on to followers. The two-step flow model challenged the previous *hypodermic needle model*, which postulated that the mass media had direct, immediate, and powerful effects on individual members of a mass audience.

Homophily is the degree to which a pair of individuals who communicate are similar. *Heterophily* is the degree to which pairs of individuals who interact are different in certain attributes. Interpersonal diffusion networks are mostly homophilous (Generalization 1). Such homophily can act as an invisible barrier to the rapid flow of innovations within a social system, as similar people interact in socially horizontal patterns.

When interpersonal diffusion networks are heterophilous, follow-ers seek opinion leaders of higher socioeconomic status, with more for-mal education, greater mass media exposure, more cosmopoliteness, greater change agent contact, and more innovativeness (Generalizations 2 through 7).

Compared to followers, opinion leaders have greater mass media ex-posure, more cosmopoliteness, greater change agent contact, greater social participation, higher social status, and more innovativeness (Generaliza-tions 8 through 13). Opinion leaders conform more closely to a system's norms than do their followers. When a social system's norms favor change, opinion leaders are especially innovative (Generalization 14).

A *communication network* consists of interconnected individuals who are linked by patterned flows of information. An individual's network links are important determinants of his or her adoption of innovations. The network interconnectedness of an individual in a social system is positively related to the individual's innovativeness (Generalization 15). *Interconnectedness* is the degree to which the units in a social system are linked by interpersonal networks.

Networks provide a certain degree of structure and stability in the predictability of human behavior. *Communication structure* is the differen-tiated elements that can be recognized in the patterned communication flows in a system. This structure consists of the cliques within a system and the network interconnections among them through bridges and liai-sons. Individuals are identified as belonging to cliques on the basis of *communication proximity*, the degree to which two linked individuals in a network have personal communication networks that overlap. A *personal network* consists of those interconnected individuals who are linked by patterned communication flows to a given individual.

Personal networks that are radial (rather than interlocking) are more open to an individual's environment and hence play a more important role in the diffusion of innovations. The information-exchange potential of communication network links is negatively related to their degree of (1) communication proximity and (2) homophily. This generalization (16) is an expression of Granovetter's theory of the "strength of weak ties." Individuals tend to be linked to others who are close to them in physical distance and who are relatively homophilous in social characteristics (Generalization 17).

The *critical mass* occurs at the point at which enough individuals have adopted an innovation that the innovation's further rate of adoption be-comes self-sustaining. The critical mass is particularly important in the diffusion of interactive innovations like e-mail, cellular telephones, and teleconferencing, where each additional adopter increases the utility of adoption for all adopters. *Interactivity* is the degree to which participants in a communication process can exchange roles in, and have control over, their mutual discourse. As more individuals in a system adopt a noninteractive innovation, it is perceived as increasingly beneficial to future adopters (this is a *sequential* interdependence effect on later adopters). However, in the case of an interactive innovation, the benefits from each additional adoption increase not only for all future adopters but also for each previous adopter (this is *reciprocal* interdependence).

A *threshold* is the number of other individuals who must be engaged in an activity before a given individual will join that activity. An innovator has a low threshold of resistance to adopting a new idea, and so few (or no) interpersonal network influences are needed for adoption. In contrast, a late-majority individual has a much higher threshold that must be overcome by near-peer network influences in order to overcome resistance to the innovation. Thresholds act for individuals in a somewhat parallel way to the critical mass at the system level. An individual is more likely to adopt an innovation if more of the other individuals in his or her personal network have adopted previously (Generalization 18).

Social learning theory states that individuals learn from others whom they observe and then imitate by following a similar (but not necessarily identical) behavior. Such social modeling frequently occurs through diffusion networks.

▪ Notes

1. Although similarities in static variables like age and other demographic characteristics obviously cannot be explained as the result of communication leading to increased homophily.

2. It is possible, however, to locate sociometric opinion leaders in surveys by means of snowball sampling in which an original sample of respondents in a system is interrogated. Then the individuals sociometrically designated by this sample are interviewed as a second sample, and so on (Rogers and Kincaid, 1981).

3. Very unobtrusive methods of measuring network links may sometimes be used, where the data were recorded for other purposes (Rogers and Kincaid, 1981). For example, an electronic mail system leaves a computer record of who talks to whom and what they said; these data can sometimes be accessed as an unobtrusive measure of network links, with the permission of the respondents.

4. Becker (1970) actually referred to these two innovations as "high adoption potential" and "low adoption potential," with the former having a larger audience of potential adopters than the latter innovation.

5. The publications bearing on the Walker study of innovativeness among the U.S. states are Walker (1966, 1971, 1973, 1976, 1977) and Gray (1973a, 1973b).

6. *Openness* is the degree to which a unit exchanges information with its environment.

7. Similar evidence of the importance of weak ties in the diffusion of information about new jobs is provided by Langlois (1977), Lin and others (1981), and Friedkin (1980) but not by Murray and others (1981). An overall summary of research findings is provided by Granovetter (1982).

8. A *bridge* is an individual who links two or more cliques in a system from his or her position as a member of one of the cliques.

9. The discussion of the critical mass draws directly on Rogers (1990 and 1991).

■ **References**

Allen, David (1983), "New Telecommunication Services: Network Externalities and Critical Mass," *Telecommunication Policy*, 12(3):257–271.

Bandura, Albert (1977), *Social Learning Theory*, Englewood Cliffs, NJ, Prentice Hall.

Becker, Marshall H. (1970), "Sociometric Location and Innovativeness: Reformulation and Extension of the Diffusion Model," *American Sociological Review*, 35:262–282.

Brewer, M. (1985), "Experimental Research and Social Policy: Must It Be Rigor versus Relevance?" *Journal of Social Issues*, 41(4):159–176.

Burt, Ronald S. (1980), "Innovation as a Structural Interest: Rethinking the Impact of Network Position on Innovation Adoption," *Social Networks*, 2:327–355.

———. (1987), "Social Contagion and Innovation: Cohesion Versus Structural Equivalence," *American Journal of Sociology*, 92:1287–1335.

Carlson, Richard O. (1965), *Adoption of Educational Innovations*, Eugene, University of Oregon, Center for the Advanced Study of Educational Administration.

Coleman, James S., Elihu Katz, and Herbert Menzel (1966), *Medical Innovation: A Diffusion Study*, New York, Bobbs-Merrill, pp. 25, 30–32, 52, 59, 79–92, 95–112, 119, 126.

Duff, Robert W., and William T. Liu (1975), "The Significance of Heterophilous Structure in Communication Flows," *Philippine Quarterly of Culture and Society*, 3:159–175.

Friedkin, Noah (1980), "A Test of Structural Features of Granovetter's Strength of Weak Ties Theory," *Social Networks*, 2:411–422.

Granovetter, Mark S. (1973), "The Strength of Weak Ties," *American Journal of Sociology*, 78:1360–1380.

———. (1978), "Threshold Models of Collective Behavior," *American Journal of Sociology*, 83:1420–1443.

———. (1982), "The Strength of Weak Ties: A Network Theory Revisited," in Peter Marsden (ed.), *Social Structure and Network Analysis*, Newbury Park, CA, Sage, pp. 105–130.

Gray, Virginia (1973a), "Innovation in the States: A Diffusion Study," *American Political Science Review*, 67:1174–1185.

———. (1973b), "Rejoinder to 'Comment' by Jack L. Walker," *American Political Science Review*, 4:1192–1193.

Gurbaxani, Vijay (1990), "Diffusion in Computing Networks: The Case of BITNET," *Communications of the ACM*, 33(12):65–75.

Hamblin, Robert L., R. B. Jacobson, and J. L. Miller (1973), *A Mathematical Theory of Social Change*, New York, Wiley.

Hamblin, Robert L., and others (1979), "Modeling Use Diffusion," *Social Forces*, 57:799–811.

Hardin, Garrett (1968), "The Tragedy of the Commons," *Science*, 162:1243–1248.

Herzog, William A., J. David Stanfield, Gordon C. Whiting, and Lynne Svenning (1968), *Patterns of Diffusion in Rural Brazil*, East Lansing, Michigan State University, Department of Communication, Diffusion of Innovations Research Report 10, p. 72.

Hölmov, P. G., and Karl-Eric Warneryd (1990), "Adoption and Use of Fax in Sweden" in M. Carnevale, M. Lucertini, and S. Nicosia (eds.), *Modeling the Innovation: Communications, Automation and Information Systems*, Amsterdam, Elsevier Science Publishers, pp. 95–108.

Katz, Elihu (1962). "Notes on the Unit of Adoption in Diffusion Research," *Sociological Inquiry*, 32:3–9.

Katz, Elihu, and Paul F. Lazarsfeld (1955), *Personal Influence: The Part Played by People in the Flow of Mass Communications*, New York, Free Press, pp. 16, 334.

Kearns, Kelvin P. (1992), "Innovations in Local Governments: A Sociocognitive Network Approach," *Knowledge and Policy*, 5(2):45–67.

Klovdahl, Alden S. (1985), "Social Networks and the Spread of Infectious Diseases: The AIDS Example," *Social Science Medicine*, 21(11):1203–1216.

Kramer, Richard (1993), "The Policies of Information: A Study of the French Minitel System," in Jorge R. Schement and Brent D. Ruben (eds.), *Between Communication and Information*, Volume 4 of *Information and Behavior*, New Brunswick, NJ, Transaction, pp. 453–486.

Krassa, M. A. (1988), "Social Groups, Selective Perception, and Behavioral Contagion in Public Opinion," *Social Networks*, 10:109–136.

Kunkel, John H. (1977), "The Behavioral Perspective of Social Dynamics," in Robert L. Hamblin and John H. Kunkel (eds.), *Behavioral Theory in Sociology*, New Brunswick, NJ, Transaction.

Langlois, Simon (1977), "Les Reseaux Personnels et la Diffusion des Informations sur les Emplois," *Researches Sociographiques*, 2:213–245.

Lazarsfeld, Paul F., Bernard Berelson, and Hazel Gaudet (1944), *The People's Choice: How the Voter Makes up His Mind in a Presidential Election*, New York, Duell, Sloan, and Pearce; reprinted 1948, 1968, New York, Columbia University Press, p. 157.

Lazarsfeld, Paul F., and Herbert Menzel (1963), "Mass Media and Personal Influence," in Wilbur Schramm (ed.), *The Science of Human Communication*, New York, Basic Books, p. 96.

Lazarsfeld, Paul F., and Robert K. Merton (1964). "Friendship as Social Process: A Substantive and Methodological Analysis," in Monroe Berger and others (eds.), *Freedom and Control in Modern Society*, New York, Octagon, pp. 23, 63.

Lin, Nan, and others (1981), "Social Resources and Strength of Ties: Structural Factors in Occupational Status Attainment," *American Sociological Review*, 46:393–405.

Liu, William T., and Robert W. Duff (1972), "The Strength of Weak Ties," *Public Opinion Quarterly*, 36:361–366.

Markus, M. Lynne (1987), "Toward a 'Critical Mass' Theory of Interactive Media: Universal Access, Interdependence and Diffusion," *Communication Research*, 14:491–511.

————. (1990), "Toward a 'Critical Mass' Theory of Interactive Media," in Janet Fulk and Charles Steinfield (eds.), *Organizations and Communication Technology*, Newbury Park, CA, Sage, pp. 194–218.

Marsden, Peter V., and Joel Podolny (1990), "Dynamic Analysis of Network Diffusion Processes," in Jerver Wessie and Hank Flap (eds.), *Social Networks Through Time*, Utrecht, Netherlands, ISOR, pp. 197–214.

McAdam, Doug (1986), "Recruitment to High-Risk Activism: The Case of Freedom Summer," *American Journal of Sociology*, 92(1):64–90.

McAdam, Doug, and Ronnelle Paulsen (1993), "Specifying the Relationship between Social Ties and Activism," *American Journal of Sociology*, 99(3):640–667.

Murray, Stephen O., and others (1981), "Strong Ties and Job Information," *Sociology of Work and Occupations*, 8:119–136.

Olson, Mancur H. (1965), *The Logic of Collective Action: Public Goods and the Theory of Groups*, Cambridge, MA, Harvard University Press.

Pitcher, Brian L., Robert L. Hamblin, and Jerry L. L. Miller (1978), "The Diffusion of Collective Violence," *American Sociological Review*, 43:23–25.

Rao, G. Appa, Everett M. Rogers, and S. N. Singh (1980), "Interpersonal Relations in the Diffusion of an Innovation in Two Indian Villages," *Indian Journal of Extension Education*, 16(1&2):19–24.

Rogers, Everett M. (1986), *Communication Technology: The New Media in Society*, New York, Free Press.

————. (1990), "The 'Critical Mass' in the Diffusion of Interactive Technologies," in M. Carnevale, M. Lucertini, and S. Nicosia (eds.), *Modeling the Innovation: Communication, Automation, and Information Systems*, Amsterdam, Elsevier, pp. 79–94.

————. (1991), "The 'Critical Mass' in the Diffusion of Interactive Technologies in Organizations," in Kenneth L. Kraemer, James I. Cash, Jr., and Jay F. Nunmaker, Jr. (eds.), *The Information System Research Challenges: Survey Research Methods*, Boston, Harvard Business School Press, pp. 245–263.

————. (1994), *A History of Communication Study: A Biographical Approach*, New York, Free Press.

Rogers, Everett M., and D. Lawrence Kincaid (1981), *Communication Networks: Toward a New Paradigm for Research*, New York, Free Press.

Rogers, Everett M., with Lynne Svenning (1969), *Modernization among Peasants: The Impact of Communication*, New York, Holt, Rinehart and Winston, pp. 230–231, 300.

Rohlfs, J. (1974), "A Theory of Interdependent Demand for a Communication Service," *Bell Journal of Economics and Management Science*, 5:16–37.

Schelling, Thomas C. (1978), *Micromotives and Macrobehavior*, New York, Norton, pp. 13, 89, 94.

Tarde, Gabriel (1903), *The Laws of Imitation*, translated by Elsie Clews Parsons, New York, Holt; reprinted 1969, University of Chicago Press, pp. 4, 27, 64, 140, 178, 221.

Valente, Thomas W. (1991), *Thresholds and the Critical Mass in Mathematical Models of the Diffusion of Innovation*, Ph.D. Thesis, Los Angeles, University of Southern California.

————. (1993), "Diffusion of Innovation and Policy Decision-Making," *Journal of Communication*, 43(1):30–41.

———. (1994), *Network Models of the Diffusion of Innovations*, Creskill, NJ, Hampton Press.

Van den Ban, A. W. (1963), *Hoe Vinden Nieuee Landbouwmethodeningand* (How a New Practice Is Introduced), *Landbouwvoorlichting*, 20:227–239.

Walker, Jack L. (1966), "The Diffusion of Innovations among the American States," *American Political Science Review*, 63:880–899.

———. (1971), "Innovation in State Policies," in Herbert Jacob and Kenneth N. Vines (eds.), *Politics in the American States: A Comparative Analysis*, Boston, Little Brown, pp. 358, 381.

———. (1973), "Comment: Problems in Research on the Diffusion of Policy Innovations." *American Political Science Review*, 67:1186–1191.

———. (1976), "Setting the Agenda in the U.S. Senate: A Theory of Problem Selection," Ann Arbor, University of Michigan, Institute of Public Policy Studies, Discussion Paper 94, pp. 26–32.

———. (1977), "Setting the Agenda in the U.S. Senate: A Theory of Problem Selection," *British Journal of Political Science*, 7:423–445.

Whyte, William H., Jr. (1954), "The Web of Word of Mouth," *Fortune*, 50:140–143, 204–212.

Williams, Frederick R., Ronald E. Rice, and Everett M. Rogers (1988), *Research Methods and the New Media*, New York, Free Press.

6

Designs for Working

Why Your Bosses Want to Turn Your New Office

into Greenwich Village

Malcolm Gladwell

1

In the early 1960s, Jane Jacobs lived on Hudson Street, in Greenwich Village, near the intersection of Eighth Avenue and Bleecker Street. It was then, as now, a charming district of nineteenth-century tenements and townhouses, bars and shops, laid out over an irregular grid, and Jacobs loved the neighborhood. In her 1961 masterpiece, "The Death and Life of Great American Cities," she rhapsodized about the White Horse Tavern down the block, home to Irish longshoremen and writers and intellectuals—a place where, on a winter's night, as "the doors open, a solid wave of conversation and animation surges out and hits you." Her Hudson Street had Mr. Slube, at the cigar store, and Mr. Lacey, the locksmith, and Bernie, the candy-store owner, who, in the course of a typical day, supervised the children crossing the street, lent an umbrella or a dollar to a customer, held on to some keys or packages for people in the neighborhood, and "lectured two youngsters who asked for cigarettes." The street had "bundles and packages, zigzagging from the drug store to the fruit stand and back over to the butcher's," and "teenagers, all dressed up, are pausing to ask if their slips show or their collars look right." It was, she said, an urban ballet.

The miracle of Hudson Street, according to Jacobs, was created by the particular configuration of the streets and buildings of the neighborhood. Jacobs argued that when a neighborhood is oriented toward the street, when sidewalks are used for socializing and play and commerce, the users of that street are transformed by the resulting stimulation: they form relationships and casual contacts they would never have otherwise. The West Village, she pointed out, was blessed with a mixture of houses and apartments and shops and offices and industry, which meant that there were always people "outdoors on different schedules and . . . in the place for different purposes." It had short blocks, and short blocks create the greatest variety in foot traffic. It had lots of old buildings, and old buildings have the low rents that permit individualized and creative uses. And, most of all, it had people, cheek by jowl, from every conceivable walk of life. Sparely populated suburbs may look appealing, she said, but without an active sidewalk life, without the frequent, serendipitous interactions of many different people, "there is no public acquaintanceship, no foundation of public trust, no cross-connections with the necessary people—and no practice or ease in applying the most ordinary techniques of city public life at lowly levels."

Jane Jacobs did not win the battle she set out to fight. The West Village remains an anomaly. Most developers did not want to build the kind of community Jacobs talked about, and most Americans didn't want to live in one. To reread "Death and Life" today, however, is to be struck by how the intervening years have given her arguments a new and unexpected relevance. Who, after all, has a direct interest in creating diverse, vital spaces that foster creativity and serendipity? Employers do. On the fortieth anniversary of its publication, "Death and Life" has been reborn as a primer on workplace design.

The parallels between neighborhoods and offices are striking. There was a time, for instance, when companies put their most valued employees in palatial offices, with potted plants in the corner, and secretaries out front, guarding access. Those offices were suburbs—gated communities, in fact—and many companies came to realize that if their best employees were isolated in suburbs they would be deprived of public acquaintanceship, the foundations of public trust, and cross-connections with the necessary people. In the 1980s, and early 1990s, the fashion in corporate America was to follow what designers called "universal planning"—rows of identical cubicles, which resembled nothing so much as a Levittown. Today, universal planning has fallen out of favor, for the same reason that the postwar suburbs like Levittown did: to thrive, an office space must have a diversity of uses—it must have the workplace equivalent of houses and apartments and shops and industry.

If you visit the technology companies of Silicon Valley, or the media companies of Manhattan, or any of the firms that self-consciously identify themselves with the New Economy, you'll find that secluded private offices have been replaced by busy public spaces, open-plan areas without walls, executives next to the newest hires. The hush of the traditional office has been supplanted by something much closer to the noisy, bustling ballet of Hudson Street. Forty years ago, people lived in neighborhoods like the West Village and went to work in the equivalent of suburbs. Now, in one of the odd reversals that mark the current economy, they live in suburbs and, increasingly, go to work in the equivalent of the West Village.

2

The office used to be imagined as a place where employees punch clocks and bosses roam the halls like high-school principals, looking for miscreants. But when employees sit chained to their desks, quietly and industriously going about their business, an office is not functioning as it should. That's because innovation—the heart of the knowledge economy—is fundamentally social. Ideas arise as much out of casual conversations as they do out of formal meetings. More precisely, as one study after another has demonstrated, the best ideas in any workplace arise out of casual contacts among different groups within the same company. If you are designing widgets for Acme.com, for instance, it is unlikely that a breakthrough idea is going to come from someone else on the widget team: after all, the other team members are as blinkered by the day-to-day demands of dealing with the existing product as you are. Someone from outside Acme.com—your old engineering professor, or a guy you used to work with at Apex.com—isn't going to be that helpful, either. A person like that doesn't know enough about Acme's widgets to have a truly useful idea. The most useful insights are likely to come from someone in customer service, who hears firsthand what widget customers have to say, or from someone in marketing, who has wrestled with the problem of how to explain widgets to new users, or from someone who used to work on widgets a few years back and whose work on another Acme product has given him a fresh perspective. Innovation comes from the interactions of people at a comfortable distance from one another, neither too close nor too far. This is why—quite apart from the matter of logistics and efficiency—companies have offices to begin with. They go to the trouble of gathering their employees under one roof because they want the widget designers to bump into the people in marketing and the people in customer service and the guy who moved to another department a few years back.

The catch is that getting people in an office to bump into people from another department is not so easy as it looks. In the 1960s and 1970s, a researcher at M.I.T. named Thomas Allen conducted a decade-long study of the way in which engineers communicated in research-and-development laboratories. Allen found that the likelihood that any two people will communicate drops off dramatically as the distance between their desks increases: we are four times as likely to communicate with someone who sits six feet away from us as we are with someone who sits sixty feet away. And people seated more than seventy-five feet apart hardly talk at all.

Allen's second finding was even more disturbing. When the engineers weren't talking to those in their immediate vicinity, many of them spent their time talking to people *outside* their company—to their old computer-science professor or the guy they used to work with at Apple. He concluded that it was actually easier to make the outside call than to walk across the room. If you constantly ask for advice or guidance from people inside your organization, after all, you risk losing prestige. Your colleagues might think you are incompetent. The people you keep asking for advice might get annoyed at you. Calling an outsider avoids these problems. "The engineer can easily excuse his lack of knowledge by pretending to be an 'expert in something else' who needs some help in 'broadening into this new area,'" Allen wrote. He did his study in the days before E-mail and the Internet, but the advent of digital communication has made these problems worse. Allen's engineers were far too willing to go outside the company for advice and new ideas. E-mail makes it even easier to talk to people outside the company.

The task of the office, then, is to invite a particular kind of social interaction—the casual, nonthreatening encounter that makes it easy for relative strangers to talk to each other. Offices need the sort of social milieu that Jane Jacobs found on the sidewalks of the West Village. "It is possible in a city street neighborhood to know all kinds of people without unwelcome entanglements, without boredom, necessity for excuses, explanations, fears of giving offense, embarrassments respecting impositions or commitments, and all such paraphernalia of obligations which can accompany less limited relationships," Jacobs wrote. If you substitute "office" for "city street neighborhood," that sentence becomes the perfect statement of what the modern employer wants from the workplace.

■ 3

Imagine a classic big-city office tower, with a floor plate of a hundred and eighty feet by a hundred and eighty feet. The center part of every floor is given over to the guts of the building: elevators, bathrooms, electrical and plumbing systems. Around the core are cubicles and interior offices, for support staff and lower management. And around the edges of the floor, against the windows, are rows of offices for senior staff, each room perhaps two hundred or two hundred and fifty square feet. The best research about office communication tells us that there is almost no worse way to lay out an office. The executive in one corner office will seldom bump into any other executive in a corner office. Indeed, stringing the exterior offices out along the windows guarantees that there will be very few people within the critical sixty-foot radius of those offices. To maximize the amount of contact among employees, you really ought to put the most valuable staff members in the center of the room, where the highest number of people can be within their orbit. Or, even better, put all places where people tend to congregate—the public areas—in the center, so they can draw from as many disparate parts of the company as possible. Is it any wonder that creative firms often prefer loft-style buildings, which have usable centers?

Another way to increase communication is to have as few private offices as possible. The idea is to exchange private space for public space, just as in the West Village, where residents agree to live in tiny apartments in exchange for a wealth of nearby cafés and stores and bars and parks. The West Village forces its residents outdoors. Few people, for example, have a washer and dryer in their apartment, and so even laundry is necessarily a social event: you have to take your clothes to the laundromat down the street. In the office equivalent, designers force employees to move around, too. They build in "functional inefficiencies"; they put kitchens and copiers and printers and libraries in places that can be reached only by a circuitous journey.

A more direct approach is to create an office so flexible that the kinds of people who need to spontaneously interact can actually be brought together. For example, the Ford Motor Company, along with a group of researchers from the University of Michigan, recently conducted a pilot project on the effectiveness of "war rooms" in software development. Previously, someone inside the company who needed a new piece of software written would have a series of meetings with the company's programmers, and the client and the programmers would send messages back and forth. In the war-room study, the company moved the client, the programmers, and a manager into a dedicated conference room, and made them stay there until the project was done. Using the war room cut the software-development time by two-thirds, in part because there was far less time wasted on formal meetings or calls outside the building: the people who ought to have been bumping into each other were now sitting next to each other.

Two years ago, the advertising agency TBWA/Chiat/Day moved into new offices in Los Angeles, out near the airport. In the preceding years, the firm had been engaged in a radical, and in some ways disastrous, experiment with a "nonterritorial" office: no one had a desk or any office equipment of his own. It was a scheme that courted failure by neglecting all the ways in which an office is a sort of neighborhood. By contrast, the new office is an almost perfect embodiment of Jacobsian principles of community. The agency is in a huge old warehouse, three stories high and the size of three football fields. It is informally known as Advertising City, and that's what it is: a kind of artfully constructed urban neighborhood. The floor is bisected by a central corridor called Main Street, and in the center of the room is an open space, with café tables and a stand of ficus trees, called Central Park. There's a basketball court, a game room, and a bar. Most of the employees are in snug workstations known as nests, and the nests are grouped together in neighborhoods that radiate from Main Street like Paris arrondissements. The top executives are situated in the middle of the room. The desk belonging to the chairman and creative director of the company looks out on Central Park. The offices of the chief financial officer and the media director abut the basketball court. Sprinkled throughout the building are meeting rooms and project areas and plenty of nooks where employees can closet themselves when they need to. A small part of the building is elevated above the main floor on a mezzanine, and if you stand there and watch the people wander about with their portable phones, and sit and chat in Central Park, and play basketball in the gym, and you feel on your shoulders the sun from the skylights and listen to the gentle buzz of human activity, it is quite possible to forget that you are looking at an office.

■ 4

In "The Death and Life of Great American Cities," Jacobs wrote of the importance of what she called "public characters"—people who have the social position and skills to orchestrate the movement of information and the creation of bonds of trust:

> A public character is anyone who is in frequent contact with a wide circle of people and who is sufficiently interested to make himself a public character. . . . The director of a settlement on New York's Lower East Side, as an example, makes a regular round of stores. He learns from the cleaner who does his suits about the presence of dope pushers in the neighborhood. He learns from the grocer that the Dragons are working up to something and need attention. He learns from the candy store that two girls are agitating the Sportsmen toward a rumble. One of his most important information spots is an unused breadbox on Rivington Street. . . . A message spoken there for any teen-ager within many blocks will reach his ears unerringly and surprisingly quickly, and the opposite flow along the grapevine similarly brings news quickly in to the breadbox.

A vital community, in Jacobs's view, required more than the appropriate physical environment. It also required a certain kind of person, who could bind together the varied elements of street life. Offices are no different. In fact, as office designers have attempted to create more vital workplaces, they have become increasingly interested in identifying and encouraging public characters.

One of the pioneers in this way of analyzing offices is Karen Stephenson, a business-school professor and anthropologist who runs a New York–based consulting company called Netform. Stephenson studies social networks. She goes into a company—her clients include J. P. Morgan, the Los Angeles Police Department, T.R.W., and I.B.M.—and distributes a questionnaire to its employees, asking about which people they have contact with. Whom do you like to spend time with? Whom do you talk to about new ideas? Where do you go to get expert advice? Every name in the company becomes a dot on a graph, and Stephenson draws lines between all those who have regular contact with each other. Stephenson likens her graphs to X rays, and her role to that of a radiologist. What she's depicting is the firm's invisible inner mechanisms, the relationships and networks and patterns of trust that arise as people work together over time, and that are hidden beneath the organization chart. Once, for example, Stephenson was doing an "X ray" of a Head Start organization. The agency was mostly female, and when Stephenson analyzed her networks she found that new hires and male staffers were profoundly isolated, communicating with the rest of the organization through only a handful of women. "I looked at tenure in the organization, office ties, demographic data. I couldn't see what tied the women together, and why the men were talking only to these women," Stephenson recalls. "Nor could the president of the organization. She gave me a couple of ideas. She said, 'Sorry I can't figure it out.' Finally, she asked me to read the names again, and I could hear her stop, and she said, 'My God, I know what it is. All those women are smokers.'" The X ray revealed that the men—locked out of the formal power structure of the organization—were trying to gain access and influence by hanging out in the smoking area with some of the more senior women.

What Stephenson's X rays do best, though, is tell you who the public characters are. In every network, there are always one or two people who have connections to many more people than anyone else. Stephenson calls them "hubs," and on her charts lines radiate out from them like spokes on a wheel. (Bernie the candy-store owner, on Jacobs's Hudson Street, was a hub.) A few people are also what Stephenson calls "gatekeepers": they control access to critical people and link together a strategic few disparate groups. Finally, if you analyze the graphs there are always people who seem to have lots of indirect links to other people—who are part of all sorts of networks without necessarily being in the center of them. Stephenson calls those people "pulsetakers." (In Silicon Valleyspeak, the person in a sea of cubicles who pops his or her head up over the partition every time something interesting is going on is called a prairie dog: prairie dogs are pulsetakers.)

■ 5

In the past year, Stephenson has embarked on a partnership with Steelcase, the world's largest manufacturer of office furniture, in order to use her techniques in the design of offices. Traditionally, office designers would tell a company what furniture should go where. Stephenson and her partners at Steelcase propose to tell a company what people should go where, too. At Steelcase, they call this "floor-casting."

One of the first projects for the group is the executive level at Steelcase's headquarters, a five-story building in Grand Rapids, Michigan. The executive level, on the fourth floor, is a large, open room filled with small workstations. (Jim Hackett, the head of the company, occupies what Steelcase calls a Personal Harbor, a black, freestanding metal module that may be—at seven feet by eight—the smallest office of a Fortune 500 C.E.O.) One afternoon recently, Stephenson pulled out a laptop and demonstrated how she had mapped the communication networks of the leadership group onto a seating chart of the fourth floor. The dots and swirls are strangely compelling—abstract representations of something real and immediate. One executive, close to Hackett, was inundated with lines from every direction. "He's a hub, a gatekeeper, and a pulsetaker across all sorts of different dimensions," Stephenson said. "What that tells you is that he is very strategic. If there is no succession planning around that person, you have got a huge risk to the knowledge base of this company. If he's in a plane accident, there goes your knowledge." She pointed to another part of the floor plan, with its own thick overlay of lines. "That's sales and marketing. They have a pocket of real innovation here. The guy who runs it is very good, very smart." But then she pointed to the lines connecting that department with other departments. "They're all coming into this one place," she said, and she showed how all the lines coming out of marketing converged on one senior executive. "There's very little path redundancy. In human systems, you need redundancy, you need communication across multiple paths." What concerned Stephenson wasn't just the lack of redundancy but the fact that, in her lingo, many of the paths were "unconfirmed": they went only one way. People in marketing were saying that they communicated with the senior management, but there weren't as many lines going in the other direction. The sales-and-marketing team, she explained, had somehow become isolated from senior management. They couldn't get their voices heard when it came to innovation—and that fact, she said, ought to be a big consideration when it comes time to redo the office. "If you ask the guy who heads sales and marketing who he wants to sit next to, he'll pick out all the people he trusts," she said. "But do you sit him with those people? No. What you want to do is put people who don't trust each other near each other. Not necessarily next to each other, because they get too close. But close enough so that when you pop your head up, you get to see people, they are in your path, and all of a sudden you build an inviting space where they can hang out, kitchens and things like that. Maybe they need to take a hub in an innovation network and place the person with a pulsetaker in an expert network—to get that knowledge indirectly communicated to a lot of people."

The work of translating Stephenson's insights onto a new floor plan is being done in a small conference room—a war room—on the second floor of Steelcase headquarters. The group consists of a few key people from different parts of the firm, such as human resources, design, technology, and space-planning research. The walls of the room are cluttered with diagrams and pictures and calculations and huge, blownup versions of Stephenson's X rays. Team members stress that what they are doing is experimental. They don't know yet how directly they want to translate findings from the communications networks to office plans. After all, you don't want to have to redo the entire office every time someone leaves or joins the company. But it's clear that there are some very simple principles from the study of public characters which ought to drive the design process. "You want to place hubs at the center," Joyce Bromberg, the director of space planning, says. "These are the ones other people go to in order to get information. Give them an environment that allows access. But there are also going to be times that they need to have control—so give them a place where they can get away. Gatekeepers represent the fit between groups. They transmit ideas. They are brokers, so you might want to put them at the perimeter, and give them front porches"—areas adjoining the workspace where you might put little tables and chairs. "Maybe they could have swinging doors with white boards, to better transmit information. As for pulsetakers, they are the roamers. Rather than give them one fixed work location, you might give them a series of touchdown spots—where you want them to stop and talk. You want to enable their meandering."

One of the other team members was a tall, thoughtful man named Frank Graziano. He had a series of pencil drawings—with circles representing workstations of all the people whose minds, as he put it, he wanted to make "explicit." He said that he had done the plan the night before. "I think we can thread innovation through the floor," he went on, and with a pen drew a red line that wound its way through the maze of desks. It was his Hudson Street.

■ 6

"The Death and Life of Great American Cities" was a controversial book, largely because there was always a whiff of paternalism in Jacobs's vision of what city life ought to be. Chelsea—the neighborhood directly to the north of her beloved West Village—had "mixtures and types of buildings and densities of dwelling units per acre . . . almost identical with those of Greenwich Village," she noted. But its long-predicted renaissance would never happen, she maintained, because of the "barriers of long, self-isolating blocks." She hated Chatham Village, a planned "garden city" development in Pittsburgh. It was a picturesque green enclave, but it suffered, in Jacobs's analysis, from a lack of sidewalk life. She wasn't concerned that some people might not want an active street life in their neighborhood; that what she saw as the "self-isolating blocks" of Chelsea others would see as a welcome respite from the bustle of the city, or that Chatham Village would appeal to some people precisely because one did not encounter on its sidewalks a "solid wave of conversation and animation." Jacobs felt that city dwellers belonged in environments like the West Village, whether they realized it or not.

The new workplace designers are making the same calculation, of course. The point of the new offices is to compel us to behave and socialize in ways that we otherwise would not—to overcome our initial inclination to be office suburbanites. But, in all the studies of the new workplaces, the reservations that employees have about a more social environment tend to diminish once they try it. Human behavior, after all, is shaped by context, but how it is shaped—and whether we'll be happy with the result—we can understand only with experience. Jane Jacobs knew the virtues of the West Village because she lived there. What she couldn't know was that her ideas about community would ultimately make more sense in the workplace. From time to time, social critics have bemoaned the falling rates of community participation in American life, but they have made the same mistake. The reason Americans are content to bowl alone (or, for that matter, not bowl at all) is that, increasingly, they receive all the social support they need—all the serendipitous interactions that serve to make them happy and productive—from nine to five.

7

Six Degrees of Lois Weisberg

She's a Grandmother, She Lives in a Big House in Chicago,

and You've Never Heard of Her. Does She Run the World?

Malcolm Gladwell

1

Everyone who knows Lois Weisberg has a story about meeting Lois Weisberg, and although she has done thousands of things in her life and met thousands of people, all the stories are pretty much the same. Lois (everyone calls her Lois) is invariably smoking a cigarette and drinking one of her dozen or so daily cups of coffee. She will have been up until two or three the previous morning, and up again at seven or seven-thirty, because she hardly seems to sleep. In some accounts—particularly if the meeting took place in the winter—she'll be wearing her white, fur-topped Dr. Zhivago boots with gold tights; but she may have on her platform tennis shoes, or the leather jacket with the little studs on it, or maybe an outrageous piece of costume jewelry, and, always, those huge, rhinestone-studded glasses that make her big eyes look positively enormous. "I have no idea why I asked you to come here, I have no job for you," Lois told Wendy Willrich when Willrich went to Lois's office in downtown Chicago a few years ago for an interview. But by the end of the interview Lois did have a job for her, because for Lois meeting someone is never just about meeting someone. If she likes you, she wants to recruit you into one of her grand schemes—to sweep you up into her world. A while back, Lois called up Helen Doria, who was then working for someone on Chicago's city council, and said, "I don't have a job for you. Well, I might have a little job. I need someone to come over and help me clean up my office." By this, she meant that she had a big job for Helen but just didn't know what it was yet. Helen came, and, sure enough, Lois got her a big job.

Cindy Mitchell first met Lois twenty-three years ago, when she bundled up her baby and ran outside into one of those frigid Chicago winter mornings because some people from the Chicago Park District were about to cart away a beautiful sculpture of Carl von Linné from the park across the street. Lois happened to be driving by at the time, and, seeing all the commotion, she slammed on her brakes, charged out of her car—all five feet of her—and began asking Cindy questions, rat-a-tat-tat: "Who are you? What's going on here? Why do you care?" By the next morning, Lois had persuaded two *Chicago Tribune* reporters to interview Cindy and turn the whole incident into a cause célèbre, and she had recruited Cindy to join an organization she'd just started called Friends of the Parks, and then, when she found out that Cindy was a young mother at home who was too new in town to have many friends, she told her, "I've found a friend for you. Her name is Helen, and she has a little boy your kid's age, and you will meet her next week and the two of you will be best friends." That's exactly what happened, and, what's more, Cindy went on to spend ten years as president of Friends of the Park. "Almost everything that I do today and 80–90 percent of my friends came about because of her, because of that one little chance meeting," Cindy says. "That's a scary thing. Try to imagine what would have happened if she had come by five minutes earlier."

It could be argued, of course, that even if Cindy hadn't met Lois on the street twenty-three years ago she would have met her somewhere else, maybe a year later or two years later or ten years later, or, at least, she would have met someone who knew Lois or would have met someone who knew someone who knew Lois, since Lois Weisberg is connected, by a very short chain, to nearly everyone. Weisberg is now the commissioner of cultural affairs for the City of Chicago. But in the course of her seventy-three years she has hung out with actors and musicians and doctors and lawyers and politicians and activists and environmentalists, and once, on a whim, she opened a second hand-jewelry store named for her grand-daughter Becky Fyffe, and every step of the way Lois has made friends and recruited people, and a great many of those people have stayed with her to this day. "When we were doing the jazz festival, it turned out— surprise, surprise—that she was buddies with Dizzy Gillespie," one of her friends recalls. "This is a woman who cannot carry a tune. She has no sense of rhythm. One night Tony Bennett was in town, and so we hang out with Tony Bennett, hearing about the old days with him and Lois."

Once, in the mid-1950s, on a whim, Lois took the train to New York to attend the World Science Fiction Convention and there she met a young writer by the name of Arthur C. Clarke. Clarke took a shine to Lois, and next time he was in Chicago he called her up. "He was at a pay phone," Lois recalls. "He said, 'Is there anyone in Chicago I should meet?' I told him to come over to my house." Lois has a throaty voice, baked hard by half a century of nicotine, and she pauses between sentences to give her-self the opportunity for a quick puff. Even when she's not smoking, she pauses anyway, as if to keep in practice. "I called Bob Hughes, one of the people who wrote for my paper." Pause. "I said, 'Do you know anyone in Chicago interested in talking to Arthur Clarke?' He said, 'Yeah, Isaac Asimov is in town. And this guy Robert, Robert. . . . Robert Heinlein.' So they all came over and sat in my study." Pause. "Then they called over to me and they said, 'Lois'—I can't remember the word they used. They had some word for me. It was something about how I was the kind of person who brings people together."

This is in some ways the archetypal Lois Weisberg story. First, she reaches out to somebody—somebody outside her world. (At the time, she was running a drama troupe, whereas Arthur C. Clarke wrote science fiction.) Equally important, that person responds to her. Then there's the fact that when Arthur Clarke came to Chicago and wanted to meet some-one Lois came up with Isaac Asimov. She says it was a fluke that Asimov was in town. But if it hadn't been Asimov it would have been someone else. Lois ran a salon out of her house on the North Side in the late 1950s, and one of the things that people remember about it is that it was always, effortlessly, integrated. Without that salon, blacks would still have social-ized with whites on the North Side—though it was rare back then, it happened. But it didn't happen by accident: it happened because a certain kind of person made it happen. That's what Asimov and Clarke meant when they said that Lois has this thing—whatever it is—that brings peo-ple together.

■ 2

Lois is a type—a particularly rare and extraordinary type, but a type nonetheless. She's the type of person who seems to know everybody, and this type can be found in every walk of life. Someone I met at a wedding (actually, the wedding of the daughter of Lois's neighbors, the Newber-gers) told me that if I ever went to Massapequa I should look up a woman named Marsha, because Marsha was the type of person who knew every-body. In Cambridge, Massachusetts, the word is that a tailor named Char-lie Davidson knows everybody. In Houston, I'm told, there is an attorney named Harry Reasoner who knows everybody. There are probably Lois Weisbergs in Akron and Tucson and Paris and in some little town in the Yukon Territory, up by the Arctic Circle. We've all met someone like Lois Weisberg. Yet, although we all know a Lois Weisberg type, we don't know much about the Lois Weisberg type. Why is it, for example, that these few, select people seem to know everyone and the rest of us don't? And how important are the people who know everyone? This second question is critical, because once you begin even a cursory examination of the life of someone like Lois Weisberg you start to suspect that he or she may be far more important than we would ever have imagined—that the people who know everyone, in some oblique way, may actually run the world. I don't mean that they are the sort who head up the Fed or General Motors or Microsoft, but that, in a very down-to-earth, day-to-day way, they make the world work. They spread ideas and information. They connect varied and isolated parts of society. Helen Dorla says someone high up in the Chicago government told her that Lois is "the epicenter of the city administration," which is the right way to put it. Lois is far from being the most important or the most powerful person in Chicago. But if you connect all the dots that constitute the vast apparatus of government and influence and interest groups in the city of Chicago you'll end up coming back to Lois again and again. Lois is a connector.

Lois, it must be said, did not set out to know everyone. "She doesn't network for the sake of networking," says Gary Johnson, who was Lois's boss years ago, when she was executive director of the Chicago Council of Lawyers. "I just think she has the confidence that all the people in the world, whether she's met them or not, are in her Rolodex already, and that all she has to do is figure out how to reach them and she'll be able to connect with them."

Nor is Lois charismatic—at least, not in the way that we think of extroverts and public figures as being charismatic. She doesn't fill a room; eyes don't swivel toward her as she makes her entrance. Lois has frizzy blond hair, and when she's thinking—between her coffee and her cigarette—she kneads the hair on the top of her head, so that by the end of a particularly difficult meeting it will be standing almost straight up. "She's not like the image of the Washington society doyenne," Gary Johnson says. "You know, one of those people who identify you, take you to lunch, give you the treatment. Her social life is very different. When I bump into her and she says, 'Oh, we should catch up,' what she means is that someday I should go with her to her office, and we'd go down to the snack bar and buy a muffin and then sit in her office while she answered the phone. For a real treat, when I worked with her at the Council of Lawyers she would take me to the dining room in the Wieboldt's department store." Johnson is an old-school Chicago intellectual who works at a fancy law firm and has a corner office with one of those Midwestern views in which, if you look hard enough, you can almost see Nebraska, and the memory of those lunches at Wieboldt's seems to fill him with delight. "Now, you've got to understand that the Wieboldt's department store—which doesn't exist anymore—was a notch below Field's, where the suburban society ladies have their lunch, and it's also a notch below Carson's," he says. "There was a kind of room there where people who bring their own string bags to go shopping would have a quick lunch. This was her idea of a lunch out. We're not talking Pamela Harriman here."

In the mid-1980s, Lois quit a job she'd had for four years, as director of special events in the administration of Harold Washington, and somehow hooked up with a group of itinerant peddlers who ran the city's flea markets. "There was this lady who sold jewelry," Lois said. "She was a person out of Dickens. She was bedraggled. She had a houseful of cats. But she knew how to buy jewelry, and I wanted her to teach me. I met her whole circle of friends, all these old gay men who had antique stores. Once a week, we would go to the Salvation Army." Lois was arguably the most important civic activist in the city. Her husband was a judge. She lived in a huge house in one of Chicago's nicest neighborhoods. Yet somehow she managed to be plausible as a flea-market peddler to a bunch of flea-market peddlers, the same way she managed to be plausible as a music lover to a musician like Tony Bennett. It doesn't matter who she's with or what she's doing; she always manages to be in the thick of things. "There was a woman I knew—Sandra—who had a kid in school with my son Joseph," Lois told me. Lois has a habit of telling stories that appear to be tangential and digressive but, on reflection, turn out to be parables of a sort. "She helped all these Asians living uptown. One day, she came over here and said there was this young Chinese man who wanted to meet an American family and learn to speak English better and was willing to cook for his room and board. Well, I'm always eager to have a cook, and especially a Chinese cook, because my family loves Chinese food. They could eat it seven days a week. So Sandra brought this man over here. His name was Shi Young. He was a graduate student at the Art Institute of Chicago." Shi Young lived with Lois and her family for two years, and during that time Chicago was in the midst of political turmoil. Harold Washington, who would later become the first black mayor of the city, was attempting to unseat the remains of the Daley political machine, and Lois's house, naturally, was the site of late-night, top-secret strategy sessions for the pro-Washington reformers of Chicago's North Side. "We'd have all these important people here, and Shi Young would come down and listen," Lois recalls. "I didn't think anything of it." But Shi Young, as it turns out, was going back up to his room and writing up what he heard for the *China Youth Daily*, a newspaper with a circulation in the tens of millions. Somehow, in the improbable way that the world works, a portal was opened up, connecting Chicago's North Side reform politics and the readers of the *China Youth Daily*, and that link was Lois's living room. You could argue that this was just a fluke—just as it was a fluke that Isaac Asimov was in town and that Lois happened to be driving by when Cindy Mitchell came running out of her apartment. But sooner or later all those flukes begin to form a pattern.

■ 3

In the late 1960s, a Harvard social psychologist named Stanley Milgram conducted an experiment in an effort to find an answer to what is known as the small-world problem, though it could also be called the Lois Weisberg problem. It is this: How are human beings connected? Do we belong to separate worlds, operating simultaneously but autonomously, so that the links between any two people, anywhere in the world, are few and distant? Or are we all bound up together in a grand, interlocking web? Milgram's idea was to test this question with a chain letter. For one experiment, he got the names of a hundred and sixty people, at random, who lived in Omaha, Nebraska, and he mailed each of them a packet. In the packet was the name and address of a stockbroker who worked in Boston and lived in Sharon, Massachusetts. Each person was instructed to write his name on a roster in the packet and send it on to a friend or acquaintance who he thought would get it closer to the stockbroker. The idea was that when the letters finally arrived at the stockbroker's house Milgram could look at the roster of names and establish how closely connected someone chosen at random from one part of the country was to another person chosen at random in another part. Milgram found that most of the letters reached the stockbroker in five or six steps. It is from this experiment that we got the concept of six degrees of separation.

That phrase is now so familiar that it is easy to lose sight of how surprising Milgram's finding was. Most of us don't have particularly diverse groups of friends. In one well-known study, two psychologists asked people living in the Dyckman public-housing project, in uptown Manhattan, about their closest friend in the project; almost 90 percent of the friends lived in the same building, and half lived on the same floor. In general, people chose friends of similar age and race. But if the friend lived down the hall, both age and race became a lot less important. Proximity overpowered similarity. Another study, involving students at the University of Utah, found that if you ask someone why he is friendly with someone else he'll say that it is because they share similar attitudes. But if you actually quiz the pairs of students on their attitudes you'll find out that this is an illusion, and that what friends really tend to have in common are activities. We're friends with the people we do things with, not necessarily with the people we resemble. We don't seek out friends; we simply associate with the people who occupy the same physical places that we do: People in Omaha are not, as a rule, friends with people who live in Sharon, Massachusetts. So how did the packets get halfway across the country in just five steps? "When I asked an intelligent friend of mine how many steps he thought it would take, he estimated that it would require 100 intermediate persons or more to move from Nebraska to Sharon," Milgram wrote. "Many people make somewhat similar estimates and are surprised to learn that only five intermediaries will—on the average—suffice. Somehow it does not accord with intuition."

The explanation is that in the six degrees of separation not all degrees are equal. When Milgram analyzed his experiments, for example, he found that many of the chains reaching to Sharon followed the same asymmetrical pattern. Twenty-four packets reached the stockbroker at his home, in Sharon, and sixteen of those were given to him by the same person, a clothing merchant whom Milgram calls Mr. Jacobs. The rest of the packets were sent to the stockbroker at his office, and of those the majority came through just two men, whom Milgram calls Mr. Brown and Mr. Jones. In all, half of the responses that got to the stockbroker were delivered to him by these three people. Think of it. Dozens of people, chosen at random from a large Midwestern city, sent out packets independently. Some went through college acquaintances. Some sent their packets to relatives. Some sent them to old workmates. Yet in the end, when all those idiosyncratic chains were completed, half of the packets passed through the hands of Jacobs, Jones, and Brown. Six degrees of separation doesn't simply mean that everyone is linked to everyone else in just six steps. It means that a very small number of people are linked to everyone else in a few steps, and the rest of us are linked to the world through those few.

There's an easy way to explore this idea. Suppose that you made a list of forty people whom you would call your circle of friends (not including family members or coworkers), and you worked backward from each person until you could identify who was ultimately responsible for setting in motion the series of connections which led to that friendship. I met my oldest friend, Bruce, for example, in first grade, so I'm the responsible party. That's easy. I met my college friend Nigel because he lived down the hall in the dormitory from Tom, whom I had met because in my freshman year he invited me to play touch football. Tom, then, is responsible for Nigel. Once you've made all the connections, you will find the same names coming up again and again. I met my friend Amy when she and her friend Katie came to a restaurant where I was having dinner. I know Katie because she is best friends with my friend Larissa, whom I know because I was told to look her up by a mutual friend, Mike A., whom I know because he went to school with another friend of mine, Mike H., who used to work at a political weekly with my friend Jacob. No Jacob, no Amy. Similarly, I met my friend Sarah S. at a birthday party a year ago because she was there with a writer named David, who was there at the invitation of his agent, Tina, whom I met through my friend Leslie, whom I know because her sister Nina is best friends with my friend Ann, whom I met through my old roommate Maura, who was my roommate because she had worked with a writer named Sarah L., who was a college friend of my friend Jacob. No Jacob, no Sarah S. In fact, when I go down my list of forty friends, thirty of them, in one way or another, lead back to Jacob. My social circle is really not a circle but an inverted pyramid. And the capstone of the pyramid is a single person, Jacob, who is responsible for an overwhelming majority of my relationships. Jacob's full name, incidentally, is Jacob Weisberg. He is Lois Weisberg's son.

This isn't to say, though, that Jacob is just like Lois. Jacob may be the capstone of my pyramid, but Lois is the capstone of lots and lots of people's pyramids, and that makes her social role different. In Milgram's experiment, Mr. Jacobs the clothing merchant was the person to go through to get to the stockbroker. Lois is the kind of person you would use to get to the stockbrokers of Sharon and also the cabaret singers of

Sharon and the barkeeps of Sharon and the guy who gave up a thriving career in orthodontics to open a small vegetarian falafel hut.

■ 4

There is another way to look at this question, and that's through the popular parlor game Six Degrees of Kevin Bacon. The idea behind the game is to try to link in fewer than six steps any actor or actress, through the movies they've been in, to the actor Kevin Bacon. For example, O. J. Simpson was in "Naked Gun" with Priscilla Presley, who was in "The Adventures of Ford Fairlane" with Gilbert Gottfried, who was in "Beverly Hills Cop II" with Paul Reiser, who was in "Diner" with Kevin Bacon. That's four steps. Mary Pickford was in "Screen Snapshots" with Clark Gable, who was in "Combat America" with Tony Romano, who, thirty-five years later, was in "Starting Over" with Bacon. That's three steps. What's funny about the game is that Bacon, although he is a fairly young actor, has already been in so many movies with so many people that there is almost no one to whom he can't be easily connected.

Recently, a computer scientist at the University of Virginia by the name of Brett Tjaden actually sat down and figured out what the average degree of connectedness is for the quarter million or so actors and actresses listed in the Internet Movie Database: he came up with 2.8312 steps. That sounds impressive, except that Tjaden then went back and performed an even more heroic calculation, figuring out what the average degree of connectedness was for everyone in the database. Bacon, it turns out, ranks only six hundred and sixty-eighth. Martin Sheen, by contrast, can be connected, on average, to every other actor, in 2.63681 steps, which puts him almost six hundred and fifty places higher than Bacon. Elliott Gould can be connected even more quickly, in 2.63601. Among the top fifteen are people like Robert Mitchum, Gene Hackman, Donald Sutherland, Rod Steiger, Shelley Winters, and Burgess Meredith.

Why is Kevin Bacon so far behind these actors? Recently, in the journal *Nature*, the mathematicians Duncan Watts and Steven Strogatz published a dazzling theoretical explanation of connectedness, but a simpler way to understand this question is to look at who Bacon is. Obviously, he is a lot younger than the people at the top of the list are and has made fewer movies. But that accounts for only some of the difference. A top-twenty person, like Burgess Meredith, made a hundred and fourteen movies in the course of his career. Gary Cooper, though, starred in about the same number of films and ranks only eight hundred and seventy-eighth, with a 2.85075 score. John Wayne made a hundred and eighty-three movies in his fifty-year career and still ranks only a hundred and sixteenth, at 2.7173. What sets someone like Meredith apart is his range. More than half of John Wayne's movies were Westerns, and that means he made the same kind of movie with the same kind of actors over and over again. Burgess Meredith, by contrast, was in great movies, like the Oscar-winning "Of Mice and Men" (1939), and in dreadful movies, like "Beware! The Blob" (1972). He was nominated for an Oscar for his role in "The Day of the Locust" and also made TV commercials for Skippy peanut butter. He was in four "Rocky" movies, and also played Don Learo in Godard's "King Lear." He was in schlocky made-for-TV movies, in B movies that pretty much went straight to video, and in pictures considered modern classics. He was in forty-two dramas, twenty-two comedies, eight adventure films, seven action films, five sci-fi films, five horror flicks, five Westerns, five documentaries, four crime movies, four thrillers, three war movies, three films noir, two children's films, two romances, two mysteries, one musical, and one animated film. Burgess Meredith was the kind of actor who was connected to everyone because he managed to move up and down and back and forth among all the different worlds and subcultures that the acting profession has to offer. When we say, then, that Lois Weisberg is the kind of person who "knows everyone," we mean it in precisely this way. It is not merely that she knows lots of people. It is that she belongs to lots of different worlds.

In the 1950s, Lois started her drama troupe in Chicago. The daughter of a prominent attorney, she was then in her twenties, living in one of the suburbs north of the city with two small children. In 1956, she decided to stage a festival to mark the centenary of George Bernard Shaw's birth. She hit up the reclusive billionaire John D. MacArthur for money. ("I go to the Pump Room for lunch. Booth One. There is a man, lurking around a pillar, with a cowboy hat and dirty, dusty boots. It's him.") She invited William Saroyan and Norman Thomas to speak on Shaw's legacy; she put on Shaw plays in theatres around the city; and she got written up in *life*. She then began putting out a newspaper devoted to Shaw, which mutated into an underground alternative weekly called the *Paper*. By then, Lois was living in a big house on Chicago's near North Side, and on Friday nights people from the *Paper* gathered there for editorial meetings. William Friedkin, who went on to direct "The French Connection" and "The Exorcist," was a regular, and so were the attorney Elmer Gertz (who won parole for Nathan Leopold) and some of the editors from *Playboy*, which was just up the street. People like Art Farmer and Thelonious Monk and Dizzy Gillespie and Lenny Bruce would stop by when they were in town. Bruce actually lived in Lois's house for a while. "My mother was hysterical about it, especially one day when she rang the doorbell and he answered in a bath towel," Lois told me. "We had a window on the porch, and he didn't have a key, so the window was always left open for him. There were a lot of rooms in that house, and a lot of people stayed there and I didn't know they were there." Pause. Puff. "I never could stand his jokes. I didn't really like his act. I couldn't stand all the words he was using."

Lois's first marriage—to a drugstore owner named Leonard Solomon—was breaking up around this time, so she took a job doing public relations for an injury rehabilitation institute. From there, she went to work for a public-interest law firm called B.P.I., and while she was at B.P.I. she became concerned about the fact that Chicago's parks were neglected and crumbling, so she gathered together a motley collection of nature lovers, historians, civic activists, and housewives and founded the lobbying group Friends of the Parks. Then she became alarmed on discovering that a commuter railroad that ran along the south shore of Lake Michigan—from South Bend to Chicago—was about to shut down, so she gathered together a motley collection of railroad enthusiasts and environmentalists and commuters and founded South Shore Recreation, thereby saving the railroad. Lois loved the railroad buffs. "They were all good friends of mine," she says. "They all wrote to me. They came from California. They came from everywhere. We had meetings. They were really interesting. I came this close"—and here she held her index finger half an inch above her thumb—"to becoming one of them." Instead, though, she became the executive director of the Chicago Council of Lawyers, a progressive bar association. Then she ran Congressman Sidney Yates's re-election campaign. Then her sister June introduced her to someone who got her the job with Mayor Washington. Then she had her flea-market period. Finally, she went to work for Mayor Daley as Chicago's commissioner of cultural affairs.

If you go through that history and keep count, the number of worlds that Lois has belonged to comes to eight: the actors, the writers, the doctors, the lawyers, the park lovers, the politicians, the railroad buffs, and the flea-market aficionados. When I asked Lois to make her own list, she added musicians and the visual artists and architects and hospitality-industry people whom she works with in her current job. But if you looked harder at Lois's life you could probably subdivide her experiences into fifteen or twenty worlds. She has the same ability to move among different subcultures and niches that the busiest actors do. Lois is to Chicago what Burgess Meredith is to the movies.

Lois was, in fact, a friend of Burgess Meredith. I learned this by accident, which is the way I learned about most of the strange celebrity details of Lois's life, since she doesn't tend to drop names. It was when I was with her at her house one night, a big, rambling affair just off the lakeshore, with room after room filled with odds and ends and old photographs and dusty furniture and weird bric-a-brac, such as a collection of four hundred antique egg cups. She was wearing blue jeans and a flowery-print top and she was smoking Carlton Menthol 100s and cooking pasta and holding forth to her son Joe on the subject of George Bernard Shaw, when she started talking about Burgess Meredith. "He was in Chicago in a play called 'Teahouse of the August Moon,' in 1956," she said, "and he came to see my production of 'Back to Methuselah,' and after the play he came up to me and said he was teaching acting classes, and asked would I come and talk to his class about Shaw. Well, I couldn't say no." Meredith liked Lois, and when she was running her alternative newspaper he would write letters and send in little doodles, and later she helped him raise money for a play he was doing called "Kicks and Company." It starred a woman named Nichelle Nichols, who lived at Lois's house for a while. "Nichelle was a marvellous singer and dancer," Lois said. "She was the lead. She was also the lady on the first . . ." Lois was doing so many things at once—chopping and stirring and smoking and eating and talking—that she couldn't remember the name of the show that made Nichols a star. "What's that space thing?" She looked toward Joe for help. He started laughing. "Star something," she said. " 'Star . . . Star Trek'! Nichelle was Lieutenant Uhura!"

■ 5

On a sunny morning not long ago, Lois went to a little café just off the Magnificent Mile, in downtown Chicago, to have breakfast with Mayor Daley. Lois drove there in a big black Mercury, a city car. Lois always drives big cars, and, because she is so short and the cars are so big, all that you can see when she drives by is the top of her frizzy blond head and the lighted ember of her cigarette. She was wearing a short skirt and a white vest and was carrying a white cloth shopping bag. Just what was in the bag was unclear, since Lois doesn't have a traditional relationship to the trappings of bureaucracy. Her office, for example, does not have a desk in it, only a sofa and chairs and a coffee table. At meetings, she sits at the head of a conference table in the adjoining room, and, as often as not, has nothing in front of her except a lighter, a pack of Carltons, a cup of coffee, and an octagonal orange ceramic ashtray, which she moves a few inches forward or a few inches back when she's making an important point, or moves a few inches to the side when she is laughing at something really funny and feels the need to put her head down on the table.

Breakfast was at one of the city's tourist centers. The mayor was there in a blue suit, and he had two city officials by his side and a very serious and thoughtful expression on his face. Next to him was a Chicago developer named Al Friedman, a tall and slender and very handsome man who is the chairman of the Commission on Chicago Landmarks. Lois sat across from them, and they all drank coffee and ate muffins and batted ideas back and forth in the way that people do when they know each other very well. It was a "power breakfast," although if you went around the table you'd find that the word "power" meant something very different to everyone there. Al Friedman is a rich developer. The mayor, of course, is the administrative leader of one of the largest cities in the country. When we talk about power, this is usually what we're talking about: money and authority. But there is a third kind of power as well—the kind Lois has—which is a little less straightforward. It's social power.

At the end of the 1980s, for example, the City of Chicago razed an entire block in the heart of downtown and then sold it to a developer. But before he could build on it the real-estate market crashed. The lot was an eyesore. The mayor asked for ideas about what to do with it. Lois suggested that they cover the block with tents. Then she heard that Keith Haring had come to Chicago in 1989 and worked with Chicago high-school students to create a giant five-hundred-foot-long mural. Lois loved the mural. She began to think. She'd long had a problem with the federal money that Chicago got every year to pay for summer jobs for disadvantaged kids. She didn't think it helped any kid to be put to work picking up garbage. So why not pay the kids to do arts projects like the Haring mural, and put the whole program in the tents? She called the program Gallery 37, after the number of the block. She enlisted the help of the mayor's wife, Maggie Daley, whose energy and clout were essential in order to make the program a success. Lois hired artists to teach the kids. She realized, though, that the federal money was available only for poor kids, and, Lois says, "I don't believe poor kids can advance in any way by being lumped together with other poor kids." So Lois raised money privately to bring in middle-income kids, to mix with the poor kids and be put in the tents with the artists. She started small, with two hundred and sixty "apprentices" the first year, 1990. This year, there were more than three thousand. The kids study sculpture, painting, drawing, poetry, theatre, graphic design, dance, textile design, jewelry-making, and music. Lois opened a store downtown, where students' works of art are sold. She has since bought two buildings to house the project full time. She got the Parks Department to run Gallery 37 in neighborhoods around the city, and the Board of Education to let them run it as an after-school program in public high schools. It has been copied all around the world. Last year, it was given the Innovations in American Government Award by the Ford Foundation and the Harvard School of Government.

Gallery 37 is at once a jobs program, an arts program, a real-estate fix, a schools program, and a parks program. It involves federal money and city money and private money, stores and buildings and tents, Maggie Daley and Keith Haring, poor kids and middle-class kids. It is everything, all at once—a jumble of ideas and people and places which Lois somehow managed to make sense of. The ability to assemble all these disparate parts is, as should be obvious, a completely different kind of power from the sort held by the mayor and Al Friedman. The mayor has key allies on the city council or in the statehouse. Al Friedman can do what he does because, no doubt, he has a banker who believes in him, or maybe a lawyer whom he trusts to negotiate the twists and turns of the zoning process. Their influence is based on close relationships. But when Lois calls someone to help her put together one of her projects, chances are she's not calling someone she knows particularly well. Her influence suggests something a little surprising—that there is also power in relationships that are not close at all.

■ 6

The sociologist Mark Granovetter examined this question in his classic 1974 book "Getting a Job." Granovetter interviewed several hundred professional and technical workers from the Boston suburb of Newton, asking them in detail about their employment history. He found that almost 56 percent of those he talked to had found their jobs through a personal connection, about 20 percent had used formal means (advertisements, headhunters), and another 20 percent had applied directly. This much is not surprising: the best way to get in the door is through a personal contact. But the majority of those personal connections, Granovetter found, did not involve close friends. They were what he called "weak ties." Of those who used a contact to find a job, for example, only 16.7 percent saw that contact "often," as they would have if the contact had been a good friend; 55.6 percent saw their contact only "occasionally"; and 27.8 percent saw the contact "rarely." People were getting their jobs not through their friends but through acquaintances.

Granovetter argues that when it comes to finding out about new jobs—or, for that matter, gaining new information, or looking for new ideas—weak ties tend to be more important than strong ties. Your friends, after all, occupy the same world that you do. They work with you, or live near you, and go to the same churches, schools, or parties. How much, then, do they know that you don't know? Mere acquaintances, on the other hand, are much more likely to know something that you don't. To capture this apparent paradox, Granovetter coined a marvellous phrase: "the strength of weak ties." The most important people in your life are, in certain critical realms, the people who aren't closest to you, and the more people you know who aren't close to you the stronger your position becomes.

Granovetter then looked at what he called "chain lengths"—that is, the number of people who had to pass along the news about your job before it got to you. A chain length of zero means that you learned about your job from the person offering it. A chain length of one means that you heard about the job from someone who had heard about the job from the employer. The people who got their jobs from a zero chain were the most satisfied, made the most money, and were unemployed for the shortest amount of time between jobs. People with a chain of one stood second in the amount of money they made, in their satisfaction with their jobs, and in the speed with which they got their jobs. People with a chain of two stood third in all three categories, and so on. If you know someone who knows someone who knows someone who has lots of acquaintances, in other words, you have a leg up. If you know someone who knows someone who has lots of acquaintances, your chances are that much better. But if you know someone who has lots of acquaintances—if you know someone like Lois—you are still more fortunate, because suddenly you are just one step away from musicians and actors and doctors and lawyers and park lovers and politicians and railroad buffs and flea-market aficionados and all the other weak ties that make Lois so strong.

This sounds like a reformulation of the old saw that it's not what you know, it's who you know. It's much more radical than that, though. The old idea was that people got ahead by being friends with rich and powerful people—which is true, in a limited way, but as a practical lesson in how the world works is all but useless. You can expect that Bill Gates's godson is going to get into Harvard and have a fabulous job waiting for him when he gets out. And, of course, if you play poker with the mayor and Al Friedman, it is going to be a little easier to get ahead in Chicago. But how many godsons can Bill Gates have? And how many people can fit around a poker table? This is why affirmative action seems pointless to so many people: It appears to promise something—entry to the old-boy network—that it can't possibly deliver. The old-boy network is always going to be just for the old boys.

Granovetter, by contrast, argues that what matters in getting ahead is not the quality of your relationships but the quantity—not how close you are to those you know but, paradoxically, how many people you know whom you aren't particularly close to. What he's saying is that the key person at that breakfast in downtown Chicago is not the mayor or Al Friedman but Lois Weisberg, because Lois is the kind of person who it really is possible for most of us to know. If you think about the world in this way, the whole project of affirmative action suddenly starts to make a lot more sense. Minority-admissions programs work not because they give black students access to the same superior educational resources as white students, or access to the same rich cultural environment as white students, or any other formal or grandiose vision of engineered equality. They work by giving black students access to the same white students as white students—by allowing them to make acquaintances outside their own social world and so shortening the chain lengths between them and the best jobs.

This idea should also change the way we think about helping the poor. When we're faced with an eighteen-year-old high-school dropout whose only career option is making five dollars and fifty cents an hour in front of the deep fryer at Burger King, we usually talk about the importance of rebuilding inner-city communities, attracting new jobs to depressed areas, and reinvesting in neglected neighborhoods. We want to give that kid the option of another, better-paying job, right down the street. But does that really solve his problem? Surely what that eighteen-year-old really needs is not another marginal inducement to stay in his neighborhood but a way to get out of his neighborhood altogether. He needs a school system that provides him with the skills to compete for jobs with middle-class kids. He needs a mass-transit system to take him to the suburbs, where the real employment opportunities are. And, most of all, he needs to know someone who knows someone who knows where all those good jobs are. If the world really is held together by people like Lois Weisberg, in other words, how poor you are can be defined quite simply as how far you have to go to get to someone like her. Wendy Willrich and Helen Doria and all the countless other people in Lois's circle needed to make only one phone call. They are well-off. The dropout wouldn't even know where to start. That's why he's poor. Poverty is not deprivation. It is isolation.

■ 7

I once met a man named Roger Horchow. If you ever go to Dallas and ask around about who is the kind of person who might know everyone, chances are you will be given his name. Roger is slender and composed. He talks slowly, with a slight Texas drawl. He has a kind of wry, ironic charm that is utterly winning. If you sat next to him on a plane ride across the Atlantic, he would start talking as the plane taxied to the runway, you would be laughing by the time the seat-belt sign was turned off, and when you landed at the other end you'd wonder where the time had gone.

I met Roger through his daughter Sally, whose sister Lizzie went to high school in Dallas with my friend Sara M., whom I know because she used to work with Jacob Weisberg. (No Jacob, no Roger.) Roger spent at least part of his childhood in Ohio, which is where Lois's second husband, Bernie Weisberg, grew up, so I asked Roger if he knew Bernie. It would have been a little too apt if he did—that would have made it all something out of "The X-Files"—but instead of just answering, "Sorry, I don't," which is what most of us would have done, he paused for a long time, as if to flip through the "W"s in his head, and then said, "No, but I'm sure if I made two phone calls . . ."

Roger has a very good memory for names. One time, he says, some-one was trying to talk him into investing his money in a business venture in Spain, and when he asked the names of the other investors he recog-nized one of them as the same man with whom one of his ex-girlfriends had had a fling during her junior year abroad, fifty years before. Roger sends people cards on their birthdays: he has a computerized Rolodex with sixteen hundred names on it. When I met him, I became convicted that these techniques were central to the fact that he knew everyone—that knowing everyone was a kind of skill. Horchow is the founder of the Horchow Collection, the first high-end mail-order catalog, and I kept asking him how all the connections in his life had helped him in the business world, because I thought that this particular skill had to have been cultivated for a reason. But the question seemed to puzzle him. He didn't think of his people collection as a business strategy, or even as something deliberate. He just thought of it as something he did—as who he was. One time, Horchow said, a close friend from childhood suddenly resurfaced. "He saw my catalog and knew it had to be me, and when he was out here he showed up on my doorstep. I hadn't seen him since I was seven. We had zero in common. It was wonderful." The juxtaposition of those last two sentences was not ironic; he meant it.

In the book "The Language Instinct," the psychologist Steven Pinker argues against the idea that language is a cultural artifact—something that we learn "the way we learn to tell time." Rather, he says, it is innate. Language develops "spontaneously," he writes, "without conscious effort or formal instruction," and "is deployed without awareness of its underlying logic. . . . People know how to talk in more or less the sense that spiders know how to spin webs." The secret to Roger Horchow and Lois Weisberg is, I think, that they have a kind of social equivalent of that instinct—an innate and spontaneous and entirely involuntary affinity for people. They know everyone because—in some deep and less than conscious way—they can't help it.

■ 8

Once, in the very early 1960s, after Lois had broken up with her first husband, she went to a party for Ralph Ellison, who was then teaching at the University of Chicago. There she spotted a young lawyer from the South Side named Bernie Weisberg. Lois liked him. He didn't notice her, though, so she decided to write a profile of him for the *Hyde Park Herald*. It ran with a huge headline. Bernie still didn't call. "I had to figure out how I was going to get to meet him again, so I remembered that he was standing in line at the reception with Ralph Ellison," Lois says. "So I called up Ralph Ellison"—whom she had never met—"and said, 'It's so wonderful that you are in Chicago. You really should meet some people on the North Side. Would it be O.K. if I have a party for you?" He said yes, and Lois sent out a hundred invitations, including one to Bernie. He came. He saw Dizzy Gillespie in the kitchen and Ralph Ellison in the living room. He was impressed. He asked Lois to go with him to see Lenny Bruce. Lois was mortified; she didn't want this nice Jewish lawyer from the South Side to know that she knew Lenny Bruce, who was, after all, a drug addict. "I couldn't get out of it," she said. "They sat us down at a table right at the front, and Lenny keeps coming over to the edge of the stage and saying"—here Lois dropped her voice down very low—" 'Hello, Lois. I was sitting there like this." Lois put her hands on either side of her face. "Finally I said to Bernie, 'There are some things I should tell you about. Lenny Bruce is a friend of mine. He's staying at my house. The second thing is I'm defending a murderer.' " (But that's another story.) Lois and Bernie were married a year later.

The lesson of this story isn't obvious until you diagram it culturally: Lois got to Bernie through her connections with Ralph Ellison and Lenny Bruce, one of whom she didn't know (although later, naturally, they became great friends) and one of whom she was afraid to say that she knew, and neither of whom, it is safe to speculate, had ever really been connected with each other before. It seems like an absurdly roundabout way to meet someone. Here was a thirtyish liberal Jewish intellectual from the North Side of Chicago trying to meet a thirtyish liberal Jewish intellectual from the South Side of Chicago, and to get there she charted a cross-cultural social course through a black literary lion and an avant-garde standup comic. Yet that's a roundabout journey only if you perceive the worlds of Lenny Bruce and Ralph Ellison and Bernie Weisberg to be impossibly isolated. If you don't—if, like Lois, you see them all as three points of an equilateral triangle—then it makes perfect sense. The social instinct makes everyone seem like part of a whole, and there is something very appealing about this, because it means that people like Lois aren't bound by the same categories and partitions that defeat the rest of us. This is what the power of the people who know everyone comes down to in the end. It is not—as much as we would like to believe otherwise—something rich and complex, some potent mixture of ambition and energy and smarts and vision and insecurity. It's much simpler than that. It's the same lesson they teach in Sunday school. Lois knows lots of people because she likes lots of people. And all those people Lois knows and likes invariably like her, too, because there is nothing more irresistible to a human being than to be unqualifiedly liked by another.

Not long ago, Lois took me to a reception at the Museum of Contemporary Art, in Chicago—a brand-new, Bauhaus-inspired building just north of the Loop. The gallery space was impossibly beautiful—cool, airy, high-ceilinged. The artist on display was Chuck Close. The crowd was sleek and well groomed. Black-clad young waiters carried pesto canapés and glasses of white wine. Lois seemed a bit lost. She can be a little shy sometimes, and at first she stayed on the fringes of the room, standing back, observing. Someone important came over to talk to her. She glanced up uncomfortably. I walked away for a moment to look at the show, and when I came back her little corner had become a crowd. There was her friend from the state legislature. A friend in the Chicago Park District. A friend from her neighborhood. A friend in the consulting business.

A friend from Gallery 37. A friend from the local business-development group. And on and on. They were of all ages and all colors, talking and laughing, swirling and turning in a loose circle, and in the middle, nearly hidden by the commotion, was Lois, clutching her white bag, tiny and large-eyed, at that moment the happiest person in the room.

8

Knowing What We Know

Supporting Knowledge Creation and Sharing

in Social Networks

Rob Cross, Andrew Parker, Laurence Prusak, and Stephen P. Borgatti

Crafting an Answer

"So the call came in late on Thursday afternoon and right away I wished I hadn't answered the phone. We had received a last-second opportunity to bid on a sizable piece of work that the Partner on the other end of the line really wanted to pursue. I had no clue how to even begin looking for relevant methodologies or case examples, so my first move was to tap into my network to find some relevant info and leads to other people or databases. And I relied pretty heavily on this group over the next couple of days. Seth was great for pointing me to other people and relevant information; Paul provided ideas on the technical content of the project, while Jeff really helped in showing me how to frame the client's issues in ways that we could sell. He also helped navigate and get buy-in from the client given his knowledge of their operations and politics. . . . I mean the whole game is just being the person that can get the client what they need with [the firm's] resources behind you. This almost always seems to mean knowing who knows what and figuring out a way to bring them to bear on your client's issue."

—Anonymous Interviewee

The way in which this manager relied on his network to obtain information and knowledge critical to the success of an important project is common and likely resonates with your own experience. Usually when we think of where people turn for information or knowledge we think of databases, the Web, intranets and portals or other, more traditional, repositories such as file cabinets or policy and procedure manuals. However, a significant component of a person's information environment consists of the relationships he or she can tap for various informational needs. For example, in summarizing a decade worth of studies, Tom Allen of Massachusetts Institute of Technology (MIT) found that engineers and scientists were roughly five times more likely to turn to a person for information than to an impersonal source such as a database or a file cabinet. In other settings, research has consistently shown that who you know has a significant impact on what you come to know, as relationships are critical for obtaining information, solving problems, and learning how to do your work.

Particularly in knowledge-intensive work, creating an informational environment that helps employees solve increasingly complex and often ambiguous problems holds significant performance implications. Frequently such efforts entail knowledge-management initiatives focusing on the capture and sharing of codified knowledge and reusable work products. To be sure, these so-called knowledge bases hold pragmatic benefits. They bridge boundaries of time and space, allow for potential reuse of tools or work products employed successfully in other areas of an organization, and provide a means of reducing organizational "forgetting" as a function of employee turnover. However, such initiatives often undervalue crucial knowledge held by employees and the web of relationships that help dynamically solve problems and create new knowledge.

As we move further into an economy where collaboration and innovation are increasingly central to organizational effectiveness, we must pay more attention to the sets of relationships that people rely on to accomplish their work. Certainly we can expect emerging collaborative technologies to facilitate virtual work and skill-profiling systems to help with the location of relevant expertise. However, as was so poignantly demonstrated by reengineering, technology alone can only accomplish so much in the pursuit of business performance. Improving efficiency and effectiveness in knowledge-intensive work demands more than sophisticated technologies—it requires attending to the often idiosyncratic ways that people seek out knowledge and learn from and solve problems with other people in organizations.

With this in mind, we initiated a research program to determine means of improving employees' ability to create and share knowledge in important social networks. In the first phase of our research, we assessed the characteristics of relationships that 40 managers relied on for learning and knowledge sharing in important projects. In the second phase, we systematically employed social network analysis to map these dimensions of relationships among strategically important networks of people in various organizations. Working with a consortium of Fortune 500 companies and government organizations, we developed empirical support for relational characteristics that facilitate knowledge creation and sharing in social networks, as well as insight into social and technical interventions to facilitate knowledge flow in these networks.

■ Supporting Knowledge Creation and Sharing in Social Networks

In the first phase of our research we asked 40 managers to reflect on a recent project that was important to their careers and indicate where they obtained information critical to the project's success. As can be seen in figure 8.1, these managers overwhelmingly indicated (and supported with

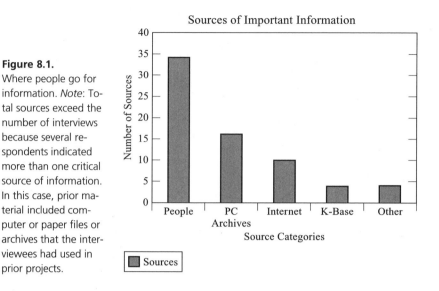

Figure 8.1.
Where people go for information. *Note*: Total sources exceed the number of interviews because several respondents indicated more than one critical source of information. In this case, prior material included computer or paper files or archives that the interviewees had used in prior projects.

Sources of Important Information

vivid stories) that they received this information from other people far more frequently than impersonal sources such as their personal computer archives, the Internet, or the organization's knowledge-management database. And we found this in an organization that most industry analysts heralded as a knowledge-management exemplar because of its investment in technology. This is not to say that the firm's leading-edge technical platform and organizational practices for capturing, screening, and archiving knowledge were not helpful. It is just to point out that "impersonal" information sources were primarily leveraged only after the managers had been unsuccessful in obtaining relevant knowledge from colleagues (or when directed to a point in the database by a colleague).

We also asked the managers to identify the people most important to them in terms of information or knowledge acquired for that project and had them carefully describe these relationships. Four features emerged that distinguished effective from ineffective relationships: (1) knowing what another person knows and thus when to turn to them; (2) being able to gain timely access to that person; (3) willingness of the person sought out to engage in problem solving rather than to dump information; and (4) a degree of safety in the relationship that promoted learning and creativity. An in-depth review of these dimensions is beyond our scope here; however, a summary of these relational features and representative quotes can be found in table 8.1.

The managers we interviewed indicated that these four dimensions were key characteristics of relationships that were effective for acquiring information, solving problems, or learning. In contrast, they also re-

Table 8.1
Relational Qualities that Promote Effective Knowledge Sharing

Relational Dimensions	Impact on Knowledge Seeking	Representative Quote
Knowledge	Knowing what someone else knows (even if we are initially inaccurate and calibrate over time) is a precursor to seeking out a specific person when we are faced with a problem or opportunity. For other people to be options we must have at least some perception of their expertise.	"At [Company X] we had access to background information and you know lots of case studies and approaches that were really well written up. I had no experience though of actually applying this approach on an engagement. So what was specifically useful to me was to talk with Terry, who I knew had done several of these engagements. He helped me work some of the content in the database into a workable approach. I was lucky I knew him and could leverage some of his experience . . ."
Access	However, knowing what someone else knows is only useful if one can get access to their thinking in a sufficiently timely fashion. Access is heavily influenced by the closeness of one's relationship as well as physical proximity, organizational design, and collaborative technology.	"I have gotten less frustrated the more I have worked with him because I know how to get ahold of him. It took me a while to figure out that he was a phone guy and not an e-mail guy. And I have also learned how to ask him for help and what I can expect. It was important to learn what I could rely on him for and how to get his attention to make the relationship, which was initially frustrating, an important one for me . . ."
Engagement	People who are helpful in learning interactions actively think with the seeker and engage in problem solving. Rather than dump information, these people first understand the problem *as experienced by the seeker* and then shape their knowledge to the problem at hand.	"Some people will give you their opinion without trying to either understand what your objectives are or understand where you are coming from or be very closed in their answer to you. [She] is the sort of person who first makes sure she understands what the issue is. I have been around people who give you a quick spiel because they think they are smart and that by throwing some framework or angle up they can quickly wow you and get out of the hard work of solving a problem. [She], for all her other responsibilities and stature within the firm, is not like that."
Safety	Finally, those relationships that are safe are often most effective for learning purposes. Being able to admit a lack of knowledge or to diverge in a conversation often results in creativity and learning.	"[He] is always looking for the positive spin on something. I mean, even if he thinks that is garbage and if he really thought that, he would make this known but in a positive way. So he might say, 'Well I think we might be a little off track on that and her's why' and then say why and of course there is learning that comes from that."

counted numerous times when learning or knowledge sharing did not happen because of one of the above dimensions not existing in the relationship (e.g., someone knew what they needed to know but did not make himself or herself accessible). Further, a separate quantitative study demonstrated that these dimensions consistently predict whom people seek out for informational purposes, even after controlling for such features as education or age similarity, physical proximity, time in an organization, and formal hierarchical position. With the importance of these four relational characteristics established, the second step of our research was to use social network analysis to map information flow, as well as these relational characteristics, among strategically important groups to improve knowledge creation and sharing.

■ Social Network Analysis

Social network analysis (SNA) provides a rich and systematic means of assessing informal networks by mapping and analyzing relationships among people, teams, departments, or even entire organizations. Though managers are often adamant that they know their organization, studies are showing that they have different levels of accuracy in understanding the networks around them. By virtue of their position in the hierarchy, managers are frequently far removed from the day-to-day work interactions that generate an organization's informal structure and so may have a very inaccurate understanding of the actual patterns of relationships. And the potential for inaccurate perceptions is only increased by our transition into a world of virtual work and telecommuting, where employees are engaged in work relationships increasingly invisible to superiors. Social network analysis can provide an X ray of the way in which work is or is not occurring in these informal networks.

Mapping Information Flow among Executives

We conducted a social network analysis of executives in the exploration and production division of a large petroleum organization. This group was in the midst of implementing a distributed technology to help transfer knowledge across drilling initiatives and was also interested in assessing their ability as a group to create and share knowledge. As a result, we were asked to conduct a social network analysis of information flow among the top 20 executives within the Exploration and Production Division. As can be seen in figure 8.2, this analysis revealed a striking contrast between the group's formal and informal structures.

Three important points quickly emerged for this group in relation to sharing information and effectively leveraging their collective expertise. First, the social network analysis identified midlevel managers who were

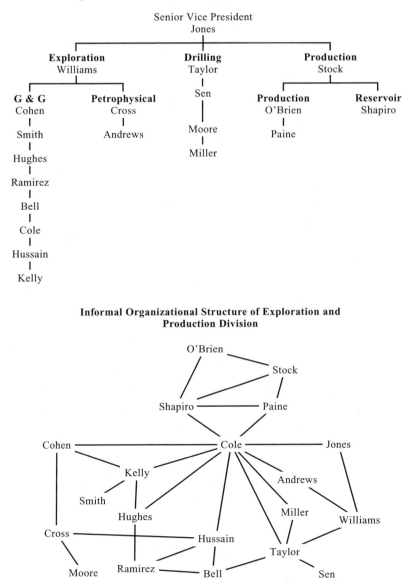

Formal Organizational Structure of Exploration and Production Division

Senior Vice President
Jones

Exploration — Williams
Drilling — Taylor
Production — Stock

G & G — Cohen
Petrophysical — Cross
Sen
Production — O'Brien
Reservoir — Shapiro

Smith
Andrews
Moore
Paine

Hughes
Miller

Ramirez

Bell

Cole

Hussain

Kelly

Informal Organizational Structure of Exploration and Production Division

O'Brien

Stock

Shapiro — Paine

Cohen — Cole — Jones

Kelly

Andrews

Smith

Hughes

Miller

Williams

Cross

Hussain

Taylor

Moore Ramirez — Bell Sen

Figure 8.2.
Formal versus informal structure in a petroleum organization. *Note*: Names have been disguised at the request of the company.

critical in terms of information flow within the group. A particular surprise came from the very central role that Cole played in terms of both overall information flow within the group and his being the only point of contact between members of the production division and the rest of the network. A facilitated session with this executive team revealed that over time Cole's reputation for expertise and responsiveness had resulted in his becoming a critical source for all sorts of information. Through no fault of his own, the number of informational requests he received and the number of projects he was involved in had grown excessive, which not only caused him stress but also frequently slowed the group as a whole, because Cole had become a bottleneck.

The social network analysis also revealed the extent to which the entire network was disproportionately reliant on Cole. If he were hired away, the efficiency of this group as a whole would be significantly impacted as people in the informal network reestablished important informational relationships. Of course, people would find ways to reconnect to obtain necessary information. However, the social network diagram made it very clear that if Cole left, the company would lose both his valuable knowledge *and* the relationships he had established that in many ways were holding the network together. As a result, a central intervention that came from this analysis was to reallocate many of the informational requests coming to Cole to other members in the group. Simply categorizing various informational requests that Cole received and then allocating ownership of these informational or decision domains to other executives served to both unburden Cole and make the overall network more responsive and robust.

Just as important, the social network analysis helped to identify highly peripheral people who essentially represented untapped expertise and thus underutilized resources for the group. In particular, it became apparent that many of the senior people had become too removed from the day-to-day operations of this group. For example, figure 8.2 reveals that the most senior person (Jones) was one of the most peripheral in the informal network. This is a common finding. As people move higher within an organization, their work begins to entail more administrative tasks that make them both less accessible and less knowledgeable about the day-to-day work of their subordinates. However, in this case our debriefing session indicated that Jones had become too removed, and his lack of responsiveness frequently held the entire network back when important decisions needed to be made. In this case, the social network diagram helped to make what could have been a potentially difficult conversation with this executive nonconfrontational, and resulted in more of his time being committed back to the group.

Finally, the social network analysis demonstrated the extent to which the production division (the subgroup on the top of the diagram) had become separated from the overall network. Several months before this analysis, these people had been physically moved to a different floor in the building. Upon reviewing the network diagram, many of the executives realized that this physical separation had resulted in loss of a lot of the serendipitous meetings that occurred when they were co-located. In this case, the executives decided that they needed to introduce more structured meetings to compensate for this recent loss of serendipitous communication (and they also adopted an instant messaging system to promote communication).

Beyond Information Flow

In addition to mapping information flow, we also use social network analysis to assess the relational characteristics of *knowledge, access, engagement,* and *safety* among a group. Sometimes, if we have only mapped an information network and find that certain people are not as connected as they should be, it is difficult to tell what to do. Simply proposing more or better communication is the oldest consulting recommendation in the book—and no one today really needs more meetings. By analyzing the dimensions of relationships that precede or lead to effective knowledge sharing, we can offer more precise ways to improve a network's ability to create and share knowledge. For example, if it is discovered that the *knowledge* network is sparse, it might make sense to consider a skill-profiling system or new staffing practices—technical and social interventions designed to help a network know what it knows. In contrast, if the *access* network is sparse, then it might make sense to consider peer feedback or technical means of connecting distributed workers (e.g., video conferencing or instant messaging) to make sure that people within the network have access to each other in a timely fashion.

Throughout our research we have found organizations employing various practices to promote these relational dimensions in important networks. We have summarized some of these initiatives in figure 8.3, and now turn to specific case examples where we used social network analysis to assess these relational dimensions.

Initiatives Promoting Knowledge Sharing in Human Networks

Knowledge Dimension: Do We Know What We Know?
- British Telecommunication's global effort to expand product lines and services was hampered because all of its six industry sectors were acting as silos. Employees in one industry sector were not aware of the knowledge and expertise of employees in the other sectors. To overcome this

lack of awareness, they introduced virtual communities of practice that were connected through the Knowledge Interchange Network (KIN). This increased awareness of experts via the distributed technology and improved cross-sector collaboration.

- IBM Global Services, the management consulting division of IBM, has a strategic drive to ensure that the best expertise is brought to bear on client projects. To help employees better understand "who knows what" in this complex and distributed workforce, they have adopted Tacit Systems EKG profiling system. This technology actively mines e-mail (that the employees permit the system to assess) and distributed databases to categorize kinds of knowledge that are being requested/shared and by whom. Though limited to electronic communications, the system is then able to generate and make available a profile of an employee's expertise that others in the organization can then seek out as necessary.
- Recently the World Bank made a strategic decision to reposition itself away from being a lending organization to being a provider of knowledge and services (a "Knowledge Bank"). In order for its employees to meet the needs of its member organizations, it was necessary to increase awareness of the expertise throughout the organization. A critical step in this process has been to hold regular Knowledge Fairs, where people from each department and/or thematic group set up booths which inform others of their expertise. These events help also to increase people's awareness of the experience of employees throughout the bank.

Access Dimension: Can We Access What We Know in a Sufficiently Timely Fashion?
- Alcoa, the world's leading producer of aluminum, wanted to improve access between its senior executives. When designing their new headquarters they focused on open offices, family-style kitchens in the center of each floor, and plenty of open spaces. Previously, top executives would interact only with a couple of people in the elevator and those they had scheduled meetings with. Now, executives bump into each other more often and are more accessible for serendipitous conversations. This change in space has increased general accessibility and narrowed the gap between top executives and employees.
- Shearman & Sterling, a top New York law firm, wanted to make its attorneys more accessible to each other in order to use the full expertise of staff on client cases. They implemented Same Time, an instant messaging system, throughout the organization. This system quickly began to overcome barriers of physical distance that often precluded serendipitous interaction. It also allowed attorneys to send messages to each other while simultaneously being on conference calls with opposing counsel. The increased accessibility of their attorneys meant that the firm's human capital could be more effectively used.
- IBM Global Services has incorporated knowledge creation, sharing, and reuse measurements into performance metrics. Performance metrics and incentives, particularly at the executive rank, have driven collaborative behavior into the day-to-day work practices of executive networks. Further, knowledge sharing has been incorporated into personal business commit-

ments, which are required for certification and effect promotion decisions. This encourages employees at all levels to be collaborative with and accessible to each other.

Engagement Dimension: Do We Effectively Engage with Each Other in Problem Solving?

- Deep sea oil drilling is a very expensive business, with lost production for a day costing up to $250,000. To minimize costs, British Petroleum has initiated a peer assist program that brings experts together to brainstorm with project teams. The peer assist program allows experts with relevant knowledge and experience to collaborate with and advise teams initiating a drilling project (or facing an important milestone). Peer assists facilitate active engagement in problem solving among the most current and relevant expertise that this organization has at a given point in time.
- An important issue for Skandia is improving the probability and frequency of innovation. Skandia has "Future Centers," where employees can come together informally and discuss ideas about new products or ideas for the future of the organization. These brainstorming sessions can very often produce new ideas about products and directions for the organization.
- At Aventis, the pharmaceutical company formed with the merger of Rhone Poulenc Rorer and Hoechst Marion Russel, they employ the GET program (Global Experience Transfer) to facilitate engagement between the marketing and research and development organizations. Selected employees from the R&D function and the Commercial Operations functions of specific therapeutic units are paired and go through a rotation program in each functional unit (with each employee alternating in the mentoring role). This process facilitates engagement in problem solving by developing a shared context between the functions and the integrating social networks at a critical functional boundary.

Safety Dimension: How Do We Promote Safety in Relationships?

- Buckman Laboratories, a highly successful chemical company, aspires to support front-line workers with the knowledge they need to help the customer. At Buckman, they have introduced a code of ethics that explicitly states that every employee has the right to talk to any other employee. This code has helped build an atmosphere of trust and decreased barriers between hierarchical levels in the organization.
- Russell Reynolds Associates, one of the world's premier executive search firms, believes a large part of its success is derived from the extent to which its recruiters and researchers share knowledge about candidates and openings. In an attempt to counter knowledge-hoarding they have created a culture of openness, trust, and collaboration. In hiring, the company places a unique emphasis on demonstrated collaboration and trustworthiness. In orientation, all new hires engage in a 3–4 day New Associates Program that promotes cross-office collaboration. On an ongoing basis, weekly meetings within offices, monthly conference calls between the different offices, and as face-to-face meetings of action committees all serve to promote an environment of trust.
- An important issue for Johnson and Johnson is increasing knowledge

sharing throughout a highly decentralized organization that operates in over 50 countries. At Johnson and Johnson they have set up communities of practice around product areas. These communities have helped create a shared vocabulary around specific activities, a recognition of the knowledge of their peers, a higher degree of trust between employees, and communal effort on projects rather than many individuals pulling in separate directions.

Figure 8.3

Knowledge Dimension: Do We Know What We Know?

Other people can be useful to us in solving problems only if we have some awareness of their expertise. Even if we are wrong, our initial perception will determine whether and how we turn to them for information when we are faced with a new problem or opportunity. The managers we interviewed in the first phase of our research reported that people they turned to for information provided a critical extension to their own knowledge when the manager had at least a semi-accurate understanding of her or his contact's expertise. As a result, assessing this relational knowledge of "who knows what" at a network level provides insight into the potential for members of a network to be able to tap others with relevant expertise when faced with a new problem or opportunity.

Supporting New Product Development

We analyzed a network of immunologists in a Fortune 250 pharmaceutical company to determine "who knows what." By virtue of effectively integrating highly specialized knowledge in the drug development process, this group of people held the potential to provide strategic advantage to the organization. However, they also dealt with many impediments to effective collaboration in that they were dispersed across five geographic sites and four hierarchical levels and attempting to integrate very different kinds of expertise. One telling view of this network emerged when we mapped the *knowledge* relation to get a better understanding of who understood and valued other people's expertise in this group.

What we found was that the *knowledge* network was very sparse compared with others that we had seen, indicating that an impediment to this group effectively creating and sharing knowledge was that they did not know what each other knew. Two characteristics of this group seemed to result in the sparse pattern. First, the group was physically dispersed, which precluded serendipitous interactions that help people learn colleagues' expertise and skills. Second, the group housed deep specialists who often struggled to find overlap with their colleagues. Stories emerging in interviews indicated that even when there were opportunities to incorporate each other's expertise, this was often not done, because one group of specialists did not know enough about what another group did to be able to "see" a way to involve them in projects.

Conducting the social network analysis provided several intervention opportunities. A facilitated session with leaders allowed them to assess and discuss the relative isolation of the specialties, as well as more pointed concerns about certain members' expertise not being tapped while other members appeared to be bottlenecks in sharing information. As a result of the discussion around this social network, various changes were made to the group's operations. First, a variety of internal projects—ranging from process improvement to a project-tracking database—were jointly staffed with people from various locations. This move forced people to work together and so begin to develop an appreciation of each other's unique skills and knowledge. Second, several new communication forums were created—including weekly status calls, a short update e-mail done weekly, and a project-tracking database that helped each person keep up-to-date on what other members of the group were doing. Finally, some simple changes in project management practices and restructuring of the project leaders' responsibilities helped people to connect around them.

Facilitating Merger Integration

In another scenario we assessed the top leadership network of a Fortune 250 organization (i.e., top 126 executives of this conglomerate). This was an organization that had grown by acquisition over the course of several years, with the strategic intent that acquired companies would combine their expertise in developing and taking to market new products and services. The chief executive officer (CEO) of this organization had become acutely aware of the need to create a leadership network that knew enough of what others in the conglomerate knew to be able to combine the appropriate resources in response to new opportunities. As there was some evidence that this was not happening, he asked us to conduct a social network analysis of his top executives across these acquired organizations.

Mapping information flow among these executives showed that there was only limited collaborative activity in pockets of the organization and that in general this lack of collaboration was a product of people not knowing what other people knew. In fact, we found that the problem was so significant that a key executive indicated not only that he or she did not know what a specific person in another division did but also that he or she did not even know what that division did. Despite alignment of the organization's formal structure, this lack of collective awareness of "who knows what" was having a significant impact on the organization's ability to execute strategically.

Two interventions were undertaken to begin helping to integrate this group. First, on a technical front, a customized technology was introduced for this group that combined a skill-profiling system with a new collab-orative environment where executives posted project information. This system was quickly used, as the CEO pushed people into adopting it and also made it the primary forum by which these executives began to get information they needed to run their business. In addition, action-learning sets were employed on internal projects. People from across these divi-sions were staffed together on small teams that each attacked a given project, but they were instructed to do so with reflective exercises, as the point of the initiative was both to solve problems for the company and to create connections across the executive team.

Creating Awareness of "Who Knows What"

Overall, we are finding that it is important for organizations to pay atten-tion to how strategic networks of employees develop an understanding of their collective knowledge. In more staid times, working relationships developed as a product of interaction over longer time periods. This is not so in today's business environment. Given the rapid turnover many companies experience today, it is important to find ways to help people become better connected so the organization can get the true benefit of their expertise more quickly. This is often a process that can be improved by focusing on the way that new people are brought into a group. Gen-erally what most organizations do when hiring a new person is to hold orientation courses that teach the person about the computer system, ben-efits, and, perhaps, the culture and history of the company. It is rare to find practices that teach the group what the newcomers know. This is a critical shortcoming in increasingly project-based work, where people will be brought into the center of the network primarily as a result of what other people understand about their expertise and so how to tap it when new problems or opportunities arise.

However, knowingly or unknowingly, some organizations we worked with were employing different mechanisms that built this awareness of "who knows what." For example, on a technical front many organizations are implementing skill-profiling systems or corporate yellow pages. On an organizational front, organizations such as the World Bank have or-ganized their employees into thematic groups that have help desks that anyone connected with the organization can contact. The individuals staff-ing the help desks are able to route people to others within the thematic group who have expertise on a particular subject. Other companies and government organizations have regular Knowledge Fairs where teams, communities, or departments can set up booths and distribute information about the expertise that they have. Although this forum has limited scope, it has proven effective in increasing awareness of the projects and knowl-edge activities taking place within the different departments and com-munities of the organization.

Access Dimension: Can We Access What We Know in a Sufficiently Timely Fashion?

Of course, knowing that someone else knows something of relevance does little good if we cannot gain access to their thinking in a timely fashion. Critical issues on which we may turn to others for help or advice often require turnaround within increasingly tight time frames. As with the *knowledge* dimension, we have found it helpful to map the *access* relation at a network level to understand who is able to reach whom in a sufficiently timely fashion.

Assessing Access in a Global Consulting Practice

We conducted a network analysis of the global consumer goods practice within a major consulting firm. One of the more telling networks in this analysis was the diagram reflecting who was sufficiently accessible to whom among this group of 46 people spread through Europe and the United States Despite the entire practice reporting to one overall partner and being subject to a common strategy, performance measurement, and reward practices, we found significant clustering in the network when we assessed who was accessible to whom. The social network analysis of accessibility showed three tightly knit groups rather than one integrated network—two in North America and one in Europe—that were all highly centralized around different partners. In fact, only three employees served to bridge these fiefdoms, and these were not the people in charge of the group. Rather, they had been through rotating work assignments and so developed relations with many others in the network.

A first intervention for this organization was reconsidering staffing practices to help integrate people from the different locations on both client projects and internal initiatives. A key concern lay with developing relationships throughout the overall practice to improve knowledge sharing and the location of relevant expertise for both sales efforts and client engagements. Further, increasing overall connection within the network also reduced the extent to which the practice was exposed by the potential for any of these three central people leaving. In this and many other examples, we have consistently found that a network view makes it clear that, should certain central people in a network leave, they take more than just what they know—they also fundamentally affect the connectivity of the entire group.

The two groups in the United States represented another challenge for management. It turned out that the majority of people in these two groups not only had offices in the same building but also were interspersed along the same corridor. What we discovered in interviews was a political problem that had emerged and resulted in tensions between two subgroups. While management had suspected there were problems, the visual representation of the network diagram clearly showed the extent to which these issues were impeding the ability of the overall group to effectively leverage the expertise of its members. Various steps were taken to help resolve the problem, including executive coaching, revised performance management practices, an extensive off-site planning session, and organizational development (OD) interventions to help the group integrate.

Accessibility after a Transition to Teams

Reorganizations often shift the location and the accessibility of specific expertise concurrently. For example, we worked with one commercial lending organization in a transition from a functional to a team-based structure. To minimize inefficiencies resulting from cross-functional hand-offs in the commercial lending process, the organization shifted to a team-based structure that co-located lenders, analysts, and servicers in industry teams. Before the transition, these groups had been housed together on different floors and so were able to tap into each other's functional knowledge with relative ease. With the redesign, it was far more difficult for inexperienced people to learn the basics of their function and for experienced lenders and analysts to engage in collaborative problem-solving efforts on the more creative aspects of commercial lending (e.g., structuring a specific transaction).

Social network analysis showed that four months after the transition to teams, several key people had become significantly overburdened, as they were heavily sought out by both their past functional colleagues and their new team members. In particular, we found that the people who were reputed experts in their area were tapped for advice to such an extent that they were falling behind on their own work. While in the functional department these interactions were more controlled and observable, in the team-based environment it was difficult for management to see how instrumental these opinion leaders really were to the success of the whole system. In fact, from a cursory review of their individual performance metrics (e.g., loans serviced or loans booked), these people experienced a fairly significant decline in productivity. Further, the longer hours that these people were working, in tandem with declining individual performance metrics that influenced their bonus calculations, served to undermine their own morale. As a result of these findings, several steps were taken—such as new staffing practices, better orientation materials (to help bring new people up to speed more effectively), and a reallocation of tasks within teams.

Managing Accessibility

Through the course of our research we have found that many organizations struggle with the notion of accessibility as people increasingly work from diverse locations. By and large, most solutions that companies considered were technical in nature and included such things as e-mail, asynchronous and synchronous collaborative environments, video conferencing, and instant messaging. However, we generally find that organizational design considerations and cultural norms are the more powerful indicators of who is accessible to whom.

Performance management systems promoting individualistic behaviors seem to be one of the primary drivers of sparse, disconnected networks. Further, we often find that hierarchy, though more of a trait of organizational culture, has a marked impact on who is able to access whom. Again, this is a telling indicator for organizations trying to become more flexible and effective at information sharing. Some organizations have taken interesting steps to promote access across hierarchy, such as making knowledge sharing a part of their mission or code of ethics. At Buckman Laboratories, all associates are empowered to speak with any associate at any level, and they are supported by a communication technology that gives each employee access to all other employees. Other organizations are beginning to turn to creative uses of physical space to promote both intentional and serendipitous interactions among high-end knowledge workers. For example, Chrysler has gone full circle (from dispersion back to co-location) by recently bringing all the people involved in new car development into one building so that they can have face-to-face access to each other.

Engagement Dimension: How Do We Improve Engagement in Problem Solving?

One of the most interesting findings from our interviews with the 40 managers in the first phase of our research was the importance of the person sought out for information being willing to cognitively engage with the information seeker. People who were willing to engage in problem solving helped seekers to create knowledge with sufficient understanding and clarity that they could take action on it. And when we say engaging in problem solving, we do not mean a significant time investment on the part of the person sought out. Rather, we mean a simple two-step behavior whereby those contacted for information first ensured that they understood the other person's problem and then actively shaped what they knew to the problem at hand. In short, these people taught rather than dumped information on the seeker—a behavior that if developed among a network can improve the effectiveness with which people learn from each other.

Integrating Specialized Expertise in Problem Solving

We conducted one network analysis of a specialist group supporting the internal knowledge management efforts of a global computer manufacturer. This group of 18 people was a virtual team that had been formed to combine expertise in both the technical and organizational/strategic aspects of knowledge management. While members of the group claimed to know and have access to each other's expertise, a quick review of the *engagement* network showed that in fact the group was having little success in integrating their expertise. Rather, what became apparent was a strong split in the network because of unique skill bases.

Despite people technically knowing at a high level what the skills and knowledge of people in the other discipline were, there were only two connections between the two groups on the *engagement* relation. This clustering was a significant concern, as it is in engagement in problem solving that true learning takes place and people effectively integrate specialized expertise in projects—rather than just doing what they know or have done before. Interviews revealed that each group's depth of specialization and the fact that they were virtual and so had little slack, face-to-face time to interact made it difficult for them to find common ground. Aside from the leader of the group, who had experience with both subgroups, there was little common language or occupational values that existed between the two subgroups.

Several organizational learning interventions have been undertaken in this group to help build engagement and trust. As always, a key component of these interventions has been the use of various network diagrams in facilitated sessions to help the group create common awareness and make sense of productive and unproductive dynamics. Further, a shift in performance measurement was made to encourage joint problem solving and to de-emphasize individual project metrics. While in the midst of these initiatives, the group plans to periodically assess the engagement network and intervene as appropriate to improve their operations over time.

Supporting Engagement of Specialists in New Product Development

In another scenario, we conducted a network analysis of 78 members of a drug development community of practice. The community, which was geographically dispersed across eight sites in the United States and Europe, included people from the drug discovery stage all the way to clinical development. The analysis indicated that within this highly dispersed community there were many people who did not know each other. It also became apparent that, although the people within each functional unit engaged with each other on matters relevant to the community, there was little engagement between the functions. This was a critical problem for this group, given the need to combine unique expertise to effectively develop and market a specific drug.

Further, the network proved to be highly centralized around a few individuals. The six most central people resided in the main U.S. site. Although they had many connections to people within the site, they did not engage as often with community members in the European locations.

There were also several people who were totally disconnected from the group, which resulted in their skills and expertise being lost to the community. In this instance, a new collaborative technology was introduced that had both synchronous and asynchronous features. In addition, different project management practices and a new role within the community were initiated to help bridge functional areas of expertise. Finally, the network diagrams were used to convince management to support staged face-to-face forums focusing on specific problems. These forums helped the different functional areas find common ground while solving problems critical to the success of a project.

Engagement in Human Networks

Overall, as with the access dimension, we found that many of the things organizations were doing that had an impact on engagement were technical in nature and included synchronous technologies such as VP Buddy, Same Time, or white boarding applications that allow for dispersed engagement in a common problem. In many ways, instant messaging does seem to support the serendipitous kinds of interactions that are lost when employees are not co-located. However, there are limitations in the ability of these applications to richly convey knowledge across media that provide relatively few cues in comparison to face-to-face interactions. Videoconferencing for visual interaction between people in different locations does seem to help. This has been particularly important at British Petroleum, where experts have been able to assist technicians who are working on oil rigs thousands of miles away.

British Petroleum is also unique in its recognition of the importance of engagement in problem solving early in projects where learning from others' experiences can have a disproportionate impact on the trajectory and success of a project. For example, BP has instituted a peer-review process in its drilling initiatives as an effective way to tap into others' knowledge. Before engaging in any significant task, the individual or group invites peers to provide input. Because the focus is performance, those with the most relevant knowledge and recent experiences are tapped to participate. Through this peer-review process, not only is performance on the task at hand improved but also people become much more aware of the unique skills and abilities of others. This awareness creates a natural reason for meeting and developing the needed norms of reciprocity and trust that make engagement and sharing of expertise a natural process.

Safety Dimension: How Do We Promote Safety in Relationships?

Finally, the managers we interviewed in the first phase of our research indicated that safe relationships offered certain advantages in problem solving. First, they provided more learning, as people were not overly concerned about admitting a lack of knowledge or expertise. Asking someone for help often requires that the seeker have some degree of trust in the person sought out for information. Such trust often shapes the extent to which people will be forthcoming about their lack of knowledge, as defensive behaviors can knowingly and unknowingly block learning in critical interactions. Second, several of the managers indicated that in more safe relationships they could be more creative. An important feature of these relationships was that they were more willing to take risks with their ideas and felt that this often resulted in more creative solutions.

Safety Promotes Learning in High-End Knowledge Work

Social network analysis provides us with a means of understanding the extent to which information and knowledge seeking is a safe behavior in important groups. For example, we assessed the *safety* network in the information resources group supporting a key research and development function of a Fortune 500 manufacturing organization. This group of 34 people was composed of two organizational units that had recently been merged under one leader. The *safety* network represented an interesting point of intervention here because, unlike many networks we have seen the *knowledge, access,* and *engagement* networks were all very well connected, whereas the safety network was not.

Interestingly enough, the safety network split into two groups that reflected the two departments that had been merged several months before this analysis. This is a common finding in both restructuring and merger scenarios. We often have found that communication networks (i.e., network diagrams developed from asking people who they typically communicate with) form quickly in restructuring or merger scenarios. However, what simply assessing communication patterns obscures is the time and effort that must be put into developing trust among a group, if we truly want people to learn from each other. Safety is important and highly predictive of who is sought out when one engages in problem solving and so exposes a lack of knowledge or allows someone else to shape the course of a solution. Relationships that are safe, and therefore useful for deeper levels of knowledge sharing and true learning, take time to develop.

In this specific network analysis, there were two interesting points. First, two people who were low in the hierarchy had become important ambassadors between the groups. Several amusing anecdotes were discovered in our interviews, whereby people that were senior in this group often went to these more junior people when they needed information from a colleague in the other subgroup. A light-hearted but very effective intervention was created by using these anecdotes along with the network diagram in a facilitated session debriefing the overall group. Playfully illuminating the way in which members of each group had stereotyped the other, and the inefficiencies that this caused, resulted in a productive discussion of a potentially charged issue.

Second, there were different levels of safety between the two groups. In part this seemed to be a product of the physical environment, as the more tightly connected group had all worked in an open-space environment that allowed frequent, face-to-face communication. We also found that leadership style differed in the two groups before the restructuring. In general, the degree of safety within networks of relationships is often a product of leadership style and organizational (or sometimes occupational) culture. The behaviors that leaders exhibit and those they reward shape the extent to which people will be forthcoming about their lack of knowledge on various topics. This varied widely by organization. In some, safety was never considered a concern, because it was an accepted norm to doggedly seek out the most relevant knowledge for the success of a given project. In others, safety was a critical concern, and employees were very cautious about exposing a lack of knowledge.

Just as important, our interviews indicated that relationships need time and some space (physical, cognitive, and social) to develop a sense of safety. Although communication technologies such as e-mail are helpful in maintaining relationships, we have found that when an organization wants to create relationships it is important to increase the opportunity for face-to-face interactions between people. For example, though often chided, organizations that have instigated a program of brown-bag lunches find that this process is effective for the development of safe relationships between people. One organization we worked with encouraged face-to-face contact by monthly meetings between different groups of researchers. These meetings consisted of a discussion session in the morning and a working session in the laboratory in the afternoon and allowed for a free flow of ideas within the context of a real working environment.

■ A Combined Network View and Organizational Learning

In addition to looking at each of the networks individually, it is also instructive to assess the dimensions cumulatively to get a better understanding of a network's underlying learning potential. In doing this, we can analyze networks where pairs of relationships exist (e.g., both knowledge and access) or networks where all of the relationships exist (e.g., knowledge, access, engagement, and safety). For example, we conducted a social network analysis of 38 employees constituting the telecommunications consulting practice of a Big Five accountancy. We first assessed the knowledge network to better understand who in this network of people indicated that they knew and valued other's expertise. Though relatively sparse, we found that the knowledge network showed a healthy, integrated pattern without distinct subgroups. However, the network diagram took on added life when we also considered the access network, where each person rated his or her colleagues on the extent to which they were accessible in a time frame sufficient to help solve problems. Ultimately, both knowledge and access relations must be present for information sharing in a group to be effective. By combining the networks from these two questions, we had a view of the potential of a person to obtain information from others when faced with a new problem or opportunity.

Several things were interesting in this network. First, we noticed a fairly marked decline in the number of connections among the group in comparison to the knowledge network. While many central people remained central, several people higher in the hierarchy shifted out to the periphery of the network. As people move higher in an organization, their work begins to entail more administrative tasks, which makes them both less accessible and less knowledgeable about the day-to-day work of their subordinates. What network analysis affords in this picture is an opportunity to assess whether those in positions of formal authority are sufficiently central to the flow of knowledge, as well as to identify those people who truly are influential knowledge brokers in the group.

The third question asked of the 38 consultants was who in the group they could count on to actively engage in problem solving. When the engagement network was added we were assessing a network where a line was drawn between two people *only* if all three dimensions of a relationship existed (knowing what the others know, having access to their thinking and being willing to engage in problem solving). With the addition of the engagement network, we found a significant decrease in connections, which is not trivial in terms of the network's ability to solve problems. As outlined in the initial interviews, it is often those people who are willing to engage in problem solving who help both create actionable knowledge (rather than information overload) and ensure that we are solving the right problem. The final question we asked of this consulting practice determined with whom each person felt safe discussing work-related issues. With the incorporation of the safety network there is very little change. This is because the safety network in this group was the densest of all the networks. Ultimately, this was a sound indicator of the culture of this group for knowledge creation and is obviously not a place we would look to intervene. It is also important to note that based on our experiences, a dense safety network is not typical.

Interventions from a Combined Network View

Analyzing the combined network (i.e., knowledge + access + engagement + safety) provides a great deal of insight into who is critical as well as who is currently less utilized within a group in terms of knowledge creation and sharing. Understanding who is central to a group indicates people who might be either bottlenecks or highly valued knowledge resources upon whom the group is reliant. Only interviews providing an in-depth understanding of a network can tell, but these people do pose interesting questions to management. Has the group become too reliant on these people should they decide to leave? Are these people hoarding information and so are bottlenecks in terms of the group's knowledge creation and sharing activities? In contrast, should these people be rewarded for the somewhat invisible role they play in supporting a group from a knowledge perspective?

If we discover that people are central in these networks for legitimate reasons, management has an opportunity to begin acknowledging the work that these people do for the group. In the words of one of the people central in the telecommunications practice, "I spend about an hour and a half every day responding to calls and other informational requests . . . [and] . . . none of that time gets seen in my performance metrics." Network analysis makes such interactions that are critical to a group visible, thus providing an opportunity for management to acknowledge these people and the critical role they play. For example, management might choose to better support knowledge creation and sharing by offering central people such things as:

- Monies for efforts that might stimulate knowledge flow in a group via face-to-face meetings, or to purchase technologies such as groupware.
- Cognitive and social space to allow room for both individual and collective creativity and bonding to occur.
- Executive focus such as rewarding or promoting network-enabling people to both acknowledge their efforts and signal the importance of this kind of work to others within the organization.

In addition to understanding why some people are central or core individuals, we also find it important to better understand why some people are peripheral in these networks. It might be that people in these positions do not know what we thought they knew when they were hired. In these cases, they are peripheral for a legitimate reason and so reflect development or restaffing opportunities. Alternatively, it might be that these people are peripheral because they are relatively new and the organization's assimilation processes do little to help them integrate into a network of colleagues. The important feature of this combined network view is that we can isolate why people are peripheral. Being peripheral because one is inaccessible is a different coaching process than if one is not considered safe.

Finally, on a more conceptual level, the combined network view offers unique purchase on the elusive concept of organizational learning. Some scholars have claimed that an organization has learned when, through its processing of information, its range of potential behaviors has changed. Thus, if we are interested in promoting an organization's ability to react to new opportunities, we need to account for the ways in which people in networks become able to leverage each others' knowledge. Changes in the knowledge, access, engagement, and safety relationships underlying a network's future information processing behavior provide one means of both descriptive and prescriptive traction on organizational learning. Organizations have often been claimed to be path-dependent or constrained by what they know. Such notions as absorptive capacity, core rigidities, or architectural knowledge have been claimed to lead to this path-dependence over time. While critically important, this work has often been done at a level of abstraction that makes interventions questionable. In contrast, the combined view of these networks provides some idea as to precisely whose knowledge is primarily responsible for what a group is likely to learn over time.

■ Conclusion

A critical resource embedded within organizations is the knowledge that workers bring to work on a day-to-day basis. However, aside from human resource policies targeted to the attraction, development, and retention of identified valuable workers, there has been little effort put into systematic ways of working with the knowledge that is embedded in social networks. Given the extent to which people rely on their own knowledge and the knowledge of their contacts to solve problems, this is a significant shortcoming. By introducing social network analysis to understand how a given network of people create and share knowledge, we are able to make these interactions visible and thus actionable.

In applying these ideas in various organizations, we have found it particularly important to identify points of knowledge creation and sharing that hold strategic relevance within an organization. Typical domains yielding benefit include senior management networks, communities of practice and collaborative initiatives such as new product development, R&D units, or joint ventures and alliances. It is particularly fruitful to map collaborative relationships that cross boundaries of some form. Such boundaries might be hierarchical, functional, geographical, or even organizational, as in joint-venture or merger-and-acquisition scenarios. Understanding how knowledge flows (or more frequently does not flow) across these various boundaries within an organization can yield critical insight into where management should target efforts to promote collaboration that has a strategic payoff for the organization.

Much of the emphasis on organizational knowledge today (at least in terms of practice) is focused on efforts to capture, screen, store, and codify knowledge. To get a more popular view of what many organizations are doing under the rubric of knowledge management we suggest some of the following publications: T. Davenport & L. Prusak, *Working Knowledge* (Boston, MA: Harvard Business School Press, 1998); C. O'Dell & C. J. Grayson, *If Only We Knew What We Know* (New York: Free Press, 1998); T. Stewart, *Intellectual Capital: The New Wealth of Organizations* (New York: Doubleday, 1997); and R. Ruggles, "The State of the Notion: Knowledge Management in Practice," *California Management Review*, 1998, 40(3), 80–89.

Of course, our own perspective is that knowledge embedded in human networks is too often overlooked in these initiatives. Two streams of literature heavily influenced our thinking here. First is the rich ethnographic evidence accumulating within the situated-learning and community-of-practice traditions. This work is making clear the large degree to which people learn how to do their work not from impersonal sources of information but through interactions with other people. Some important work in this tradition includes J. S. Brown & P. Duguid, "Organizational Learning and Communities-of-Practice: Toward a Unified View of Working Learning and Innovation," *Organization Science,* 1991, 2(1), 40–57; J. Brown & P. Duguid, *The Social Life of Information* (Boston: Harvard Business School Press, 2000); J. Lave & E. Wenger, *Situated Learning: Legitimate Peripheral Participation* (Cambridge, UK: Cambridge University Press, 1991); J. Orr, *Talking about Machines* (Ithaca, NY: Cornell University Press, 1996); and E. Wenger, *Communities of Practice* (Oxford: Oxford University Press, 1998).

The second stream of literature influential in our thinking came from the social network tradition, which has also shown, with very different methods, the extent to which information that affects what we do largely comes from other people. Some important works on how social networks influence information flow and diffusion in networks include G. Simmel, *The Sociology of Georg Simmel* (New York: Free Press, 1950); R. Burt, *Structural Holes* (Cambridge, MA: Harvard University Press, 1992); M. Granovetter, "The Strength of Weak Ties," *American Journal of Sociology*, 1973, 78, 1360–1380; T. Allen, *Managing the Flow of Technology* (Cambridge, MA: MIT Press, 1984); P. Monge & N. Contractor, "Emergence of Communication Networks," forthcoming in F. Jablin and L. Putnam (Eds.), *Handbook of Organizational Communication*, 2nd ed. (Thousand Oaks, CA: Sage); and E. Rogers, *Diffusion of Innovations*, 4th ed. (New York: Free Press, 1995).

Part III

Managerial Implications of Social

Networks in Organizations

9

Informal Networks

The Company behind the Chart

David Krackhardt and Jeffrey R. Hanson

Many executives invest considerable resources in restructuring their companies, drawing and redrawing organizational charts only to be disappointed by the results. That's because much of the real work of companies happens despite the formal organization. Often what needs attention is the *informal* organization, the networks of relationships that employees form across functions and divisions to accomplish tasks fast. These informal networks can cut through formal reporting procedures to jump start stalled initiatives and meet extraordinary deadlines. But informal networks can just as easily sabotage companies' best laid plans by blocking communication and fomenting opposition to change unless managers know how to identify and direct them. Learning how to map these social links can help managers harness the real power in their companies and revamp their formal organizations to let the informal ones thrive.

If the formal organization is the skeleton of a company, the informal is the central nervous system driving the collective thought processes, actions, and reactions of its business units. Designed to facilitate standard modes of production, the formal organization is set up to handle easily anticipated problems. But when unexpected problems arise, the informal organization kicks in. Its complex webs of social ties form every time colleagues communicate and solidify over time into surprisingly stable networks. Highly adaptive, informal networks move diagonally and elliptically, skipping entire functions to get work done.

Managers often pride themselves on understanding how these networks operate. They will readily tell you who confers on technical matters and who discusses office politics over lunch. What's startling is how often they are wrong. Although they may be able to diagram accurately the social links of the five or six people closest to them, their assumptions about employees outside their immediate circle are usually off the mark. Even the most psychologically shrewd managers lack critical information about how employees spend their days and how they feel about their peers. Managers simply can't be everywhere at once, nor can they read people's minds. So they're left to draw conclusions based on superficial observations, without the tools to test their perceptions.

Armed with faulty information, managers often rely on traditional techniques to control these networks. Some managers hope that the authority inherent in their titles will override the power of informal links. Fearful of any groups they can't command, they create rigid rules that will hamper the work of the informal networks. Other managers try to recruit "moles" to provide intelligence. More enlightened managers run focus groups and host retreats to "get in touch" with their employees. But such approaches won't rein in these freewheeling networks, nor will they give managers an accurate picture of what they look like.

Using network analysis, however, managers can translate a myriad of relationship ties into maps that show how the informal organization gets work done. Managers can get a good overall picture by diagramming three types of relationship networks:

- The advice network shows the prominent players in an organization on whom others depend to solve problems and provide technical information.
- The trust network tells which employees share delicate political information and back one another in a crisis.
- The communication network reveals the employees who talk about work-related matters on a regular basis.

Maps of these relationships can help managers understand the networks that once eluded them and leverage these networks to solve organizational problems. Case studies using fictional names, based on companies with which we have worked, show how managers can bring out the strengths in their networks, restructure their formal organizations to complement the informal, and "rewire" faulty networks to work with company goals.

■ The Steps of Network Analysis

We learned the significance of the informal network 12 years ago while conducting research at a bank that had an 80 percent turnover rate among its tellers. Interviews revealed that the tellers' reasons for leaving had less to do with the bank's formal organization than with the tellers' relationships to key players in their trust networks. When these players left, others followed in droves.

Much research had already established the influence of central figures in informal networks. Our subsequent studies of public and private companies showed that understanding these networks could increase the influence of managers outside the inner circle. If they learned who wielded power in networks and how various coalitions functioned, they could work with the informal organization to solve problems and improve performance.

Mapping advice networks, our research showed, can uncover the source of political conflicts and failure to achieve strategic objectives. Because these networks show the most influential players in the day-to-day operations of a company, they are useful to examine when a company is considering routine changes. Trust networks often reveal the causes of nonroutine problems such as poor performance by temporary teams. Companies should examine trust networks when implementing a major change or experiencing a crisis. The communication network can help identify gaps in information flow, the inefficient use of resources, and the failure to generate new ideas. They should be examined when productivity is low.

Managers can analyze informal networks in three steps. Step one is conducting a network survey using employee questionnaires. The survey is designed to solicit responses about who talks to whom about work, who trusts whom, and who advises whom on technical matters. It is important to pretest the survey on a small group of employees to see if any questions are ambiguous or meet with resistance. In some companies, for example, employees are comfortable answering questions about friendship; in others, they deem such questions too personal and intrusive. The following are among the questions often asked:

- Whom do you talk to every day?
- Whom do you go to for help or advice at least once a week?
- With one day of training, whose job could you step into?
- Whom would you recruit to support a proposal of yours that could be unpopular?
- Whom would you trust to keep in confidence your concerns about a work-related issue?

Some companies also find it useful to conduct surveys to determine managers' *impressions* of informal networks so that these can be compared with the actual networks revealed by the employee questionnaires. In such surveys, questions are posed like this:

- Whom do you think Steve goes to for work-related advice?
- Whom would Susan trust to keep her confidence about work-related concerns?

The key to eliciting honest answers from employees is to earn their trust. They must be assured that managers will not use their answers against them or the employees mentioned in their responses and that their immediate colleagues will not have access to the information. In general, respondents are comfortable if upper-level managers not mentioned in the surveys see the results.

After questionnaires are completed, the second step is cross-checking the answers. Some employees, worried about offending their colleagues, say they talk to *everyone* in the department on a daily basis. If Judy Smith says she regularly talks to Bill Johnson about work, make sure that Johnson says he talks to Smith. Managers should discount any answers not confirmed by both parties. The final map should not be based on the impressions of one employee but on the consensus of the group.

The third step is processing the information using one of several commercially available computer programs that generate detailed network maps. (Drawing maps is a laborious process that tends to result in curved lines that are difficult to read.) Maps in hand, a skilled manager can devise a strategy that plays on the strengths of the informal organization, as David Leers, the founder and CEO of a California-based computer company, found out.

■ Whom Do You Trust?

David Leers thought he knew his employees well. In 15 years, the company had trained a cadre of loyal professionals who had built a strong regional reputation for delivering customized office information systems (see figure 9.1). The field design group, responsible for designing and installing the systems, generated the largest block of revenues. For years it had been the linchpin of the operation, led by the company's technical superstars, with whom Leers kept in close contact.

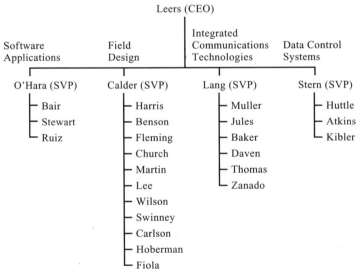

Figure 9.1.
The formal chart shows who's on top

But Leers feared that the company was losing its competitive edge by shortchanging its other divisions, such as software applications and integrated communications technologies. When members of field design saw Leers start pumping more money into these divisions, they worried about losing their privileged position. Key employees started voicing dissatisfaction about their compensation, and Leers knew he had the makings of a morale problem that could result in defections.

To persuade employees to support a new direction for the company, Leers decided to involve them in the planning process. He formed a strategic task force composed of members of all divisions and led by a member of field design to signal his continuing commitment to the group. He wanted a leader who had credibility with his peers and was a proven performer. Eight-year company veteran Tom Harris seemed obvious for the job.

Leers was optimistic after the first meeting. Members generated good discussion about key competitive dilemmas. A month later, however, he found that the group had made little progress. Within two months, the group was completely deadlocked by members championing their own agendas. Although a highly effective manager, Leers lacked the necessary distance to identify the source of his problem.

An analysis of the company's trust and advice networks helped him get a clearer picture of the dynamics at work in the task force. The trust map turned out to be most revealing. Task force leader Tom Harris held a central position in the advice network—meaning that many employees relied on him for technical advice (see figure 9.2). But he had only *one* trust link with a colleague (see figure 9.3). Leers concluded that Harris's weak position in the trust network was a main reason for the task force's inability to produce results.

In his job, Harris was able to leverage his position in the advice network to get work done quickly. As a task force leader, however, his technical expertise was less important than his ability to moderate conflicting views, focus the group's thinking, and win the commitment of task force members to mutually agreed upon strategies. Because he was a loner who took more interest in computer games than in colleagues' opinions, task force members didn't trust him to take their ideas seriously or look out for their interests. So they focused instead on defending their turf.

With this critical piece of information, the CEO crafted a solution. He did not want to undermine the original rationale of the task force by declaring it a failure. Nor did he want to embarrass a valued employee by summarily removing him as task force head. Any response, he concluded, had to run with the natural grain of the informal organization. He decided to redesign the team to reflect the inherent strengths of the trust network.

Referring to the map, Leers looked for someone in the trust network who could share responsibilities with Harris. He chose Bill Benson, a

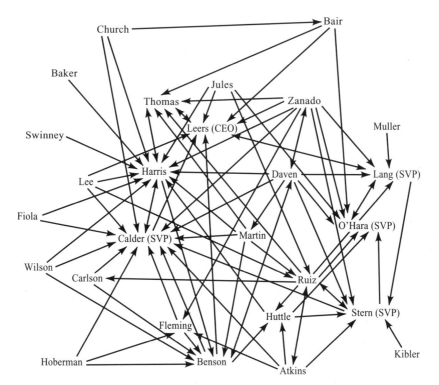

Figure 9.2.
The advice network reveals the experts

warm, amiable person who occupied a central position in the network and with whom Harris had already established a solid working relationship. He publicly justified his decision to name two task force heads as necessary, given the time pressures and scope of the problem.

Within three weeks, Leers could see changes in the group's dynamics. Because task force members trusted Benson to act in the best interest of the entire group, people talked more openly and let go of their fixed positions. During the next two months, the task force made significant progress in proposing a strategic direction for the company. And in the process of working together, the task force helped integrate the company's divisions.

A further look at the company's advice and trust networks uncovered another serious problem, this time with the head of field design, Jim Calder.

The CEO had appointed Calder manager because his colleagues respected him as the most technically accomplished person in the division. Leers thought Calder would have the professional credibility to lead a diverse group of very specialized design consultants. This is a common

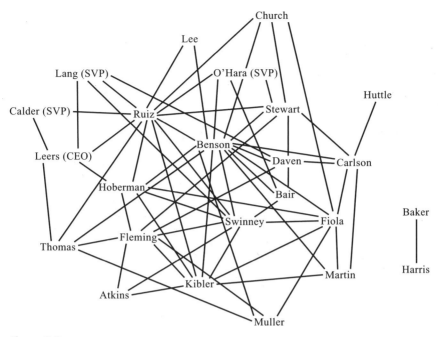

Figure 9.3.
But when it comes to trust . . .

practice in professional service organizations: make your best producer the manager. Calder, however, turned out to be a very marginal figure in the trust network. His managerial ability and skills were sorely lacking, which proved to be a deficit that outweighed the positive effects derived from his technical expertise. He regularly told people they were stupid and paid little attention to their professional concerns.

Leers knew that Calder was no diplomat, but he had no idea to what extent the performance and morale of the group were suffering as a result of Calder's tyrannical management style. In fact, a map based on Leers's initial perceptions of the trust network put Calder in a central position (see figure 9.4). Leers took for granted that Calder had good personal relationships with the people on his team. His assumption was not unusual. Frequently, senior managers presume that formal work ties will yield good relationship ties over time, and they assume that if *they* trust someone, others will too.

The map of Calder's perceptions was also surprising (see figure 9.5). He saw almost no trust links in his group at all. Calder was oblivious to *any* of the trust dependencies emerging around him—a worrisome characteristic for a manager.

The information in these maps helped Leers formulate a solution.

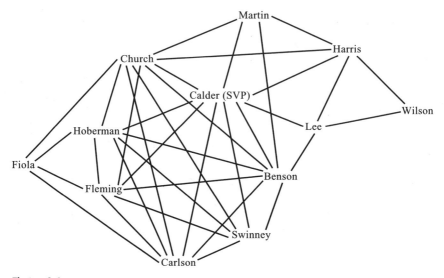

Figure 9.4.
How the CEO views the trust network

Again, he concluded that he needed to change the formal organization to reflect the structure of the informal network. Rather than promoting or demoting Calder, Leers cross-promoted him to an elite "special situations team," reporting directly to the CEO. His job involved working with highly sophisticated clients on specialized problems. The position took better advantage of Calder's technical skills and turned out to be good for him socially as well. Calder, Leers learned, hated dealing with formal management responsibilities and the pressure of running a large group.

Leers was now free to promote John Fleming, a tactful, even-tempered employee, to the head of field design. A central player in the trust network, Fleming was also influential in the advice network. The field group's performance improved significantly over the next quarter, and the company was able to create a highly profitable revenue stream through the activities of Calder's new team.

■ Whom Do You Talk To?

When it comes to communication, more is not always better, as the top management of a large East Coast bank discovered. A survey showed that customers were dissatisfied with the information they were receiving about banking services. Branch managers, top managers realized, were not communicating critical information about available services to tellers. As a result, customers' questions were not answered in a timely fashion.

Fleming ————————————————————— Hoberman

Figure 9.5.
The trust network according to Calder

Management was convinced that more talking among parties would improve customer service and increase profits. A memo was circulated ordering branch managers to "increase communication flow and coordination within and across branches and to make a personal effort to increase the amount and effectiveness of their own interpersonal communications with their staffs."

A study of the communication networks of 24 branches, however, showed the error of this thinking. *More* communication ties did not distinguish the most profitable branches; the *quality* of communication determined their success Nonhierarchical branches, those with two-way communication between people of all levels, were 70% more profitable than branches with one-way communication patterns between "superiors" and staff.

The communication networks of two branches located in the same city illustrated this point. Branch 1 had a central figure, a supervisor, with whom many tellers reported communicating about their work on a daily basis. The supervisor confirmed that employees talked to her, but she reported communicating with only half of these tellers about work-related matters by the end of the day. The tellers, we later learned, resented this one-way communication flow. Information they viewed as critical to their success flowed up the organization but not down. They complained that the supervisor was cold and remote and failed to keep them informed. As a result, productivity suffered.

In contrast, Branch 2 had very few one-way communication lines but many mutual, two-way lines. Tellers in this branch said they were well-informed about the normal course of work flow and reported greater satisfaction with their jobs.

After viewing the communication map, top management abandoned the more-is-better strategy and began exploring ways of fostering mutual communication in all the branches. In this case, management did not recast the formal structure of the branches. Instead, it opted to improve relationships within the established framework. The bank sponsored miniseminars in the branches, in which the problems revealed by the maps were openly discussed. These consciousness-raising sessions spurred many supervisors to communicate more substantive information to tellers. District managers were charged with coming up with their own strategies for improving communication. The bank surveyed employees at regular intervals to see if their supervisors were communicating effectively, and supervisors were informed of the results.

The communication network of a third branch surfaced another management challenge: the branch had divided itself into two distinct groups, each with its own culture and mode of operation. The network map showed that one group had evolved into the "main branch," consisting of tellers, loan officers, and administrative staff. The other group was a kind of "sub-branch," made up primarily of tellers and administrators. It turned out that the sub-branch staff worked during nonpeak and Saturday hours, while main-branch employees worked during peak and weekday hours. The two cultures never clashed because they rarely interacted.

The groups might have coexisted peacefully if customers had not begun complaining about the sub-branch. The main-branch staff, they reported, was responsive to their needs, while the sub-branch staff was often indifferent and even rude. Sub-branch employees, it turned out, felt little loyalty to the bank because they didn't feel part of the organization. They were excluded from staff meetings, which were scheduled in the morning, and they had little contact with the branch manager, who worked a normal weekday shift.

The manager, who was embedded in the main branch, was not even aware that this distinct culture existed until he saw the communication network map. His challenge was to unify the two groups. He decided not to revamp the formal structure, nor did he mount a major public-relations campaign to integrate the two cultures, fearing that each group would reject the other because the existing ties among its members were so strong. Instead, he opted for a stealth approach. He exposed people from one group to people from the other in the hopes of expanding the informal network. Although such forced interaction does not guarantee the emergence of stable networks, more contact increases the likelihood that some new ties will stick.

Previously planned technical training programs for tellers presented the opportunity to initiate change. The manager altered his original plans for on-site training and opted instead for an off-site facility, even though it was more expensive. He sent mixed groups of sub-branch and main-branch employees to programs to promote gradual, neutral interaction and communication. Then he followed up with a series of selective "staff swaps" whereby he shifted work schedules temporarily. When someone from the main branch called in sick or was about to go on vacation, he elected a substitute from the sub-branch. And he rescheduled staff meetings so that all employees could attend.

This approach helped unify the two cultures, which improved levels of customer satisfaction with the branch as a whole over a six-month period. By increasing his own interaction with the sub-branch, the manager discovered critical information about customers, procedures, and data systems. Without even realizing it, he had been making key decisions based on incomplete data.

As managers become more sophisticated in analyzing their communication networks, they can use them to spot five common configurations. None of these are inherently good or bad, functional or dysfunctional. What matters is the *fit*, whether networks are in sync with company goals. When the two are at odds, managers can attempt to broaden or reshape the informal networks using a variety of tactics.

Imploded Relationships

Communication maps often show departments that have few links to other groups. In these situations, employees in a department spend all their time talking among themselves and neglect to cultivate relationships with the rest of their colleagues. Frequently, in such cases, only the most senior employees have ties with people outside their areas. And they may hoard these contacts by failing to introduce these people to junior colleagues.

To counter this behavior, one manager implemented a mentor system in which senior employees were responsible for introducing their apprentices to people in other groups who could help them do their jobs. Another manager instituted a policy of picking up the tab for "power breakfasts," as long as the employees were from different departments.

Irregular Communication Patterns

The opposite pattern can be just as troubling. Sometimes employees communicate only with members of other groups and not among themselves. To foster camaraderie, one manager sponsored seasonal sporting events, with members of the "problem group" assigned to the same team. Staff meetings can also be helpful if they're really used to share resources and exchange important information about work.

A lack of cohesion resulting in factionalism suggests a more serious underlying problem that requires bridge building. Initiating discussions among peripheral players in each faction can help uncover the root of the problem and suggest solutions. These parties will be much less resistant to compromise than the faction leaders, who will feel more impassioned about their positions.

Fragile Structures

Sometimes group members communicate only among themselves and with employees in one other division. This can be problematic when the contribution of several areas is necessary to accomplish work quickly and spawn creativity. One insurance company manager, a naturally gregarious fellow, tried to broaden employees' contacts by organizing meetings and cocktail parties for members of several divisions. Whenever possible, he introduced employees he thought should be cultivating working relationships. Because of his warm, easygoing manner, they didn't find his methods intrusive. In fact, they appreciated his personal interest in their careers.

Holes in the Network

A map may reveal obvious network holes, places you would expect to find relationship ties but don't. In a large corporate law firm, for example, a group of litigators was not talking to the firm's criminal lawyers, a state of affairs that startled the senior partner. To begin tackling the problem, the partner posed complex problems to criminal lawyers that only regular consultations with litigators could solve. Again, arranging such interactions will not ensure the formation of enduring relationships, but continuous exposure increases the possibility.

"Bow Ties"

Another common trouble spot is the bow tie, a network in which many players are dependent on a single employee but not on each other. Individuals at the center knot of a bow tie have tremendous power and control within the network, much more than would be granted them on a formal organizational chart. If the person at the knot leaves, connections between isolated groups can collapse. If the person remains, organizational processes tend to become rigid and slow and the individual is often torn between the demands of several groups. To undo such a knot, one manager self-consciously cultivated a stronger relationship with the person at the center. It took the pressure off the employee, who was no longer a lone operative, and it helped to diffuse some of his power.

In general, managers should help employees develop relationships within the informal structure that will enable them to make valuable contributions to the company. Managers need to guide employees to cultivate the right mix of relationships. Employees can leverage the power of informal relationships by building both strong ties, relationships with a high frequency of interaction, and weak ties, those with a lower frequency. They can call on the latter at key junctures to solve organizational problems and generate new ideas.

■ Testing the Solution

Managers can anticipate how a strategic decision will affect the informal organization by simulating network maps. This is particularly valuable when a company wants to anticipate reactions to change. A company that wants to form a strategic SWAT team that would remove key employees from the day-to-day operations of a division, for example, can design a map of the area without those players. If removing the central advice person from the network leaves the division with a group of isolates, the manager should reconsider the strategy.

Failure to test solutions can lead to unfortunate results. When the trust network map of a bank showed a loan officer to be an isolate, the manager jumped to the conclusion that the officer was expendable. The manager was convinced that he could replace the employee, a veteran of the company, with a younger, less expensive person who was more of a team player.

What the manager had neglected to consider was how important this officer was to the company's day-to-day operations. He might not have been a prime candidate for a high-level strategy team that demanded excellent social skills, but his expertise, honed by years of experience, would have been impossible to replace. In addition, he had cultivated a close relationship with the bank's largest client—something an in-house network map would never have revealed. Pictures don't tell the whole story; network maps are just one tool among many.

The most important change for a company to anticipate is a complete overhaul of its formal structure. Too many companies fail to consider how such a restructuring will affect their informal organizations. Managers assume that if a company eliminates layers of bureaucracy, the informal organization will simply adjust. It will adjust all right, but there's no guarantee that it will benefit the company. Managers would do well to consider what type of redesign will play on the inherent strengths of key players and give them the freedom to thrive. Policies should allow all employees easy access to colleagues who can help them carry out tasks quickly and efficiently, regardless of their status or area of jurisdiction.

Experienced network managers who can use maps to identify, leverage, and revamp informal networks will become increasingly valuable as companies continue to flatten and rely on teams. As organizations abandon hierarchical structures, managers will have to rely less on the authority inherent in their title and more on their relationships with players in their informal networks. They will need to focus less on overseeing employees "below" them and more on managing people across functions and disciplines. Understanding relationships will be the key to managerial success.

10

The People Who Make Organizations Go—or Stop

Rob Cross and Laurence Prusak

We're all familiar with the truism "It's not what you know, it's who you know." Managers invariably use their personal contacts when they need to, say, meet an impossible deadline, get advice on a strategic decision, or learn the truth about a new boss. Increasingly, it's through these informal networks—not just through traditional organizational hierarchies—that information is found and work gets done. Social networks can be powerful political tools as well; few managers can resist the temptation to use their connections to discredit business initiatives they dislike or to support proposals they favor.

Most corporations, however, treat informal networks as an invisible enemy—one that keeps decisions from being made and work from getting done. To many senior executives, these intricate webs of communication are unobservable and ungovernable—and, therefore, not amenable to the tools of scientific management. As a result, executives tend to work around informal networks or, worse, try to ignore them. When they do acknowledge the networks' existence, executives fall back on intuition—scarcely a dependable tool—to guide them in nurturing this social capital.

It doesn't have to be that way. It is entirely possible to develop informal networks systematically. In fact, our research suggests that if senior managers focus their attention on a handful of key role-players in the group, the effectiveness of any informal network can be enhanced. After analyzing informal networks at more than 50 large organizations over the past five years, we've identified four common role-players whose performance is critical to the productivity of any organization.

First, there are *central connectors*, who link most people in an informal network with one another. They aren't usually the formal leaders within a unit or department, but they know who can provide critical information or expertise that the entire network draws on to get work done. Then there are *boundary spanners*, who connect an informal network with other parts of the company or with similar networks in other organizations. They take the time to consult with and advise individuals from many different departments—marketing, production, or R&D, for instance—regardless of their own affiliations. *Information brokers* keep the different subgroups in an informal network together. If they didn't communicate across the subgroups, the network as a whole would splinter into smaller, less-effective segments. Finally, there are *peripheral specialists*, who anyone in an informal network can turn to for specialized expertise.

Despite the enormous influence these role-players wield within an organization, they are often invisible to senior managers. Because senior executives rely on gut feel, gossip, or formal reporting structures for their information about their managers and employees, they often misunderstand the links between people, especially in large and globally distributed corporations. And because there are so many informal networks in an organization, the problem is exacerbated. So the first step in managing informal networks is to bring them into the open. That can be done through a well-established technique called *social network analysis*, a graphical tool that maps out the relationships in an organization. (For an explanation of the tool and how it can be applied in business, see the sidebar "Who's Who?")

Who's Who?

Over the past two decades, much has been written about the role and importance of informal networks from a variety of academic perspectives, including sociology, social psychology, anthropology, and epidemiology. Drawing on those disciplines, social scientists have developed and honed a powerful tool called *social network analysis*, a technique that lets users identify and map informal networks of people. In fact, David Krackhardt and Jeffrey R. Hanson wrote a detailed description of social network analysis in "Informal Networks: The Company behind the Chart" (*Harvard Business Review*, July–August 1993), in which they argued that this tool could be logically applied to business. Indeed, some organizations are already using social network analysis to recognize and manage their informal networks.

Although it may be tempting for senior executives to map all the informal networks in a company at one go, this may be overkill. It is more effective if executives first identify the functions or activities where connectivity is most needed to improve productivity and then map the corresponding networks. These priority areas—say, the development of a new product line or the integration of a recent acquisition—normally follow from the company's strategic objectives.

The next step is to collect information from people to map sets of relationships within the priority areas. While those data can be obtained in various ways, from tracking e-mail to observing people, the most efficient way is to administer a 10-to-20-minute questionnaire. The questions asked will depend on the kind of network you want to uncover. In most companies, senior managers are most interested in assessing how information flows. For instance, they want to know "To whom do you talk regularly about work? From whom do you get your technical information? And from whom do you get your political information?" Some organizations map networks of trust ("Whom do you trust in this group to keep your best interests in mind?") or networks of energy ("When you interact with this person, how does it affect your energy level?"). Other organizations choose to map activities such as decision making ("To whom do you turn for advice before making an important decision?") or innovation ("With whom are you most likely to discuss a new idea?"). In short, the ability to map networks of relationships is virtually limitless and can be tailored to the needs of each organization.

The survey can be pretested on a small sample of employees to determine if they would respond positively or if the poll would be seen as an unwanted intrusion. Safeguards such as guaranteeing confidentiality and cross-checking responses can be built into the process to ensure that employees' privacy is protected and that they are answering honestly.

The information collected from the surveys is then used to create network maps that illustrate the relationships between the members of a group. Software programs are used to generate such maps since it is almost impossible to draw them by hand. Reading the maps is easy. Typically, each line on a network map indicates a link between two people, while the arrows show the direction of the relationship. In an information network, an incoming arrow indicates that someone is being sought out for information or advice and an outgoing arrow signals that someone is seeking information or advice.

If an informal network has more than 50 members, it may be a good idea to focus on the subnetworks in the group. Subgroups form for a variety of reasons—formal reporting structures, political tensions, or physical locations—and can have a major impact on a network's performance. Executives must analyze why there are such splits in the informal network before planning their interventions.

Finally, it is essential to conduct interviews with the key role-players indicated in the map. Although the roles are reflected in the number and nature of interactions among members of the group, they cannot be simply read off a map: Sometimes a person plays more than one role in a network, and, often, that same person may play different roles in different networks.

Once these network maps have been drawn, executives can start asking the right questions of the right people. Do the employees in one business unit have problems getting vital data from another business unit? Maybe that's because one of the central connectors in the informal network is hoarding information. Is the unit too isolated from other parts of the organization? Perhaps the boundary spanners aren't talking to the right people outside the group. Is the unit losing its technical expertise in a key area? It could be that a peripheral specialist needs to be drawn more closely into the network. In the following pages, we describe the four roles in detail and suggest ways that executives can transform ineffective informal networks into productive ones.

The first person you notice when you look at a network map is the person everyone in the group talks to the most. Take a look at figure 10.1, which depicts how the information flows in a global pharmaceutical company we consulted with. In this informal network, Alan is clearly the central information source for almost everyone in the network. The incoming arrows on the map indicate that Alan is the go-to person for most of his colleagues, even though Lisa is the head of the department.

In most cases, the central connectors are not the formally designated go-to people in the unit. For instance, the information flows at one practice of a large technology consulting company we worked with depended almost entirely on five midlevel managers. They would, for instance, give their colleagues background information about key clients or offer ideas on new technologies that could be employed in a given project. These managers handled most technical questions themselves, and when they couldn't, they guided their colleagues to someone else in the informal network—regardless of functional area—who had the relevant expertise. Each of these central connectors spent an hour or more every day helping the other 108 people in the group. But while their colleagues readily acknowledged the connectors' importance, their efforts were not recognized, let alone rewarded, by the company. As a result, the connectors we spoke

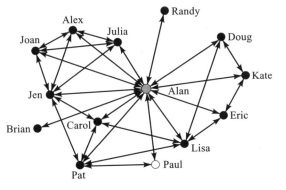

Figure 10.1.
Finding central connectors and peripheral specialists. Even though Lisa is the head of the department, Alan is considered the go-to person for information within this informal network. He plays the role of central connector. Meanwhile, Paul operates on the perimeter of the network, offering expertise to members of the group as it's needed, but not necessarily connecting with many other colleagues frequently. Paul plays the role of peripheral specialist.

with were losing heart; they told us they were planning to focus more on work that top management was inclined to reward.

Therefore, it's important to explicitly recognize the connectors. Indeed, merely acknowledging their existence by showing them the network map, and their important role in it, gives central connectors considerable gratification. But for the long term, companies need to set up tangible ways to reward the good citizenship of their connectors.

Some organizations offer spot rewards. For instance, there were few central connectors at a large engineering company we studied, so senior executives instituted a system of "above and beyond" rewards: Each time someone went out of his or her way to introduce a colleague in trouble to those who could help solve the problem, the connector was nominated for a cash reward. Although small, the bonus was paid out quickly and the effort was publicly acknowledged. This incentive helped create many more central connectors in the engineering company in a relatively short time.

Other organizations have changed aspects of their performance management systems to regularly reward central connectors. For instance, an investment bank we worked with changed the criteria for its annual bonuses: At the end of the review period, each manager's ability to link people in the bank was specifically evaluated by all the people with whom he or she worked. The most successful connectors (those who greatly improved employee communications, for instance) were awarded bigger bonuses than other managers were—a major departure from the schemes most investment banks follow, in which the managers who create the most profits get the biggest bonuses.

While most central connectors serve the company in a positive way, linking colleagues and increasing productivity, some end up creating bottlenecks that can hold back the informal network. Sometimes the connectors use their roles for political or financial gain; in other cases, they are just struggling to keep up with their own work while also fulfilling their roles in the network. Whatever the reason, it is not easy for the other members of the network to supplant an ineffective central connector because he or she is often the person around whom the network first formed. There may be little incentive for anyone else to take on this time-consuming role. Instead, the members of the network will keep buzzing around the central connector out of sheer habit—though, increasingly less often than they would like to.

A network map cannot tell you explicitly whether a central connector is creating a bottleneck. But if department members complain that their work suffers because of poor communication—citing, for instance, that they can't get information quickly enough to do their work—the organization's first task should be to get a sense of the personalities and workloads of the central connectors in that unit. Then, by using the network maps as the basis for a conversation, executives can, where necessary, coach connectors to improve their effectiveness and stop impeding the network.

In those cases where a central connector is consciously hoarding information or playing colleagues off one another, the solution usually involves altering the incentive systems that different departments or units use; conflicting reward systems can often cause such problems. Other organizational interventions, such as redesigning jobs and rotating people among different positions, can also help. At one government agency, a central connector was essentially pitting two subsets of the informal network against each other in order to enhance his own reputation in the agency. That is, the connector claimed success at integrating work between the two groups but wasn't helping the most relevant people from each subgroup connect on a given project. So the groups were not working as efficiently as they could have been. The organization decided to tackle this problem by changing the way it created project teams. Using information from a network analysis the company had conducted, executives carefully staffed new teams with members from both subsets of the informal network. That allowed members of both groups to work closely with one another and lowered the barriers among them. The central connector's stranglehold was broken even though he continued to play a key role in the informal network.

Power plays can happen, but more often, bottlenecks occur because the central connectors' jobs have grown too big for them, and they are struggling to keep up. They work at a frenetic pace and don't realize that they are slowing down others by not responding quickly enough to their colleagues or subordinates. In such cases, executives might intervene by reallocating responsibilities. For example, if a person is central to an informal network because of the depth of her knowledge in consulting or banking or software development, it may be a good idea to reassign some of her other work so that she can continue to focus on her area of expertise. Alternatively, if people are central only because they monitor information that many people need, it may be possible to make those data more widely available in other ways—for instance, using e-mail or a corporate intranet to disseminate information to everyone in the company.

We analyzed the communication flows among 200 globally dispersed professionals at a management consultancy. Two partners within the group were the central connectors, and nearly everyone in the network felt it necessary to communicate frequently with one or the other. As a result, the two were heavily overworked. Both would stay up well into the night to answer all the e-mail from their colleagues. Our network maps identified these overloaded central connectors, and changes were made to reduce the logjam. Some of the partners' work responsibilities, such as approving travel requests and reviewing all projects, were shifted to their colleagues, and several formal communication forums were created for transmitting routine information. For instance, new policies were put in place that allowed people in the network to make their own decisions—within set limits—about expenditures for travel, equipment, or service ideas. And the consultancy encouraged broader participation in weekly operational conference calls.

■ The Boundary Spanner

Every informal network has its roving ambassadors, people who serve as the group's eyes and ears in the wider world. These boundary spanners nurture connections mainly with people outside the informal network— for instance, they communicate with people in other departments within a company, at different satellite offices, and even in other organizations. As figure 10.2 indicates, Andy plays the role of a boundary spanner in an investment bank's informal network. Through his relationships with central connectors in two other informal networks, Andy serves as an efficient conduit of information; he puts most people in all the networks at less than four removes from one another.

Boundary spanners play an important role in those situations where people need to share different kinds of expertise—for instance, in establishing strategic alliances or developing new products. When we mapped the R&D department at a leading consumer-products company, we found that just 4 of the 36 researchers in the group maintained links with academics in their fields. These four boundary spanners were the sole sources of crucial knowledge for the entire team, and if any of them were to leave

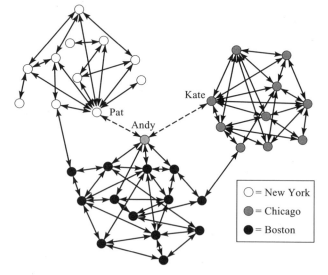

Figure 10.2.
Spotting boundary spanners. Because of his links to the central connectors in two other informal networks, Andy serves as the main conduit of information between the Boston network and groups in Chicago and New York. He plays the role of boundary spanner.

or be promoted out of R&D, the productivity of the entire group would have been hit hard.

Boundary spanners are a rare breed, however, and few networks have many of them. That's primarily because most people don't have the breadth of intellectual expertise, the wealth of social contacts, and the personality traits necessary to be accepted by vastly different groups. They may have one or two of these components but rarely have all. For instance, few marketing managers are welcomed into the heart of an R&D network, largely because the two groups value different aspects of their work.

Corporate life may not be particularly friendly to the boundary spanner, who has to spend a lot of time developing an external network. To do so, the spanner may take up projects and tasks that cut across formal boundaries in the company, and he or she may spend less time in the immediate network. If that kind of work is not welcomed by the organization, it could set back the spanner's career.

Senior executives can use network maps to check whether their boundary spanners are making the right connections—particularly with central connectors in other groups. In our investment bank example, if Andy were connected to a peripheral specialist (who, by definition, is not central to the network and works apart from most colleagues) rather than to a central connector, the average degree of separation would rise in the network. It is hard for executives to legislate who boundary spanners should build relationships with, but senior managers can shape the spanners' networks in subtle ways. At one commercial bank we consulted with, midlevel managers were asked to set new product-development goals for themselves in conjunction with the senior executives in other units. The resulting planning meetings and projects prompted the formation of close informal relationships among people who served in different functions at different levels of the bank. This created many more boundary spanners in the bank, which is what top management wanted.

A company can reap substantial benefits by recognizing its boundary spanners. Take the case of the consumer goods practice of a global consulting firm we worked with. This group was distributed across different offices in North America, Europe, and Australia. Few consultants knew their counterparts in other countries, so coordination among the offices was poor. The firm saw a dramatic improvement, however, once it recognized the few people who were informally in touch with colleagues in other offices and gave them incentives to do more of this. A network analysis was conducted to formally identify these boundary spanners, and they were increasingly assigned to projects that would require them to travel to offices on all three continents. As a result, the spanners developed larger and more reliable personal networks all over the world. Since the firm was making additional demands on them, the senior partners awarded the boundary spanners generous salary increases as well as quicker promotions. A follow-up network analysis that we conducted a year later showed that many of the groups in the firm were, indeed, much more integrated. New projects were won and old contracts were extended, partly because people were able to get the knowledge or expertise they needed from their far-flung colleagues more easily.

■ The Information Broker

In large informal networks, you may find people who connect the various subnetworks in the company. Without these information brokers, the network as a whole wouldn't exist. For instance, remove Joe from figure 10.3 and you no longer have one large informal network but rather three smaller, more tightly knit groups that are quite isolated from one another. Information brokers play a role similar to that of boundary spanners, only they do it within the social network.

Information brokers are disproportionately important to the informal network's effectiveness because they wield the power of a central con-

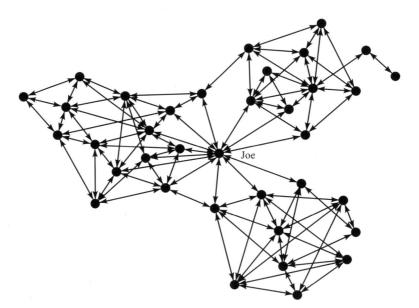

Figure 10.3.
Identifying information brokers. Joe holds the various parts of this large, informal network together. He may not have as many direct connections with colleagues as the central connectors in the network do, but he has a wealth of indirect associations. If Joe were removed, this large, informal network would splinter into three smaller, disjointed subnetworks. Joe is the information broker.

nector without necessarily possessing the number of direct links that connectors have. In fact, they are characterized by a wealth of indirect connections. (In figure 10.3, Joe is connected directly or by two degrees of separation to more than 20 people in the network.) Information brokers play such a critical role that organizations often try to manage large informal networks through them.

At one electronics company, for example, we identified eight information brokers in a community of practice of 120 people. Senior managers were so impressed by the brokers' efforts that they decided to reinforce their work by making them, their expertise, and the roles they played explicit to the whole group. The information brokers were allowed to spend 20% of their time supporting the network and were officially designated as the go-to people in their areas of expertise—electronics and various kinds of engineering. The information brokers stayed in touch with one another through bimonthly conference calls and frequent on-line chat forums, and senior managers provided collaboration software that helped them stay abreast of who knew (or was doing) what in the informal network. When the analysis was originally conducted, the members of the work community were, on average, four removes from one another. After the interventions, almost all the employees were only two links from one another—a degree of connectivity that greatly improved information sharing in the group. Thus, the organization ensured, with minimal investment, that the members of this community could leverage their collective expertise more easily and effectively.

There is, however, a degree of danger in relying too much on information brokers, whose departure could tear apart an informal network. Executives should, therefore, encourage central connectors to develop more connections with subgroups they are not adequately linked with. That way, if the need arises, a connector could take over an information broker's role in the network.

The Peripheral Specialist

Large or small, every informal network has its outsiders. Although they operate on the periphery, these people play a vital role in the network by serving as experts. They possess specific kinds of information or technical knowledge—for instance, research data, or software skills, or customer preferences—that they pass on to the other members of the group whenever it is needed. Executives typically assume that it is a bad idea for anyone to be a peripheral specialist, and they often take great pains to socialize these people. If their efforts fail, they may even conclude that such people are expendable. That can be an expensive mistake.

To be sure, many peripheral specialists could contribute more if they were tightly integrated in the informal network. In fact, many people on the periphery are new hires who are desperately trying to get better connected. But the peripheral specialists are intentionally on the edge of a network. They might be loners who do not like to work too closely with the rest of the group or people who have to invest a lot of time outside the network to stay on the cutting edge. (For a depiction of peripheral specialists' place in the network, see figure 10.1.) Integrating peripheral specialists may distract them from staying ahead in their fields; they can't stay on top of what they want to do if they are forced to sit on committees. And these frustrated specialists are likely to take their skills to a more accommodating employer.

Consider one high-tech company we worked with. Several of its leading researchers were threatening to resign. Senior management was blindsided by this news because the team had been extremely successful at developing new technologies and introducing them to the rest of the company, and their work had been handsomely rewarded and recognized. But a social network analysis showed that the organization was destroying the group because it did not recognize that most of the scientists were peripheral specialists. As the researchers came up with winning applications, senior managers started asking them to attend more internal meetings and to present their findings to large customers. As their successes increased, the demands on the researchers' time increased to such a level that they felt unable to stay at the cutting edge of their areas of expertise, let alone advance them.

In other cases, people operate on the outer fringes of a network for personal reasons. They might, for instance, be the primary caregivers in their families. If the company subtly forces these people into more activities—such as early—morning conference calls, late—evening meetings, and increased travel—they will resent having to participate and may eventually quit. Executives who value the expertise of people in these situations need to be extremely sensitive to the demands placed on them and respect the desire of such people to play only a peripheral role in the informal network.

■ Personal Network Management

Up to this point, we have presented social network analysis as a tool for viewing groups of people. But an equally powerful way to promote connectivity in the organization is to give employees customized views of their personal networks. Through social network analysis, people can identify where they need to build more or better relationships, and senior executives can coach them appropriately: Is all the manager's information coming from people above him rather than below him? Does his network include only those people who work on the same floor? Is he missing feedback from people with different perspectives?

Many characteristics can be used to analyze managers' social networks—education, gender, and age among them. But we have found that a focus on four dimensions can help managers improve their connections. The first is the extent to which managers seek out people within or outside of their functional areas. Second is the degree to which hierarchy, tenure, and location matter to the managers' social relationships. Third is the length of time managers have known their connections. And fourth is the extent to which managers' personal networks are the result of interactions that are built into their schedules (such as planned meetings) rather than ad hoc encounters in the hallways.

Letting employees get a closer look at their personal networks can help them uncover all kinds of weaknesses. For instance, we conducted a social network analysis of the information flows among the senior executives in the Americas division of a major technology company. We focused on the way information flowed among the nine senior managers and the next layer down in the organization (a group of 54 executives). In addition to assessing the effectiveness of the group, we analyzed each of the top leaders' personal networks. (This can be a particularly important exercise for senior executives, since a significant part of their jobs is to make effective decisions, and most of the information they rely on comes from people in their networks.) Let's consider two of those top nine executives, Neil and Dave, who both had significant responsibilities throughout the division.

Dave's network was smaller than Neil's, both in terms of the number of people seeking information from them (10 people for Dave, 14 for Neil) and in terms of the number of people they sought out for information (14 people for Dave, 21 for Neil). But the difference in the sizes of their networks was not as revealing as the difference in the composition of their networks. Dave tended to acquire information almost exclusively from those in his functional area; of his 10 informal contacts, 9 were from his department. By contrast, 8 of Neil's 14 informal contacts were members of his department, and 6 worked in different functional areas. Although we couldn't definitively say that Dave would have had a more adaptable network if he had forged relationships with people from a greater number of functional units, we felt it important to make him aware of this potential bias, which was likely to affect both his ability to learn and his decision making. Other aspects of Dave's network also suggested rigidity. For example, he tended to turn only to people he had known for a long time or had met because they were structured into his schedule. As a result, Dave had much less exposure to new concepts or information than Neil did.

Dave was initially surprised to find that there were such biases inherent in his personal network. But he admitted there had been instances when decisions he had made or actions he had taken had caused problems because he had not considered other perspectives. Through his own initiative, and with the help of a coaching program that senior management established, Dave set out to systematically identify and nurture the relationships he had underinvested in and to decrease his reliance on relationships he had overinvested in, thereby strengthening his personal network.

Because informal networks are not, by their very nature, part of the official hierarchy, they are often starved of resources—and the right kind of management attention. Indeed, many organizations cling to the outdated notion that as long as they indirectly create the right context—more off-sites, more company picnics, and more coffee machines in the hallways—informal networks will flourish. That is simply not enough. Social networks cannot be aligned with organizational goals through those kinds of random interventions. It is only after executives openly and systematically start working with informal networks that the groups will become more effective.

Moreover, we have found that people with strong personal networks—such as the key role-players—are more satisfied in their jobs and stay longer at their companies than employees with weak networks. Thus, working with the role-players to improve their effectiveness not only will boost productivity but will also help executives retain the people who really make their organizations tick.

11

Making Invisible Work Visible

Using Social Network Analysis to Support

Strategic Collaboration

■ Rob Cross, Stephen P. Borgatti, and Andrew Parker

Over the past decade, significant restructuring efforts have resulted in organizations with fewer hierarchical levels and more permeable internal and external boundaries. A byproduct of these restructuring efforts is that coordination and work increasingly occur through informal networks of relationships rather than through channels tightly prescribed by formal reporting structures or detailed work processes. For example, informal networks cutting across core work processes or holding together new product development initiatives are not found on formal organizational charts. Rather, these networks often promote organizational flexibility, innovation, and efficiency, as well as quality of products or services, by virtue of effectively pooling unique expertise. Supporting collaboration and work in these informal networks is increasingly important for organizations competing on knowledge and an ability to innovate and adapt.

Unfortunately, critical informal networks often compete with and are fragmented by such aspects of organizations as formal structure, work processes, geographic dispersion, human resource practices, leadership style, and culture. This is particularly problematic in knowledge-intensive settings where management is counting on collaboration among employees with different types of expertise. People rely very heavily on their network of relationships to find information and solve problems—one of the most consistent findings in the social science literature is that who you know often has a great deal to do with what you come to know.[1] Yet both practical experience and scholarly research indicate significant difficulty in getting people with different expertise, backgrounds, and problem-solving styles to effectively integrate their unique perspectives.[2] Simply moving boxes on an organizational chart is not sufficient to ensure effective collaboration among high-end knowledge workers.

Movement toward de-layered, flexible organizations and emphasis on supporting collaboration in knowledge-intensive work has made it increasingly important for executives and managers to attend to informal networks within their organizations. Performance implications of effective informal networks can be significant as the rapidly growing social capital tradition has indicated at the individual, team, and organizational levels.[3] Yet while research indicates ways managers can influence informal networks at both the individual[4] and whole network levels,[5] executives seem to do relatively little to assess and support critical, but often invisible, informal networks in organizations.[6]

Over the past eighteen months, we have conducted research to determine how organizations can better support work occurring in informal networks of employees. Working with a consortium of Fortune 500 companies and government agencies, we assessed collaboration and work in 29 informal networks from 23 different organizations. In all cases, the networks we studied provided strategic and operational value to the embedding organization by enabling employees to effectively collaborate and integrate disparate expertise. The first goal of our research was to better define scenarios where conducting a social network analysis (SNA) would likely yield sufficient benefit to justify the investment of time and energy on the part of the organization. A second goal of our work was to develop generalized insight into analyses that were informative and actionable for practitioners.

■ Assessing and Supporting Informal Networks

Put an organizational chart in front of most any employee and they will tell you the boxes and lines only partially reflect the way work gets done in their organization. Informal relationships among employees are often far more reflective of the way work happens in an organization than relationships established by position within the formal structure. However, these informal relationships are often invisible or at least only partially understood by managers—a problem that is growing with de-layering of organizations, virtual work, and globalization. While managers often think they understand the networks around them, studies show that they can vary widely in the accuracy of their network perceptions.[7] As outlined by Krackhardt and Hanson: "Although managers may be able to diagram accurately the social links of the five or six people closest to them, their assumptions about employees outside their immediate circle are usually off the mark."[8]

Social network analysis can be an invaluable tool for systematically assessing and then intervening at critical points within an informal network. Of course, social network techniques have been around for some time. The idea of drawing a picture (called a "sociogram") of who is connected to whom for a specific set of people is credited to Dr. J. L. Moreno, an early social psychologist who envisioned mapping the entire population of New York City.[9] Cultural anthropologists independently invented the notion of social networks to provide a new way to think about social structure and the concepts of role and position,[10] an approach that culminated in rigorous algebraic treatments of kinship systems.[11] At the same time, in mathematics, the nascent field of graph theory began to grow rapidly, providing the underpinnings for the analytical techniques of modern SNA.[12] The new methods were particularly embraced in sociology, where relational theoretical perspectives had been important since the dawn of the field.[13]

Today, the scholarly discipline is growing in the field of management as researchers have clearly demonstrated the extent to which informal networks pervade and effect life and work within organizations.[14] A particularly important line of inquiry in this work has been to understand forces influencing the emergence of informal networks within organizations.[15] Through such work we have learned that communication is likely to occur in homophilous[16] relationships and have evidence of the role of similarity between people in increasing the likelihood of communication.[17] At the same time, we have also learned that design of an organization can have a strong influence on the pattern of informal networks via formal structure,[18] physical proximity,[19] and nature of the task.[20]

This and other research has begun to help us think about means of assessing and supporting informal networks within organizations. Yet while clearly informing the field of management, the majority of this work is found in academic outlets often inaccessible to practitioners due to the technical nature of the publications and network terminology employed. In addition, these pieces intend to advance science and so do not as a matter of practice make clear to managers the ways in which network analysis can be applied to organizational issues. While the outcomes of such research might influence decision makers in terms of policy variables, a more contextualized perspective is needed to help practitioners apply network analysis to their specific organizational concerns.

At the most rudimentary level, we have found that visually assessing the pattern of relationships that hold a certain group together can reveal a number of interesting and actionable points. For example, identifying people that are highly central in networks (and so disproportionately impact a group by controlling information or decision making) can help a manager consider how to reallocate informational domains or decision-making rights so that the group as a whole is more effective. Alternatively, understanding who is peripheral in a network and crafting ways to engage these people is also an important means of ensuring that expertise resident in a given network is being effectively utilized. Particularly in today's age of turnover, it is increasingly important to get people connected more and more quickly so that they are productive for an organization. Furthermore, assessing junctures in networks that are fragmented across functional or hierarchical boundaries (or detecting subgroups) can be particularly informative for social or technical interventions that help to integrate disparate groups.[21]

While social network information can be obtained in a variety of ways, the most pragmatic means in organizational settings is typically through surveys. Very informative social network diagrams can be generated from 10- to 15-minute surveys assessing information or knowledge flow among members of a group. In this process, the first step is to identify an informal network where effective collaboration and knowledge sharing has a significant impact on the organization's operations or strategy. Often, these groups do not appear on a formal organizational chart, yet their ability to collaborate and pool disparate expertise is critical to the current and future success of an organization. As a result, in the first stages of an SNA it is often important to push executives beyond groups defined by the formal organizational chart to those that might cross functional or hierarchical boundaries (e.g., new product development, communities of practice, or top leadership networks). These groups often go unrecognized and unsupported even when their interactions underlie organizational capabilities or support strategically important innovation.

Conducting a social network survey is a straightforward process of obtaining a list of all people in the defined network and simply asking all members of the group to characterize their relationships with each other. In this process, it is important to ensure that the kinds of relationships measured are appropriate for the task at hand and not unnecessarily inflammatory. Organizations are very different in their tolerance for disclosure of various kinds of social relations. In some, we have been asked to map relationships of trust and power, while in others we have been asked to disguise names on all relationship diagrams (including more innocuous ones such as who works with whom). One of the most powerful ways to apply SNA as a diagnostic tool and a catalyst for change is to put people's names on a network diagram and make the diagram available to all group members as a basis for dialogue. However, such diagrams can be sensitive, depending on the kinds of network questions asked and the culture of the specific organization. As a result, we pay considerable attention to shaping the questions asked so that they are helpful to the specific issue an organization is grappling with while at the same time not unnecessarily disruptive to existing relationships.

As a guide, we have outlined several important relationships and reasons for targeting these relationships in Appendix 1. The primary focus of our research lay with establishing applications of SNA as a diagnostic tool for managers attempting to promote collaboration and knowledge sharing in important networks. Through this process, we found SNA uniquely effective in (1) promoting effective collaboration within a strategically important group; (2) supporting critical junctures in networks that cross functional, hierarchical, or geographic boundaries; and (3) ensuring integration within groups following strategic restructuring initiatives.

Promoting Effective Collaboration within a Strategically Important Group

Social network analysis can be a very effective tool for promoting collaboration and knowledge sharing within important groups such as core functions of an organization, research and development departments, and strategic business units. For example, in one global consulting organization, we worked with a highly skilled group that was commissioned to provide thought leadership and specialized support to the organization's knowledge management consultants. This group was composed of people with either advanced degrees or extensive industry experience in strategy and organizational design or technical fields such as data warehousing or information architecture. By integrating these highly specialized skill sets, leadership of the consultancy felt the firm could provide a holistic knowledge management solution that would differentiate it from competitors focusing on solely technical or organizational solutions. However, the partner leading this group felt intuitively that the team was not leveraging its abilities as effectively as possible and asked us to conduct an SNA of information flow within the group.

Our analysis confirmed the partner's intuition. As shown in the top half of figure 11.1, the information sharing network revealed not one group at all, but two distinct subgroups. Interestingly enough, the group had become divided on precisely the dimension it needed to be connected, as it was the group's unique skill sets that turned out to account for the fragmentation of this network. The group on the left side of the network was skilled in the "softer" issues of strategy or organizational design, often focusing on cultural interventions or other aspects of organizations to help improve knowledge creation and sharing. The group on the right was composed of people skilled in "harder" technical aspects of knowledge management, such as information architecture, modeling, and data warehousing.

Over time, members of these two subgroups had gravitated to each other based on common interests. These people often worked on projects together and just as important shared common work-related interests in terms of what they read, conference attendance, and working groups within the organization. The problem was that each subgroup had grown to a point of not knowing what people in the other subgroup could do in a consulting engagement or how to think about involving them in their projects. Thus, even when there were opportunities in client engagements to incorporate each other's skill sets, this was often not done because neither group knew what the other knew or how to apply their skill sets to new opportunities. This was despite the fact that the group's strategic charter was to integrate these unique skill sets and that all aspects of formal organizational design supported this mission (e.g., reporting structure, common performance metrics, and incentives).

Pre-Intervention

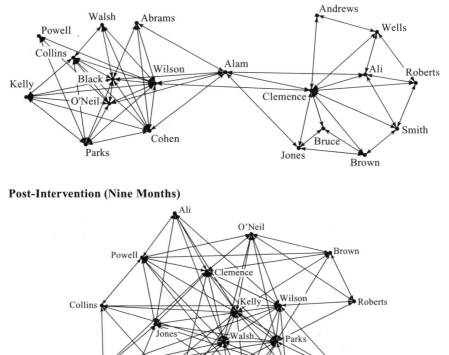

Post-Intervention (Nine Months)

Figure 11.1.
Information sharing within an expert consulting group. *Note*: Names were disguised in this example at the request of the organization.

Conducting the SNA provided several intervention opportunities. A lengthy facilitated session with this group allowed members to assess and discuss the relative isolation of the two specialties, as well as more pointed concerns about certain members' expertise not being tapped while other members appeared to be bottlenecks in sharing information. As a result of the discussion around this social network, various changes were made to the group's operations. First, a variety of internal projects—ranging from white papers to development of a project-tracking database—were jointly staffed with one person from each group. This move forced people to work together and so begin to develop an appreciation of each other's unique skills and knowledge. Second, the partner implemented mixed revenue sales goals so that each of the managers was accountable for selling projects that included both a technical and organizational component. This new policy also forced people to find ways to integrate their approaches to addressing client problems. Finally, several new communication forums were created—including weekly status calls, a short update e-mail done weekly, and a project-tracking database that helped each person keep up-to-date on what other members were doing.

The result of these interventions was significant. Over the course of the next several months, the group began to sell more work that integrated technical and organizational skills. In addition, this integration often proved to differentiate the consultancy from its competition in the sales process. Further, as can be seen in the bottom half of figure 11.1, a network analysis conducted nine months later revealed a well-integrated group that was sharing information much more effectively.

In this case, the underlying problem was that each subgroup had grown to a point of not knowing what the other group knew (and so how to even consider integrating their expertise in projects). As a result, the interventions undertaken focused on helping to develop this awareness and not simply on implementing a collaborative technology or group process intervention that ultimately would not have addressed the underlying need to create an awareness of each other's expertise. Other common factors fragmenting networks include hierarchical leadership style; physical dispersion and virtual work; politics resulting in subgroups; "not invented here" mentality resulting in networks with dense subgroups only weakly connected to other subgroups; and workflow processes or job descriptions that overload specific roles and slow the group.

Each of these issues demands a different set of interventions; however, social network analysis, combined with some interviews, makes these interactions visible, allowing for a diagnosis and an appropriate solution.

Supporting Critical Junctures in Networks That Cross Boundaries

Social network analysis can also be an effective means of pinpointing breakdowns in informal networks that cross functional, hierarchical, geographic, or organizational boundaries (e.g., merger or acquisition scenarios, new product development, or top leadership networks). People within these networks must often collaborate effectively for the organization to benefit despite the fact that they may reside in different physical locations and/or be held accountable for different financial and operational goals. Social network analysis provides insight into collaborative behavior within and across boundaries that can yield a similar purchase on performance improvement opportunities as process mapping did for reengineering in the early 1990s.[22] Reengineering generally focused on "hand-offs," decision points, and the "white space" in organizational charts to improve efficiency of work processes. Today, concern has shifted to innovation that often requires critical collaboration within and between functional units, divisions, and even entire organizations. Network analysis provides us with the means to understand where collaboration is and is not occurring.

Collaboration across Functional Boundaries

For example, we mapped the relationships of one Fortune 500 organization's top 126 executives to assess collaboration across divisions. This was an organization that had grown by acquisition over several years with the primary intent that acquired companies would combine their expertise in developing and taking to market new products and services. The CEO of this organization had become acutely aware of the need to create a leadership network that was able to recognize opportunities in one sphere of the network and know enough of what others in the conglomerate knew to be able to combine the appropriate resources in response to these opportunities. As there was some evidence that this was not happening, we were invited to come in and conduct an SNA of his top executives both within and across these acquired organizations.

While various network diagrams were generated in our assessment, the most insightful view came from a simple table demonstrating collaborative activity among this network of executives. Table 11.1 outlines the percentage of collaborative relationships that existed within and between each specific division (out of 100% possible in each cell). Looking at the table provided an opportunity to learn from practices within one division and apply these practices in others where the work of each division required similar levels of collaboration. Similarly, we were also able to determine which of the merged organizations (termed "divisions" in table

Table 11.1
Collaboration across Merged Divisions within a Conglomerate

	Div. 1	Div. 2	Div. 3	Div. 4	Div. 5	Div. 6	Div. 7	Div. 8
Division 1	**33%**							
Division 2	5%	**76%**						
Division 3	11%	18%	**45%**					
Division 4	2%	11%	21%	**38%**				
Division 5	6%	7%	12%	6%	**75%**			
Division 6	7%	2%	13%	7%	2%	**76%**		
Division 7	1%	3%	16%	6%	8%	2%	**36%**	
Division 8	10%	2%	9%	6%	3%	10%	0%	**90%**

11.1) had integrated well with other divisions. For example, a quick review of table 11.1 shows that divisions 3 and 4 had a relatively high degree of collaboration; whereas divisions 1 and 7 had minimal contact.[23]

This simple summary of collaborative activity within and between divisions provided a great deal of insight into the inner workings of the organization. The company had acquired various organizations with the intent that they collaborate in bringing their offerings to market. However, the SNA showed that there was only limited collaborative activity in pockets of the organization. Various reasons existed for this. In some settings, members of the executive team were not sure what a given division did and so did not know how to even think about involving them in their projects. In others, cultural barriers restricted people from seeking information outside of their own divisions. In some, the complementarity of product offerings that was presumed when an acquisition was made did not exist. As a result, different interventions were applied as appropriate throughout the network; however, it was the view of collaborative activity afforded by the SNA that allowed the organization to intervene appropriately at these strategic junctures.

Throughout the organizations we worked with in our research we found this kind of cross-boundary view powerful for identifying points where collaborative activity is not occurring due to organizational boundaries and for providing a more targeted approach to interventions. It is important to recognize that it is often not the case that one wants high collaborative activity among all departments within an organization. People have a finite amount of time to put into developing and maintaining relationships. With network analysis, we can begin to take a portfolio approach to considering the constellation of relationships that is worth investing time and energy to develop and maintain. For example, in the disguised scenario outlined above, it was not critical that division 1 be tightly connected to all other divisions to help the organization meet strategic objectives. To provide strategic value to the organization, division 1 really only needed to be well connected to divisions 3, 5, and 6. Thus, rather than engage in a company wide initiative to improve collaboration, more targeted and ultimately more successful interventions were employed to facilitate collaboration at specific junctures.

Mapping the pattern of information flow (or, more frequently, lack of flow) across functional barriers can yield critical insight into where management should target efforts to promote collaboration that will provide strategic benefit. Quite often, initiatives attempting to promote collaboration and learning take a cultural perspective and usually struggle with the enormity of the task at hand. In contrast, we have found that by targeting junctures in networks that hold strategic relevance for an organization, it is much more feasible to intervene where investments in collaboration yield strategic payoff for the organization. Moreover, by tracking changes in networks over time, management and network participants have a very real way of assessing the impact of interventions on both the informal network and organizational effectiveness.

Collaboration across Hierarchical Boundaries

Another type of critical boundary within organizations is not functional but hierarchical. Across the various companies in our research, we have seen very different network patterns in relation to hierarchy. Some informal networks in an organization are very similar to, and thus obviously constrained by, the organization's hierarchy. Others are more fluid and seem to place less of a constraint on whether employees follow the chain of command to obtain information. What is good or bad depends on the kind of work the organization does; however, it is interesting diagnostically to see the extent to which hierarchy conditions information flow and knowledge exchange in a given organization. Just as we analyzed collaboration across divisional boundaries in the conglomerate noted above, we can also assess collaboration and information sharing across hierarchical levels within an organization.

Alternatively, we can assess how those in positions of formal authority are embedded in larger networks within their organization. For example, we were asked to map the top leadership network of a commercial bank. However, rather than just mapping the top 9 members of the management team, we looked at information-seeking and-sharing behaviors among the top 62 executives of this organization (SVP level and above) to understand how this network was collaborating. One particularly informative view came from assessing the pattern of relationships *among* the top 9 executives and then *between* these executives and the overall top 62 executives in the institution. By pulling out the top 9 executives and mapping the flow of information among these executives, we could assess the extent to which this group was effectively collaborating as a decision-making body. Further, by considering this group in the context of the larger network of 62 people, we could also see the extent to which the executive team tapped into the larger leadership network for informational purposes or communicated decisions effectively back to this group. Figure 11.2 shows a simplified graphic portrayal of this network that identifies connections between the CEO and the remaining executives in both the executive leadership team and the bank's functional departments. In this diagram, the direction of the arrows reflects whom the CEO seeks out for information or advice and the numbers beside the arrows reflect the number of people in each department that the CEO turned to.

Diagnostically, these kinds of views are important along two fronts. First, by looking at a completed diagram showing the same relationship patterns for all members of the top management team, we can get a sense of how information tends to enter and leave this group. The bulk of in-

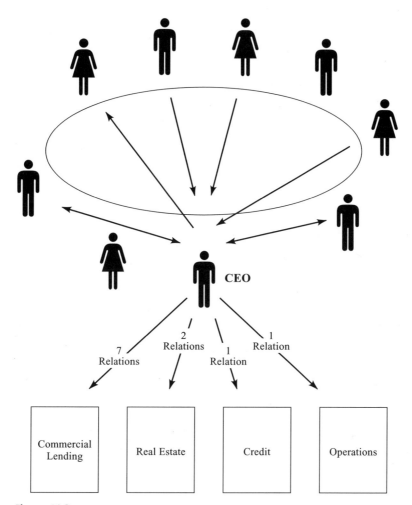

Figure 11.2.
Collaboration across hierarchical boundaries

formation that managers use to make decisions comes from meetings and conversations. Social network analysis provides a way to better understand the way in which teams might be biased in critical decisions by virtue of the kinds of information received in discussions with others. Which members of the executive team seem to reach out to various functional areas (and so likely best understand issues and concerns of these groups)? Is the executive group seeking information from (or at least listening to) these people? Are certain functional departments more sought out than others (thereby potentially representing biases in information this group relies on for strategic decisionmaking)? Given the strategic importance of the decisions that a top management team makes, understanding their sources and usage of information can provide critical insight into ways to improve their effectiveness. This of course also holds for other groups such as new product development initiatives or process redesign efforts where one hopes that the teams are effectively reaching out to relevant and balanced sources of information prior to making critical decisions.

In terms of executive development, these kinds of views can also be highly effective in uncovering potential biases in a single person's network. A long-standing finding in communication research is that people tend to interact with people that are similar to themselves on a set of socially important attributes, such as race, gender, and age.[24] This makes communication easier and often more satisfying; however, it is also a source of bias in what executives learn and think is important. In the example above, it was apparent that the CEO heavily attended to and was influenced by the concerns of the commercial lending group where he spent the bulk of his career. In private conversations after reviewing this diagram, he reflected on what he felt were ineffective tendencies in his own decisions over time due in large part to the biased way he sought information from others. As a result of the SNA of his organization, he made more concerted efforts to balance whom he sought out for information within and outside of the bank.

Ensuring Integration within Groups Following Strategic Change Initiatives

Social network analysis can also play a powerful role in assessing the health of informal structure after a change has been implemented, such as an internal restructuring or acquisition. It is well known that performance does not always improve as anticipated even when technically sound solutions are implemented. Frequently, this problem is attributed either to a misalignment somewhere in the organization's formal structure or to a failure of leadership. However, we have consistently found that a lack of social, technical, or organizational support provided to strategically important informal networks is at least as important a predictor of failure. Very often, large-scale change initiatives impair the effectiveness of established networks while at the same time doing little to help development of new relationships.

Social network analysis can be a very useful means of assessing the impact of strategic restructuring initiatives on the informal structure of an organization. For example, we conducted an SNA of the global telecommunications practice of a major consulting organization. This firm was going through a significant restructuring initiative to combine the expertise of several groups into one industry practice in order to compete more effectively with other major consulting organizations. By combining smaller practices into one global network, partners felt that the firm would be better able to provide the best and most directly relevant expertise for both sales initiatives and consulting engagements. Further, significant efficiency benefits were anticipated as consultants would be able to leverage the work of others in this practice rather than continually starting from scratch.

Of course, deriving these strategic benefits hinged on this group's willingness and ability to share information and leverage each other's expertise. Almost a year after the initial restructuring, the partner leading the practice had become increasingly concerned that the overall group was not integrating as effectively as it should. However, aside from some surface-level indicators of this problem based on sales and billable hour metrics, he had no true understanding of his practice's integration or where to begin in terms of corrective action. The practice was globally distributed and of such size that he had never even had the opportunity to meet many of the people. To get a better understanding of this network, he invited us in to conduct an SNA.

Our SNA confirmed the fragmentation of the network and provided some useful insights and information to work with in helping integrate his practice. What we immediately noticed was significant clustering in the network despite the entire practice reporting to one overall partner and being embedded within a common organizational context (i.e., strategy, performance metrics, technical infrastructure). As can be seen in figure 11.3, we found three tightly knit subgroups rather than one integrated network—two in North America and one in Europe. In fact, apart from the partner, only a handful of hierarchically lower-level employees served to bridge these subgroups because they had developed relationships when staffed on projects together.

A first intervention for this partner was to use the network diagram to create common awareness of the lack of integration among the leaders of this practice. One of the more important benefits of SNA is that it helps to make visible, and therefore actionable, the ways that work is occurring within organizations. We have worked with global groups ranging up to almost 300 people with only three or four levels of hierarchy. Clearly, the span of control combined with the physical dispersion of such groups makes it close to impossible for any one person or group of people to know what is going on or how executive decisions are affecting the work and effectiveness of these networks. Social network analysis provides a snapshot for executives that can be used to gain agreement on what problems need to be addressed in such a distributed group, what appropriate interventions need to be taken, and how to conduct a follow-up network analysis to ensure that initiatives are having the desired impact.

In this case, though formal aspects of the organization were aligned, we learned that there were no initiatives in place to help employees learn others' expertise. As a result, the organization took a number of steps to

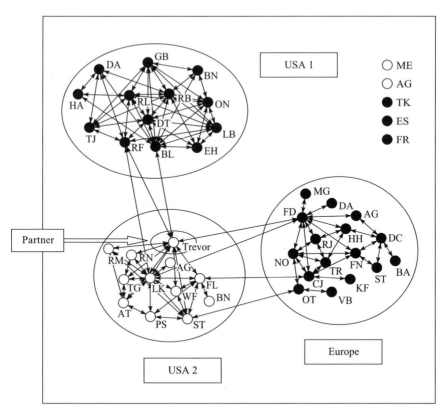

Figure 11.3.
Information sharing in a global consulting practice

help build this awareness of "who knows what." First, they redesigned their approach to staffing both client projects and internal initiatives to help integrate people from the different locations. On a technical front, they implemented a skill-profiling system and a virtual environment to promote collaboration on consulting engagements. On a social front, a series of face-to-face meetings were conducted to help people meet and learn the projects that other people were working on and the expertise that they held. This step was critical to the group's integration as it was not until people actually met face-to-face that the skill-profiling system began to be used. Finally, a shift in skills targeted in recruiting, as well as performance measurement, was made to encourage joint problem solving and deemphasize individual expertise and task accomplishment.

The two groups in the United States represented another challenge for management. It turned out that the majority of people in these two groups not only had offices in the same building but were interspersed along the same corridor. What we discovered in interviews was a political problem that had emerged and resulted in tensions between two sub-groups. While the partner leading the practice knew there were problems, the visual representation of the network diagram clearly showed the extent to which these issues were impeding the overall group. Various steps were taken to help resolve the problem, including executive coaching, revised performance management practices, and an extensive off-site planning session with organizational development interventions to help the group integrate.

In addition to altering various aspects of organizational design, other, more pointed interventions unfolded with various people in the network, depending on whether they were highly central or highly peripheral. For example, central people were interviewed to see if certain aspects of their jobs could be parceled out to others so that they were not overburdened and in danger of becoming bottlenecks. Alternatively, various approaches were taken with peripheral people to help get them integrated more effectively (depending on the specific issue that seemed to result in their being peripheral). A driving concern was to help develop relationships throughout the overall practice to improve knowledge sharing and the location of relevant expertise for both sales efforts and client engagements. Increasing connection within the network also reduced the extent to which the practice was exposed by the potential of central people leaving. In this and many other examples, we consistently find that a network view makes it clear that should certain central people in a network leave, they take more than just what they know, they also fundamentally affect the connectivity of the entire group.

Lessons from the Field

Throughout our research, we have consistently found SNA a powerful managerial tool largely because it makes visible the patterns of information sharing within and across strategically important networks. Simply reviewing these diagrams with managers usually results in myriad recommendations, as people immersed in the patterns of relationships define and resolve issues affecting group performance. In short, a picture really is worth a thousand words. Using social network diagrams as prompts in facilitated sessions can serve to identify issues that are currently hindering a group and the specific behaviors and organizational design elements requiring modification to improve group efficiency and effectiveness. Rich discussions will often evolve simply by showing network diagrams to the members of a group and asking them to diagnose the patterns they see, as well as the issues facilitating or impeding their effectiveness. Often this process simultaneously creates common awareness of problems, helps define solutions, and gains agreement on actions—all critical steps to effecting organizational change.

We have consistently found it important for groups to identify and work with people who are highly central. Often these people are central for legitimate reasons, based on, for example, workflow demands or unique expertise that a person brings to bear. Alternatively, we also find people who are central and affecting an overall network's effectiveness by virtue of either becoming overburdened by their job or having a tendency to hoard information. Network diagrams can help determine who these people are and what might be done both to allow other connections and work to occur around them to protect the organization should these people decide to go elsewhere.

It is just as important to use the network diagrams (or metrics) to identify peripheral people and find ways to improve their connections where appropriate. These people are often underutilized by the group and are also frequently at the highest risk for turnover. Given the difficulty in attracting and retaining talented employees today, we have found it highly important to find ways to move people into the central part of the network more quickly. Unfortunately, it is rare to find practices where a new person has systematic opportunities to know what other people know in the organization, and almost unheard of to find practices that teach the group what new individuals know. This is a critical shortcoming because as work becomes increasingly project-based, people are being drawn into the center of these networks primarily as a result of what central people understand about their knowledge and skills when new opportunities arise.

We have also found social network diagrams to be a powerful tool for individuals to actively shape their personal networks. While certain managerial decisions and actions can be important to facilitate development of a network, an equally critical means of effecting change is for each person in the network to actively work on improving his or her own connectivity. Where possible, a key component of our debriefing sessions focuses on getting people to use the network diagrams to assess the effectiveness of their personal networks along two dimensions. First, in terms of composition, we focus on the diversity within each person's network (e.g., "Do you rely too heavily on people from a specific functional area or hierarchical level or those that are simply closest to you?"). Second, in terms of content, we focus on the resources that people derive from these relationships (e.g., career advice, information, or other resources). Focusing on these two issues generally helps people recognize a need to invest in the development of specific kinds of relationships (and oftentimes reduce an investment being made in other relationships).

Of course, social network analysis is not a cure all. In our experience, it is important to be cautious about overcorrecting with groups. One organization we worked with believed that a group of research scientists would function more efficiently if there were greater interaction across geographical regions. As a result, they put in place several interventions to ensure that members of the department worked more closely with people in other locations within the organization. After we performed the network analysis, we noticed that as a whole the department had integrated very well across the various geographical locations but functional units within the department were not well connected with each other despite sometimes being in the same building. This overcorrection had resulted in a series of effectiveness and efficiency problems for this group. Thus, as managers consider interventions, it is important to take a balanced approach and always realize that improving some connections likely takes time away from the development and maintenance of others. People have only so much relational energy to expend.

■ Conclusion

In today's fast-paced knowledge-intensive economy, work of importance is increasingly accomplished collaboratively through informal networks. As a result, assessing and supporting strategically important informal networks in organizations can yield substantial performance benefits. In addition, network relationships are critical anchoring points for employees, whose loyalty and commitment may be more to sets of individuals in their network than to a given organization. Our research (and that of others) has found that these informal networks are increasingly important contributors to employee job satisfaction and performance. Yet, despite their importance, these networks are rarely well-supported or even understood by the organizations in which they are embedded. Social network analysis provides a means to identify and assess the health of strategically important networks within an organization. By making visible these otherwise "invisible" patterns of interaction, it becomes possible to work with important groups to facilitate effective collaboration.

Perhaps just as important, social network diagrams often serve to focus executive attention on informal networks that can be critical to organizational effectiveness. Scarce resources—ranging from funding and technology support on the one hand to executive recognition on the other—tend to go to those units that can be found on an organizational chart. Despite often not being reflective of how work is done, organizational charts and reporting relationships are the agreed-on currency of executive decision makers and their trusted advisers. Network diagrams, such as the ones shown here, can be very compelling tools with which to refocus executive attention on how organizational design decisions and leadership behaviors affect the relationships and information flows that are at the heart of how work is done. Our research has consistently shown that while social relationships cannot be mandated by management, they are strongly affected by elements under management control, such as hierarchical levels, horizontal departments, office location, project staffing, and so on. With social network analysis, managers have a means of assessing the effects of decisions on the social fabric of the organization.

■ Appendix 1   Collecting Network Data: What Questions to Ask

If Trying to Discover . . .	These Kinds of Questions Can Help . . .
Communication Network—The informal structure of an organization as represented in ongoing patterns of interaction, either in general or with respect to a given issue. *Rationale*—To understand the informal structure. It can be particularly helpful to identify subgroups or cliques that might represent political problems or individual roles in these networks such as highly central parties, isolates, and bottlenecks.	• How often do you talk with the following people regarding (topic x)? • How much do you typically communicate with each person relative to others in the group?
Information Network—Who goes to whom for advice on work-related matters. *Rationale*—Just assessing who communicates with whom does not guarantee that the interactions reflect exchanges of information important to do one's work. Particularly in efforts that require a collective to effectively pool its knowledge (e.g., new product development), it is important to understand the effectiveness with which a group traffics in information.	• How frequently have you acquired information necessary to do your work from this person in the past month? • Information I receive from this person is useful in helping to get my work done. • Who do you typically seek work-related information from? • Who do you typically give work-related information to?
Problem-Solving Network—Who goes to whom to engage in dialogue that helps people solve problems at work. *Rationale*—Interactions with other people help us think about important dimensions of problems we are trying to solve or consequences of actions we are considering. Strong problem-solving networks often ensure that people are solving the right problem thus improving both individual and network performance.	• Who do you typically turn to for help in thinking through a new or challenging problem at work? • How effective is each person listed below in helping you to think through new or challenging problems at work?
Know Network—Who is aware of whose knowledge and skills. *Rationale*—Awareness of what someone else knows dictates whether and for what problems you are likely to turn to them for help. Strong knowledge networks are an essential basis for strong information networks.	• How well do you understand this person's knowledge and skills?

Access Network—Who has access to whose knowledge and expertise.

Rationale—Just knowing someone has relevant information or knowledge does not guarantee that they will share it with you in a way that is helpful. A strong access network is often critical to ensuring effective information sharing and problem solving in a sufficiently timely fashion.

• When I need information or advice, this person is generally accessible to me within a sufficient amount of time to help me solve my problem.

■ Notes

1. For example, research has shown that relationships are critical for obtaining information, learning how to do your work, and collectively solving cognitively complex tasks. For "obtaining information," see, for example, G. Simmel, *The Sociology of Georg Simmel*, translated by K. H. Wolff (New York: Free Press, 1923, 1950); M. Granovetter, "The Strength of Weak Ties," in this volume; T. Allen, *Managing the Flow of Technology* (Cambridge, MA: MIT Press, 1977); R. Burt, *Structural Holes* (Cambridge, MA: Harvard University Press, 1992); E. Rogers, *Diffusion of Innovations*, 4th edition (New York: Free Press, 1995); and G. Szulanski, "Exploring Internal Stickiness: Impediments to the Transfer of Best Practices within the Firm," *Strategic Management Journal*, 17 (Winter 1996, Special Issue): 27–43. For "learning how to do your work," see, for example, J. Lave and E. Wenger, *Situated Learning: Legitimate Peripheral Participation* (Cambridge: Cambridge University Press, 1991); J. S. Brown and P. Duguid, "Organizational Learning and Communities-of-Practice: Toward a Unified View of Working, Learning and Innovation," *Organization Science*, 2/1 (1991): 40–57; J. S. Brown and P. Duguid, *The Social Life of Information* (Boston: Harvard Business School Press, 2000); J. E. Orr, *Talking about Machines* (Ithaca, NY: Cornell University Press, 1996); E. Wenger, *Communities of Practice* (Oxford: Oxford University Press, 1998); and E. Wenger and W. Snyder, "Communities of Practice: The Organizational Frontier," *Harvard Business Review*, 78/1 (January/February 2000): 139–145. For "collectively solving cognitively complex tasks," see, for example, K. Weick and K. Roberts, "Collective Mind in Organizations: Heedful Interrelating on Flight Decks," *Administrative Science Quarterly*, 38/3 (September 1993): 357–381; E. Hutchins, "Organizing Work by Adaptation," *Organization Science*, 2/1 (January/February 1991): 14–29; R. Moreland, L. Argote, and R. Krishnan, "Socially Shared Cognition at Work: Transactive Memory and Group Performance," in J. Nye and A. Brower, eds., *What's Social about Social Cognition* (Thousand Oaks, CA: Sage, 1996); and A. Hollingshead, "Retrieval Processes in Transactive Memory Systems," *Journal of Personality and Social Psychology*, 74/3 (1998): 659–671.

2. It is a problem to learn or act on knowledge with others who think like you (such as in a community of practice), however, it is an entirely different problem to do this in diverse social contexts, such as cross-functional teams, where people often do not share a common vision, language, metrics of performance, or even understanding of the problem itself. For example, sociologists have poignantly demonstrated how correct information can have little or no impact on critical decision processes. See I. Janis, *Groupthink: Psychological Studies of*

Policy Decisions and Fiascoes (Boston: Houghton Mifflin, 1982); C. Perrow, *Complex Organizations: A Critical Essay* (New York: McGraw-Hill, 1986); and D. Vaughn, *The Challenger Launch Decision: Risky Technology, Culture and Deviance at NASA* (Chicago: University of Chicago Press, 1996). Further, organizational theorists have shown that a person's knowledge can be role constrained (J. March and J. Olsen, "The Uncertainty of the Past: Organizational Learning under Ambiguity," *European Journal of Political Research*, 3 [1975]: 147–171; 1975; B. T. Pentland, "Organizing Moves in Software Support Hot Lines," *Administrative Science Quarterly*, 37/4 [1992]: 527–548) or not acted upon due to motivational or cognitive impediments resulting from introducing knowledge into diverse social contexts (D. Dougherty, "Interpretive Barriers to Successful Product Innovation in Large Films," *Organization Science*, 3/2 [1992]: 179–202; C. M. Fiol, "Consensus, Diversity and Learning in Organizations," *Organization Science*, 5/3 [May/June 1994]; R. J. Boland, Jr., and V. T. Ramkirshnan, "Perspective Making and Perspective Taking in Communities of Knowing," *Organization Science*, 6/4 [July/August 1995]: 350–372; Szulanski, "Exploring Internal Stickiness").

3. See, for example, J. Coleman, "Social Capital in the Creation of Human Capital," in this volume; R. Burt, *Structural Holes*; R. Burt, "The Contingent Value of Social Capital," *Administrative Science Quarterly*, 42/2 (June 1997): 339–365; M. Hansen, "The Search-Transfer Problem: The Role of Weak Ties in Sharing Knowledge across Organization Sub-Units," *Administrative Science Quarterly*, 44/1 (March 1999): 82–111; J. Podolny and J. Baron, "Resources and Relationships: Social Networks and Mobility in the Workplace," *American Sociological Review*, 62/5 (October 1997): 673–693; J. Nahapiet and S. Ghoshal, "Social Capital, Intellectual Capital, and the Creation of Value in Firms," *Academy of Management Review*, 23/2 (April 1998): 242–266; R. Leenders and S. Gabbay, *Corporate Social Capital and Liability* (Boston: Kluwer, 1999); D. Cohen and L. Prusak, *In Good Company: How Social Capital Makes Organizations Work* (Boston: Harvard Business School Press, 2000); and N. Lin, *Social Capital: A Theory of Social Structure and Action* (Cambridge: Cambridge University Press, 2001).

4. W. Baker, *Networking Smart: How to Build Relationships for Personal and Organizational Success* (New York: McGraw-Hill, 1994); W. Baker, *Achieving Success through Social Capital* (San Francisco, CA: Jossey-Bass, 2000).

5. See, for example, D. Krackhardt, "The Strength of Strong Ties: The Importance of *Philos* in Organizations," in this volume; D. Krackhardt, "Constraints on the Interactive Organization as an Ideal Type," in this volume; D. Krackhardt and J. R. Hanson, "Informal Networks: The Company behind the Chart," in this volume.

6. To be sure, academics and practitioners have discussed shifts to network forms via mechanisms such as joint ventures, partnerships, strategic alliances, and R&D consortia for some time now (R. Miles and C. Snow, "Network Organizations: New Concepts for New Forms," *California Management Review*, 28/3 [Spring 1986]: 62–73; R. Miles and C. Snow, *Fit, Failure, and the Hall of Fame* [New York: Free Press, 1994]: R. Miles and C. Snow, "The New Network Firm: A Spherical Structure Built on a Human Investment Policy," *Organizational Dynamics*, 23/4 [Spring 1995]: 4–18; C. Handy, *The Age of Paradox* [Boston: Harvard Business School Press, 1994]; C. Heckscher, "Defining the Post-Bureaucratic Type," in Heckscher and Donnellon, eds., *Post-Bureaucratic Organization*; J. Gal-

braith, *Designing Organizations: An Executive Briefing on Strategy, Structure, and Process* [San Francisco, CA: Jossey-Bass, 1995]). Such forms are presumed to allow for the effective integration of knowledge and capabilities across organizational entities. However, there has been much less practical attention paid to how informal networks of employees in either traditional or networked organizations facilitate or impede organizational effectiveness.

7. See, for example, D. Krackhardt, "Cognitive Social Structures," *Social Networks*, 9 (1987): 109–134; D. Krackhardt, "Assessing the Political Landscape: Structure, Cognition, and Power in Organizations," *Administrative Science Quarterly*, 35/2 (June 1990): 342–369; and T. Casciaro, "Seeing Things Clearly: Social Structure, Personality, and Accuracy in Social Network Perception," *Social Networks* 20 (1998): 331–351.

8. Krackhardt and Hanson, "Informal Networks," 104.

9. J. L. Moreno, *Who Shall Survive?* (Washington, DC: Nervous and Mental Disease Publishing Company, 1934).

10. S. F. Nadel, *The Theory of Social Structure* (New York: Free Press, 1957); J. C. Mitchell, "The Concept and Use of Social Networks," in J. Clyde Mitchell, ed., *Social Networks in Urban Situations* (Manchester: Manchester University Press, 1969).

11. H. C. White, *An Anatomy of Kinship* (Englewood Cliffs, NJ: Prentice Hall, 1963); J. P. Boyd, "The Algebra of Group Kinship," *Journal of Mathematical Psychology*, 6 (1969): 139–167.

12. F. Harary, *Graph Theory* (Reading, MA: Addison-Wesley, 1969).

13. E. Durkheim, *The Division of Labor in Society*, translated by G. Simpson (New York: Free Press, 1893, 1933); G. Simmel, *Conflict and Web of Group Affiliations*, translated by K. H. Wolff and R. Bendix (New York: Free Press, 1922, 1955).

14. See, for example, J. Lincoln, "Intra- and Interorganizational Networks," in S. B. Bacharach, ed., *Perspectives in Organizational Sociology* (Greenwich, CT: JAI Press, 1982), pp. 1–38; B. Wellman and S. D. Berkowitz, *Social Structures: A Network Approach* (Greenwich, CT: JAI Press, 1997); N. Nohria and R. G. Eccles, eds., *Networks in Organizations: Structure, Form, and Action* (Boston, MA: Harvard Business School Press, 1992); and S. Andrews and D. Knoke, eds., *Networks in and around Organizations, Research in the Sociology of Organizations*, 16 (Greenwich, CT: JAI Press, 1999).

15. P. R. Monge and E. M. Eisenberg, "Emergent Communication Networks," in F. Jablin, L. Putnam, K. Roberts, and L. Porter, eds., *Handbook of Organizational Communication* (Newbury Park, CA: Sage, 1987); P. Monge and N. Contractor, "Dualisms in Leadership Research," in F. Jablin and L. Putnam, eds., *The New Handbook of Organizational Communication: Advances in Theory, Research, and Methods* (Thousand Oaks, CA: Sage, 2000).

16. Homophily refers to the extent to which communicating individuals are similar (P. Lazarsfeld and R. Merton, "Friendship as a Social Process," in M. Berger, ed., *Freedom and Control in Modern Society* [New York: Octagon, 1964]).

17. See, for example, T. Zenger and B. Lawrence, "Organizational Demography: The Differential Effects of Age and Tenure Distributions on Technical Communication," *Academy of Management Journal*, 32/2 (June 1989): 353–376; H. Ibarra, "Homophily and Differential Returns: Sex Differences in Network Structure and Access in an Advertising Firm," *Administrative Science Quarterly*, 37/3

(September 1992): 422–447; H. Ibarra, "Race, Opportunity, and Diversity of Social Circles in Managerial Networks," *Academy of Management Journal*, 38/3 (June 1995): 673–703: and M. McPherson, L. Smith-Lovin, and J. Cook, "Birds of a Feather: Homophily in Social Networks," *Annual Review of Sociology*, 27 (2001): 415–444.

18. See, for example, Lincoln, "Intra- and Interorganizational Networks"; W. Stevenson, "Formal Structure and Networks of Interaction within Organizations," *Social Science Research*, 19 (1990): 113–131; W. B. Stevenson and M. Gilly, "Problem-Solving Networks in Organizations: Intentional Design and Emergent Structure," *Social Networks*, 22 (1993): 92–113; and D. Brass, "Being in the Right Place: A Structural Analysis of Individual Influence in an Organization," *Administrative Science Quarterly*, 29/4 (December 1984): 518–539.

19. See, for example, Allen, *Managing the Flow of Technology*; and P. Monge, L. Rothman, E. Eisenberg, K. Miller, and K. Kirste, "The Dynamics of Organizational Proximity," *Management Science*, 31/9 (September 1985): 1129–1141.

20. A. Bavelas, "Communication Patterns in Task-Oriented Groups," *Journal of Acoustical Society of America*, 22 (1950): 725–730; H. Leavitt, "Some Effects of Certain Communication Patterns on Group Performance," *Journal of Abnormal and Social Psychology*, 46 (1951): 38–50; M. Shaw, "Communication Networks," in L. Berkowitz, ed., *Advances in Experimental Social Psychology* (New York: Academic Press, 1964).

21. Social network researchers have also developed a wide range of quantitative analyses and tools for assessing networks. They are beyond the scope of this article, so readers interested in more depth on this front should turn to J. Scott, *Social Network Analysis*, 2nd edition (Thousand Oaks, CA: Sage, 2000), or S. Wasserman and K. Faust, *Social Network Analysis: Methods and Applications* (Cambridge: Cambridge University Press, 1994), for an introductory treatment.

22. G. Rummler and A. Brache, *Improving Performance: How to Manage the White Space on the Organization Chart* (San Francisco, CA: Jossey-Bass, 1990); M. Hammer and J. Champy, *Reengineering the Corporation: A Manifesto for Business Revolution* (New York: HarperBusiness, 1993); M. Hammer and S. Stanton, *The Reengineering Revolution: A Handbook* (New York: HarperBusiness, 1995).

23. A side benefit of our research program has been development of an extensive database that can be used for benchmarking purposes.

24. See, for example, P. Marsden, "Homogeneity in Confiding Relations," *Social Networks*, 10 (1988): 57–76; K. Carley, "A Theory of Group Stability," *American Sociological Review*, 56/3 (June 1991): 331–354; Ibarra, "Homophily"; Ibarra, "Race"; and D. Brass, "A Social Network Perspective on Human Resources Management," *Research in Personnel and Human Resources Management*, 13 (1995): 39–79.

12

A Social Network Perspective on Human Resources Management

Daniel J. Brass

As a net is made up of a series of ties, so everything in this world is connected by a series of ties. If anyone thinks that the mesh of a net is an independent, isolated thing, he is mistaken. It is called a net because it is made up of a series of interconnected meshes, and each mesh has its place and responsibility in relation to the other meshes.
—Buddha

Introduction

It is, of course, highly appropriate that the study of personnel and human resources management in fact focuses on individuals in organizations; and, it is to the credit of my industrial/organizational psychology friends that so much progress has occurred in the recruitment, selection, training, appraisal, compensation, and career development of employees. However, to focus on the individual in isolation, to search in perpetuity for the elusive personality or demographic characteristic that defines the successful employee is, at best, failing to see the entire picture. At worst, it is misdirected effort continued by the overwhelming desire to develop the perfect measurement instrument. There is little doubt (at least in my mind) that the traditional study of personnel and human resources management has been dominated by the perspective that focuses on the individual or the organization in isolation. We are, of course, continually reminded of the need for an interactionist perspective; that is, that the responses of actors are a function of both the attributes of the actors and their environments (cf. Schneider, 1983). Although our research sometimes seems to ignore this dictum, the predominant model in human resources management has been one of matching the characteristics of the worker with the characteristics of the organization (Betz, Fitzgerald, & Hill, 1989). The characteristics of the organization, or more recently, the organization's strategy (Snell, 1992; Wright & McMahan, 1992), defines the relevant individual attributes to be considered in recruitment, selection, training, appraisal, and compensation and promotion. Even with this "matching model," the environment is little more than a context for individual interests, needs, values, motivation, and behavior. Beginning with Cattell and Binet, our human resources management task has been to develop methods of measuring these individual differences.

I do not mean to suggest that individuals do not differ in their skills and abilities and their willingness to use them. I, too, revel in the tradition of American individualism. I will not dismiss the dispositional approach or the lure of "macro organizational psychology" (Staw & Sutton, 1993) to suggest that individuals are merely the "actees" rather than the actors (Mayhew, 1980). I do not wish to climb out on that limb and hand my I/O friends the saw. Rather, I wish to suggest an alternative perspective, that of social networks, which does not focus on attributes of individuals (or of organizations). The structural perspective of social networks instead focuses on relationships rather than actors (the links rather than the nodes). The difference is not a micro/macro one, nor a political/rational one. The difference is the focus on relations rather than attributes; on structure rather than isolated individual actors. The social network perspective assumes that actors (whether they be individuals, groups, or organizations; rational or political) are embedded within a web (or network) of interrelationships with other actors. It is this intersection of relationships that defines an individual's role, an organization's niche in the market, or simply an actor's position in the social structure. It is these networks of relationships that provide opportunities and constraints, that are as much, or more, the causal forces as the attributes of the actors.

I begin with some examples of social networks, and, assuming that most readers are unfamiliar with social network research, I provide a brief, general primer on social networks. I then attempt to provide a heuristic social network theory, followed by consideration of the antecedents and consequences of social networks. Throughout I take a broad view of human resources management, including topics and issues that might more appropriately be labeled organizational behavior. I attempt to note the research that has been done and suggest directions for future research. My overall goal is to introduce the social network perspective to the study of human resources management.

■ Social Networks

Consider the diagrams in figure 12.1. One does not need to be an expert on social networks to suggest that the center node (position A) in figure 12.1a is the most powerful position. When shown this simple picture, few people ask whether the nodes represent individuals or groups, or whether the lines represent communications, friendship, or buy-sell transactions. Nor does anyone ask if the lines are of differing strengths or intensities, or whether they represent restricted, repeated, or symmetric interactions.

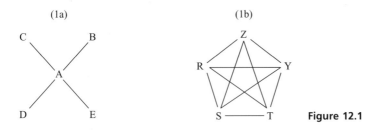

(1a) (1b)

Figure 12.1

Most people simply look at the diagram and declare that position A is the most powerful.

If pressed to explain why they had picked position A as the most powerful, most people could articulate an intuitive notion of centrality. They might suggest that position A is at the "center" of the group, that position A has access to all the other positions, or that the other positions are dependent on position A; that is, they must "go through" position A in order to "reach" each other. They might conclude that position A "controls" the group; A is not dependent on any one other position, and all the other positions are dependent on position A. Thus, most people have an intuitive idea of what social networks are, what centrality is, and how both might relate to power. Consequently, few people would be surprised to learn that their intuitive prediction has been supported in a number of settings (see Brass 1992 for a review).

Now consider both figure 12.1a and 12.1b. Which set of positions (12.1a or 12.1b) would have the most turnover? Which set of positions would perform best? Which position would have the highest level of job satisfaction? Consider the larger network in figure 12.2. Which position (e.g., consider A and Z) would be more likely selected? Recruited? Promoted? Receive the highest performance appraisal? Can you suggest a set of positions that will have similar attitudes? Where will conflict arise in this figure 12.2 network?

In order to hypothesize answers to any or all of these questions, you were forced to adopt a structural, network perspective. That is, figures 12.1 and 12.2 provide no information other than the structural arrangement of positions. We do not know the values, attitudes, personality, or abilities of any of the "positions." We do not even know if the positions represent individuals (although you probably assumed that based on the questions asked). And, you may have relied upon a particular theory in justifying your selections. Regardless of your assumptions or theories, the exercise illustrates a structural, network perspective. You arrived at answers based upon the relationships shown. You adopted a social network perspective, and, it is this perspective that I wish to illustrate further. We begin with some basic information about social networks.

Although many intuitive definitions exist, we define a network as a

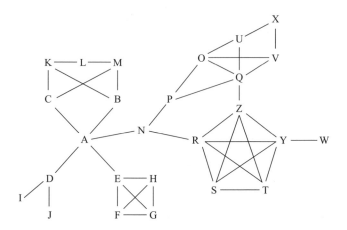

Figure 12.2

set of nodes and the set of ties representing some relationship, or lack of relationship, between the nodes. In the case of social networks, the nodes represent actors (i.e., individuals, groups, organizations). Often included in this definition is the assumption that these linkages as a whole may be used to interpret the social responses of the actors (Mitchell, 1969). The links often involve some form of interaction, such as communication, or represent a more abstract connection, such as trust or friendship, which implies interaction. Although the particular content of the relationships represented by the ties is limited only by the researcher's imagination, typically studied are flows of information (communication), expressions of affect (friendship), goods and services (workflow), and influence (advice). We consider ties that are repeated over time, thus establishing a relatively stable pattern of network interrelationships. Small networks are often depicted graphically, as in figure 12.2.

The basic building block of social network analysis is the relationship. That is, the focus is on the link, or lack of a link, rather than the actors. In addition to the content of the relationships, several ways to characterize the links have been measured by social network researchers. Table 12.1 indicates typical measures of links, or ties.

Although each of the measures in table 12.1 can be used to describe a particular link between two actors, the measures can be aggregated and assigned to a particular actor or used to describe the entire network. For example, we might note that 30% of actor A's ties are symmetric, or 50% are strong ties. For the entire network, we might note that 70% of all ties are reciprocated, or that 40% of the ties are multiplex.

In addition to the aggregated measures of ties, other social network measures are typically assigned to individual actors. Some of these measures are listed in table 12.2. It is important to keep in mind that these measures are not attributes of isolated individual actors; rather, they represent

Table 12.1
Typical Social Network Measures of Ties

Measure	Definition	Example
Indirect links	Path between two actors is mediated by one or more others	A is linked to B, B is linked to C; thus A is indirectly linked to C through B
Frequency	How many times, or how often the link occurs	A talks to B 10 times per week
Stability	Existence of link over time	A has been friends with B for 5 years
Multiplexity	Extent to which two actors are linked together by more than one relationship	A and B are friends, they seek out each other for advice, and they work together
Strength	Amount of time, emotional intensity, intimacy, or reciprocal services (frequency or multiplexity often used as measure of strength of tie)	A and B are close friends or spend much time together
Direction	Extent to which link is from one actor to another	Work flows from A to B, but not from B to A
Symmetry (reciprocity)	Extent to which relationship is bidirectional	A asks B for advice, and B asks A for advice

the actor's relationship within the network. If any aspect of the network changes, the actor's relationship within the network also changes.

Also included in table 12.2 are some typical roles or classifications of actors based on their patterns of relationships. Some of these roles, such as bridge and liaison, are dependent upon identifying groups or clusters of actors within the network. There are two typical methods of grouping actors, a relational method often called *cohesion*, and a structural method referred to as *structural equivalence*. The relational cohesion approach clusters actors based on the frequency, intensity, and/or strength of their ties to each other. The resulting groups are often referred to as cliques. For example, the R-S-T-Y-Z connections in figure 12.2 (or the E-F-G-H group) might be considered a cohesive clique. Each of the actors is connected to all the others. This relational, cohesion method is typically used when identifying the roles listed in table 12.2. For example, in figure 12.2, actors W,I, or J would be considered isolates; actor N is a gatekeeper; actor Q might be considered a bridge.

The structural equivalence approach is based on the notion that actors may occupy similar positions within the network structure, although they may not be directly connected to each other. For example, two organizations in the same industry may have similar patterns of links to suppliers and customers but may not have any direct connection between them-

Table 12.2
Typical Social Network Measures Assigned to Individual Actors

Measure	Definition
Degree	Number of direct links with other actors.
Indegree	Number of directional links to the actor from other actors (incoming links).
Outdegree	Number of directional links from the actor to other actors (outgoing links).
Range (diversity)	Number of links to different others (others are defined as different to the extent that they are not themselves linked to each other, or represent different groups or statuses).
Closeness	Extent to which an actor is close to, or can easily reach, all the other actors in the network. Usually measured by averaging the path distances (direct and indirect links) to all others. A direct link is counted as 1, indirect links receive proportionately less weight.
Betweenness	Extent to which an actor mediates, or falls between, any other two actors on the shortest path between those two actors. Usually averaged across all possible pairs in the network.
Centrality	Extent to which an actor is central to a network. Various measures (including degree, closeness, and betweenness) have been used as indicators of centrality. Some measures of centrality weight an actor's links to others by the centrality of those others.
Prestige	Based on asymmetric relationships, prestigious actors are the object rather than the source of relations. Measures similar to centrality are calculated by accounting for the direction of the relationship (i.e., in degree).
Rules	
Star	An actor who is highly central to the network.
Liaison	An actor who has links to two or more groups that would otherwise not be linked, but is not a member of either group.
Bridge	An actor who is a member of two or more groups.
Gatekeeper	An actor who mediates or controls the flow (is the single link) between one part of the network and another.
Isolate	An actor who has no links or relatively few links to others.

selves. The two organizations are said to occupy similar structural positions in the network; that is, to be structurally equivalent. In a communication network, structurally equivalent actors may communicate with similar others but not necessarily communicate with each other. In figure 12.2, actors B and C are structurally equivalent.

As was the case with measures of links, measures typically assigned to actors can be aggregated to describe the entire network. For example, measures of network density usually report the ratio of links to all possible links. The reachability of the network might be measured by the average number of links required for any actor in the network to reach any other actor. An example of a centralized network might include a few central actors with many connections, and many other actors with only a few links, those links being primarily to the central actors. A decentralized network would be characterized by actors who all have similar centrality scores. In figure 12.1, network (a) would be described as centralized, while network (b) would be described as decentralized. The size of a network is usually expressed in terms of the numbers of actors. Some typical measures used to describe entire networks are listed in table 12.3.

Table 12.3
Typical Social Network Measures Used to Describe Entire Networks

Measure	Definition
Size	Number of actors in the network.
Inclusiveness	Total number of actors in a network minus the number of isolated actors (not connected to any other actors). Also measured as the ratio of connected actors to the total number of actors.
Component	Largest connected subset of network nodes and links. All nodes in the component are connected (either direct or indirect links), and no nodes have links to nodes outside the component.
Connectivity (reachability)	Extent to which actors in the network are linked to one another by direct or indirect ties. Sometimes measured by the maximum, or average, path distance between any two actors in the network.
Connectedness	Ratio of pairs of nodes that are mutually reachable to total number of pairs of nodes.
Density	Ratio of the number of actual links to the number of possible links in the network.
Centralization	The difference between the centrality scores of the most central actor and those of all other actors in a network is calculated and used to form ratio of the actual sum of the differences to the maximum sum of the differences.
Symmetry	Ratio of number of symmetric to asymmetric links (or to total number of links) in a network.
Transitivity	Three actors (A, B, C) are transitive if whenever A is linked to B and B is linked to C, then C is linked to A. Transitivity is the number of transitive triples divided by the number of potential transitive triples (number of paths of length 2).

At what level of analysis is the study of social networks? We might be tempted to base our answer on the actors involved (i.e., individuals, groups, and organizations). However, the social network paradigm focuses on relationships (links) rather than actors (nodes). Thus, our normal method of classifying levels by actors does not apply to networks. For example, the individual level of analysis does not seem to exist. That is, at least two actors are needed to form a link. The idea of a network implies more than one link. Thus, while the dyad is the building block of the network, one link connecting two actors would not be considered a network. Therefore, a minimum of two links connecting three actors is required in order to have a network and establish such notions as indirect links and paths.

An exception to this formulation might be encountered by measuring an ego, or egocentric, network. An ego network is composed of one actor's relationships to others and is measured from the perspective of the individual actor. The study of ego networks arises from methodological considerations as well as theoretical ones. For example, in large sociological surveys, it is not always possible to obtain information from all actors in the network. Theoretically, ego networks provide one individual's perception of his or her network.

In the case where an actor had only one relationship to one other actor, that one relationship might be used to describe the actor's ego network. However, as noted in our previous definition, networks also include the absence of relationships. Thus, the actor whose ego network included only one relationship might be compared to other actors whose ego networks involved many relationships.

Even in most ego networks, more than one relationship exists. For example figure 12.1a might represent actor A's ego network, indicating that A has four relationships (i.e., with actors B, C, D, and E). The social network approach further assumes that A's relationship with B may be affected by A's relationship with C, D, or E, or by all three. Thus, rather than focus only the A-B relationship, it must be considered in the context of the A-C, A-D, and A-E relationships. For example, A might be able to provide E with information that A obtained from B. Or, A might be less dependent upon B because he has relationships with C, D, and E.

As opposed to the study of ego networks, whole network studies attempt to measure the relationships among all actors in the network. The advantage of the whole network approach lies in the assumption that the presence of absence of a relationship between two other actors may affect the relationship between an actor and one or both of the others. For example, let us assume now that figure 12.1a represents the whole network, rather than the ego network of actor A. By obtaining information from B, C, D, and E, as well as A, we know that B is not directly linked to C, D, or E; C is not directly linked to D or E; and D is not directly linked to E. How would the absence of a relationship between E and F (for example) affect the relationship between A and any of the others? Assuming that this is a communication network, the lack of communication between B and C means that A mediates or controls the flow of any information between B and C. Because B and C do not talk to each other, it is additionally likely that the information obtained by A from B and C will not be redundant. Another possibility is that A may broker the relationship between B and C, playing one against the other. This would not be possible if B communicated directly with C. To understand how A is affected by the relationship between B and C requires a network perspective.

In summary, although the building blocks of networks are dyadic relationships, the unit of analysis is not the dyad. Rather, the focus is on the relationships among the dyadic relationships (i.e., the network). Thus, we return to our definition of a network as the presence or absence of two or more relationships among three or more actors. I refer to this as the network level of analysis.

When the actors in the network are people, I refer to this as the interpersonal network level of analysis. The intergroup network level of analysis refers to relationships among groups, and the interorganizational network level of analysis will be used when the actors in the network are organizations. Groups may refer to cliques or coalitions, as well as functional task groups, and I distinguish organizations from groups by defining organizations as containing two or more groups.

The claim is often made that a social network perspective integrates micro and macro approaches to organizational studies (Wellman, 1988). Consistent with this claim is the advantage it offers of simultaneously studying the whole as well as the parts. As table 12.1 illustrates, the dyadic relationships are measured in a variety of ways and are used to compose the network. They are, in a sense, the parts that form the whole, and, as table 12.2 shows, we can assign network properties to individual actors. These measures are inherently cross-level as they combine actor and network. They represent the relative position of a part within the whole. In addition, actors can be clustered (based on their relationships within the network) into groups or cliques. Thus, researchers can simultaneously address actor, group of actors, and network characteristics. For example, a researcher might ask, to what extent does an actor's centrality within a highly central clique in a decentralized network affect that actor's power?

■ Social Network Theory

Some would suggest that "social network theory" is an oxymoron. Perhaps the most frequent criticism of the approach is that it represents a set of techniques and measures devoid of theory. Just as tables 12.1, 12.2, and

12.3 illustrate, it is often easier to catalog the measures then to provide a theoretical explanation for the emergence and persistence of social networks. More often, the measures are used to operationalize constructs suggested by theory. For example, the measurement of weak ties might be used to operationalize Weick's (1976) concept of loosely coupled systems (Beekun & Glick, 1991). Thus, social networks are often seen as a technique rather than a theory. Wellman (1988) and Scott (1991) provide excellent reviews of the history and development of the network paradigm.

Perhaps it is more accurate to state that a single social network theory does not exit than to suggest that social network analysis is theoretical. Network analysis has been applied to a variety of theories. For example, a cursory review of recent social network articles in organization studies reveals the use of such theories as resource dependence (Brass, 1984), social information processing (Rice & Aydin, 1991), transaction costs (Aldrich, 1982), exchange theory (Cook, 1982), role theory (Barley, 1990), cognitive dissonance (Krackhardt & Porter, 1985), social comparison (Kilduff, 1990, 1992), population ecology (Oliver, 1988), institution theory (Galaskiewicz & Wasserman, 1989), and others (Fulk & Boyd, 1991).

More directly, Burt (1982) has offered a fully elaborated cognitive comparison theory of social networks, with particular emphasis on structural equivalence, and recently, a theory of "structural holes" (Burt, 1992). Galaskiewicz (1979) has combined Homans's (1950) exchange theory with Coleman's (1973) purposive action model to articulate how networks form. Carley (1991) has developed a "costructural" theory of group stability based on social networks. Carley and Krackhardt (1990) have begun to develop a social network theory of asymmetric relationships. Granovetter (1985) has offered a theory of economic action and social structure. Graph theory (Harary, 1959) has been long associated with network analysis, as has Granovetter's (1973) theory of strong and weak ties. Thus, while there may not be a single, agreed upon theory of social networks, there is no lack of theory when it comes to social network research.

Ignoring the rigorous requirement of theory construction, and without being so presumptuous as to suggest a theory of social networks, let me attempt to sketch an heuristic overview of the emergence and persistence of social networks in organization. Most of this overview relies on the writings of the above authors. Following Barley's (1986, 1990) and Monge and Eisenberg's (1987) explications, I focus on structuration theory (Giddens, 1976).

As Wellman (1988) noted, social networks have been often synonymous with the structural paradigm in anthropology and sociology. Social workers often have been equated with, or used to represent, social structure. Behavior, attitudes, norms, status, and so forth have been interpreted in terms of the structure rather than the inherent properties of the actors.

Similar structures produce similar outcomes. At the extreme, "the pattern of relationships is substantially the same as the content" (Wellman, 1988, p. 25). Without adopting this extreme position, it is nevertheless appropriate to look to a theory such as structuration (Giddens, 1976) to provide a general basis for understanding networks.

I begin with the simple observation that people interact and communicate, and assume that all interaction involves communication, be it intended or unintended. Interaction can be purposeful, coincidentally random, or forced or constrained by factors external to the actors. Various reasons have been offered for why people interact (e.g., to satisfy social as well as other needs, to obtain desired outcomes, and so forth.) In a general sense, let us summarize these reasons by assuming that people interact in order to make sense of, and successfully operate on, their environment. When the interaction is helpful in this regard, the interaction continues and a relationship is formed. Although initial interaction may be random, repeated interaction is not.

Repeated interaction leads to social structure. As Barley (1990) notes, ". . . while people's actions are undoubtedly constrained by forces beyond their control and outside their immediate present, it is difficult to see how any social structure can be produced or reproduced except through ongoing action and interaction" (pp. 64–65). Thus, we define social structure as representing relatively stable patterns of behavior, interaction, and interpretation. These patterns emerge, and become institutionalized, as recurrent interaction over time takes on the status of predictable, socially shared regularities, that is, "taken-for-granted facts" (Barley, 1990, p. 67). People then behave within these institutionalized patterns as if these structures were external to, and a constraint upon, their interaction. The constrained behavior, in turn, underwrites and reinforces the observed and socially shared structural patterns. These shared structural patterns also facilitate interaction, just as language facilitates communication.

However, just as everyday speech reinforces the grammatical rules of language, it also gradually modifies the language as new words and syntax are used and reused and eventually are incorporated as acceptable additions. In the same sense, interactions which occur within the constraints of structure can gradually modify that structure. For example, those persons disadvantaged by the current structural constraints may actively seek to change them (Zeitz, 1980), or environmental shocks may provide the occasion for major restructuring (Barley, 1986, 1990; Burkhardt & Brass, 1990; Tushman & Anderson, 1986).

The above explanation is decidedly individualistic in nature. In suggesting the emergence and modification of social structure via individual agency, I have emphasized a micro, psychological orientation. Conversely, we might have taken a more macro, sociological approach by suggesting that social structure exists and that it constrains most individual attempts to modify it. Thus, actors are largely "actees" (Mayhew, 1980), whose behavior, attitudes, values, and so forth are determined, or at least constrained, by their positions in the social structure.

In either case, we are attempting to merge the micro and the macro, the individual and the structure. Thus, I do not ignore individual agency nor the structural constraints which may at times render it useless. Structure and behavior are intertwined, each affecting the other. Thus, we proceed to explore the causes and outcomes of communication networks in relation to organizations. Following Monge and Eisenberg (1987), we underscore the dynamic nature of structuration theory, noting that distinctions between causes and outcomes are often nonexistent.

■ Social Neworks: Antecedents

Actor Similarity

Social psychologists and sociologists are quite familiar with the tendency for similar people to interact. A good deal of research has supported this proposition, and it is a basic assumption in many theories (Blau, 1977; Davis, 1966; Granovetter, 1973; Homans, 1950). Similarity has been operationalized on such dimensions as age, sex, education, prestige, social class, tenure, and occupation (Carley, 1991; Coleman, 1957; Ibarra, 1993; Laumann, 1966; Lazerfield & Merton, 1954; Marsden, 1988; McPherson & Smith-Lovin, 1987). For example, Brass (1985a) found two largely segregated networks (one predominately men, the other women) in an organization. Similarity is thought to ease communication, increase predictability of behavior, and foster trust and reciprocity.

Ibarra (1992) also found evidence for homophily (i.e., interaction with similar others) in her study of men's and women's networks in an advertising agency. In distinguishing types of networks, she found that women had social support and friendship network ties with other women, but they had instrumental network ties (e.g., communication, advice, influence) with men. Men, on the other hand, had homophilous ties (with other men) across multiple networks, and these ties were stronger.

Although most of the above studies focused on interpersonal networks, there is some evidence that actor similarity also affects linkages across organizational boundaries. Perceived similarity (religion, age, ethnic and racial background, and professional affiliation) among executives has been shown to influence interorganizational linkages (Galaskiewicz, 1979; Schermerhorn, 1977).

Although social network measures were not included, research on relational and organizational demography (Tsui, Egan, & O'Reilly, 1992; Tsui & O'Reilly 1989; Wagner, Pfeffer, & O'Reilly, 1984) have employed the similarity attraction assumptions. These studies show that relational differences on such demographics as age and tenure are related to commitment and turnover. The greater the difference between an individual's age and the ages of others in his/her group, the more likely that person is to quit. Likewise, groups with greater variation in relative age have higher levels of turnover. Ease of communication and social integration are the assumed mediating-variables in these studies. Following this reasoning, Zenger and Lawrence (1989) found that technical communication in a research division of an electronics firm was related to age and tenure distributions.

We can extend these actor similarities to include personality and ability. As Tosi (1992) has noted, these personality orientations are likely to manifest themselves with respect to interactions with others. Thus, in combination with age, sex, status, and so forth we would expect similarity of personality and ability to be related to the interpersonal network patterns of interaction.

We also would expect the characteristics of the links between actors to be related to the degree of actor similarity. Communication between two dissimilar actors is likely to be infrequent, not reciprocated, less salient to either, asymmetric, unstable, uniplex rather than multiplex, and weak. Similarity of actors also may be positively related to the density or connectedness of the network. We emphasize actor similarity, and later, attitude similarity, because both are key to such human resources practices as recruitment, selection, and performance appraisal.

It is important to note that similarity is a relational concept; an individual can only be similar with respect to another individual, and in relation to dissimilar others. That is, interaction is influenced by the degree to which an individual is similar to other individuals relative to how similar he or she is with everyone else. Due to culture, selection and socialization processes, and reward systems, an organization may exhibit a modal demographic or personality pattern. Kanter (1977) has referred to this process as "homosocial reproduction." Thus, an individual's similarity in relation to the modal attributes of the organization (or the group) may determine the the extent to which he or she is central or integrated in the interpersonal network.

The above discussion implies that interaction in organizations is emergent and unrestricted. However, organizations are by definition organized. Labor is divided. Positions are formally differentiated both horizontally (by technology, workflow, task design) and vertically (by administrative hierarchy), and means for coordinating among differentiated positions are specified. Because communication and interaction are fundamental means, and results of coordination, it follows that social networks are influenced by the prescribed vertical and horizontal differentiation and the resulting need for coordination. Formally differentiated positions locate individuals and groups in physical space and at particular points in the workflow and hierarchy of authority, thereby restricting their opportunity to interact with some and facilitating interaction with others.

Vertical Differentiation and Coordination

Vertical differentiation refers to the formal, prescribed hierarchy of authority, or administrative structure, within an organization. Because it would be difficult for a superior and subordinate directly linked by the formal hierarchy to avoid interacting, it would not be surprising for the "informal" social network to shadow the formal hierarchy of authority.

Lincoln and Miller (1979) found support for this proposition when considering both instrumental, work-related communication networks and friendship networks. Noting how the formal hierarchy of authority encourages coordination and mediation of subordinate interaction by superiors, they found that rank was related to centrality (closeness) in both networks. Although sex and race were more strongly related to the friendship network, their results emphasize the extent to which differentiation constrains friendship as well as instrumental ties.

Horizontal Differentiation and Coordination

Horizontal differentiation refers to the way in which the tasks are formally divided and workers assigned to task positions. Coupled with the means to coordinate these differentiated task positions, this might be referred to as the workflow or technology. Therefore, we would expect social networks to be influenced by the workflow requirements, or technology, of the organization. Burkhardt and Brass (1990) found that communication patterns in an organization changed when the organization adopted a new technology. Recent changes in communication technology, such as electronic mail, have generated increased interest in their effects on communication networks (Fulk & Steinfield, 1990).

Physical and Temporal Proximity

To the extent that formal vertical and horizontal differentiation and coordination locate actors in physical and temporal space (departmentalization, assignment to work shifts), we can expect additional effects on social networks. For example, actors scheduled to work at the same time are more likely to communicate. Festinger, Schacter, and Back (1950) established the link between physical proximity and amount of interaction. Although the use of telephones and electronic mail may moderate the relationship between proximity and interaction, proximate ties are easier to maintain and more likely to be strong, stable links (Monge & Eisenberg, 1987).

Organizational Structure

It is a small jump from vertical and horizontal differentiation and coordination to organizational structure. In fact, many definitions equate organizational structure with vertical and horizontal differentiation and coordination. Thus, the above discussion might be grouped as easily under the "organizational structure" heading. Likewise, organizational structure has been equated with social networks. For example, the often referenced definition of structure provided by James and Jones (1976) seems to imply a network orientation. They define organizational structure as "the enduring characteristics of an organization reflected by the distribution of units within an organization and their systematic relationship to each other." Although the network view of organizational structure differs from the traditional emphasis on such variables as centralization, formalization, and size, it is consistent with Weick's (1979) notion that organizations consist of patterned, repeated interactions among social actors. Thus, rather than suggest that organizational structure influences interaction/ communication networks, I equate the two. I view the emergent interaction patterns resulting from the more prescribed differentiation and coordination as organizational structure. We note that social network measures can easily be applied to describe structure (Krackhardt, 1993), whether it is group, organizational, or industry structure.

Following Burns and Stalker (1961), organizational structure often has been defined as organic or mechanistic. Mechanistic organizations are characterized as rigid in structure with many rules and procedures, tightly coupled subsystems, and a well-defined, centralized hierarchy of authority. Organic organizations are loosely coupled with flexible means of coordination, few rules and procedures, and a decentralized authority system. To the extent that they are, in part, defined by their means of differentiation and coordination, the above propositions apply. We would expect to find differences in network patterns between mechanistic and organic organizations.

A logical extension of some of the above discussion is that the social network will overlap more closely with the formally prescribed structure in a mechanistic organization than in an organic organization. Tichy and Fombrun (1979) found support for this proposition, although their sample included only a small number of managers in three organizations. They also found higher density and connectedness in the interpersonal interaction network of the organic organization. Their analyses found fewer dense clusters and lower status differences within the clusters in the organic system as compared to the two mechanistic systems. Similarly, in a study of 36 agencies, Shrader, Lincoln, and Hoffman (1989) found that organic organizations were characterized by networks of high density, connectivity, multiplexity, and symmetry and a low number of clusters.

In general, these results suggest more unrestricted, flexible interaction in organic as compared to mechanistic organizations.

Size

The size of an organization (number of employees) will also affect the network patterns. The number of possible ties greatly increases ($n(n-1)/2$) with increases in size (n). For example, a network of 5 actors contains 10 possible links, whereas a network of 50 actors has 1,225 possible links. Thus, as the size of the network increases, density naturally decreases. Most network measures attempt to account for size so that comparisons can be made across networks of differing size.

Organization Life Cycle

In an excellent review of communication networks, Monge and Eisenberg (1987) have hypothesized that networks may be affected by an organization's stage in its life cycle. Networks may be more emergent (less stable and less likely to follow prescribed structure) during the early stages of development. As the organization matures, patterns become more stable and formalized, much as the previous discussion of structuration theory (Giddens, 1979) would suggest.

Environment

To the extent that the organizational environment is the salient influence on the organic/mechanistic character of the organization (or subsystem), and environment and organization are appropriately matched, we would expect the same social network patterns described above to apply. That is, decentralized, high-density, high interconnectedness patterns (figure 12.1b) are likely when units face complex, dynamic environments. Simple, stable environments will more likely foster centralized, low-density patterns (figure 12.1a).

Other environmental factors that may affect interpersonal, intergroup, or interorganizational networks include industry, national culture, and mergers and acquisitions. Organizational structures often differ by industry. To the extent that organizations within an industry face similar volatility, this would be expected. However, according to institutional theory (DiMaggio & Powell, 1983), organizations often mimic other organizations. For example, Galaskiewicz and Wasserman (1989) found that under conditions of uncertainty, nonprofit organizations were likely to mimic those organizations to which they had some interpersonal link. However, in an interorganizational network study, Oliver (1988) found more support for the strategic choice than either the population ecology or institutional perspectives.

National culture also may be reflected in social network patterns. For example, French employees prefer weak links at work, whereas Japanese workers tend to form strong, multiplex ties (Monge & Eisenberg, 1987). Given the Japanese group orientation to decision making, as opposed to the individualistic emphasis in most U.S. firms, we might expect density and interconnectedness to be greater in Japanese companies. Lincoln, Hanada, and Olson (1981) postulated a model of personal ties and work satisfaction based on national origin. They found that vertical differentiation was positively related to personal ties and work satisfaction for Japanese and Japanese Americans. Horizontal differentiation had negative effects on these workers.

As might be expected, mergers and acquisitions represent environmental jolts that can substantially change network patterns within an organization. Danowski and Edison-Swift (1985) found dramatic changes in electronic mail usage following a merger. However, these changes were temporary, as employees reverted to premerger patterns after a short time.

Summary

A variety of factors can have an effect on social networks. Obviously, the influences are complex and the effects cross levels of analysis. I have identified interpersonal factors, such as actor similarity, and organizational level factors, such as vertical and horizontal differentiation and coordination, and have focused on the differences between mechanistic and organic organizations. Additional influences remain to be explored. In addition, few studies have examined more than one influence. Multivariate studies are needed to begin to understand the complex interactions involved among the factors.

■ Social Networks: Outcomes

Returning to our structuration theory orientation, we note that established patterns of interaction become institutionalized and take on the quality of socially shared, structural facts. Thus, network patterns emerge, become routinized, and act as both constraints on, and facilitators of, behavior. We now turn our attention to the consequences of these networks. We begin with attitude similarity and power and politics because explanations of these consequences are relevant to the discussion of human resources practices that follow.

Attitude Similarity

Just as we noted the propensity for similar actors to interact, theory and research have also noted that those who interact become more similar.

Although actors cannot become more similar on demographics such as sex and age, they can adopt similar attitudes to those with whom they interact, or who occupy similar positions in the social network. Thus, most social network studies have focused on attitude similarity.

Erickson (1988) provides the theory and research concerning the "relational basis of attitudes." She argues that people are not born with their attitudes, nor do they develop them in isolation. Attitude formation and change occur primarily through social interaction. As people attempt to make sense of reality, they compare their own perceptions with those of others, in particular, similar other. For example, Kilduff (1990) found that MBA students made similar decisions as their perceived friends regarding job interviews with organizations. Differences in attitudes of dissimilar others have little effect; disagreements can be attributed to the dissimilarity and may even be used to reinforce one's own attitudes.

Following Erickson (1988), Rice and Aydin (1991) found that attitudes about new technology were similar to those with whom employees communicated frequently and immediate supervisors. However, one interesting finding was that estimates of others' attitudes were not correlated with others' actual (reported) attitudes. In another study, Rentsch (1990) found that members of an accounting firm who interacted with each other had similar interpretations of organizational events and that these meanings differed qualitatively across different interaction groups. Krackhardt and Kilduff (1990) found that friends had similar perceptions of others in the organization, even when controlling for demographic and positional similarities. Danowski (1980) got mixed results on the relationship between connectivity and attitude uniformity. Innovation groups displayed homogeneity in attitudes, but production groups did not.

In a longitudinal study following a technological change, Burkhardt (1994) found attitude similarity among both structurally equivalent actors and those with direct links. Walker (1985) found that structurally equivalent individuals had similar cognitive judgments of means-ends relationships regarding product success. Galaskiewicz and Burt (1991) found similar evaluations of nonprofit organizations among structurally equivalent contributions officers, and structural equivalence explained these contagion effects much better than a relational cohesion approach. Structural equivalence does not hinge on direct interaction/communication among actors. Rather, the similarity in attitudes stems from actors occupying similar positions or roles in the network. According to Burt (1982), actors cognitively compare their own attitudes and behaviors with those of others occupying similar roles rather than being influenced by direct communications from others in dissimilar roles.

Taking a slightly different approach, Dean and Brass (1985) argued that highly central employees, by virtue of their greater number of links, would be exposed to more diversity of opinion than peripheral employees. They found that central employees' attitudes about job characteristics were more similar to observable reality as measured by the perceptions of an outside observer. They argued that increased interaction leads to a convergence of perceptions similar to observable reality.

Job Satisfaction

Perhaps the most frequently researched attitude in organizational studies is job satisfaction. Despite the attention to job satisfaction in the small-group laboratory network studies of the 1950s (see Shaw, 1964, for review), there have been surprisingly few social network studies addressing job satisfaction in organizations. The early laboratory studies found that central actors were more satisfied than peripheral actors in these small (typically five-person) groups. In one of the few organizational studies, Roberts and O'Reilly (1979) found that relative isolates (zero or one link) in the communication network were less satisfied than participants (two or more links). However, Brass (1981) found no relationship between centrality (closeness) in the workflow of workgroups or departments and employee satisfaction. Centrality within the entire organization's workflow was negatively related to satisfaction in this sample of nonsupervisory employees. Brass (1981) suggested that this latter finding may be due to the routine jobs associated with the core technology of the organization. He found that job characteristics mediated the relationship between workflow network measures and job satisfaction. Similarly, Ibarra and Andrews (1993) found that centrality in advice and friendship networks was related to perceptions of autonomy. Moch (1980) also found that integration in the work network (two or more links) was associated with job characteristics and internal motivation. However, isolates with high growth needs reported high job involvement.

In a recent study of 47 managers in an entrepreneurial firm, Kilduff and Krackhardt (1993) found a negative relationship between centrality (betweenness) in the friendship network and job satisfaction. However, they also found that managers whose cognitive maps of the social networks were more schema-consistent were more satisfied and committed. Schema consistency referred to the tendency to perceive friendship ties as reciprocated (symmetric) and transitive (e.g., if A is a friend of B and C, than B and C are also friends). Combining these findings, Kilduff and Krackhardt (1993) argued that mediating the relationships between actors (betweenness centrality) who are not themselves friends may create conflicting expectations and stress.

The negative relationship found by Kilduff and Krackhardt (1993), coupled with the lack of significant relationships noted by Brass (1984), point out the fact that interaction is not always positive. Since Durkheim (1997, 1951) argued that social integration promotes mental health, there has been a long history of equating social interaction with social support (Wellman, 1992). Yet we have all experienced the obnoxious coworker, the demanding boss, the uncooperative subordinate, or the annoying neighbor. When possible, we tend to avoid interaction with these people, thereby producing a positive correlation between interaction and friendship. However, as previously noted, antecedents such as physical proximity and vertical and horizontal differentiation and coordination place constraints on the voluntary nature of social interaction in organizations. The possibility that such "required" interaction may involve negative outcomes suggests the need for further research on the negative side of social interaction.

Although more research is needed, these limited results suggest that there may be an optimum degree of centrality in social networks that is neither too little nor too great as regards satisfaction. Isolation is probably negatively related to satisfaction, while a high degree of centrality may lead to conflicting expectations, communication overload, and stress. Future research might investigate the effects of multiplexity, the extent to which two actors are linked together by more than one relationship. For example, an employee may feel forced to agree to the work-related demands of a friend in order to maintain the friendship. Failure to maintain one relationship may result in the loss of the other.

Power and Politics

Ferris and Judge (1991) have proposed a political influence perspective on human resources management as a complementary, counter model to the rationality and objectivity assumptions inherent in many of the traditional approaches. Such a perspective assumes that organizations are arenas for competing interests of individuals and groups (Pfeffer, 1989). In reviewing the research supporting the political perspective, Ferris and Judge focus on the effects of impression management and behavioral tactics. Although I consider some of these political factors in reference to particular topics, my agenda in this section is to add the structural, network perspective to those reviewed by Ferris and Judge.

A structural network perspective on power and influence has been the topic of much research. The finding that central network positions are associated with power has been reported in small, laboratory workgroups (Shaw, 1964), in interpersonal networks in organizations (Brass, 1984, 1985a, Brass & Burkhardt, 1993; Burkhardt & Brass, 1990; Fombrun, 1983; Krackhardt, 1990; Tushman & Romanelli, 1983); in organizational buying systems (Bristor; 1993; Ronchetto, Hutt, & Reingen, 1989); in intergroup networks in organizations (Astley & Zajac, 1990; Hinings, Hickson, Pennings, & Schneck, 1974); in interorganizational networks (Boje & Whetten, 1981; Galaskiewicz, 1979); in professional communities (Breiger, 1976), and community elites (Laumann & Pappi, 1976).

Theoretically, actors in central network positions have greater access to, and potential control over, relevant resources, such as information in the case of a communication network. Actors who are able to control relevant resources, and thereby increase others' dependence on them, acquire power. In addition to increasing others' dependence on them, actors must also decrease their dependence on others. They must have access to relevant resources that is not controlled or mediated by others. Thus, two measures of centrality, closeness (representing access) and betweenness (representing control), correspond to resource dependence notions (Brass, 1984). Both measures have been shown to contribute to the variance in reputational measures of power and promotions in organizations (Brass, 1984, 1985a). In addition, simple degree-centrality measures of the size of one's ego network (symmetric and asymmetric) have been associated with power (Brass & Burkhardt, 1992, 1993; Burkhardt & Brass, 1990).

Knoke and Burt (1983) have emphasized the distinction between symmetric and asymmetric ties, arguing that being the object of the relation rather than the source is an indication of superordination. They refer to measures that distinguish between source and object as measures of prestige. The difference between symmetric measures of centrality and asymmetric measures of prestige may be the difference between leaders and followers. Although their analyses showed the symmetric centrality measures to be highly correlated with the asymmetric prestige measures, Knoke and Burt found that only the prestige measure predicted early adoption of a medical innovation. Similarly, Burkhardt and Brass (1990) found that all employees increased their closeness centrality (symmetric measure) following the introduction of new technology. However, the early adopters of the new technology increased their indegree prestige and their power significantly more than the later adopters.

Studying an interpersonal network of nonsupervisory employees, Brass (1984) found that links beyond the workgroup and workflow requirements (prescribed vertical and horizontal coordination) were related to influence. In particular, closeness to the dominant coalition in the organization was strongly related to power and promotions. The dominant coalition was identified by a clique analysis of the interaction patterns of the top executives in the company. Brass (1985a) also found that men were more closely linked to the dominant coalition (composed of four men) and were perceived as more influential than women. Assuming that power positions in most organizations are dominated by men, women may be forced to forgo any preference for homophily in order to build connections with the dominant coalition. Thus, the organizational context places constraints on preferences for homophily, especially for women and minorities (Ibarra, 1993).

Brass (1985a) found further evidence of the effects of organizational structure on interaction patterns and power. Women who were part of integrated formal workgroups (at least two men and two women) and who were linked (closeness) to the men's network (only male employees considered) were perceived as more powerful than women who were not. Interestingly, men who were closely linked to the women's network (only women employees considered) were also perceived as more influential than men who were not.

Blau and Alba (1982) found that ties linking different workgroups increased one's power. Similarly, Brass (1984) found that centrality within departments was a better predictor of power than centrality within subgroups. Both studies (Blau & Alba; Brass, 1984) and Ibarra (1992) found that group membership was related to individual power.

In integrating the structural perspective with the behavioral perspective outlined by Ferris and Judge (1991), Brass and Burkhardt (1993) found that network position was related to behavioral tactics used, that both network position and behavioral tactics were independently related to perceptions of power, and that each (structure and behavior) mediated the relationship between the other and power. In suggesting that network position represented potential power (i.e., access to resources), and that behavioral tactics represented the strategic use of resources, they concluded that behavioral tactics increased in importance as network position decreased in strength. Consistent with structuration theory, their results also supported the argument that behavioral tactics are used to secure privileged positions in the network.

In other applications of social networks, Krackhardt (1990) found that the accuracy of individual cognitive maps of the social network in an organization was related to perceptions of influence. That is, power was related to the degree to which an individual's perception of the interaction network matched the "actual" social network. In a case analysis, Krackhardt (1992) also demonstrated how a lack of knowledge of the social networks in a firm prevented a union from successfully organizing employees.

The relation between networks and coalitions in organizations also has been the focus of several authors (Bacharach & Lawler, 1980; Murnighan & Brass, 1991; Stevenson, Pierce, & Porter, 1985; Thurman, 1979). Murnighan and Brass demonstrated how coalitions are formed one actor at a time and require the founder to have an extensive ego network of weak ties. Thurman described how leveling counter coalitions are formed through existing social network ties.

At the interorganizational network level of analysis, Stern (1979) used such network concepts as loose coupling and multiplexity to explain coalitions and power among colleges and universities. This historical analysis demonstrated how networks can be used to explain the transformation of the National Collegiate Athletic Association (NCAA) from a loose, voluntary confederation into a dominant, independent control agent over collegiate athletics.

Recruitment

The application of social networks to the traditional human resources practices of recruitment and selection begins with the simple assumption that both parties (i.e., the individual and the organization) must know of each other. As most people assume, the use of networks, as contrasted with employment agencies or job listings, can be a valuable aid in both job search and recruitment, particularly for high-paying, high-responsibility jobs such as managerial positions (Granovetter, 1982). In a classic example of the strength of weak ties, the people in Granovetter's study were able to find jobs more effectively through weak ties (acquaintances) than strong ties or formal listings (Granovetter, 1982). Granovetter argued that an actor's acquaintances (weak ties) are less likely to be linked to one another than are an actor's close friends (strong ties). An actor's set of weak ties will form a low-density, high-diversity network, one rich in nonredundant information. Although the lines in figure 12.2 do not indicate the strength of the tie (friend or acquaintence), we note that actor A is connected to several others who are not themselves connected. A set of strong ties will be densely interconnected and will likely represent a high degree of redundant information. For example, in figure 12.2, actor T is connected to others (R, S, Y, and Z) who are themselves connected. It is unlikely that actor R would provide information about a job opportunity that is different from the information provided by actor S. Thus, individuals have greater access to more and different job opportunities when relying on weak ties.

Later findings (Lin, Ensel, & Vaughn, 1981) modified and emphasized this notion. They found that weak ties used in finding jobs were associated with higher occupational achievement when the weak ties connected the job seekers to those of higher occupational status. Thus, the effectiveness of weak ties rests in the diversity and nonredundancy of the information they provide.

Although weak ties may be effectively used to cross occupational statuses, strong ties may be the mechanism behind homosocial reproduction in organizations (Kanter, 1977). As previously noted, actor similarity can be a powerful influence on the development of social networks and repeated interaction can lead to attitude similarity. Strong ties (friends) are likely to be related to both. For example, in a study of graduate business students, Kilduff (1990) found that students who perceived each other to be similar, or who indicated they were friends, tended to interview with the same organizations. These results held up even when controlling for academic concentration (e.g., finance, marketing, etc.) and job preference.

Likewise, organizations may establish recruiting networks based on actor and attitude similarity. Previous hires act as links that facilitate recruiting and likely promote homosocial reproduction. That is, recruiters seek out those whom they believe will "fit in" well in the organization. Fit is often based on actor similarity.

Selection

In adopting a political perspective on human resources, both Pfeffer (1989) and Ferris and Judge (1991) noted that selection is not entirely the result of abilities and competences. In moving beyond the rationality assumption, Pfeffer suggested that credentials and hiring standards are often the result of political contests within organizations. Those in power seek to perpetuate their power and further build coalitions and alliances by setting criteria and selecting those applicants most like themselves. Thus, as in the case of recruiting via the use of networks, selection may also largely depend on network ties. This is particularly true when the qualified applicant pool is large or when hiring standards are ambiguous. In such cases, similarity between applicant and recruiter may be an important basis of the selection choice. Because of the overlap between social networks and actor and attitude similarity, selection research might fruitfully pursue the effects of patterns of social relationships on hiring decisions.

Burt (1992) provided an interesting analysis of hiring practices in an organization in which conflict had escalated to the point of shootings and bomb threats. In consulting for the CEO, Burt and colleagues attempted to guide the senior executives past the debilitating attributions of personality and attributes to reach the underlying social network of the organization. Burt used the archival data provided in the application forms of current employees to trace the historical pattern of hirings and match it to the warring factions in the company. The social network data came from questions on the application forms of 1,721 current employees asking them (a) whether they knew anyone (i.e., friends, acquaintances, or relatives) working for the firm, (b) how they learned about the job opening, and (c) names of references. Added to the network analyses were the addresses of employees. Analyses of the social connections show how a lower-level manager, since fired, had virtually taken control of the company years earlier by hiring family, friends, and friends of friends, almost exclusively from a particular geographical location (his community). The conflicts arose between those people obligated to the lower-level manager and others hired from a rival community. Studying the social network patterns also provided possible solutions for resolving the conflict by identifying as possible mediators those employees with links to both groups (Burt & Ronchi, 1989). The case analysis provides a rich example of the political perspective, actor similarity, and a social network analysis of selection.

Socialization

Following selection into an organization, the process of socialization often begins. As noted above, interaction has been shown to positively relate to attitude similarity. Thus, the social networks of new employees may be a key to their socialization into the organization. Two related studies dealing with the socialization of new employees (Jablin & Krone, 1987; Sherman, Smith, & Mansfield, 1986) indicate that network involvement is a key process in assimilation of new employees. In an earlier study of communication roles, Roberts and O'Reilly (1979) found that participants (i.e., two or more links to others) were more satisfied and committed to the organization than isolates (i.e., less than two links). Eisenberg, Monge, and Miller (1984) found that network participation was related to organizational commitment for salaried employees but that only high involvement was related to commitment for hourly employees. However, due to the cross-sectional nature of these studies, it is impossible to know whether integration into the network leads to commitment, or vice versa. Position in the network and socialization and commitment are likely to be reciprocally causal, as our structuration assumptions would suggest.

Training

Despite the volumes written about training, to my knowledge there is little that addresses social networks or provides a structural perspective on training. As in the case of job search, awareness of training opportunities may be the result of network ties. In particular, weak ties will provide a diversity of knowledge of training and may be the source of novel, or innovative, information. If we view training as acquiring new and innovative ideas and skills, and consider the implementation of training as the adoption and implementation of these skills, we might turn to the adoption of innovation literature to provide some network insights into training.

Much writing has focused on the process of innovation and the role of social networks in adoption and diffusion of innovations (cf. Burt, 1982; Rogers, 1971; Tushman, 1977; Tushman & Anderson, 1986). It is generally agreed that innovation requires diverse and novel information. If so, an actor is more likely to get that novel information via weak ties. A member of a closely knit, dense clique of strong ties (e.g., actor S in figure 12.2) is less likely to be exposed to diverse, novel perspectives than an actor with weak ties to a number of different social groups. Thus, Burt (1992) argued that the size of one's network is much less important than the diversity of one's contacts. Supporting this theory are the findings that cosmopolitans (i.e., actors with external ties which cross social boundaries) are more likely to introduce innovations than are locals (Rogers). Likewise, central actors, sometimes identified as "opinion leaders," are unlikely to be early adopters of innovations when the innovation is not consistent with the established norms of the group (Rogers). Similarly, Tushman and Anderson noted that radical technological change (competence destroying) does not often originate with the dominant, industry-leading organization. The research and theory emphasize the importance of boundary spanning roles, or weak ties in the social network (Tushman).

As with an innovation, once training is introduced or adopted, the diffusion of the training (or the spread of new ideas and skills) can be predicted by social network relationships. Some controversy exists over whether diffusion is best predicted by a relational cohesion (direct interaction links) approach or a structural equivalence perspective. The relational cohesion approach suggests that the most central actors should be the first to experience training. For example, in figure 12.2, the most efficient diffusion of training might occur if we trained actors A and Z first. However, Burt (1987) has argued that persons occupying structurally equivalent roles in the network (for example, actors B and C in figure 12.2) are likely to similarly adopt the innovation regardless of whether they directly communicate with each other. His reanalysis of the classic adoption of tetracycline by doctors supports his arguments.

In a more recent study, Burkhardt and Brass (1990) investigated the introduction, training, and diffusion of a major technological change in an organization. They found that centrality in the existing network was not related to early use of the new system. Those who were early adopters increased both their centrality and power in the organization as the technology was implemented. The diffusion process closely followed the network patterns following the change, with structurally equivalent employees adopting at similar times.

In a similar study of the introduction of a new computer technology, Papa (1990) found that productivity following the change was positively related to interaction frequency, network size, and network diversity (i.e., number of different departments and hierarchical levels contacted). Frequency, size, and diversity also predicted the speed at which the new technology was learned (time to reach 110% of past productivity). Papa argued that training programs can provide basic operating information but that much of the learning about a new technology occurs after training as employees attempt to apply the training. His results supported the proposition that learning is an active process of information exchange. Communicating with others to gather and understand information had a positive effect on productivity, even when controlling past performance.

An alternative network perspective on training would be to view it as an opportunity to build social connections among participants. For example, if we consider college as a training experience, the advantage of network connections made as cohorts proceed through the college experience becomes obvious. Deep and lasting connections develop as people go through the rites of transition together (Trice & Morand, 1989). In some cases, such as police forces and military units, training is intentionally designed to develop strong ties among participants (Van Maanen, 1975). Likewise, corporations have recently emphasized teamwork and building strong, trusting relationships among team members in intensive training programs such as "Outward Bound," where executives spend prolonged periods of time in the wilderness. Even when training involves only short periods of time, network connections are formed. Organizations may wish to use training to build connections across diverse, heterogeneous groups in anticipation of the future formation of cross-functional teams. In the context of training, connections may be based on similar training experiences rather than actor similarity on attributes such as race, sex, or age.

An example of this management strategy is related by Krackhardt and Hanson (1993). Upon learning of two distinct subcultures in the organization, top management scheduled off-site training that intentionally mixed members of the two conflicting groups. This was followed by "staff swaps," whereby members of one group substituted for vacationing or ill members of the other group, and vice versa (Krackhardt & Hanson, p. 110). Although structured interaction does not always lead to stable links, the previously noted antecedents suggest that it increases the possibility. Longitudinal research which maps network connections formed during training may provide useful organizational insights.

Performance Appraisal

Although the traditional human resources approach to performance appraisal has focused on methods of increasing accuracy and reliability, recent research has taken a political perspective. As in the case of selection, performance evaluations by supervisors may incorporate a variety of non-performance-related factors (Longenecker, Sims, & Gioia, 1987). Although some of the results are mixed, actual and perceived similarity in attitudes, values, and demographics between supervisor and subordinate has been shown to result in higher performance ratings (see Ferris & Judge, 1991, for review). As noted above, similarity is both an antecedent and consequence of social network connections. We would expect that strong links between supervisors and subordinates would result in higher performance evaluations.

The multiplexity of relationships between the supervisor and subordinate may also have an effect on performance evaluations. Multiplexity refers to the extent to which two actors are linked by more than one relationship. For example, the supervisor and subordinate may be linked by friendship as well as communication and workflow links. Providing a poor performance evaluation (work link) may create stress, or result in the loss of the other relationship (friendship). Thus, to maintain the friendship, the supervisor may provide higher performance evaluations.

In addition, a social network perspective suggests that the analysis of performance appraisal be extended beyond the dyadic level to assess the larger network. An analysis of supervisor-subordinate similarity might fruitfully be extended to include differences among subordinates. For example, if a white, male supervisor has all white, male subordinates, race and gender similarity will not differentiate performance evaluations. The network perspective would encourage researchers to simultaneously search for supervisor-subordinate similarity and subordinate-subordinate difference. Similarities and differences may be readily apparent from an analysis of the social network patterns of the group. Continuing with our structuration framework, patterns of interaction may be both an antecedent and a consequence of performance evaluations (i.e., poor evaluations may decrease supervisor-subordinate interactions).

Looking again beyond the supervisor-subordinate dyad, the network perspective suggests that performance evaluations of the supervisors might have an effect on their evaluations of their subordinates. Likewise, evaluations on each subordinate may be made relative to evaluations of the other subordinates. These possibilities suggest that much could be learned by mapping a network of performance evaluations on the network of interactions.

Combining the social network/power relationships discussed above with performance evaluations suggests a direction for further research. Subordinates who are in network positions to control the flow of information to and from their supervisors (high betweenness centrality) may be able to use their "gatekeeping" position to influence performance evaluations. Such an analysis involves attention not only to the existence of connections but also to the absence of connections.

Equity of performance evaluations is another issue that has been closely tied to traditional attempts to increase accuracy and reliability. Perceptions of inequity are particularly salient when rewards are tied to evaluations. According to equity theory (Adams, 1965), employees compare their perceived input/outcome ratios with their perceptions of others' input/outcome ratios. The problem of testing equity predictions outside the laboratory has been the large number of possible "others" that might be considered for possible comparison. The social network perspective provides a possible solution to the problem of identifying comparison others. According to a network perspective, choice of comparison others is both facilitated and constrained by the network of relationships. Krackhardt and Brass (1994) have predicted that structurally equivalent individuals, and individuals with strong ties, are likely to make social comparisons of equity. For example, in figure 12.2, actor B would likely compare inputs and outcomes with actor C. Further, Krackhardt's focus on cognitive maps of networks (i.e., individual perceptions of network relations) may be a better predictor of comparison others than the actual network relations (Kilduff & Krackhardt, 1993; Krackhardt, 1987, 1990; Krackhardt & Brass).

Performance

Although we have assumed a political perspective in much of the discussion of performance appraisal, the social network perspective does not necessarily require such a perspective. Thus, we move to the effects of networks on performance, noting that performance, as measured by supervisory ratings, may contain political aspects. The network perspective on performance invites us to analyze the pattern of relationships rather than view individuals' performance in isolation. As is the case with interdependent tasks in organizations, relationships with others affect performance.

At the interpersonal network level of analysis, Roberts and O'Reilly (1979) found that participants (i.e., two or more links to others) were better performers than isolates (i.e., less than two links). Although Brass (1981) found no significant correlations between centrality in the workflow and performance, he found that job characteristics (e.g., task variety and autonomy) mediated this relationship. That is, centrality in the workgroup's workflow was positively related to job characteristics, which in turn were positively related to both satisfaction and performance. Centrality within the entire organization's workflow network (rather than the smaller workgroups) was negatively related to job characteristics (Brass, 1981). Brass argued that the latter jobs were routinized, mechanistic jobs in the technical core, buffered by more complex, uncertain jobs on the boundary of the organization. In a later study, Brass (1985b) used network techniques to identify pooled, sequential, and reciprocal interdependencies within workgroups. He found that performance varied according to combinations of technological uncertainty, job characteristics, and interaction patterns. The results suggest that the relationship between interpersonal interaction and performance is a complex one dependent upon horizontal differentiation and coordination requirements (i.e., tasks, technology, workflow).

This conclusion in consistent with small-group-laboratory network studies of the early 1950s (see Shaw, 1964, for a review). Although these early laboratory studies were highly controlled and simplistic, some consistent findings emerged. Centralized communication networks (e.g., figure 12.1a) resulted in more efficient performance when tasks were simple and routine. Decentralized networks (e.g., figure 12.1b) were better at performing complex, uncertain tasks. That is, performance is better when the communication structure matches the information processing requirements of the task.

Career Development

Getting ahead in organizations has often been said to be a matter of "who you know, not what you know." This statement is typically made in a cynical, derogatory way because it emphasizes the importance of "social capital" as compared to "human capital" (e.g., personal attributes such as education, intelligence, attractiveness, etc.) (Burt, 1982). Likewise, the "old boys' network" has received much negative attention, especially in relation to the careers of women and minorities. The emphasis on social capital is contrary to the individualistic values of western cultures such as the United States. That is, most of us believe that achievement and rewards should be contingent on individual effort and abilities. These are the same values that drive much of the research in human resources management. The focus is on the identification and measurement of individual attributes. Despite the individualism apparent throughout our system of education, most managers' careers are contingent on what they can effectively accomplish in connection with others. As Mintzberg (1973) has noted, the myth of managerial work is that it occurs in isolation. Most of a manager's roles involve social relationships. Thus, the social network framework provides a useful perspective for focusing on the importance of social relationships in careers.

To the extent that acquiring power and influence is related to upward mobility and success, much of the previous discussion of social networks and power applies. For example, in one of the few longitudinal studies of social networks, Brass (1984, 1985a) found that network indicators of power also related to promotions of previously nonsupervisory employees over a three-year period.

The popular press has noted the importance of "networking" as well as the advantages of having mentors in organizations. The intuitive advantages of building a large network have seldom been questioned, although little systematic research has actually addressed this prescription. Rather than simply building relationships randomly, two strategies (a weak tie and a strong tie strategy) are possible given the constraints of organizational structure.

Let us assume that all relationships require maintenance time and that strong, close relationships require more time than weak (acquaintance) relationships. The question arises as to whether managers should develop a close personal relationship with a mentor or highly connected other (i.e., a strong tie strategy emphasizing closeness centrality) or attempt to develop many weaker relationships with disconnected others (i.e., a weak tie strategy emphasizing betweenness centrality and structural holes). The strong tie, closeness strategy allows an employee to be central by virtue of a few direct links to others who have many direct links. The employee has access to resources such as information via the indirect links of the highly connected other (mentor). Assuming a limit to the number of direct links that an employee can maintain, having links to central others is more efficient than links to peripheral others. In figure 12.2, actor Q has indirect connection to others by virtue of being connected to actor Z. Likewise, actor D has access to others via his/her connection to highly central actor A. However, the reliance on indirect links creates a dependency on the highly connected other (mentor) to mediate the flow of resources.

Adopting the weak tie strategy, Burt (1992) has argued that the size of one's network is not as important as the diversity of one's contacts. He has argued that structural autonomy (which is, similar to the notion of betweenness centrality) can be obtained by managers taking advantage of "structural holes." A structural hole is defined as the absence of link between two contacts who are both linked to the manager. Burt (1992) has noted the advantages of the *tertius gaudens* (i.e., "the third who benefits"). Not only does the *tertius* gain nonredundant information from the contacts (i.e., the strength of weak ties argument), but the *tertius* is in a position to control the information flow between the two (i.e., broker the relationship) or play the two off against each other. The *tertius* profits from the disunion of others. Although the strength of ties is not indicated in figure 12.2 actor A's links suggest a weak tie, structural hole strategy. Actor A is linked to actors who are not themselves linked.

Using the criterion of early promotions, Burt (1992) found the weak tie strategy (presence of structural holes) to be more effective for a sample of 284 managers in a large, high-technology firm, except in the case of women and newly hired managers. For women, the strong tie strategy worked best. However, because the network data were not longitudinal, it is impossible to discern whether the networks were the result of early promotions or the cause of early promotions.

In another study, Kilduff and Krackhardt (1994) demonstrated the power of strong ties. They found that a friendship link to a prominent person in an organization tended to boost an individual's performance reputation. In comparing the cognitive maps of the network with the actual network, they found that the perceived network, rather than the actual network, significantly predicted reputations. Thus, it appears that individuals may acquire power by "basking in the reflected glory" of prominent others. Likewise, Brass (1984, 1985a) found that links to supervisors and closeness to the dominant coalition were related to promotions.

While being closely linked to a powerful other may result in "basking in the reflected glory," it may also result in being perceived as "second fiddle." In the latter case, one's own talents are diminished in the presence of a powerful other (i.e., one is perceived as "riding the coattails" or "second fiddle"). The difference in perceptions, and the difference in career advantage, may be the result of the stage of one's career, boundaries to entry, and/or the type of organization. Early in one's career, strong connections to a mentor are perceived as an indication of potential success. However, later in one's career, one is expected to successfully perform on one's own, and to mentor others. Early in a career, the mentor provides access to the network. As Burt's (1992) analyses suggest, women or newly hired managers may face barriers to entry in established networks. Thus, a strong connection to a powerful, well-connected mentor may overcome such barriers. This idea is consistent with Brass's (1984) results in a non-supervisory sample, in which links to the dominant coalition were related to promotions. Also, Burt's (1992) managerial sample was drawn from a high-technology firm facing a rapidly changing environment, whereas Brass was studying a relatively more bureaucratic newspaper publishing organization. The dynamic environment and matrix organization in the high-technology firm may naturally favor the diversity-of-information advantage of the weak tie, structural hole strategy.

In figure 12.2, note that actor N's relationships appear to capture both strategies. Although the strength of the ties are not indicated, actor N is connected to highly central others (A, R, and P) who are not themselves connected. Thus, actor N connects three relatively distinct groups and has indirect access to almost everyone. One in such a position is typically called a gatekeeper and scores very high on betweenness centrality. N's connections to central others also result in a high closeness centrality score.

Turnover

In a study of fast-food restaurants, Krackhardt and Porter (1986) found that turnover did not occur randomly but in structurally equivalent clusters in the perceived interpersonal communication network. That is, turnover was a function of the social network context. In a related study, Krackhardt and Porter (1985) looked at the effects of turnover on the attitudes of those who remained in the organization. In this longitudinal study, the closer the employee was to those who left, the more satisfied and committed the remaining employee became. The authors argued that remaining employees cognitively justified their decision to stay by increasing their satisfaction and commitment.

Research on relational and organizational demography (Tsui, Egan, & O'Reilly, 1992; Tsui & O'Reilly, 1989; Wagner, Pfeffer, & O'Reilly, 1984; Zenger & Lawrence, 1989) has shown that similarity in age and tenure among group members is related to turnover. In combination with our previous review of the similarity/attraction literature, we can predict that similarity leads to increased communication, which, in turn, is negatively related to turnover. McPherson, Popielarz, and Drobnic (1992) supported this prediction. In voluntary organizations, they found that network ties within a group were associated with reduced turnover while ties outside the group (weak ties) increased turnover.

Conflict

In a study of intergroup networks in twenty organizations, Nelson (1989) found that low-conflict organizations were characterized by a high number of strong ties between members of different groups. Analyzing the overall pattern of ties, Nelson argued that the interaction networks were significantly different for high- and low-conflict organizations. In a case analysis, Lincoln and Miller (1979) noted how conflict in an organization was readily apparent from the social network patterns. Although further research on conflict is needed, it appears that intergroup conflict in organizations is negatively related to the percentage of strong ties which cross group boundaries.

■ Conclusion

Overall, I have attempted to demonstrate how a social network perspective can contribute to our understanding of personnel and human resources management, and organizations. As the set of nodes and the set of ties which represent the presence or absence of some relationship between the nodes, the network can be used to describe many structures. The nodes, or actors, can be people, roles, groups, organizations, industries, or even nations. The ties may represent communication, friendship, kinship, authority, economic exchange, information exchange, or any other relationship. Thus, the social structure of any organization can be viewed as a network. Networks bridge the micro and macro levels of analysis so that we can simultaneously study the whole and the parts. More important, the network perspective focuses on the relationships rather than the attributes of the actors. I have attempted to outline the antecedents of social networks and to show how social networks may affect such human resource practices as recruitment, selection, training, socialization, performance appraisal, careers, and turnover. From an applied perspective, we can identify effective and ineffective social network structures and change those influences which affect those patterns. By noting the influences and outcomes we can more effectively manage organizations.

What does the future hold for organizations and human resources management? Those who see increased acceleration of change in the environment, increased uncertainty, and increased information processing requirements have suggested the emergence of a new organizational form—the "network" organization (Baker, 1993; Miles & Snow, 1986; Nohria & Eccles, 1993). This post industrial form is radically different, with relations based on neither hierarchy nor market (Granovetter, 1985; Powell, 1990). The trends are apparent: increasing globalization of the world economy, increasing diversity in the workforce, rapid entry and exit of both competitors and technologies, flexible, computer-assisted design and manufacturing of customized products and services, and unprecedented risk (Nohria & Eccles). Bureaucratic, vertically integrated organizations are being replaced by small, flexible organizations engaging in joint ventures.

Snow and Snell (1993) provide a description of network organizations and the role of human resources management. Unlike traditional organizations, the network organization will be a temporary "configuration of independent business units linked together by contracts" (Snow & Snell, p. 461). Managing human resources in a network organization may involve identifying, locating, and organizing "temporary employees" across organizational and international boundaries. Human resource managers will likely become human resource "brokers," bringing together the right mix of people to successfully offer a product or service. And that mix may be used only temporarily as environments and technologies rapidly change. Needed resources are contracted for through an ongoing network of extraorganizational connections. Human resource management will require identifying and nurturing potential relationships, which may change with each product cycle. Employee files may become databases of information about people and companies outside the organization who are available for "employment" on a short-term, contractual basis. Permanent employees may be only a small group of generalists characterized by their ability to quickly adapt to change and to broker synergistic relationships across interdepartmental and interorganizational teams. The network organization places additional importance on relationships. As one network organization executive said, "Our business is one of relationships" (*Business Week*, 1986, p. 64).

The social network perspective may provide the framework for understanding the "network" organization of the future. As presented here, it is not offered as a substitute or a competing perspective to the traditional focus on individual attributes in human resources management. As I have previously noted, much of the progress in research and application has been achieved via the traditional emphasis on the identification and measurement of individual attributes. Yet it has been estimated that the average adult maintains more than 1,000 informal ties (mutually recognizable others). Research on the "small world" phenomenon (Travers & Milgram, 1969) has shown that two randomly selected people can "reach" each other through a path of a surprising few number of links. As the epigraph suggests, we are a network of social interdependencies. Further progress can be achieved by combining these perspectives with the traditional approaches and methodologies. In adding the social network perspective, we answer the call for a broader perspective in human resources management and increase our understanding of the complexities of behavior in organizations.

■ References

Adams, J. S. (1965). Inequity in social change. In L. Berkowitz (Ed.), *Advances in experimental social psychology* (pp. 267–300). New York: Academic Press.
Aldrich, H. (1982). The origins and persistence of social networks. In P. V. Mars-

den & N. Lin (Eds.), *Social structure and network analysis* (pp. 281–293). Beverly Hills, CA: Sage.

Astley, W. G., & Zajac, E. J. (1990). Beyond dyadic exchange: Functional interdependence and sub-unit power. *Organization Studies, 11*, 481–501.

Racharach, S. B., & Lawler, E. J. (1980). *Power and politics in organizations*. San Francisco: Jossey-Bass.

Baker, W. E. (1993). The network organization in theory and practice. In N. Nohria & R. Eccles (Eds.), *Networks and organizations: Structure, form, and action* (pp. 397–429). Boston: Harvard Business School Press.

Barley, S. R. (1986). Technology as an occasion for structuring: Evidence from observations of CT scanners and the social order of radiology departments. *Administrative Science Quarterly, 31*, 78–108.

Barley, S. R. (1990). The alignment of technology and structure through roles and networks. *Administrative Science Quarterly, 35*, 61–103.

Beekun, R. I., & Glick, W. H. (1991). *Moving beyond the literary metaphor of loose coupling: A network analysis approach*. Working paper MS# 89-008.

Betz, N. E., Fitzgerald, L. F., & Hill, R. E. (1989). Trait-factor theories: Traditional cornerstone of career theory. In M. B. Arthur, D. T. Hall, & B. S. Lawrence (Eds.), *Handbook of career theory* (pp. 26–40). New York: Cambridge University Press.

Blau, J. R., & Alba, R. D. (1982). Empowering nets of participation. *Administrative Science Quarterly, 27*, 363–379.

Blau, P. M. (1977). *Inequality and heterogeneity*. New York: Free Press.

Boje, D. M., & Whetten, D. A. (1981). Effects of organizational strategies and contextual constraints on centrality and attributions of influence in interorganizational networks. *Administrative Science Quarterly, 26*, 378–395.

Brass, D. J. (1981). Structural relationships, job characteristics, and worker satisfaction and performance. *Administrative Science Quarterly, 26*, 331–348.

Brass, D. J. (1984). Being in the right place: A structural analysis of individual influence in an organization. *Administrative Science Quarterly, 29*, 518–539.

Brass, D. J. (1985a). Men's and women's networks: A study of interaction patterns and influence in an organization. *Academy of Management Journal, 28*, 327–343.

Brass, D. J. (1985b). Technology and the structuring of jobs: Employee satisfaction, performance, and influence. *Organizational Behavior and Human Decision Processes, 35*, 216–240.

Brass, D. J., & Burkhardt, M. E. (1992). Centrality and power in organizations. In N. Nohria & R. Eccles (Eds.), *Networks and organizations: Structure, form, and action* (pp. 191–215). Boston: Harvard Business School Press.

Brass, D. J., & Burkhardt, M. E. (1993). Potential power and power use: An investigation of structure and behavior. *Academy of Management Journal, 36*, 441–470.

Breiger, R. L. (1976). Career attributes and network structure: A blockmodel study of biomedical research specialty. *American Sociological Review, 41*, 117–135.

Bristor, J. M. (1993). Influence strategies in organizational buying: The importance of connections to the right people in the right places. *Journal of Business-to-Business Marketing, 1*, 63–98.

Burkhardt, M. E. (1994). Social interaction effects following a technological change: A longitudinal investigation. *Academy of Management Journal, 37*, 869–898.

Burkhardt, M. E., & Brass, D. J. (1990). Changing patterns or patterns of change: The effect of a change in technology on social network structure and power. *Administrative Science Quarterly, 35*, 104–127.

Burns, T., & Stalker, G. M. (1961). *The management of innovation.* London: Tavistock.

Burt, R. S. (1982). *Toward a structural theory of action.* New York: Academic Press.

Burt, R. S. (1987). Social contagion and innovation: Cohesion versus structural equivalence. *American Journal of Sociology, 92*, 1287–1335.

Burt, R. S. (1992). *Structural holes: The social structure of competition.* Cambridge, MA: Harvard University Press.

Burt, R. S., & Ronchi, D. (1989, August 13–16). *Contested control in a large manufacturing plant.* Paper presented at Academy of Management Meetings, Washington, DC.

Business Week. (1986, March 3). And now, the post-industrial corporation, pp. 64–71.

Carley, K. (1991). A theory of group stability. *American Sociological Review, 56*, 331–354.

Carley, K., & Krackhardt, D. (1990, February 15–18). *Emergent asymmetric behavior: A sociocognitive examination of asymmetric relationships.* Paper presented at Sunbelt X International Social Network Conference, San Diego.

Coleman, J. S. (1957). *Community conflict.* New York: Free Press.

Coleman, J. S. (1973). *The mathematics of collective action.* Chicago: Aldine.

Cook, K. S. (1982). Network structures from an exchange perspective. In P. V. Marsden & N. Lin (Eds.), *Social structure and network analysis* (pp. 177–199). Beverly Hills, CA: Sage.

Danowski, J. A. (1980). Group attitude uniformity and connectivity of organizational communication networks for production, innovation, and maintenance content. *Human Communication Research, 6*, 299–308.

Danowski, J. A., & Edison-Swift, P. (1985). Crisis effects on intraorganizational computer-based communication. *Communication Research, 12*, 251–270.

Davis, J. A. (1966). Structural balance, mechanical solidarity, and interpersonal relations. In J. Berger, M. Zelditch, & B. Anderson (Eds.), *Sociological theories in progress* (Vol. 1, pp. 74–101). Boston: Houghton-Mifflin.

Dean, J. W., & Brass, D. J. (1985). Social interaction and the perception of job characteristics in an organization. *Human Relations, 38*, 571–582.

DiMaggio, P. J., & Powell, W. W. (1983). The iron cage revisited: Institutional isomorphism and collective rationality in organizational fields. *American Sociological Review, 48*, 147–160.

Durkheim, E. (1997/1951). *Suicide: A study in sociology.* (Translated by J. A. Spaulding & G. Simpson). New York: Free Press.

Eisenberg, E. M., Monge, P. R., & Miller, K. I. (1984). Involvement in communication networks as a predictor of organizational commitment. *Human Communication Research, 10*, 179–201.

Erickson, B. H. (1988). The relational basis of attitudes. In B. Wellman & S. D. Berkowitz (Eds.), *Social structures: A network approach* (pp. 99–121). New York: Cambridge University Press.

Ferris, G. R., & Judge, T. A. (1991). Personnel/human resources management: A political influence perspective. *Journal of Management, 17*, 447–488.

Festinger, L., Schachter, S., & Back, K. (1950). *Social pressures in informal groups: A study of human factors in housing.* Palo Alto, CA: Stanford University Press.

Fombrun, C. J. (1983). Attributions of power across a social network. *Human Relations, 36*, 493–508.

Fulk, J., & Boyd, B. (1991). Emerging theories of communication in organizations. *Journal of Management, 17*, 407–446.

Fulk, J., & Steinfield, C. (1990). *Organizations and communication technology.* London: Sage.

Galaskiewicz, J. (1979). *Exchange networks and community politics.* Beverly Hills, CA: Sage.

Galaskiewicz, J., & Burt, R. S. (1991). Interorganizational contagion in corporate philanthropy. *Administrative Science Quarterly, 36*, 88–105.

Galaskiewicz, J., & Wasserman, S. (1989). Mimetic processes within an interorganizational field: An empirical test. *Administrative Science Quarterly, 34*, 454–479.

Giddens, A. (1976). *New rules of sociological method.* London: Hutchinson.

Giddens, A. (1979). *Central problems in social theory.* London: Macmillan.

Granovetter, M. (1973). The strength of weak ties. *American Journal of Sociology, 78*, 1360–1380.

Granovetter, M. (1982). The strength of weak ties: A network theory revisited. In P. V. Marsden & N. Lin (Eds.), *Social structure and network analysis* (pp. 105–130). Beverly Hills, CA: Sage.

Granovetter, M. (1985). Economic action and social structure: The problem of embeddedness. *American Journal of Sociology, 91*, 481–510.

Harary, F. (1959). Graph theoretic methods in the management sciences. *Management Science, 5*, 387–403.

Hinings, C. R., Hickson, D. J., Pennings, J. M., & Schneck, R. E. (1974). Structural conditions of intraorganizational power. *Administrative Science Quarterly, 19*, 22–44.

Homans, G. C. (1950). *The human group.* New York: Harcourt Brace.

Ibarra, H. (1992). Homophily and differential returns: Sex differences in network structure and access in an advertising firm. *Administrative Science Quarterly, 37*, 422–447.

Ibarra, H. (1993). Personal networks of women and minorities in management: A conceptual framework. *Academy of Management Review, 18*, 56–87.

Ibarra, H., & Andrews, S. B. (1993). Power, social influence and sense-making: Effects of network centrality and proximity on employee perceptions. *Administrative Science Quarterly, 38*, 277–303.

Jablin, F. M., & Krone, K. J. (1987). Organizational assimilation. In C. Berger & S. H. Chaffee (Eds.), *Handbook of communication science* (pp. 711–746). Newbury Park, CA: Sage.

James, L. R., & Jones, A. P. (1976). Organizational structure: A review of structural dimensions and their conceptual relationships with individual attitudes and behavior. *Organizational Behavior and Human Performance, 16*, 74–113.

Kanter, R. M. (1977). *Men and women of the corporation.* New York: Basic Books.

Knoke, D., & Burt, R. S. (1983). Prominence. In R. S. Burt & M. J. Miner (Eds.), *Applied network analysis: A methodological introduction* (pp. 195–222). Beverly Hills, CA: Sage.

Kilduff, M. (1990). The interpersonal structure of decision making: A social comparison approach to organizational choice. *Organizational Behavior and Human Decision Processes, 47,* 270–288.

Kilduff, M. (1992). The friendship network as a decision-making resource: Dispositional moderators of social influences on organizational choice. *Journal of Personality and Social Psychology, 62,* 168–180.

Kilduff, M., & Krackhardt, D. (1993). Schemas at work: Making sense of organizational relationships. Unpublished manuscript.

Kilduff, M., & Krackhardt, D. (1994). Bringing the individual back in: A structural analysis of the internal market for reputation in organizations. *Academy of Management Journal, 37,* 87–108.

Krackhardt, D. (1987). Cognitive social structures. *Social Networks, 9,* 109–134.

Krackhardt, D. (1990). Assessing the political landscape: Structure, cognition, and power in organizations. *Administrative Science Quarterly, 35,* 342–369.

Krackhardt, D. (1992). The strength of strong ties: The importance of *Philos*. In N. Nohria & R. Eccles (Eds.), *Networks and organizations: Structure, form, and action* (pp. 216–239). Boston: Harvard Business School Press.

Krackhardt, D. (1993). Graph theoretical dimensions of informal organizations. In K. Carley & M. Prietula (Eds.), *Computational organizational theory.* New York: Lawrence Erlbaum Assoc.

Krackhardt, D., & Brass, D. J. (1994). Intra-organizational networks: The micro side. In S. Wasserman & J. Galaskiewicz (Eds.), *Social networks.* Beverly Hills, CA: Sage.

Krackhardt, D., & Hanson, J. R. (1993, July-August). Informal networks: The company behind the chart. *Harvard Business Review,* pp. 104–111.

Krackhardt, D., & Kilduff, M. (1990). Friendship patterns and culture: The control of organizational diversity. *American Anthropologist, 92,* 142–154.

Krackhardt, D., & Porter, L. W. (1985). When friends leave: A structural analysis of the relationship between turnover and stayers' attitudes. *Administrative Science Quarterly, 30,* 242–261.

Krackhardt, D., & Porter, L. W. (1986). The snowball effect: Turnover embedded in communication networks. *Journal of Applied Psychology, 71,* 50–55.

Lazarsfeld, P. F., & Merton, R. K. (1954). Friendship as social process: A substantive and methodological analysis. In M. Berger, T. Able, & C. Page (Eds.), *Freedom and control in modern society.* New York: Octagon.

Laumann, E. O. (1966). *Prestige and association in an urban community: An analysis of an urban stratification system.* New York: Bobbs-Merrill.

Laumann, E. O., & Knoke, D. (1987). *The organizational state.* Madison: University of Wisconsin Press.

Laumann, E. O., & Pappi, F. U. (1976). *Networks of collective action: A perspective on community influence systems.* New York: Academic Press.

Lin, N., Ensel, W. M., & Vaughn, J. C. (1981). Social resources and strength of ties: Structural factors in occupational status attainment. *American Sociological Review, 46,* 393–405.

Lincoln, J. R., Hanada, M., & Olson, J. (1981). Cultural orientation and individual reactions to organizations: A study of employees of Japanese-owned firms. *Administrative Science Quarterly, 26*, 93–115.

Lincoln, J. R., & Miller, J. (1979). Work and friendship ties in organizations: A comparative analysis of relational networks. *Administrative Science Quarterly, 24*, 181–199.

Longenecker, C. O., Sims, H. P., & Gioia, D. A. (1987). Behind the mask: The politics of employee appraisal. *Academy of Management Executive, 1*, 183–193.

Marsden, P. V. 1988. Homogeneity in confiding relations. *Social Networks, 10*, 57–76.

Mayhew, B. H. (1980). Structuralism versus individualism: Part 1, Shadowboxing in the dark. *Social Forces, 59*, 335–375.

McPherson, J. M., Popielarz, P. A., & Drobnic, S. (1992). Social networks and organizational dynamics. *American Sociological Review, 57*, 153–170.

McPherson, J. M., & Smith-Lovin, L. (1987). Homophily in voluntary organizations: Status distance and the composition of face-to-face groups. *American Sociological Review, 52*, 370–379.

Miles, R. E., & Snow, C. C. (1986). Network organizations: New concepts for new forms. *California Management Review, 28*, 62–73.

Mintzberg, H. (1973). *The nature of managerial work.* New York: Harper & Row.

Mitchell, J. C. (1969). *Social networks in urban situations.* Manchester: University of Manchester Press.

Moch, M. K. (1980). Job involvement, internal motivation, and employees' integration into networks of work relationships. *Organizational Behavior and Human Performance, 25*, 15–31.

Monge, P. R., & Eisenberg, E. M. (1987). Emergent communication networks. In F. M. Jablin, L. L. Putman, K. H. Roberts, & L. W. Porter (Eds.), *Handbook of organizational communication: An interdisciplinary perspective* (pp. 304–342). Newbury Park, CA: Sage.

Murnighan, J. K., & Brass, D. J. (1991). Intraorganizational coalitions. In M. Bazerman, B. Sheppard, & R. Lewicki (Eds.), *Research on negotiations in organizations* (Vol. 3, pp. 283–307). Greenwich, CT: JAI Press.

Nelson, R. E. (1989). The strength of strong ties: Social networks and intergroup conflict in organizations. *Academy of Management Journal, 32*, 377–401.

Nohria, N., & Eccles, R. G. (1993). Face-to-face: Making network organizations work. In N. Nohria & R. Eccles (Eds.), *Networks and organizations: Structure, form, and action* (pp. 288–308). Boston: Harvard Business School Press.

Oliver, C. (1988). The collective strategy framework: An application to competing predictions of isomorphism. *Administrative Science Quarterly, 33*, 543–561.

Papa, M. J. (1990). Communication network patterns and employee performance with a new technology. *Communication Research, 17*, 344–368.

Pfeffer, J. (1989). A political perspective on careers: Interests, networks, and environments. In M. B. Arthur, D. T. Hall, & B. S. Lawrence (Eds.), *Handbook of career theory* (pp. 380–396). New York: Cambridge University Press.

Powell, W. W. (1990). Neither market nor hierarchy: Network forms of organization. In B. M. Staw & C. L. Cummings (Eds.), *Research in organizational behavior* (Vol. 12, pp. 295–336). Greenwich, CT: JAI Press.

Rentsch, J. R. (1990). Climate and culture: Interaction and qualitative differences in organizational meanings. *Journal of Applied Psychology, 75*, 668–681.

Rice, R. E., & Aydin, C. (1991). Attitudes toward new organizational technology: Network proximity as a mechanism for social information processing. *Administrative Science Quarterly, 36*, 219–244.

Roberts, K. H., & O'Reilly, C. A., III. (1979). Some correlates of communication roles in organizations. *Academy of Management Journal, 22*, 42–57.

Rogers, E. M. (1971). *Communication of innovations*. New York: Free Press.

Ronchetto, J. R., Hutt, M. D., & Reingen, P. H. (1989). Embedded influence patterns in organizational buying systems. *Journal of Marketing, 53*, 51–62.

Schermerhorn, J. R. (1977). Information sharing as an interorganizational activity. *Academy of Management Journal, 20*, 148–153.

Schneider, B. (1983). Interactional psychology and organizational behavior. In L. L. Cummings & B. M. Staw (Eds.), *Research in organizational behavior* (Vol. 5, pp. 1–32). Greenwich, CT: JAI Press.

Scott, J. (1991). *Social network analysis: A handbook*. London: Sage.

Shaw, M. E., (1964). Communication networks. In L. Berkowitz (Ed.), *Advances in experimental social psychology* (Vol. 1, pp. 111–147). New York: Academic Press.

Sherman, J. D., Smith, H. L., & Mansfield, E. R. (1986). The impact of emergent network structure on organizational socialization. *Journal of Applied Behavioral Science, 22*, 53–63.

Shrader, C. B., Lincoln, J. R., & Hoffman, A. N. (1989). The network structures of organizations: Effects of task contingencies and distributional form. *Human Relations, 42*, 43–66.

Snell, S. A. (1992). Control theory in strategic human resource management: The mediating effect of administrative information. *Academy of Management Journal, 35*, 292–327.

Snow, C. C., & Snell, S. A. (1993). Staffing as strategy. In N. Schmitt & W. C. Borman (Eds.), *Personnel selection in organizations* (pp. 448–477). San Francisco: Jossey-Bass.

Staw, B. M., & Sutton, R. I. (1993). Macro organizational psychology. In J. K. Murnighan (Ed.), *Social psychology in organizations: Advances in theory and research* (pp. 350–384). Englewood Cliffs, NJ: Prentice Hall.

Stern, R. N. (1979). The development of an interorganizational control network: The case of intercollegiate athletics. *Administrative Science Quarterly, 24*, 242–266.

Stevenson, W. B., Pierce, J. L., & Porter, L. W. (1985). The concept of coalition in organization theory and research. *Academy of Management Review, 10*, 256–268.

Thurman, B. (1979). In the office: Networks and coalitions. *Social Networks, 2*, 47–63.

Tichy, N. M., & Fombrun, C. (1979). Network analysis in organizational settings. *Human Relations, 32*, 923–965.

Tosi, H. L. (1992). *The environment / organization / person contingency model: A Meso approach to the study of organizations*. Greenwich, CT: JAI Press.

Travers, J., & Milgram, S. (1969). An experimental study of the "small world" problem. *Sociometry, 32*, 425–443.

Trice, H. M., & Morand, D. A. (1989). Rites of passage in work careers. In M. B. Arthur, D. T. Hall, & B. S. Lawrence (Eds.), *Handbook of career theory* (pp. 397–416). New York: Cambridge University Press.

Tsui, A. E., Egan, T. D., & O'Reilly, C. A., III. (1992). Being different: Relational demography and organizational attachment. *Administrative Science Quarterly, 37,* 549–579.

Tsui, A. E., & O'Reilly, C. A., III. (1989). Beyond simple demographic effects: The importance of relational demography in superior-subordinate dyads. *Academy of Management Journal, 32,* 402–423.

Tushman, M. L. (1977). Special boundary roles in the innovation process. *Administrative Science Quarterly, 22,* 587–605.

Tushman, M. L., & Anderson, P. (1986). Technological discontinues and organizational environments. *Administrative Science Quarterly, 31,* 439–465.

Tushman, M. L., & Romanelli, E. (1983). Uncertainty, social location and influence in decision making: A sociometric analysis. *Management Science, 29,* 12–23.

Van Maanen, J. (1975). Police socialization: A longitudinal examination of job attitudes in an urban police department. *Administrative Science Quarterly, 20,* 207–228.

Wagner, G. W., Pfeffer, J., & O'Reilly, C. A., III. (1984). Organizational demography and turnover in top-management groups. *Administrative Science Quarterly, 29,* 74–92.

Walker, G. (1985). Network position and cognition in a computer firm. *Administrative Science Quarterly, 30,* 103–130.

Weick, K. E. (1976). Educational organizations as loosely coupled systems. *Administrative Science Quarterly, 21,* 1–19.

Weick, K. E. (1979). *The social psychology of organizing.* Reading, MA: Addison-Wesley.

Wellman, B. (1988). Structural analysis: From method and metaphor to theory and substance. In B. Wellman & S. D. Berkowitz (Eds.), *Social structures: A network approach* (pp. 19–61). New York: Cambridge University Press.

Wellman, B. (1992). Which types of ties and networks provide what kinds of social support? In E. J. Lawler (Ed.), *Advances in group processes* (Vol. 9, pp. 207–235). Greenwich, CT: JAI Press.

Wright, P. M., & McMahan, G. C. (1992). Theoretical perspectives for strategic human resource management. *Journal of Management, 18,* 295–320.

Zeitz, G. (1980). Interorganizational dialectics. *Administrative Science Quarterly, 25,* 72–88.

Zenger, T. R., & Lawrence, B. S. (1989). Organizational demography: The differential effects of age and tenure distributions on technical communications. *Academy of Management Journal, 32,* 353–376.

13

Constraints on the Interactive Organization

as an Ideal Type

■ David Krackhardt

Some men see things as they are and say, Why; I dream things that never were
and say, Why not.
—*Robert Kennedy, 1968*

Expressed in the theme of this book [C. Hecksher and A. Donnellon, *The Post Bureaucratic Organization*, the book from which this chapter is reproduced] is a hope, a desire for a better organization than the one we have experienced for generations, the infamous bureaucracy. I am sympathetic with this hope. All of us who have studied organizations have encountered the debilitating effects of bureaucratic forms, whether managed well or not. And progress is made, as the Kennedy quote in the epigraph suggests, by dreamers who are willing to let go of the way of the past and peer into the neverland of what could be.

Dreams motivate. They liberate us from the institutional constraints of history and social inertia so that we can explore new, unimaginable landscapes. But dreams also conveniently leave out the obstacles and problems that reality so rudely interjects. Thus, dreams do not guarantee success. And although the last two words "Why not" from the above quote are presumably rhetorical, one could take them literally and suggest that dreams should be scrutinized for loopholes. The answer to the question. "Why not?" may just be, "Because it won't work."

It is not my purpose here to prejudge the viability of the post bureaucratic form. But, if it is to succeed, we must explore the obstacles to its evolution, the possible constraints to its existence. If we can anticipate the sources of resistance to its survival, we will have a better chance of nurturing it along until it can predominate among its alternatives.

This chapter is built around two questions: (1) Can the ideal post bureaucratic form exist? and (2) If it could exist, would we want it to?

The characteristics of interactive forms are described in the Heckscher-Applegate "Introduction" and narrowed down in the Heckscher chapter "Defining the Post-Bureaucratic Type" [in *The Post-Bureaucratic Organization*]. Although I see differences in the various chapters about what ideal type might entail, there are characteristics that emerge as dominant in this proposed form.

Foremost among these defining characteristics is the reliance on informal relations, or associations, that cut across, or perhaps replace, formal channels established by the organization. This theme is prominent in the definition of the organic organization (Burns & Stalker, 1961): "The organic form . . . is characterized by . . . a network structure of control, authority, and communication."

In the interactive form, this characteristic is taken one step further: "It is a matter of knowing who to go to for a particular problem or issue." This theme is localized to the team level, where the definitions and boundaries of teams are adapted to meet the current needs of the organization. Moreover, the interactive relations are extended beyond the organization to include highly mobile personnel, joint ventures, and other forms of collaborations beyond the traditional organizational boundaries.

I would start by noting that there are three "laws" of social systems that are likely to place great constraints on the likelihood that the "ideal" interactive form could exist. These laws are the Law of N-Squared, the Law of Propinquity, and the Iron Law of Oligarchy.

The Law of *N*-Squared

The Law of N-Squared simply states that the number of possible links in a social system goes up approximately as the square of the number of elements in the system. With 10 people, there are 90 possible links ($=10 \times 9$, assuming asymmetric links are possible); with 20 people there are 380 possible links; 100 people produce 9,900 possible links; 1,000 people produce 999,000 links; and so on.

It is quite easy to extrapolate from these numbers to note that any organization of a moderate size (say, 1,000 employees) has no chance of being a fully connected network (cf. Harrison, in press). At Harvard University, for example, to expect that a professor's secretary be connected to the Harvard baseball team's assistant batting coach is unreasonable. There are cognitive and time limitations on the employee's part that prevent this from occurring. Not only is this asking too much of the employee, it is asking too much of the organization to ensure that all n-squared connections are extant.

In contrast, one could argue that the ideal is simply a lack of barriers to links and not a full set of activated links. That is, if a particular secretary has a task that requires information from the batting coach, then the question is how easily the secretary could access the coach to get the information. In this case, the interactive form would be characterized by many (but not all) temporary connections, presumably randomly distributed throughout the organization.

If we allow for this milder definition of barriers rather than a complete set of activated connections, we may still refer to the effective barriers produced by lack of knowledge of who the person should be going to for any particular piece of advice. The interactive form has no advantage over the traditional bureaucracy if everyone still only interacts with their supervisor out of ignorance of others as a resource.

But, what if everyone has access to an information technology—a kind of superdirectory—that tells them which person is the best to go to for help or advice. Now, the Law of N-Squared presents a different kind of constraint. Such an ideal type may not result in egalitarian interactions, because some people are more expert than others. In this eventuality, what we observe is that the unlucky soul who knows the most, is the best resource, will be inundated with interactions. The constraint, then, is not that people are unable to go to whomever they want; it is that the recipients of these requests will not have the personal resources to handle all the traffic. After all, even the best organizational form cannot squeeze out more than 24 hours in a day.

Thus, the Law of N-Squared, I argue, is an immutable constraint on the interaction capabilities of the organization. But, even if it were not, the organization would still have to face the next two laws of social systems that constrain equal access.

The Law of Propinquity

The Law of Propinquity differs from the preceding law in that it was deduced from consistent empirical findings. This law states that the probability of two people communicating is inversely proportional to the distance between them. In fact, the results often imply a stronger statement. In a study of R&D labs, where intergroup communication is essential to the groups' vitality and productivity, Tom Allen (1977, pp. 236–240) found striking evidence across a set of seven labs: "One might . . . expect [communication frequency] to decay at a more than linear rate [with distance]. It is the actual rate of decay that is surprising. Probability of weekly communication reaches a low asymptotic level within the first twenty-five or thirty meters."

One might expect that such face-to-face communications are affected by distance because of people's unwillingness to transgress the physical distance necessary to communicate beyond that. What has been surprising is the more recent research results that point to the robustness of this law even with the widespread use of modern communication technology, such as the phone or electronic mail, where physical distance should not create such a firm barrier. As Kraut, Galegher, and Egido (1990) have noted:

> Many studies have shown that communication frequency declines sharply, even exponentially, with the distance between the potential communicators, and that this decline is relatively independent of the technology through which the communication is occurring. . . . These findings can be partly explained by the idea that individuals who need to communicate are geographically clustered, and that the association of proximity with communication frequency is an artifact of this clustering. But data indicate that the association between communication frequency and proximity holds even when the need for communication between collaborators is held constant. (pp. 10–11)

I observed an example of this in a major investment bank in New York. As part of a larger reorganization, a group of 24 specialists from different parts of the firm were put together as a team to facilitate communication and reduce response time for problem solving. This group was considered a high-powered team that would lead the way out of the doldrums that the division found itself in.

Because of space constraints, different parts of this team were located in three different nearby buildings and on three floors in each building. The understanding was that the team members, each versatile with computer mail, would all communicate with each other on a regular basis, either by phone, e-mail, or in person (walking between buildings was common).

I asked each member how often they communicated with other members of the team. There was a strong preference to talking to people on the same floor. More than 60% of the communication occurred within the same floor, and most of the rest within the same building.

Moreover, I asked people to list the names of other members of the team whom they do not currently talk to very often but who would be of help to them in getting their job done if they did talk to them. I call this the "cry for help" question. The first interesting result was that people listed more names in response to this question than they did to the question about who they actually talked to, even though a primary purpose of forming the group was to encourage more communication. Second, the pattern of these "cry for help" nominations was even more strongly related to physical proximity. Only one of these responses was to someone within the same floor of a building; and 86% of the nominations bridged across buildings. That is, although some communication leaked from one building to the next, the barriers to effective communication access were highly related to physical proximity—despite the formal admonitions to communicate more and the advanced communication technology at their disposal.

What implications does this law have for the ideal interactive form? At a minimum, this law underscores a difficulty organizations will have in establishing unrestricted communication access, since the laws of physics prohibit everyone crowding into a sufficiently small space. It is quite likely that, no matter what the social, cultural, and formal norms are about being a "completely connected network," communication patterns will localize geographically.

The Law of N-Squared is a mathematical law with biological limitations. The Law of Propinquity exposes physical limitations. But perhaps the most intractable laws are those that deal with the inherent way humans relate and respond to each other: the social laws. The past 100 years of social science has produced precious few such laws, because of the ubiquitous inconsistency and creativity in human behavior. But the Iron Law of Oligarchy has been so named because it seems to recur despite the best efforts of good willed participants to suppress it. I now turn to this third constraint on the viability of the interactive form.

The Iron Law of Oligarchy

The term *oligarchy* is literally translated from the Greek to mean "rule by the few." It is this inequality in power that the interactive form attempts to squelch. Yet some social theorists, including Michels and Pareto, have observed that groups, even devoutly democratic ones, seem to evolve into an oligarchical structure, with power relinquished by the majority to a small handful of "leaders."

Pareto (1942, vol. 1, p. 62) argued that democratic socialism led to a new "elite" class of leaders, called the "political class." He lauded the leaders who were able to stand up to the masses and their criticisms of their rule; such was a display of courage and demonstrated that the leader deserved his or her status. But Pareto's view was that this elite class, in a democratic socialist state, would be fluid, and this fluidity would keep the rulers from straying far from the interests of the nonruling class.

Michels (1915/1949) went further. In a carefully documented historical account of democratic socialist experiments, he noted that differential interests develop within any social system:

> By a universally applicable social law, every organ of the collectivity, brought into existence through the need for the division of labor, creates for itself, as soon as it becomes consolidated, interests peculiar to itself. The existence of these special interests involves a necessary conflict with the interests of the collectivity. Nay, more, social strata fulfilling peculiar functions tend to become isolated, to produce organs fitted for the defence of their own peculiar interests. In the long run they tend to undergo transformation into distinct classes. (p. 389)

His sympathies were with the democratic socialists. But he begrudgingly concluded after reviewing the evidence of many well-intended attempts at true egalitarian reform: "Thus, the majority of human beings, in a condition of eternal tutelage, are predestined by tragic necessity to submit to the dominion of a small minority, and must be content to constitute the pedestal of an oligarchy" (p. 390).

Michels's pessimistic theory comes only after a volume of detailed observations of conditions that lead him to his inevitable conclusion. He noted that cooperative effort through organization (i.e., division of labor) is more efficient than individuals in accomplishing complex goals. He outlined the technical infeasibility of all the members of the cooperative being aware of and making decisions regarding all matters of concern to everyone. He also noted the psychological advantages to having a political leader: People like a leader who can inspire them, organize them to accomplish more than they could otherwise. And, finally, he noted that these same leaders, once virtuous and selfless, become addicted to their power and engage in behaviors that perpetuate it rather than benefit the followers who thrust them into power in the first place.

The modern question for us as organization theorists, then, is whether these preconditions and forces, psychological and sociological, still operate today. Certainly, we would not deny that organized cooperative effort is more efficient. Nor would we argue, I think, that it makes sense for everyone in a collective of any reasonable size to have all information contained in the whole system and to collectively discuss and participate in every decision.

What about Michels's claim that people like to abdicate their power to leaders? This may be a point of contention. But I know of no evidence to suggest that it is not true. Although clearly people do not like the feeling of being "controlled" (Langer, 1983), they do like being inspired by the Martin Luther Kings and John Kennedys of the world. That is, although they will not abdicate their power to just anyone, once they find someone whom they can trust (and depend on), they gladly abdicate.

I am reminded of the work of McClelland (1987; McClelland & Burnham, 1976). He made a career out of developing people's "need for achievement," a sense of fulfillment derived from facing a challenge and accomplishing a task by yourself. Yet, to his surprise (and dismay, I think), he found that achievement motives did not contribute to the success of the large organization manager. Rather, he found that the key to success was a high need for power. More striking, he found that managers who exhibited a high need for power (and who used it judiciously) had the most satisfied subordinates. He concluded that having a powerful superior enabled the employees to be more effective themselves, giving them a stronger sense of accomplishment.

McCarthy (1987), in a study of worker participation in a high-tech manufacturing firm, found that programs designed to increase participation in the workplace were regularly resisted by the very people who were to supposedly benefit from these programs. Although she found several reasons for this resistance, one that dominated was that employees did not want the increased responsibility of participating in more decisions than they already had to make. They had work to do, and these additional responsibilities were not part of the psychological contract in their job.

Finally, there was the experiment by the grand master of participation, Douglas McGregor, author of Theory Y management. It may be recalled that he spent several years as president of Antioch College implementing his Theory Y participative management philosophy. Antioch is a progressive liberal arts school, a prime candidate for such an experiment. If it could succeed anywhere, it should succeed there with a highly self-motivated, achievement-oriented, intellectual student body and faculty. But, as McGregor was to later admit, his attempt at creating a Theory Y culture and organization failed, and he returned to his post at MIT as a professor.

What about Michels's last condition, that is, the inevitable psychological "metamorphosis" that leaders undergo when they become ensconced in their position of power? Again, I know of no systematic evidence to refute this suggestion. However, stories abound about failures. For example, Rath Meat Packing was a company bought out by the employees. Employees sat on the board of directors, and the former union president became president of the company. Within three years, the president became a bitterly distrusted leader who returned to the hated practices of the previous management, including the practice of laying off employees in order to make the firm more efficient and preserve his job (Hammer & Stern, 1984).

Michels was writing about social movements and governments. But the forces behind his Iron Law of Oligarchy are equally applicable to organizations of all types, including business organizations. Whether his law is immutable or only represents a formidable challenge to the formation of a true interactive form is a question we cannot answer. But it is at least a formidable challenge.

Although these three "laws" are compelling in themselves, I will offer a fourth barrier to the emergence of the ideal interactive form. This argument does not constitute a law, as provided in the prior three examples, but it does constitute a credible objection. The objection stems from what we know about networks in organizations.

The Property of the Emergent Organization

An inherent principle of the interactive form is that networks of relations span across the entire organization, unimpeded by preordained formal structures and fluid enough to adapt to immediate technological demands. These relations can be multiple and complex. But one characteristic they share is that they *emerge* in the organization, they are not pre-planned.

I propose that we must first agree on the fundamental process by which these networks emerge before we can agree on what effect they might have. To clarify this point, I will outline a model network formation based on a three-dimensional model of relation types. I will characterize these relational dimensions as dependence, intensity, and affect.

By *dependence* I mean the degree that one person is dependent on another in the performance of his or her task or work assignment. A relation that characterizes a high degree of dependence indicates that the relation is critical to the person in order for the person to effectively do their job. Low dependence indicates a relation that may be incidental to the accomplishment of their work.

Such dependence may change from one time to the next. And dependency does not guarantee interaction. That is, one could be dependent on another for information but the former does not have access to the latter.

Intensity is the extent to which the two parties interact with each other, both in frequency and duration. Strong intensity would be characteristic of coworkers who work side-by-side each day, collaborating in their work. If such collaboration facilitated their respective work performance, then such links would also be highly dependent. If their interactions were merely social, and their work performance is not enhanced by these interactions, then their relation would be characterized by strong intensity but low dependence.

As Granovetter (1973) has so well articulated, low-intensity ties, or weak ties, are not necessarily dysfunctional for the firm. First, they are relatively low cost to the individuals to maintain. Second, weak ties, relative to strong ties, tend to form between distal parts of the organization. And, finally, two people with a strong tie tend to have access to the same information and the same sources of information, making their tie redundant. By contrast, weak ties often provide sources of relatively new, different, even contradictory information. This richness allows weak ties frequently to be the source of creative, innovative, and adaptive exchanges.

Affect, the third dimension, captures how a person feels about another in the relationship. Such evaluations can vary from strong (trust, love, hate, reverence) to relatively mild levels, even indifference. Note that the focus here is on the strength of the affect as well as whether it is positive or negative.

Again, the relationship between two people can be characterized by strong or weak feelings with any combination of dependency and intensity. However, I propose that overall patterns tend to emerge over time as a function of the relationship between these three factors. The process by which these emergent networks form is my next point of departure.

Dependency → Intensity

Task dependence creates a demand, a need for interaction. An employee faced with a need for information, or resources, or permission will attempt to fill that need by seeking someone who can provide it. If the dependence persists, interaction with that person who fills the need will increase over time.

Intensity → Affect

One of the most enduring findings in social psychology is that prolonged interactions induce affective evaluations, even emotional responses. Two people who interact only sparingly can maintain neutral evaluations of each other. If they are induced to interact frequently, they will tend to form stronger emotional bonds through the experience. Over time, each party learns what to expect from the other, resulting in feelings of trust, respect, and even strong friendship.

Sometimes these experiences form negative emotional bonds. One party may "learn" that another is untrustworthy, unreliable, perhaps sinister in intentions, or just unlikable. But whether the feelings are positive or negative, they tend to grow in strength as the parties interact more frequently.

If the frequent interaction results in stronger positive evaluations of the other person, this will reinforce the connection, inducing more intense (frequent and durable) interactions. It will also tend to reinforce the dependency, especially the perception of dependency, since the employee feels comfortable that the need created by the dependency can be readily filled. Thus, a relationship characterized by positive affect will tend to endure and that link in the network will be *stabilized*.

Conversely, a negative evaluation will tend to encourage the employee to reduce the frequency and duration of interaction. If the dependency is sufficiently strong, reduced interaction may not be an option. In such a case, the employee will be motivated to reduce the dependency in the relationship (for example, by finding another means of getting the information or resources, or by reducing the perceived need for the information or resources). Thus, negative affect will tend to shorten the life of—or *destabilize*—a link.

In aggregate, then, structures of relations will emerge as a result of this process. Those parts of the structure that are reinforced with positive affect will form a stable core to the overall network. Unstable links will tend to disappear over time and be replaced by others.

What are the implications of this model for the interactive form? It suggests that networks are not particularly fluid over time. In particular, the parts of the network that depend on *trust*, are particularly stable. Trusting relations take time to form and then once formed are difficult to break.

There is evidence that the network that people see and recall is the stable part of the network, and not the transitory, low-intensity part. That is, the network that people experience as helping them, or the network they actively draw on to do their work in the organization, is the network of stable, recurring relations.

Given this is true, then the idea of a fluid, truly organic network structure may be difficult to obtain. People as a matter of habit and preference are likely to seek out their old standbys, the people they have grown to trust, the people they always go to and depend on, to deal with new problems, even though they may not be the ones best able to address those problems.

I now turn to the final point I raised at the beginning of this chapter: If we *could* wave a magic wand and create a purely interactive organization, would we want to?

■ Constraints on the Idea of the Ideal

Simon wrote a small piece in 1962 called "The Architecture of Complexity," in which he proposed that many social, biological, chemical, and physical systems share a tendency to be "hierarchical." By hierarchical he meant that these systems were "nearly decomposable" into subsystems, which in turn were decomposable into smaller subsystems, and so on.

His claim was not based on simple observation, however. He noted that such hierarchical systems were inherently more robust against adverse outside forces. As an example, he described two watchmakers. The first had a process that was very fast but required that all 100 parts in the watch be assembled in one sitting. He could assemble a watch in an hour, if he were not interrupted. The second had a process that was slower (it took two hours to assemble the watch) but was based on building 10 subassemblies to the watch that could remain completed as each subassembly was finished. That is, if he were interrupted after half an hour, he might have completed two subassemblies that would not be lost as a result of the interruption.

Simon then shows how the second "hierarchical" watchmaker would be able to make in order of magnitude more watches in a year than the first, given even a modest interruption rate. Thus, according to Simon's theory, hierarchies are evolutionarily superior to alternative forms of systems. His paper started a minifield in systems theory called *hierarchy theory*. Simon is not the only proponent of hierarchies as more efficient and fit for environmental competition than nonhierarchical forms. Although I think we all believe that there are dysfunctions to hierarchical forms, there are some efficiencies also. Burns and Stalker (1961) recognized this in their original formulation of the organic versus mechanistic dichotomy.

One approach has been to suggest that organic forms may be more effective in some environments, whereas mechanistic and hierarchical forms are better in others. But I suggest a second approach. It is possible that organizations are inherently inefficient in either extreme. Overly bureaucratized organizations are too rigid to deal with the fast-changing world. But overly dense networked firms have inefficiencies of their own. I have found, for example, in a study of a set of bank branches, that the density of communications relations is negatively (although not strongly) related to profitability in the branch. My follow-up interviews in those branches with dense communications also reveal low morale and a good deal of experienced chaos.

Perhaps, then, there is a curvilinear relation between the degree of interaction of an organization and the organization's effectiveness. This would lead us to a new path of research. Perhaps the attributes defining the interactive form have different curvilinear shapes, with each having a different maximum point on the curve. Discovering those maximum points is not as theoretically appealing as holding up an ideal type to which we all aspire. But in the long run it may be the more profitable path.

■ References

Allen, T. J. (1977). *Managing the flow of technology: Technology transfer and the dissemination of technology information within the research and development organization.* Cambridge, MA: MIT Press.

Burns, T., & Stalker, G. M. (1961). *The management of innovation.* London: Tavistock.

Granovetter, M. (1973). The strength of weak ties. *American Journal of Sociology, 78,* 1360–1380.

Hammer, T., & Stern, R. (1984). *Labor representation on company boards of directors: Effective worker participation.* Working paper. New York: Cornell University.

Harrison, B. (in press). *Lean and mean: The changing landscape of corporate power in the age of flexibility.* New York: Basic Books.

Kennedy, R. (1968, June 9). *New York Times,* p. 56.

Kraut, R., Galegher J., & Egido, C. (1990). *Informal communication and scientific work.* Working paper. Pittsburgh, PA: Carnegie Mellon University.

Langer, E. J. (1983). *The psychology of control.* Beverly Hills, CA: Sage.

McCarthy, S. A. (1987). *Theoretical and empirical perspectives on nonparticipation at work: Levels of nonparticipation in a Company Quality Circle Program.* Ph.D. dissertation. Cornell University, New York.

McClelland, D. (1987). *Human motivation.* Cambridge, UK: Cambridge University Press.

McClelland, D. C., & Burnham, D. H. (1976). Power is the great motivator. *Harvard Business Review,* pp. 100–110.

Michels, R. (1915/1949). *Political parties: A sociological study of the oligarchical tendencies of modern democracy.* Glencoe, IL: Free Press.

Pareto, V. (1942). *The mind and society.* New York: Harcourt, Brace.

Simon, H. A. (1962, December). The architecture of complexity. *Proceedings of the American Philosophical Society, 106,* 5.

■ Index

absent ties, 110–12, *fig. 4.1*, 121, 125n3
absolute authority, 35–36
access, 18, 25, 36, 42, 203
access dimension, 210, *table 8.1*, 215, 216–17, *fig. 8.3*, 221–23, 228–30
accessibility, 141
access networks, 279
accuracy scores, 89, 94, *tables 3.1–2*, 97, 99, 104n2
acquaintance circles, 115–16, 126n12, 126–27n17
action-learning sets, 220
actions, 57–59, 66–67, 71, 77
actor similarity, 294–96
Adams, J. S., 310
Adler, P. S., 5, 7
adoption behavior, 141–50, *fig. 5.2*, 156–71, *figs. 5.4–5*, 175n4
advice networks, 239–40, 247, *fig. 9.2*
    managerial implications and, 236–37
    as strong ties, 86, 87–89, 92, *fig. 3.3*, 94–95, *table 3.1*, 97, 100–103
affect, 331–32
affective attachment, 83–85, 87, 101–3
affirmative action, 203
AIDS, 150–52, *fig. 5.3*
air conditioners, 150, 162
Alba, R. D., 304
Alcoa, 216, *fig. 8.3*
Aldrich, H., 292
Allegheny County, Penn., 130–31, *fig. 5.1*
Allen, David, 162
Allen, Thomas, 5, 7, 182–83, 208, 326
Anderson, P., 293, 307–8

Andrews, S. B., 301
Antiope, 170
ARPANET, 159–60
Art Institute of Chicago, 194
Asian immigrants, 70–71
Asimov, Isaac, 192, 194
Astley, W. G., 302
asynchronous technologies, 225
attitude similarity, 299–301
Australian National University, 151
Aventis, 217, *fig. 8.3*
axone density, 126n13
Aydin, C., 292, 300

Bacharach, S. B., 304
Back, Kurt W., 22, 51n4, 64, 114–15, 296
Bacon, Kevin, 197
Bain, Alexander, 167
Baird, L., 3
Baker, Wayne E., 58, 315
balance theory, 83, 85, 100–101, 104n1, 111–12
Bandura, Albert, 172
Banfield, Edward, 64
Barber, Bernard, 16, 20
Barkey, Karen, 34–35
Barley, S. R., 292, 293
Barnes, J. A., 117, 125n4
Becker, Gary, 62, 114
Becker, Marshall H., 143–44, 175n4
Beekun, R. I., 292
Beers, M., 3
benefit-rich networks, 19–22
Ben-Porath, Yoram, 58

diamond markets, 60, 68
differentiation strategy, 46
diffusion networks, 111–16, 118–19,
    120, 130–75, *fig. 5.2, table 5.1*
Di Lellio, Anna, 51–52n8
DiMaggio, Paul, 3, 298
discontinuance, 162–63
disharmony, 83, 85
distributive justice, 59
Dixon, N., 3
domestic clusters, 28
Donnellon, A., 324
Doria, Helen, 190, 192, 204
Drobnic, S., 314
drop-out rates, 50n2, 72–75, *tables 2.1–*
    2, 79–80nn4–6
Drucker, P., 3
Duff, Robert W., 155
Dugas, Gaetan, 151
Duguid, P., 3
Dumin, Mary, 16
Durkheim, Emile, 51n6, 301
dyadic ties, 110, 131, 135, 137, 291

Eccles, R. G., 5, 315
economic bargaining, 34, 52n9
Edison-Swift, P., 299
educational innovations, 142–43
effective networks, 117. *See also*
    efficient-effective networks
effective norms, 65–68, 77
efficient-effective networks, 24–28, *figs.*
    1.3–5, 33, 51nn4–5
Egan, T. D., 294, 314
Egido, C., 327
egocentric networks, 116–19, 121,
    126n13, 290
Eisenberg, E. M., 292, 294, 296, 298,
    299, 307
electronic mail systems
    diffusion networks and, 159, 162–63,
        171, 175n3
    in knowledge creation and sharing,
        216, *fig. 8.3*, 223, 225, 227
    office design and, 183
Ellison, Ralph, 205–6
embeddedness, 58, 71, 85
emergent organizations, 330–33
emic friends, 86

emotional intensity, 82–83, 110
empirical generalization, 57, 79n1
empirical indicators
    of entrepreneurial opportunities, 39–
        40
    of redundancy, 22–23, *fig. 1.2*
energy scarcity argument, 53–54n14
engagement dimension, 210, *table 8.1*,
    215, 217, *fig. 8.3*, 223–25, 228–30
engine of action, 57
Ensel, Walter M., 16, 83, 305
entrepreneurs, 36–40, *fig. 1.7*, 45–46, 52–
    53nn10–13
environment, 298–99
Epstein, A., 117
Erickson, B. H., 300
Erickson, E., 83
Erie County, Ohio, 133
etic *philos*, 86
event history analysis, 149
exchange of roles, 157
exchange theory, 59
executive coaching, 222
expectations, 63–65
extended networks, 117
external communication, 140–41
external networks, 255

face-to-face contact, 133, 141, 223, 224,
    225, 227
family
    social capital in, 70–73, *table 2.1*, 79–
        80nn3–6
    strength of weak ties and, 121
family planning innovations, 149–50,
    155, 164–66, *fig. 5.5*
Farmer, Art, 198
farmer opinion leaders, 136, 142, 146
fashion, 166
Faust, K., 4
fax, 159, 167–68
F-connection, 58
Feld, Scott L., 51n4, 125–26n10
Ferris, G. R., 302, 304, 306, 309
Festinger, Leon, 22, 29, 51n4, 64, 296
Filipino housewives, 155
financial capital, 13–15, 70, 73, 74, *table*
    2.1, 79–80n4
Fischer, Claude S., 16, 20, 51n4, 86

interlocking personal networks, 153, 155

International Herald Tribune, 60

International Network of Social Network Analysts, 4

INTERNET, 159–61

interorganizational networks, 144–45, 304

interpersonal debt, 19–20, 24

interpersonal networks, 134, 135–36, 145–50, *fig. 5.2*, 153, 155, 157, 172, 173–74

interpersonal ties, 109–24, 124–25nn1–4

interracial ties, 116

intimacy, 82–83, 110

investment capital, 14, 18

iron law of oligarchy, 328–30

irregular communication patterns, 245

isolates, 94, 114–15, 131, 147–48, *fig. 5.2*, 165, 247, 287

Jablin, F. M., 307

Jacobs, Jane, 127n19, 180–81, 183, 184, 185, 186, 188–89

Jacobson, R. B., 172

James, L. R., 297

job changers, 29, 118–19, 126–27nn14–17, 154, 175n7, 202

job satisfaction, 301–2

Johnson, Gary, 193

Johnson and Johnson, 217–18, *fig. 8.3*

Jones, A. P., 297

J. P. Morgan, 185

Judge, T. A., 302, 304, 306, 309

Kahn El Khalili market (Cairo, Egypt), 61, 64

Kanter, R. M., 295, 305

Kapferer, B., 111, 117, 124–25n2

Karposi's Sarcoma, 150

Katz, Elihu, 65, 77, 114, 120, 133, 140, 145–48, 149, 167

Kearns, Kelvin P., 135

Kennedy, Donald, 168

Kennedy, John, 329

Kennedy, Robert, 324

Kerckhoff, A., 114–15

Kerr, S., 3

Keyes, L. C., 120–21

Kilby, Peter, 37, 53n13

Kilduff, Martin, 104n1, 292, 300, 301, 305, 310, 313

Kincaid, D. Lawrence, 149–50, 164–66, 175nn2–3

King, Martin Luther, Jr., 329

Kirzner, Israel M., 52n10

Klovdahl, Alden S., 151–52

Knoke, D., 303

knowledge creation and sharing, 7, 208–30, *fig. 8.1, fig. 8.3*

    strategic collaboration and (*see* strategic collaboration)

knowledge dimension, 210, *table 8.1*, 215–16, 218–20, 227–30

Knowledge Fairs, 216, *fig. 8.3*, 220

Knowledge Interchange Network (KIN), 216, *fig. 8.3*

knowledge networks, 278

Korean villages, 149–50, 164–66, *fig. 5.5*

Korte, Charles, 116

Krackhardt, David, 5, 84, 86, 88–89, 102, 104nn1–3, 249, 262, 292, 300, 301, 304, 309, 310, 313, 314

Kramer, Richard, 171

Krassa, M. A., 164

Kraut, R., 327

Krone, K. J., 307

Kruskal, Joseph B., 104n4

Kwon, S., 5, 7

laboratory schools, 142–43

labor-market study, 117–19, 126–27nn14–17

Langer, E. J., 329

Langlois, Simon, 175n7

Laumann, Edward, 110, 111, 294, 302

Lawler, E. J., 304

law of *N*-Squared, 325–26, 328

law of oligarchy, 328–30

law of propinquity, 326–28

Lawrence, B. S., 295, 314

Lazarsfeld, Paul F., 16, 50n2, 65, 77, 100, 120, 133, 135, 140–41, 294

leadership, 120. *See also* opinion leadership

leadership networks, 219

Leenders, R., 5, 7

legislators, 64–65

Leinhardt, Samuel, 122–23, 125n6
leisure clusters, 28
Le Monde, 170
Lenin, V. I., 63
Leopold, Nathan, 198
liaison roles, 126n11
Light, Donald, 126–27n17
Lin, Nan, 16, 63, 83, 175n7, 305
Lincoln, J. R., 5, 296, 297, 299, 315
Lingoes, J. C., 104n4
Linné, Carl von, 190
Lipset, Seymour, 69
Liu, William T., 155
local bridges. *See* bridges
logic of collective action, 161–62
Longenecker, C. O., 309
loose-knit networks, 117
Los Angeles Police Department, 185

MacArthur, John D., 198
macro network models, 122–24
Mansfield, E. R., 307
marginal figures, 114–15, 118, 126n11
Marks, Stephen R., 53–54n14
Markus, M. Lynne, 158, 163
Marsden, Peter V., 16, 20, 22, 149, 294
Massachusetts Institute of Technology (MIT), 182, 208
mass communication flows, 120, 131, 133–34
mass media, 133–34, 140–41, 172
matching models, 283–84
Mayer, Adrian, 117
Mayer, Phillip, 109, 123
Mayhew, B. H., 284, 294
Mazur, B., 125n6
McAdam, Doug, 156–57
McCarthy, S. A., 329
McClelland, David C., 37, 40, 329
McGregor, Douglas, 330
McMahan, G. C., 283
McPhee, W. N., 100
McPherson, J. M., 294, 314
MDS (multidimensional scale), 94, 104n4
measles immunization programs, 143, 175n4
mechanistic organizations, 297
medical drugs, 145–49, *fig. 5.2*
medieval European villages, 162

Menzel, Herbert, 114, 133, 145–48, 149
merger integration, 219–20, 226, 267
Merry, Sally, 67
Merton, Robert K., 34, 53–54n14, 66, 69, 135, 294
Michels, R., 328–30
micro-macro linkages, 122–24
Miles, R. E., 315
Milgram, Stanley, 109, 115–16, 194–96, 316
Mill, James, 70
Mill, John Stuart, 70
Miller, Jerry L., 172, 296, 315
Miller, K. I., 307
Miller, N., 114
Mine, Alain, 170
Minitel, 169–71
Mintzberg, H., 312
Mississippi Freedom Summer project, 156–57
Mitchell, Cindy, 190–91, 194
Mitchell, J. Clyde, 109, 286
mobility, 29, 73–74, 80n5, 119
Moch, M. K., 301
modern math, 130–31, *fig. 5.1*
Mohrman, A., 3
Mohrman, S., 3
Monge, P. R., 5, 292, 294, 296, 298, 299, 307
monomorphism, 140
Monotype Club, 69
Morand, D. A., 308
Moreno, J. L., 4, 262
Morgan, J. P., 185
motivation, 37–40, 52–53nn11–13, 84, 85, 118, 126–27n17
multiplex relations, 69, 74, 79n2, 124–25n2
Murnighan, J. K., 304
Murray, Stephen O., 175n7
Museum of Contemporary Art (Chicago, Ill.), 206
mutual choice, 112, 122–24, 125n6

National Labor Relations Board (NLRB), 91–92, 98
national league states, 144–45
National Science Foundation, 130
Nature, 197

Russell Reynolds Associates, 217, *fig. 8.3*
Russian workers' cells, 63

safety dimension, 210, *table 8.1*, 215, 217–18, *fig. 8.3*, 225–27, 228–30
Same Time, 216, *fig. 8.3*, 225
sanctions, 65–68, 76
Saroyan, William, 198
Schachter, Stanley, 22, 51n4, 64, 296
Schelling, Thomas C., 161
Schermerhorn, J. R., 294
Schneck, R. E., 302
Schneider, B., 283
school superintendents, 130–31, *fig. 5.1*
Schreuder, Hein, 51–52n8
Schultz, Theodore, 62
Schuman, H., 111
Schumpeter, Joseph A., 37, 52–53nn10–11
Scott, J., 4, 292
screening devices, 18–19, 27
secondary contacts, 24–26, *fig. 1.3*, 40–45
secondary structural holes, 40–45, 46, *fig. 1.8*
selection, 306
self-designating method, 139, *table 5.1*
"Senate Club," 65
sequential interdependence, 158, 159, 162, 175
sexual networks, 150–52, *fig. 5.3*
Shapero, Albert, 118
Shapiro, Susan, 79n2
Shaw, M. E., 301, 302, 311
Shearman & Sterling law firm, 216, *fig. 8.3*
Sherman, J. D., 307
Shi Young, 194
Shrader, C. B., 297
sidewalk life, 180–81, 188–89
Sieber, Sam D., 53–54n14
Silicon Systems, 87–88, 91–103, *figs. 3.2–4*, *tables 3.1–2*
Silicon Valley, 181, 186
Simmel, Georg, 33, 34, 50n2, 51nn6–7, 52n9, 124–25n2
Simon, H. A., 333

simplex relations, 69, 79n2
Sims, H. P., 309
Singh, S. N., 136
siting contacts, 20–22, *fig. 1.1*
six degrees of separation, 190–207
size of networks, 20–21, 24, 27–28, *fig. 1.5*, 298
Skandia, 217, *fig. 8.3*
skill-profiling systems, 220
Small, Albion, 51n7
small-world investigations, 115–16, 194
Smith, H. L., 307
Smith-Lovin, L., 294
SNA. *See* social network analysis
SNCC (Student Nonviolent Coordinating Committee), 156
Snell, S. A., 283, 315–16
Snow, C. C., 315–16
snowball sampling, 175n2
Snyder, W., 4
social capital, 5, 7, 13–17, 46, 50–51n3
   human capital and, 57–79, *tables 2.1–2*, 79–80nn3–6
social capital theory, 16
social clubs, 69, 121
social cohesion, 119, 120–21
social distance, 113–16, 117, 125–26nn9–10
socialization, 307
social learning theory, 171–73, 175
social modeling, 172
social network analysis (SNA), 4–9, 16, 212–30, 249–50, 258–59
   office design and, 185
   strategic collaboration and, 261–79
social networks, 283–316, *figs. 12.1–2*, *tables 12.1–3*
   closure of, 66–68, *fig. 2.1*
social network theory, 291–94
social structures
   of competitive arena, 13–50, 50n1
   social capital and, 66–70, 76
   strength of weak ties and, 119–22
socioeconomic status, 141, 155
sociometric method, 109, 114–15, 122–23, 125n6, 137–39, 146–47, *table 5.1*, 175n2
Solomon, Leonard, 199

Travers, Jeffrey, 116, 316
Trice, H. M., 308
Trow, M., 69
trust networks, 236–37, 239–41, 247
trustworthy contacts, 19–20, 24, 36
  in knowledge creation and sharing, 225–27
  social capital and, 60, 62, 63–65, 68, 77
  strength of weak ties and, 120
  strong ties and, 84, 85, 102–3
T.R.W., 185
Tsui, A. E., 294, 314
Tushman, M. L., 293, 302, 307–8
two-step flow models, 133–34, 140, 173

Ullmann-Margalit, Edna, 66
Ulrich, D., 3
uncertainty, 35, 84, 143–44
underinvestment, 76–77
union certification campaign, 86, 89, 91–103
University of Arizona, 156, 172
University of California at Berkeley, 159–60
University of Chicago, 142
University of Michigan, 184
U.S. Department of Defense, 160
U.S. Department of Education, 130
U.S. state governments, 144–45

Valente, Thomas W., 149, 164, 166
Van den Ban, A. W., 136
Van Maanen, J., 309
Vaughn, John C., 16, 83, 305
vertical differentiation and coordination, 296
video conferencing, 223, 225
Von Krogh, G., 3
voting behavior, 133, 156–57
VP Buddy, 225

Wagner, G. W., 294, 314
Walker, G., 300
Walker, Jack L., 144–45, 175n5
Walster, E., 110
Warneryd, Karl-Eric, 168
war rooms, 184, 188

Washington, Harold, 193–94, 199
Wasserman, S., 4, 292, 298
Watts, Duncan, 197
weak ties, 63, 156, 305
Weber, Max, 37, 53n13
Weick, K. E., 292, 297
Weisberg, Bernie, 204–6
Weisberg, Jacob, 196, 204
Weisberg, Joe, 199–200
Weisberg, Lois, 190–94, 196, 198–202, 203–7
Wellman, B., 291, 292–93, 301
Wenger, E., 4
West End social structure, 119–22
West Village (New York, N.Y.), 180–81, 183, 184, 188–89
Whetten, D. A., 302
White, Harrison C., 29
white boarding applications, 225
Whiting, Gordon C., 142
Whyte, William H., Jr., 150
Wilken, Paul H., 53n13
Williams, Frederick R., 157–58
Williamson, Oliver, 58
Willrich, Wendy, 190, 204
Wirth, Louis, 124
Wish, Myron, 104n4
Wolfe, Richard, 127n18
workers' cells, 63
working-class communities, 119–22
workplace design, 181–89
World Bank, 216, *fig. 8.3*, 220
World Science Fiction Convention, 191
World War II, 133
Wright, P. M., 283
Wrong, Dennis, 58

X rays, 186, 212

Yale University, 159
Yancey, W., 83
Yates, Sidney, 199

Zajac, E. J., 302
Zeitz, G., 293
Zelizer, Viviana A., 51–52n8
Zenger, T. R., 295, 314
zeroblocks, 29